Partisan Diary

Partisan Diary

A Woman's Life
in the Italian Resistance

ADA GOBETTI

TRANSLATED AND EDITED
BY JOMARIE ALANO

OXFORD
UNIVERSITY PRESS

OXFORD
UNIVERSITY PRESS

Oxford University Press is a department of the University of Oxford.
It furthers the University's objective of excellence in research, scholarship,
and education by publishing worldwide.

Oxford   New York
Auckland   Cape Town   Dar es Salaam   Hong Kong   Karachi
Kuala Lumpur   Madrid   Melbourne   Mexico City   Nairobi
New Delhi   Shanghai   Taipei   Toronto

With offices in
Argentina   Austria   Brazil   Chile   Czech Republic   France   Greece
Guatemala   Hungary   Italy   Japan   Poland   Portugal   Singapore
South Korea   Switzerland   Thailand   Turkey   Ukraine   Vietnam

Oxford is a registered trademark of Oxford University Press
in the UK and certain other countries.

Published in the United States of America by
Oxford University Press
198 Madison Avenue, New York, NY 10016

Ada Gobetti, Diario partigiano
© 1956, 1996, Giulio Einaudi editore s.p.a., Torino
English translation © Oxford University Press 2014

Library of Congress Cataloging-in-Publication Data
Gobetti, Ada, 1902–1968. [Diario partigiano. English]
Partisan diary : a woman's life in the Italian Resistance / Ada Gobetti ; translated and edited by
Jomarie Alano.
pages cm
Includes index.
ISBN 978–0–19–938054–1 (hardback)—ISBN 978–0–19–938055–8 (ebook)—ISBN
978–0–19–938056–5 (ebook)   1. World War, 1939–1945—Underground movements—
Italy.   2. Gobetti, Ada, 1902–1968—Diaries.   3. World War, 1939–1945—Personal narratives,
Italian.   4. World War, 1939–1945—Participation, Female.   5. World War, 1939–1945—
Women.   6. Italy—History—German occupation, 1943–1945.   I. Title.
D802.I8M32513 2014
940.53'45092—dc23
[B]
2014007046

1 3 5 7 9 8 6 4 2
Printed in the United States of America
on acid-free paper

In memory of my father, Enrico Michael Alano,
and my father-in-law, Mark Gilmour Treat
—J.A.

CONTENTS

ACKNOWLEDGMENTS

My thanks go first of all to Carla Gobetti, Ada Gobetti's daughter-in-law and president of the Centro studi Piero Gobetti in Turin, Italy. Signora Gobetti has supported my research on Ada Gobetti from its very inception by supplying access to uncatalogued materials, gifts of books and journals, interviews, and introductions to other individuals who knew Ada Gobetti, not to mention sharing her own personal memories. She will be very happy to see this translation of the *Diario partigiano* come to fruition so that Ada's words and experiences in the *Resistenza*, along with those of her late husband, Paolo Gobetti, can reach an English-speaking audience for the first time.

I am also extremely grateful to Ersilia Alessandrone Perona, director of the Istituto piemontese per la storia della Resistenza e della società contemporanea 'Giorgio Agosti' in Turin, for the expert advice and countless hours of her time she has given me for many years, and especially for the invitation to speak about Ada Gobetti and her "life of resistance" at a conference in Turin in May 2012, entitled "Giellismo e azionismo: Cantieri aperti."

Members of the staff at the Centro studi Piero Gobetti, especially Franca Ranghino and Piera Tachis, were always there to find a missing piece of information, scan a photograph, or make a contact for me. I have deep respect for their research skills and treasure their friendship. I also appreciate the efforts of Pietro Polito, director of the Centro, who invited me to speak about my translation of the *Diario partigiano* in Turin in May 2012. The Centro is located on 6 Via Fabro, the "house of miracles" where Ada Gobetti welcomed so many who fought in the *Resistenza*.

I have been fortunate to have the opportunity to meet and interview two women who fought in the *Resistenza* with Ada Gobetti and figured prominently in the *Diario*. Bianca Guidetti Serra spoke to me about the Gruppi di difesa della donna and shared a scrapbook containing clippings about her work and that of other women in the *Resistenza*. The late Frida Malan, who co-edited with Ada the clandestine newspaper *La Nuova Realtà* beginning in February 1945, shared her experiences as a partisan in the *Resistenza*. Both women remained active in politics in Turin and fought for women's rights long after the war was over.

Cesare Alvazzi drove me to Ada's former home in Meana in the Susa Valley outside of Turin, where he had been among the many partisans who used this home as a base of operations. He is the Cesare of the *Diario*, Paolo's good friend, whose family home in Oulx provided a safe haven for Ada Gobetti and her family. How else would I have known that partisans carried both a gun and an umbrella when they were in the mountains?

Thank you to my mother, Franceschina Santilli Alano, and my husband, William Mark Treat, for reading every word of this translation; to Celia Applegate for making valuable suggestions about style; and to Valeria Dani for extensive help with vocabulary. Thank you also to Paula Schwartz for believing in the importance of my work on Ada Gobetti, including the biography I am writing, and to Stanislao Pugliese for wanting so much to see the *Diario* translated into English. *Un abbraccio* for my dear friend Bruna Ponso, who sent newspaper clippings and the latest editions of Ada Gobetti's books from Turin and provided warm hospitality during my frequent visits to her native city. Nancy Toff, my editor at Oxford University Press in New York, and Antonella Tarpino and Anna Dellaferrera at Giulio Einaudi editore in Turin worked tirelessly to make the publication of this translation possible, and I appreciate it very much.

Finally, a special thank-you goes to Andrea Ferrero, owner and chef of the delightful Cafe Torino in Warrenton, Virginia. Originally from Turin, Andrea answered all of my questions about the translation, including the Piedmontese expressions that I could not translate. He shared various legends that appear as references in the *Diario,* and helped me with usage specific to the Piedmont region. Sometimes we worked while he was making *gnocchi* in the kitchen; at other times, we sat at a table in his restaurant, and he helped me between customers. Thanks to Andrea, words came to life. This translation is better because of him.

The dedication is in memory of two men who served bravely during World War II: my father, Enrico Michael Alano, who was with the 88th Infantry Division or "Blue Devils" in Italy, and my father-in-law, Mark Gilmour Treat, who was a pilot in the 70th Bomb Squadron of the Army Air Corps and served in the Pacific Theatre. We miss your goodness and your love. The diaries you kept have given our family a personal account of your service. Now your granddaughter, Anastasia Mary Treat, will know something of the grandfathers she never met. Thank you.

PREFACE

The first edition of the *Diario partigiano* by Ada Gobetti Marchesini Prospero was published in Turin, Italy, by Giulio Einaudi editore, in 1956. It won the Premio Prato, an annual prize for a work inspired by the *Resistenza*, that year. I based my translation on the 1996 edition, the text of which is identical to the original 1956 edition.

The Einaudi family name has a prominent place in the history of antifascism in Italy. Luigi Einaudi, father of Giulio and his brother Mario, was professor of economics at the University of Turin from 1900 to 1943. Piero Gobetti, Ada's first husband and a courageous antifascist journalist who wrote openly against Mussolini from the outset, was among his pupils. A fervent opponent of Mussolini's fascist regime, Luigi Einaudi edited the *Rivista di Storia Economica* (Review of Economic History), one of the many journals suppressed by the Fascists. He fled to Switzerland in 1943 and returned after the end of World War II. Luigi Einaudi served as the first president of the Republic of Italy from 1948 to 1955.

Giulio Einaudi founded his publishing house in 1933. Its symbol, the ostrich, came from that of the journal *La Cultura*, of which he was the last editor before the journal was suppressed by Mussolini's fascist regime in 1935. An ardent antifascist and believer in the preservation of Italian culture, Giulio Einaudi collaborated with the Turinese group of the Giustizia e Libertà movement. On May 15, 1935, he was arrested along with the prominent antifascist thinkers and intellectuals Massimo Mila, Leone Ginzburg, Vittorio Foa, Franco Antonicelli, Norberto Bobbio, Cesare Pavese, Carlo Levi, and Luigi Salvatorelli. He was imprisoned and then sent into *confino* (internal exile) but later was able to bring the works of these individuals to light, along with those of the founder of the Italian Communist Party Antonio Gramsci, writers Natalia Ginzburg and Italo Calvino, and Holocaust survivor Primo Levi. Giulio Einaudi editore also published Piero Gobetti's complete works.

Mario Einaudi came to the United States in 1933 in protest against fascist rule in Italy, and he continued his antifascist activities from the United States during World War II. He joined the Cornell University faculty in 1945 and later became Goldwin Smith Professor of Government. In 1961 he founded the Center for International Studies, which was renamed the Mario Einaudi Center for International Studies in 1991. The Einaudi Center houses the Cornell Institute for European Studies, where I have been a visiting scholar for the past several years, thanks to the efforts of Susan Tarrow and Sydney Van Morgan and their belief in my research on Ada Gobetti. The Institute for European Studies maintains its connections with Turin through the Cornell in Turin program.

I hope that this translation of Ada Gobetti's *Diario partigiano* will contribute to the history of antifascism in Italy so important not only to Ada and Piero Gobetti but to the Einaudi family as well.

LIST OF ACRONYMS

Acronym	English Translation
ACC	Allied Control Commission
Acspg	Archives of the Centro studi Piero Gobetti
Anpi	National Association of Italian Partisans
Cln	Committee of National Liberation
Clnai	Committee of National Liberation of Northern Italy
Cmrp	Piedmontese Regional Military Command
Cvl	Volunteer Corps for Liberty
FdG	Young People's Front
Fdif	Women's International Democratic Federation
Ffi	French Domestic Forces (French Resistance)
Gap	Groups for Patriotic Action
Gddd	Women's Defense and Assistance Groups
GL	Justice and Liberty
Gmo	Mobile Operations Group
Mfgl	Women's Movement of "Justice and Liberty"
Pci	Italian Communist Party
Pd'A	Action Party
Psi	Italian Socialist Party
Udi	Union of Italian Women
Uff	Union of French Women

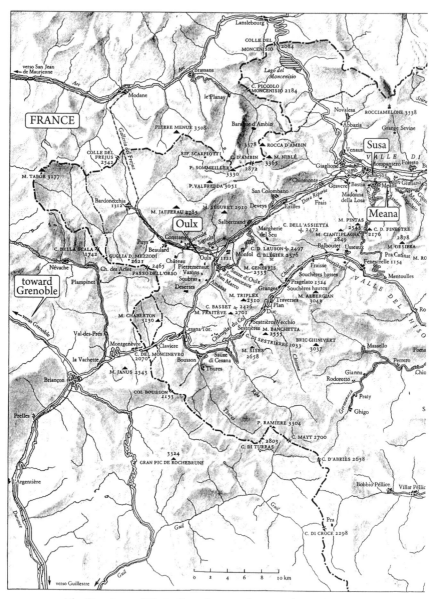

The Province of Turin from Susa to the French Border

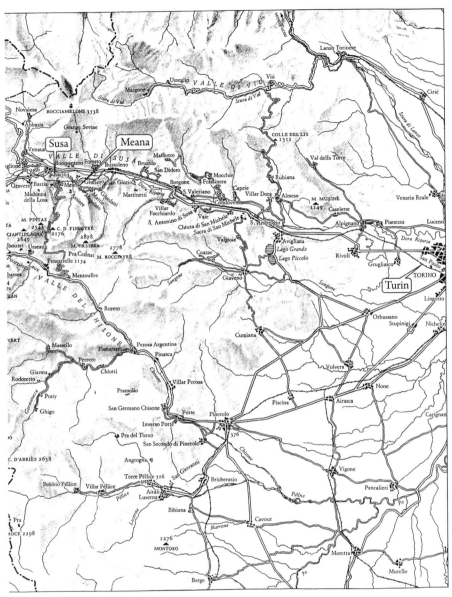

The Province of Turin from Turin to Susa

These maps represent the Province of Turin in the Piedmont Region of Italy. The Susa Valley, less than thirty kilometers west of Turin, formed a path of communication with France, making it extremely valuable to both the Germans and the partisans. Ada Gobetti's home in Meana, already a familiar meeting place for antifascists during the 1930s, was an important base of operations for many partisans during the *Resistenza*. The numbers represent elevations in meters. Ada Marchesini Gobetti and Goffredo Fofi, *Diario partigiano* (Turin: Einaudi, 1972).

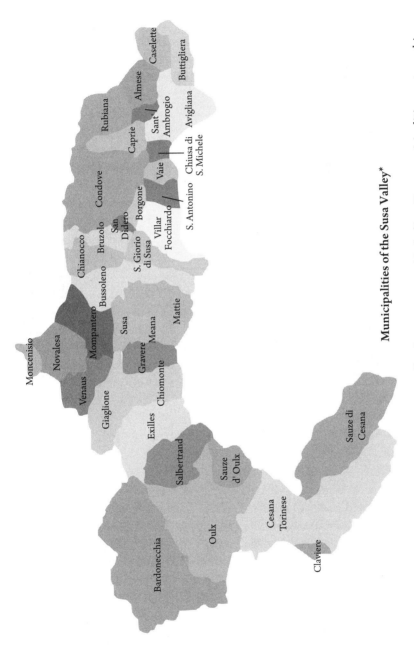

Municipalities of the Susa Valley*

This map shows the administrative divisions within the Susa Valley, known as *comuni* in Italian. These municipalities, or townships, are named after their principal towns or villages.

* For additional information about the Susa Valley, see www.conisa.it/IlConisaComuni.asp

Introduction

Ada Gobetti, a noted Italian translator, educator, politician, and women's rights activist, received the Silver Medal for Military Valor for her participation in the Italian Resistance, or *Resistenza*, the fight to liberate Italy from German occupation during the final years of World War II.[1] An ardent antifascist, she engaged actively in the principal noncommunist antifascist movement, called Giustizia e Libertà (Justice and Liberty, or GL) in the 1930s, and figured among the founders of its political heir, the Partito d'Azione (Action Party or Pd'A) in 1942.

Ada Gobetti's *Diario partigiano* is both diary and memoir. From the entry of the Germans into Turin on September 10, 1943, to the beginning of the insurrection of Turin on April 25, 1945—a little over twenty months—Ada recorded an almost daily account of events, reactions, sentiments, and personalities. She took notes in a cryptic English that only she could understand as a measure designed to keep the Germans and Fascists from reading the diary should it be discovered, and in order not to compromise her family and other partisans.[2] Thus a translation of the *Diario* from Italian to English brings us around full circle to the original language of her notes.[3]

In keeping a diary during the *Resistenza*, Ada continued a pattern she developed early in her life of writing down impressions of everyday events and recording important milestones. It was the Italian senator and philosopher Benedetto Croce, a longtime friend and mentor and foremost signatory of the Manifesto of the Antifascist Intellectuals in 1925, who encouraged Ada to convert into a book her notes chronicling her experiences as a partisan. Isolated in Naples and unable to correspond with her for the entire period of the German occupation, Croce wanted to read a firsthand account of the *Resistenza* in northern Italy. She began drafting her partisan memoirs in 1947, Italo Calvino recalled in his foreword to the original edition, "when her impressions were still warm and vivid," so that they could be "read by her old friend."[4] After the final diary entry, Ada added several pages where she reflected on the insurrection. These were written on April 28, 1949, the fourth anniversary of the liberation of Turin. In a letter to Croce in September 1950, Ada promised to copy her partisan memoirs for him, and was grateful that he wanted to read them because his opinion would be "valuable and enlightening."[5] She sent them over the course of the next year, and received Croce's very favorable impression in December 1951:

> I believe that your text is of great importance to the history of what happened in Piedmont, of all the efforts, events, and anxieties that made up the actions of the partisans. This part of the story does not have adequate treatment in the accounts of battles or military facts...it is fortunate when someone who narrates her own role can write pages like you have written, beautiful for their depth of sentiment and for the rare ability you have to rise above yourself and reach a heroic state of mind....Therefore you can be happy with the work you have accomplished.[6]

Croce then suggested how to present her work so that it would be accessible to her readers.

The *Diario partigiano* is exceptional both as a distinctive historical document and as a first-rate piece of literature. From a political and military point of view, the *Diario* provides firsthand knowledge of how the partisans in the Piedmont region fought, what obstacles they encountered, and who joined the struggle against the Nazis and the Fascists.[7] Often their success depended on the cooperation of everyday people, such as the concierge, landlord, or shopkeeper. Individuals with special skills in printing, typography, or engineering became essential to the dissemination of printed information or the transmitting of radio-telegraphic messages using International Morse Code.[8] Young people, most of whom had known nothing but fascism for their entire lives, played an essential role, not only through acts of sabotage but also by running errands between partisan groups and recruiting other young people to join the cause. The mountainous terrain and long winters of the Alpine regions where they fought and the ever-present threat of reprisals by German occupiers and their fascist partners exacerbated problems with organization among the various partisan groups.[9] So arduous was their fight that key military events—Italy's declaration of war on Germany, the fall of Rome, and the Allied landings on D-Day—appear in the diary as remote and almost unrelated events.

Ada Gobetti captures the anxieties and frustrations of everyday individuals and important leaders as they pursued their struggle against the Nazis and the Fascists. She writes of the heartbreak of mothers who lost their sons or watched them set out on dangerous missions of sabotage, relating it to her own worries about her son, Paolo, a young man by then and a very active partisan. She relates humorous incidents of longtime antifascists, eager to express noble sentiments but unsure of how to translate them into action. She reflects on the relationship between antifascist thought of the 1920s, in particular the ideas of her late husband Piero Gobetti, who published openly against fascism, and the armed struggle in which she and her family were participating. Beautiful descriptions of nature, often in stark contrast to the death and destruction around her, help to place the reader inside her story.

Although the *Resistenza* represented a culmination of more than twenty years of antifascist activity for Ada Gobetti, it also brought the beginning of an awareness of the specific talents, needs, and rights of Italian women, more than a hundred thousand of whom participated in the *Resistenza*.[10] This realization led her to organize other Italian women against the German occupiers and the fascist oppressors, found an underground women's newspaper, and solidify her views regarding women as a political force. Ada traces her personal coming of age with respect to women's issues and writes about how she was able to involve other women in the effort. She would work with women through two principal organizations. One, the Gruppi di difesa della donna e per l'assistenza ai combattenti per la libertà, or Gddd, begun in late 1943, claimed to unite women of all the antifascist parties in the struggle for liberation. The other, the Movimento femminile 'Giustizia e Libertà,' or Mfgl, came about through efforts of Ada Gobetti and others in the Action Party in 1944. Unlike the fascist women's organizations, which were conceived of by Mussolini and his men and operated under strict state surveillance and regulation, the Gddd and the Mfgl were founded, organized, and directed by women. In the case of the Gddd, moreover, local groups sprang up more or less spontaneously throughout northern Italy after November 1943. The women who participated braved extreme danger, worked despite hunger and cold, and constantly had to be aware of the possibility of arrest, torture, or execution at the hands of the German occupiers or their fascist collaborators.[11] The *Diario partigiano* tells their story.

Ada Prospero was born in Turin on July 23, 1902, the child of immigrants from Switzerland and Bosnia. Her parents, Giacomo Prospero and Olimpia Biacchi, owned a store that sold some of the finest fruits and vegetables in the city of Turin, and is said to have supplied the Queen Mother. She attended a prestigious and demanding classical *liceo* (secondary school), unusual for a girl of her time. At the age of eleven, she was already learning four languages, Italian, Latin, Greek, and French, and studying piano and voice. Seventeen-year-old Piero Gobetti, who lived in the same apartment building, invited sixteen-year-old Ada Prospero to work with him on a student periodical, *Energie Nove* (New Energies), that would "consist of the arts, literature, philosophy, social questions, etc.," and whose editorial staff would comprise young people exclusively.[12] He asked for her collaboration on the journal. Ada agreed not only to work with Piero on *Energie Nove* but also to study together.

Intellectual companionship blossomed quickly into romance. On October 30, 1918, only six weeks after their correspondence began, Ada Prospero and Piero Gobetti became engaged. The period of their courtship closely paralleled the rise to power of Benito Mussolini.

During her eight-year relationship with Piero, Ada witnessed firsthand the brutality of the Fascists and watched the increasing control of the fascist state over the lives of its citizens. When Mussolini seized control of the Italian government with the March on Rome of October 1922, Piero wasted no time in publishing openly his opposition to Mussolini. After their marriage in January 1923, Ada and Piero spent their honeymoon traveling extensively in Italy, meeting important political figures, and visiting Benedetto Croce at his home in Naples. No sooner had they returned to Turin than fascist thugs arrived in February to arrest Piero along with his father and the typographer who printed Piero's antifascist journal, *La Rivoluzione Liberale* (The Liberal Revolution), under the pretext of "belonging to subversive groups who plot against the state."[13] The correspondence and list of subscribers for the journal were confiscated. Ada described this first visit by the fascist police: "They persisted in looking for the invisible ink in my only bottle of cologne water, and they took away as 'subversive works' *The Republic* of Plato and *The Anarchy of Vittorio Alfieri* by Colosso."[14] After his release, Piero began a publishing house that over the next two years would become a voice of militant antifascism. When Piero called for the dismissal of Mussolini after socialist leader Giacomo Matteotti was assassinated on June 10, 1924, a squadron of Fascists appeared at their doorstep and beat Piero so severely that he suffered a permanent heart lesion.

Piero continued to protest openly and courageously against the fascist regime. His wife accompanied him as they fled from place to place in Italy and abroad. She watched her young husband's health deteriorate as the Fascists continued to pursue him. Despite these problems, Ada continued her schooling, earning her degree in philosophy from the Faculty of Letters and Philosophy at the University of Turin in June 1925, writing a thesis on Anglo-American pragmatism under Professor Annibale Pastore. An edict of November 1925 ordered Piero to cease all editorial activity. Around the same time, he suffered a heart attack. One month later, their son, Paolo, was born. Piero decided to go into exile in Paris, where a number of other antifascist intellectuals had already fled, and continue to publish from there. Ada was to join him after he found a place for them to live. Shortly after his arrival in Paris, however, Piero contracted bronchitis. He died on February 16, 1926, leaving Ada and their infant son alone. He was not quite twenty-five years old.

After Piero's death, Ada taught English in several private schools, acquired a solid reputation as a translator, and raised Paolo by herself. It was during this time that she developed a deep friendship with Benedetto Croce and his family. Such a friendship provided her with a prominent intellectual figure to guide her scholarly development and a second family with which to share summer vacations in Meana in the Susa Valley west of Turin.

In June 1937, Ada married Ettore Marchesini, brother of her longtime friends Maria, Ada, and Nella and an engineer working in Turin. Cesare Alvazzi, a friend of Paolo's and a partisan in the *Resistenza*, admired Ettore for his willingness to be a "nonprotagonist," remaining in the background, but supporting Ada unreservedly while she became more and more active as a public figure. He remembered Ettore for his strength of character, intelligence, and unassuming manner.[15]

During the 1930s, Ada engaged in an eclectic variety of resistance activities. She translated important works from English into Italian not only as a means to earn a living but also to bring important historical and literary works to an Italian people rapidly closing its mind to literature from abroad. Her translation of Herbert Albert Laurens Fisher's *A History of Europe* was censored by the fascist Ministry of Popular Culture in 1939 because of its severe criticisms of Adolf Hitler.[16] She wrote an antifascist children's book entitled *Storia del gallo Sebastiano: ovverosia il tredicesimo uovo* (The story of Sebastiano the rooster, otherwise known as the thirteenth egg) which was published in 1940.[17] She also pursued more traditional clandestine activities during this time, namely providing a place for antifascist colleagues to meet, keeping communication lines open among other antifascist individuals, producing and distributing leaflets attacking Mussolini's regime, contacting Italian antifascists living in France, and participating in the underground Giustizia e Libertà movement in Turin.

From June 10, 1940, when crowds gathered in the Piazza Venezia in Rome to hear Mussolini's declaration that Italy would enter World War II on the side of Germany, to the fall of Mussolini on July 24–25, 1943, Ada continued her activities in Giustizia e Libertà and helped to found the Action Party in 1942. Her principal academic project during this time was a manuscript on Alexander Pope, the eighteenth-century rationalist poet and satirist.[18] After the fall of Mussolini, Ada and many of her antifascist colleagues began the transition from clandestine activities to open resistance against the Nazis and the Fascists.

On September 9, the day after the announcement of the armistice between the Badoglio government and the Allies, Germany sent additional forces across the Italian border and occupied all of northern and central Italy, including Rome and extending almost as far south as Naples. German forces amounted to eighteen divisions by the beginning of October. Mussolini, rescued from imprisonment by German paratroopers on September 12, set up a puppet government on September 23 that was officially named the Italian Social Republic, but called the Republic of Salò after the town on Lake Garda in the north where the former leader sought refuge. On October 13, Badoglio's government declared war on Germany. In the meantime, leaders from the antifascist parties, including the Communist, Socialist, Christian Democratic, Liberal, and Action parties, banded together in Rome under the moderate socialist Ivanoe Bonomi to form the Comitato di liberazione nazionale (Committee of National Liberation, or Cln) and united in opposition to the Badoglio government and Mussolini's Republic of Salò. Each of these three governments—Badoglio's "legitimate government," Mussolini's Republic of Salò, and the Cln—claimed to be the true government of Italy. Although the British and the Americans recognized the Badoglio government, they also set up administrative units in areas they conquered and eventually established the Allied Control Commission (ACC) in November 1943 to administer military units and deal with Italian officials. Following the lead of the Cln, similar liberation committees sprang up in other cities, most importantly the Committee of National Liberation of Northern Italy (Clnai) in Milan in September 1943. The Cln of Turin often depended on information provided by Ada and her colleagues.

After their first meeting with fellow antifascists in Turin in September 1943, Ada, her second husband, Ettore Marchesini, and her son, Paolo Gobetti, accepted an assignment to work in the Susa Valley. Others would go to the nearby Pellice or Cuneese Valleys. Ada's home in Meana would serve as a refuge for partisans until the end of the war. Her landlord, Mario Cordola, offered his friendship and cooperation, making it possible for her to use the home as a haven for those who fought the Nazis and the Fascists throughout the *Resistenza*. Ada's activities in the Susa Valley ran the gamut from official duties to everyday tasks. One duty was to make contacts with local people and enlist them in the cause, which she called "taking the pulse" of the local men and women to see if they would work with them. For example, she helped to establish Teta's store in Susa, owned by villager Celestina Roglio, as a reference point for partisans and as a place to hide weapons. With her language skills, she acted as an interpreter between English officers and partisan commanders. She found places to deposit clandestine newspapers. She investigated arrests. She wrote of posting Cln flyers in Meana to warn young men born in 1925 not to present themselves for the draft. Sometimes Ada acted as a liaison between leaders of the various partisan formations. Her position of responsibility is evident in the personal contacts she had with important military leaders, known by their underground names as Braccini, Duccio, Lieutenant Ferrero, Laghi, Longo, Marcellin, and Valle, who had the greatest respect for her.[19]

At other times, Ada performed the simple task of making meals of *polenta*, *castagne* (chestnuts), and potatoes for her family and other partisans, many of whom would spend the night at her home in Meana. Ettore, ever supportive of Ada's endeavors, also contributed immensely to their clandestine activities. Using his expertise as an engineer, he devised radio-telegraphic links for communications and constructed the equipment to make false identification cards. Among his many feats as a partisan, Paolo engaged in acts of sabotage, searched for and hid weapons, and joined the formations in the Pellice Valley for a time. He also took advantage of the Nazi roundups to get local residents of Meana to become active in the *Resistenza*. As Massimo Mila observed, the "principal singularity of the events that are narrated in this book is in the maintaining of a bizarre and very tight familial nucleus, in the midst of events that make this little family of intellectuals—mother, son, and step-father—into a den of terrorists—or as they said then—of bandits."[20]

Ada acted as a liaison between Turin and the GL formations in the Susa Valley and in other places in the Piedmont region, holding the titles of "Inspectress of the GL Military Command" and "Political Commissary of the Fourth Alpine Division."[21] Despite the danger, throughout the German occupation many individuals who opposed the Nazis and the Fascists used Ada's home at 6 Via Fabro in Turin as a safe haven, a place to eat and sleep, and a meeting place for groups of resisters. Journalist E. G. Vichos described how Ada directed courier and information services out of her home in Turin: "Allied parachutists, saboteurs, informers spread amongst the ranks of the enemy, and Allied ex-prisoners who wanted to join the partisans, all knew about the 'house of miracles' where they knew they could find maps, munitions, explosives, information, comfort, and whatever else they needed to conduct the unrestrained attack without a headquarters."[22] Frequently, Ada herself brought orders from the partisan commands in the city to the leaders of the various brigades in the mountains. She went back and forth between Turin and Meana several times a week, on the train, on her bicycle, and even on foot. She also continued to teach, which most likely served as a ruse for her antifascist activities. The friendship and loyalty of Espedita Martinoli, the concierge at her home in Turin, was essential for Ada's resistance activities in the city. The loyal employee would warn Ada of impending roundups and divert Fascists or Germans seeking to search the house.

On New Year's Eve 1944, Ada left for France with a group of seven other partisans. They would climb across the Alps through the Passo dell'Orso and carry important documents to the French and Allied commands in Grenoble, which had been liberated a few months before. They also hoped to establish a permanent communications link with the Allies. When Ada returned from France at the end of February 1945, she had to face new complexities that had arisen with respect to the partisans in the Susa Valley because the Allies were pressuring them to form a single command. She continued to work incessantly until the partisans liberated Turin on April 28.

After the war ended, Ada's experience as a resister developed into a constructive political and social activism. Alessandro Galante Garrone, a Piedmontese magistrate and historian who was in the *Resistenza* with Ada, remembered how she worked incessantly without holding back, even sacrificing her health, because of her dedication to the many civil battles of the postwar period.[23] In her capacity as vice mayor of Turin, the first woman to hold such a position in Italy, Ada labored diligently to effect positive reforms in the schools and fought openly for the rights of women and children in Italian society. She was a leading figure in the Unione donne italiane (Union of Italian Women or Udi) in Italy and a founder of the multinational Federazione democratica internazionale delle donne (the Women's International Democratic Federation or Fdif). She witnessed the birth of the Italian Republic, officially proclaimed on June 18, 1946, after the first election where women could vote, and worked to integrate women into the decision-making process of the country. Ada became deeply involved in the international women's rights movement, traveling to Paris, Berlin, and China as a representative from Italy. She also wrote extensively on child rearing and devoted much of the remainder of her life to pedagogical activities to promote a "democratic education" for both children and parents. Through her children's stories, books and articles for parents, and ideas for school reform, Ada would mold a new generation. Perhaps this generation of children—the first in nearly twenty-five years not to be schooled under fascism—along with their parents could finally break the legacy of fascism.

Ada's diary was one of her most important legacies. By recording her memories as they happened and publishing them in her *Diario partigiano*, she changed what we know about the *Resistenza* and the German occupation of Italy. It is easy to romanticize the *Resistenza*, recalling tales of partisans in the hills carrying out acts of sabotage and women hiding documents from the Germans under maternity clothes. Certainly Italians who wished to forget their support of Mussolini have mythologized their level of involvement in the *Resistenza*. Moreover, some Italians turned antifascist only after the German occupation that began in September 1943. Of the "true" antifascists, many idealized pre-fascist Italy, exaggerated its level of democracy, and simply hoped for a return to the prewar status quo. But like Piero Gobetti, Ada believed fascism had its roots in pre-1922 liberalism. Many Fascists equated the defeat of fascism with the defeat of the Italian nation.[24] In contrast, Ada and many of her antifascist colleagues believed that defeating fascism was a first step in the creation of a new Italian national identity. Yet despite her idealistic observations about solidarity and unity, she knew Italy had to break completely from its pre-fascist past in order to create a more democratic society. She believed that the *Resistenza* would be a model for the creation of a new Italian state.

Though Ada wrote frequently in the *Diario* about the beauty of the human solidarity that existed during the period of the *Resistenza*, where priests worked alongside Communists for freedom from the Nazis and the Fascists, a closer analysis of her experiences demonstrates that the antifascist movement was by no means unified. During the partisan war, Ada used her significant skills in conflict resolution for everything from settling petty differences to mitigating serious disagreements in ideology. Cooperation among the antifascist parties during the *Resistenza* disguised the differences in their political ideologies that became evident again after the war. Action Party leader Leo Valiani held that the Liberals and the Christian Democrats wanted to restore the parliamentary government of pre-fascist Italy, while the Communists, Socialists, and Actionists wanted to establish a republic that reflected a new political system.[25] From the time Alcide De Gasperi left office in 1953 to Ada's death on March 14, 1968, Italy changed prime ministers eleven times, testifying to the turmoil plaguing the government of Italy.[26] Left-wing demonstrations in the 1960s and student militancy, such as that which erupted in Turin at the close of 1967, reminded former activists of the *Resistenza* that most of their goals for postwar Italy had not been realized.[27] Although she continued to believe in the values of the *Resistenza* until she died, Ada Gobetti recognized in the student protests of 1967–68 glaring evidence that the *Resistenza* had not yet created a postwar Italy that reflected political and social regeneration.[28]

Seeing Ada Gobetti as a mother during the *Resistenza*, one of many mothers whose teenage sons had joined the partisans, illustrates the depth to which she would sacrifice for a future of freedom and democracy. Motherhood provided the connecting thread between the antifascist struggle of the 1920s that she experienced with Piero Gobetti, the battle of the *Resistenza* that she shared with her son Paolo, and the postwar Italy that she wanted to create, where young people like Paolo would be able to make their own choices and pursue their dreams without encumbrance. The mother-son relationship between Ada and Paolo, who toiled side by side during the *Resistenza*, contrasted completely with the fascist conception of mothers as servants of the state. Moreover, motherhood became a mechanism for her to teach other mothers, through her example, to turn their grief into activism for the public good. The maternal feelings that she expressed did not merely reflect her personal hurt and anguish. In her desire to attract women to become active participants in the struggle for liberty during the *Resistenza* and beyond, she used motherhood as a common ground on which to build a society and a lasting peace. Motherhood, with its absence of political, class, or religious connotations and its universal appeal, became a valuable tool toward acceptance of her ideas by other women. The solidarity with other mothers that she felt during the *Resistenza* became a personification of the human solidarity she believed would be the basis for a democratic society in the future. In her capacity as a mother, Ada created a bond with other mothers. She understood the fears that mothers faced. Although she insisted that she was not a pacifist, she used motherhood to demonstrate the negative impact of war on family and society. She gave new meaning to the concept of maternity, which contrasted greatly with the fascist view.[29]

Though at first Ada thought men and women who participated in the *Resistenza* had the same goals, she grew to realize that women had something of their own to offer the partisan struggle. Moreover, their fight had broader implications. Italian women fought for the liberation of their country from the Nazis and the Fascists, but many also sought the liberation of women in Italian society. Although some women became involved through male members of their families, others followed the lead of women like Ada and entered the public sphere of their own accord. Through her leadership role in women's organizations during the *Resistenza*, she learned that women represented a strong political force for change. She believed women's role in the *Resistenza* would encourage political involvement to better Italian society after the war.

In her effort to ensure a proper place for women who had participated in the *Resistenza*, Ada Gobetti had to wage a battle against the way the *Resistenza* was being remembered by politicians who sought only to glorify the past for personal or party agendas and historians who reconstructed the *Resistenza* without crediting women for their extraordinary contribution. Italian women did not simply participate in a movement made up primarily of men who carried arms; nor did they only engage in activities that supported those of the men. Despite the cultural and political obstacles to Italian women participating in the public sphere, these women played an active role in the *Resistenza,* creating their own form of resistance and affecting the military and political nature of the *Resistenza* by their very participation.[30]

With the publication of the *Diario partigiano*, Ada Gobetti shared her own experiences in the *Resistenza* and in so doing also illuminated the actions of countless other participants. Her autobiographical account is not necessarily representative of other Italian women's experiences during the 1943–1945 period, however, which depended on factors such as degree of political involvement, party affiliation, and geographic location in the South (which was occupied by the Allies) or in the North (which fell under German occupation).[31] The antifascist music critic and historian Massimo Mila said the *Diario* carried people back to the "first reasons" for their political struggle and to the realism that was "the beauty of the Italian Resistance," during a period when "workers and bourgeois, intellectuals and farmers, set about on an undertaking that was unusual for all of them...without...changing themselves, without becoming adventurers and misfits, but remaining...workers, farmers, writers, clerks, professionals, and businessmen, even if they learned to become perfect partisans."[32] Others who fought in the *Resistenza* with Ada noted in the *Diario* the absence of hatred or cruelty toward the enemy and a deep sense of compassion for all those affected by war.[33] The *Diario* shows that resistance went far beyond armed resistance. Moreover, it describes the actions of ordinary people who met, organized, and worked together despite their often vastly different political ideologies.[34]

The *Diario* also described antifascists who did not work in solidarity, but exhibited skepticism and distrust, which Ada tried to mitigate. *Resistenza* leader Giorgio Agosti admitted that he began reading the *Diario* with some diffidence, thinking it would be the same as other partisan stories, replete with technical information and political discussions. Surprisingly, he found beautiful descriptions of life that continued and the optimism that he always associated with Ada.[35] After reading the *Diario*, Ada Della Torre, who was a *staffetta* (courier) in the *Resistenza* and worked closely with Ada, wrote to her friend of the importance of writing so that they did not forget the positive experience of the *Resistenza* and of her hope that others would do the same.[36]

The changing political climate in Italy between the end of the war in 1945 and the publication of the *Diario* in 1956 may have influenced what Ada Gobetti chose to include in the *Diario*. Of the five parties that had formed the Cln during the *Resistenza* only the Christian Democratic, Communist, and Socialist Parties played a significant role in Italian politics after 1946. By the beginning of 1946, support for the Action Party, Ada's party, had waned considerably. In the municipal elections held in Turin on November 10, 1946, no representative of the nearly defunct Action Party was elected to the eighty-member Turin City Council. After Christian Democrat Alcide De Gasperi formed his third government in January 1947, he set out to exclude the Communists and their socialist allies from his coalition government. In support of De Gasperi's action, on May 31, 1947, the Constituent Assembly confirmed the end of the antifascist coalition.[37] With the demise of the Action Party, Ada had remained independent for almost ten years. Though she was idealistic, Ada was also very practical. It would have been totally unrealistic of her, as a woman in a male-dominated society, to think she could somehow rejuvenate such a party. Without the Action Party as a viable option, the Communist Party seemed closest to Ada Gobetti's radical ideas regarding women's rights and social reform. She joined the Communist Party at the beginning of 1956 and made one simple statement about her decision: "One cannot remain a spectator all one's life; one must know how to choose, and assume one's own responsibilities."[38] Paolo Spriano, the partisan who went to France with Ada in the winter of 1945 who later became a historian of the Italian Communist Party, called her choice one that was "meditated on for a long time"; it was "the fruit of that ideological bent that had animated her entire life as a militant antifascist and her sympathy for the popular classes."[39] In the *Diario*, she demonstrated admiration both for her Action Party colleagues and for many Communists, and praised the organizational abilities of the Communists in particular.

The *Diario* also does not tell us much about Ada Gobetti's intimate feelings, except when they involve Paolo. She rarely expresses concern for her own life; her fears are confined to worries about Paolo. Sometimes her anguish over Paolo may appear excessive, but she came to the *Resistenza* with an unusual life-changing event in her past. She lost her husband when she was only twenty-three, an age when most people do not consider death a reality. Though eighteen-year-old Paolo seems fearless, Ada knows that she can lose him also.

She never mentions that in June 1944 Field-Marshall Kesselring commanded that "the fight against the partisans...be carried out with all means at (their) disposal and with utmost severity" or that the German commander ordered that "every act of violence committed by partisans" be "punished immediately." At the end of July 1944, Kesselring issued more detailed orders against the partisans and civilians who helped them. He told his soldiers to shoot civilians who supplied partisans with food, shelter, or military information (spying), activities that many women pursued. Civilians would also be shot if they hid or transported ammunition, or if they failed to report immediately to the German authorities weapons or ammunition concealed by others. Moreover, Kesselring commanded that, where partisan bands operated in large numbers, hostages (preferably relatives of partisans or able-bodied sympathizers) were to be taken first from the population of the district in which they appeared. If soldiers were fired at from any locality, the village would be burned to the ground. Finally, all civilians captured in battles with partisans and in the course of the reprisals would be sent to collecting centers for transfer to the Reich as laborers. Ada Gobetti was "guilty" of every one of these violations, as were many other women.

Another gap in her autobiographical account is that she does not present any overt opinions about the Holocaust in the *Diario*, except to express some concern for Jewish individuals who were helping the cause of the *Resistenza*. No Italian Jews were deported to Auschwitz or similar camps under Mussolini, but this situation changed after the German occupation, when more than 6,800 Jews in Italy were deported and gassed.[40] Yet Ada never mentions that her close friends Lisetta Giua and Vittorio Foa, frequent visitors to her home in Turin, were Jewish. Moreover, Alberto Salmoni, who accompanied Paolo on his first trip to France and joined Ada and the group of seven other partisans who went to France at the end of 1944, was Jewish as well. Though Ada admits that she did not hear of Auschwitz until she was in Grenoble in early 1945, she does allude at times to the danger Jews faced. Yet she never expresses any fear of reprisal for her close association with several Italian Jews.

When Ada accepted the Premio Prato for the *Diario partigiano*, she stated that the *Resistenza* was not a historical cycle that was concluded, but represented a permanent obligation.[41] Journalist Alda Radaelli once asked her what she thought about all the celebrations that were taking place on the anniversary of the *Resistenza*. She replied:

> It seems to me that they are wrapping it up with a beautiful label to send it to the museum. Why cut it out as a single and unrepeatable moment, speak of it as a point of arrival instead of a point of departure? Its validity lies in the fact that conformity could not survive: new

situations imposed new solutions, and this is what we must make young people understand. If we knew how to analyze that period with its contrasts, limits, and mistakes, we would give them the possibility of a choice, and we would not see them sink lifelessly into a loss of will power nor wander hopelessly in search of something solid, nor fold up in morose and gangster-like forms. They will find the same moral imperative that we had: like every stage of man has a maturity of its own, so every epoch of history has its own duty for young people, that can be expressed in forms and modes that are completely different, but that will always have the same creative and innovative impulse.[42]

Ada Gobetti never wanted to use the *Resistenza* to assuage national guilt. She held Italians responsible for fascism. Despite her nostalgic longing for the solidarity she experienced during the *Resistenza*, she advocated an in-depth analysis of its strengths and weaknesses, successes and failures. I hope that this translation of the *Diario partigiano* will help to enrich our understanding of the Italian experience, and that of Italian women in particular, during the *Resistenza*.

Notes

1. Historians have long debated the meaning of the *Resistenza*. Claudio Pavone's master-piece, recently translated into English, analyzes the *Resistenza* as a civil war, a class war, and a patriotic war. Claudio Pavone, *Una guerra civile: Saggio storico sulla moralità nella Resistenza* (Turin: Bollati Boringhieri, 1991).
2. The term "partisan," often used interchangeably with "patriot," has a variety of mean-ings. The Allied Control Commission defined *patriots* as "persons in the ranks of genuine bands who have carried out arms against the enemy, engaged in sabotage or secured important military information for the benefit of the Allied war effort." *New York Times*, 22 July 1944, 4:4, as quoted in Charles F. Delzell, *Mussolini's Enemies: The Italian Anti-Fascist Resistance* (Princeton: Princeton University Press, 1961), 410 and n. 72. In Ada's diary, however, the partisans were not working for the Allies, but rather to oust the Germans and the Fascists. Some partisans had been active in the antifascist under-ground for many years; others joined the cause after the German invasion. Some were armed; others "fought" with nonviolent means.
3. Ada Gobetti Marchesini Prospero, *Diario partigiano* (1956; reprint, with an introduc-tion by Goffredo Fofi, a foreword by Italo Calvino, and a postscript by Bianca Guidetti Serra, Turin: Giulio Einaudi editore, s.p.a., 1996). The 1956 edition is stamped "Saggi 202" on the page following the title page, and has three pages introducing the diary, simply signed "L'Editore." Fofi's introduction to the 1996 edition is followed by three pages entitled "Nota," signed by Italo Calvino and dated 1956. Calvino died in 1985; his comments in the 1996 edition are a reproduction of those signed "L'Editore" in the 1956 edition. There was also an edition aimed at a juvenile audience and meticulously edited by Goffredo Fofi. Ada Marchesini Gobetti and Goffredo Fofi, *Diario partigiano* (Turin: Einaudi, 1972.)
4. Italo Calvino, forward to *Diario partigiano* (1996), 13.
5. Ada Gobetti, Turin, to Benedetto Croce, 21 September 1950, in *Mezzosecolo* 7 (1987–1989): 218. The entire correspondence between Ada Gobetti and Benedetto Croce has

been reprinted in Ada Gobetti and Benedetto Croce, "Carissima Ada, Gentilissimo Senatore: Carteggio, Ada Gobetti-Benedetto Croce, 1928–1952," ed. Sergio Caprioglio, *Mezzosecolo* 7 (1987–1989): 46–227.

6. Benedetto Croce, Naples, to Ada Gobetti, 26 December 1951, *Mezzosecolo* 7: 222–223.

7. Ada Gobetti uses the term "Nazi-Fascist" in the *Diario* only rarely, perhaps because the term was so controversial. Claudio Pavone argues that "once the figure of the Fascist enemy was redefined alongside the figure of the German enemy, the unifying category of 'Nazi-Fascist' was not always sufficient to hold them together, even if it felt very accurate to most members of the Resistance and was not invalidated by the fact that the Fascist was the servant of the German; in fact, it was not a matter of an occasional servant, but of a servant morally and politically consonant with the master." Pavone, *Una guerra civile*, 266.

8. The International Morse Code was an adaption of the Morse Telegraphic Code, which altered the digital pattern for various characters to make them clearer and easier to transmit over radio. These messages were often encrypted as well so that the enemy would not understand them.

9. By 1944, four principal bands of partisans existed in the Piedmont region: the Garibaldini (Communists); the Matteotti (Socialists); the Giustizia e Libertà, or GL (Actionists); and the Autonomi (Autonomous forces, but often staffed by Christian Democrats or Liberals).

10. Figures cannot be exact, given the clandestine nature of resistance in general and the fluidity with which some women moved between military and nonmilitary activities. Some sources indicate that more than 70,000 belonged to the Gruppi di difesa della donna and 35,000 were partisans or troops in the field. More detailed reports show that 4,723 women had responsibilities for political organization and propaganda; 4,633 were arrested, tortured, and tried; 2,750 were deported to Germany; 1,750 were wounded; 623 were executed or killed in combat; and 512 held the title of Commanding Officer or Battle Inspector. These figures were taken from Bianca Guidetti Serra, "Quello che scrivevano le donne della Resistenza sui loro giornali," in *1945, Il voto alle donne*, ed. Laura Derossi (Milan: Franco Angeli, Consiglio Regionale del Piemonte, 1998), 102, who indicated that she obtained her numbers from the 1964 edition of Luigi Longo, *Un popolo alla macchia* and Camilla Ravera, "La donna nella lotta contro il fascismo e per la democrazia," *Il Congresso di Parigi*, single issue edited by the Federazione democratica internazionale delle donne (March 1946), 13. At the special session of the Turin City Council held on 25 April 1995 to mark the fiftieth anniversary of the liberation of Turin, Council President Domenico Carpanini put the total figure of women who participated in the *Resistenza* at 120,000. Domenico Carpanini, *50° Anniversario della Liberazione* (Turin: Città di Torino, 25 April 1995), 24. Perry R. Willson has estimated the number to be much higher, possibly reaching two million. See Perry R. Willson, "Saints and Heroines: re-writing the history of Italian women in the resistance," in Tim Kirk and Anthony McElligott, eds., *Opposing Fascism: Community, Authority and Resistance in Europe* (New York: Cambridge University Press. 1999), 180.

11. For an analysis of the women's clandestine newspapers, see Bianca Guidetti Serra, "Quello che scrivevano le donne della resistenza sui loro giornali," 102–134. For a study of the Gruppi di difesa della donna, see Jomarie Alano, "Armed with a Yellow Mimosa: Women's Defense and Assistance Groups in Italy, 1943–1945," *Journal of Contemporary History*, 2003, *38*(4): 615–631.

12. Piero Gobetti, Turin, to Ada Prospero, 14 September 1918, in Ada and Piero Gobetti, *Nella tua breve esistenza: Lettere 1918–1926*, ed. Ersilia Alessandrone Perona (Turin: Giulio Einaudi editore, 1991), 5.

13. Paolo Gobetti, Pietro Polito, Marco Scavino, and Ivana Solavagione, eds., *Racconto Interrotto: Piero Gobetti nel ricordo degli amici* (Turin: Centro studi Piero Gobetti, 1992), 73.

14. Ada Marchesini Gobetti, "Come nacque la 'Rivoluzione Liberale,' *Resistenza e Giustizia e Libertà* (January 1968): 3.

15. Cesare Alvazzi, interview by author, Susa, Italy, 11 November 2001.

16. H. A. L. Fisher, *A History of Europe* (London: Eyre and Spottiswoode, 1935). Ada Gobetti's translation appeared in three volumes with the following citation: H. A. L. Fisher, "Storia antica e medievale," *Storia d'Europa,* vol. 1, traduzione di Ada Prospero (Bari: Laterza, 1936), 438 pages. H. A. L. Fisher, "Rinascimento-Riforma-Illuminismo," *Storia d'Europa*, vol. 2, traduzione italiana di Ada Prospero (Bari: Laterza, 1936), 398 pages. H. A. L. Fisher, "L'Esperimento liberale," *Storia d'Europa*, vol. 3, traduzione italiana di Ada Prospero (Bari: Laterza, 1937), 488 pages.

17. Margutte (Ada Prospero), *Storia del gallo Sebastiano ovverosia il tredicesimo uovo* (Milan: Garzanti, 1940). For an analysis of this children's story, see Jomarie Alano, "Anti-Fascism for Children: Ada Gobetti's Story of Sebastiano the Rooster," *Modern Italy* (February 2012): 69–83.

18. Ada Prospero, *Il poeta del razionalismo settecentesco: Alessandro Pope* (Bari: Laterza, 1943). Pope wrote *Essays on Criticism* (1711), *The Rape of the Lock* (1712), *Essays on Man* (1733–1734) and *Moral Essays* (1731–1735). Pope is also the author of everyday sayings such as "To err is human, to forgive divine" and "Fools rush in where angels fear to tread."

19. Paolo Braccini was a university professor and representative of the Action Party in the first Piedmontese Military Command, headed by Giuseppe Perotti. Both men were condemned by the Special Tribunal, executed in Turin on 5 April 1944, and decorated with the gold medal for military valor. Duccio (Tancredi Galimberti) was regional commander of the GL formations in the Piedmont region. Killed by the Fascists on 3 December 1944, Galimberti was decorated with the gold medal for military valor. Lieutenant Ferrero (Vittorio Morone) commanded formations in the Susa Valley. Laghi (Giulio Bolaffi), an Italian Jew, commanded the entire IV Alpine GL Division. Longo (Germano Chiapusso) was commander of the GL forces in the Susa Valley. Maggiorino Marcellin, a former ski instructor, was commander of the Autonomous forces of the Chisone Valley. Valle (Egidio Liberti) was chief of staff of the GL Regional Military Command.

20. Massimo Mila, "Una famiglia di partigiani," *L'Unità* (10 June 1956).

21. Bianca Guidetti Serra, "Idee, opere, incontri e stagioni di una donna 'fatta di fuoco'," *Il Giornale dei Genitori* (July–August 1988): 5.

22. E. G. Vichos, "Una donna d'Italia: Ada Gobetti Marchesini," *Pensiero e Azione*, Ancona (15 January 1946).

23. Alessandro Galante Garrone, "Ada Gobetti: Il filo della rivolta," *l'Astrolabio* (24 March 1968): 33.

24. Pavone, *Una guerra civile*, 169.

25. Charles F. Delzell, "The Italian Anti-Fascist Resistance in Retrospect: Three Decades of Historiography," *Journal of Modern History* 47 (March 1975): 71.

26. Giuseppe Pella from August 1953 to January 1954, Amintore Fanfani from January 1954 to February 1954, Mario Scelba from February 1954 to July 1955, Antonio Segni from July 1955 to May 1957, Adone Zoli from May 1957 to June 1958, Amintore Fanfani from July 1958 to February 1959, Antonio Segni from February 1959 to March 1960, Fernando Tambroni from March 1960 to July 1960, Amintore Fanfani from July 1960 to June 1963, Giovanni Leone from June 1963 to December 1963, and Aldo Moro from December 1963 to June 1968. Denis Mack Smith, *Modern Italy: A Political History* (Ann Arbor: University of Michigan Press, 1997), 499.

27. Paul Ginsborg, *A History of Contemporary Italy: Society and Politics, 1943–1988* (London, Penguin Books, 1990), 71.

28. David Forgacs, "Fascism and Antifascism Reviewed: Generations, History, and Film in Italy after 1968," in Helmut Peitsch, Charles Burdett, and Claire Gorrara, *European Memories of the Second World War* (New York: Berghahn Books, 1999), 187.

29. See Anna Rossi Doria, *Diventare cittadine: il voto delle donne in Italia* (Florence: Giunti, 1996), 53.

30. See Perry R. Willson, "Women, War and the Vote: Gender and Politics in Italy," *Women's History Review* 7, no. 4 (1998): 619; Anna Bravo and Anna Maria Bruzzone, *In guerra*

senza armi: Storie di donne, 1940–1945 (Rome-Bari: Gius. Laterza & Figli, 1995); and Mirna Cicioni, "'In order to be considered we must first have fought': Women in the Italian Resistance," in *Never Give In: The Italian Resistance and Politics*, ed. Alastair Davidson and Steve Wright (New York: Peter Lang, 1998), 100.

31. Ersilia Alessandrone Perona, "Sincronia e diacronia nelle scritturi femminili della seconda guerra mondiale," 122–124. Iris Origo also wrote a diary of her experiences in the *Resistenza* and published it under the title *War in Val D'Orcia, 1943–1944* (London: J. Cape, 1951).

32. Mila, "Una famiglia di partigiani."

33. Elvira Pajetta, review of *Diario partigiano*, in *Fiaccola Ardente* (June 1956).

34. Maria Tanini, "Nel *Diario partigiano* una puntigliosa difesa del 'quotidiano'," *Il Giornale dei Genitori* (July–August 1988): 43.

35. Giorgio Agosti, *Dopo il tempo del furore: Diario 1946–1988*, ed. Aldo Agosti (Turin: Giulio Einaudi editore, 2005), 66–67.

36. Ada Della Torre Ortona, n.p., to Ada Gobetti, 18 September, n.d., Acspg, Fondo Ada Gobetti.

37. Ginsborg, *A History of Contemporary Italy*, 112.

38. Ada Gobetti, as quoted in Bianca Guidetti Serra, "Una donna, una persona," *Mezzosecolo* 7: 376.

39. Paolo Spriano, "Una donna del secondo Risorgimento nazionale," *L'Unità* (16 March 1968).

40. Susan Zuccotti, *The Italians and the Holocaust: Persecution, Rescue, and Survival* (Lincoln: University of Nebraska Press, 1987), 57, xxvi.

41. Luigi Balestrieri, "A 'mamma' Gobetti il Premio Prato 1956," *Patria Indipendente*, 6 January 1957.

42. Alda Radaelli, "Un giorno a Reaglie," *Il Giornale dei Genitori* (Summer 1968): 12.

Partisan Diary

ADA GOBETTI

I dedicate these memories to my friends, both near and far, to those of twenty years and to those of only an hour. Because friendship—a link of solidarity founded not on kinship nor homeland nor intellectual tradition, but on the simple human rapport of feeling close to one another in a crowd of many—appears to me to have been the profound significance, the symbol of our battle. Perhaps it truly was. Only if we are able to preserve it, perfect it, or recreate it, after so many mistakes and so much disgrace, will we be able to understand that this unity, this friendship, was not and must not be only a means to achieving something else, but is a value in and of itself, because in it is perhaps the meaning of mankind. Only then will we be able to rethink our past and see again the faces of our friends, alive and dead, without melancholy and without despair.

10–12 September 1943

I think I must have begun my story at that moment—around four o'clock in the afternoon of 10 September 1943—when, while I was distributing leaflets with Paolo, Ettore, and Lisetta at the corner of Via Cernaia and Corso Galileo Ferraris, with incredulous eyes, I saw a string of German automobiles pass by.[1]

At first, during Badoglio's forty days, I truly did not take it seriously.[2] Excitement, a continuous celebration, yes. From the first moment, on the morning of 26 July, when I heard the news on the radio in Meana, gradually, confusedly, first in Czechoslovakian, then in Greek, I reacted with almost hysterical laughter. Then the precipitous return to Turin, and the house filled with people, and all the friends who could see each other freely at last, and those who, day after day, returned from *confino*, from exile, from prison—Rossi and Ginzburg, Venturi and Foa.[3] The excitement of the first semi-clandestine press. A whirlwind in which it was wonderful to feel myself drawn, a joy that seemed just compensation for so many years of isolation. I plunged into "working" with

[1] Paolo Gobetti was the son of Ada and Piero Gobetti. Ettore Marchesini was Ada's second husband and brother of dear friends Maria, Ada, and Nella Marchesini. When she was a law student in Turin in 1941, Lisetta Giua had organized other students into what eventually became a nucleus of the Pci's Fronte della Gioventù (Young People's Front). See Jane Slaughter, *Women and the Italian Resistance, 1943–1945* (Denver: Arden Press, 1997), 46.

[2] I believe Ada meant Badoglio's forty-five days, the period between Mussolini's fall on 25 July 1943 to the armistice of 8 September 1943.

[3] *Confino* was a punishment conferred under fascism by which offenders were sent to remote locations in Italy in a type of domestic exile. Ernesto Rossi was part of the group who published the antifascist newspaper *Non Mollare* in Florence, along with Carlo Rosselli and Gaetano Salvemini. Leone Ginzburg, a Russian-born immigrant and the first Italian professor of Russian literature, served as Piero Gobetti's mentor for his writings on Russian novelists and intellectuals. He died under torture in the Regina Coeli prison in Rome in 1944 because of his antifascist activities. See Nadia Urbinati, introduction to Piero Gobetti, *On Liberal Revolution* (New Haven: Yale University Press, 2000), xl n. 26. Franco Venturi was the famous historian of the Enlightenment. Vittorio Foa was a lawyer convicted by the Special Tribunal as a member of the Giustizia e Libertà movement and representative of the Action Party in the Committee of National Liberation (Cln) of the Piedmont region.

the friends I found around me, those with whom I had remained in touch, or come into contact in the preceding years, and who to some extent espoused Piero's ideas, without fully understanding them very well, without even trying to understand, with pure sentimental attachment and enthusiasm, full of faith. Today, when I think about it again, it seems impossible that, despite my age and experience, I was able to be so much like a young girl in those days, so superficial and free, almost with a spirit of innocence, a state of mind of being on vacation. (I believe, however, that this was the state of mind of many among us.) Perhaps the only serious thing was the feeling that, as on the most wonderful vacation, all this "could not last," and the waiting for something that would otherwise and more profoundly engage us.

Therefore that day, when I saw the German automobiles pass by, suddenly I had the feeling that the vacation was over. It was not that I was aware of the reality of the situation, not even partially. On the contrary, I continued to reason with my customary foolish, subconscious optimism: certainly the German automobiles were carrying some parliamentarians, the proposals would be rejected, and Turin would be protected.

People crowded around us. One of my most poignant memories of that day was the anxiety of the passersby who, seeing us with the printed sheets in our hands, believed us to be well informed about secret things and questioned us, hoping to know, to understand. They were pitiful in their isolation, in their abandonment. Left to themselves, with neither material nor moral weapons, without direction, without one watchword. Yet, if a hand were extended to them, who knows how many of those who turned to us with such touching hope would have known how to forget their ineffective selves and become "companions" in the highest sense of the term. I wanted to hold out a hand to them, but I was neither better off nor better prepared than they. I continued to say stupid words of encouragement, watching the façade of the Camera del Lavoro.[4] Only a few hours had passed since the morning's meeting. That joy, that enthusiasm of feeling truly close to one another in a crowd of many, that sense of fraternity acquired through common hope and common suffering, was it possible that such strength had been an illusion? Yet every time I lowered my eyes again to the leaflets that I had in my hand, the printed words ("resistance," "desire for revolution," "liberty," "justice") appeared to me to be more and more futile, pitiful, and unreal.

---

[4] Ada gave this description of the Camera del Lavoro: "Built with contributions from the workers, the Camera del Lavoro was...on Galileo Ferraris between Carlo Promis, Papacino, and Sebastiano Valfrè Streets. Burned and occupied by the Fascists in 1921, leftist union members retook it after 25 July 1943. It was from its balcony that on 10 September, after the armistice, representatives of the various parties incited the Turinese people to resist the German occupation." Ada Gobetti, *Camilla Ravera. Vita in carcere e al confino con lettere e documenti* (Parma. Ugo Guanda, 1969), 10 n. 1.

Renato Martorelli was the one who convinced us that it was almost absurd to hope. This was also the last time I saw him.[5] (How many faces—noble, dear faces like his—appear for an instant in these pages, and then disappear into a shadow, never to return.) He was with someone else and came toward me, determined, his habitually pale face marked by worry and fatigue: "Leave. What is there left to do? Adami Rossi has handed the city over to the Germans. Leave quickly."[6]

The crowd around us began to thin out. We went away reluctantly, still incredulous. At home, a young man who was listening to the radio greeted us excitedly: "Farinacci is speaking from Monaco. They have reconstructed the Fascist Party. It is a true incitement to civil war!"[7] I shrugged my shoulders with a sense of annoyance. At that moment, Monaco and Farinacci mattered little to me. I thought there were more urgent things to do right now, like burn documents, especially the cards of those who were registered in the "Volunteers of the Armed Nation" for the "Italian Resistance Front." A heavy physical weariness began to weigh on me. While Lisetta made me a cup of coffee, I set about collecting the dangerous documents.

Meanwhile Paolo was arguing heatedly with some friends: "We have to do something. We cannot surrender like this. Let's remove the rails; let's raise the barricades," he shouted with a tone of desperation that rang strangely in his still young voice. It was the first time his heart had been broken. It was the first time when, as a young fellow, he had loved something and believed in something, in that strong desire to resist that he felt inside instinctively. Now he did not want to believe that this faith and this love had been illusory.

Ettore arrived with the news that one of his colleagues had found a gun. What should he do with it? "Take it," I said quickly. Ettore went away again, running, and Paolo disappeared behind him.

The documents were burning. The study was deserted. In the dining room— as if they were obeying an instinctive need for greater prudence—they held a kind of war council. Andreis, Agosti, Foa, Venturi, and Peccei were there. Luigi Scala was also there—Scala, who had been released from his long imprisonment only two days before, and whom I was to see again for a moment three years later, on his return from Mauthausen, so physically destroyed that not even his indomitable spirit could save him.[8]

---

[5] Renato Martorelli was a lawyer and representative of the Socialist Party on the Piedmontese Military Committee. Killed by the Germans in 1944, he was decorated posthumously with the gold medal for military valor.

[6] General Enrico Adami Rossi was the military commander of Turin.

[7] Roberto Farinacci, a loyal Fascist and party secretary from 1925 to 1926, became part of Mussolini's puppet administration at Salò. Denis Mack Smith called him "one of the more crude and brutish of the hierarchy." Mack Smith, *Modern Italy*, 326.

[8] On 29 April 1932, the Special Tribunal sentenced Mario Andreis and Luigi Scala to eight years in prison. Andreis was a student of economics and a leader in the Action Party. Scala was a professor of natural sciences who joined the GL movement in 1930 and who, after his release

Decisions were made quickly. We had to disappear, break up, and yet keep in touch with each other secretly. It remained to be seen what forms the police offensive would take, and how it would be possible to work. One group would go into the Pellice Valley, another into the Cuneese Valley. For the time being, we would move into the Susa Valley, to Meana.

Someone arrived, panting, with the news that a car laden with SS was about to arrive at my house, on Via Fabro. I shrugged my shoulders again. It seemed quite unlikely to me that the SS would attach so much importance to us. Nevertheless, we agreed that it would be prudent to disappear as quickly as possible. I agreed, unwillingly, that we too would have to spend that night at the Vigna Allason.[9] We said goodbye quickly, without particular emotion. I too went downstairs to the front door. Ettore had arrived, carrying a '91 model gun with which I had learned to shoot as a little girl, during the other war. "Bury it in the cellar," I suggested, caressing the long barrel fleetingly. It stayed in the cellar for twenty months until, during the nights of the insurrection, it was used to fire at the last German tanks.

But where was Paolo? "He went to the Valdocco barracks to see if he could find more weapons," said Ettore. I ran there too, somewhat anxiously. He was there indeed, with a small crowd that, bewildered and powerless, watched the soldiers at the window, "confined" in the barracks. "Poor boys," commented the women. Someone yelled, "Run away! Go home, to your mothers! After all, you do not want to be taken by the Germans!" The soldiers were looking at them, tentative and uncertain. How could we find our bearings in this world in ruins where even the only remaining benchmarks of discipline, patriotism, and honor, which had already been wavering for some time, were now breaking down tragically?

Meanwhile someone passed by with a coil of rawhide. He was clearing out an abandoned military warehouse nearby. So just as the morning's heroic aura had appealed to what was loftiest, now a sense of dissolution reinforced man's baser instincts. The little crowd dispersed rapidly, taking advantage of the opportunity to flee that was afforded it. The soldiers remained alone to stare at the deserted street with empty and melancholy eyes.

We did not see any weapons nearby. We went home in silence, heavy with sadness. As we went back in, the house seemed like an abandoned

from prison in August 1943, became active in the Action Party in Turin. He was deported to Mauthausen a few months later. Giorgio Agosti was a magistrate, a member of the Piedmontese Military Committee of the Action Party, and regional political representative of the GL formations in the Piedmont region. Aurelio Peccei was an industrial manager and political organizer of the Action Party.

    [9] The home of Barbara Allason (1877–1968), the celebrated Turinese writer, journalist, scholar of German literature, and close friend of Ada and Piero Gobetti. In her memoirs, *Memorie di una*

battlefield: cinders, torn-up documents, cigarette ashes everywhere, and two Beretta revolvers and a hundred cartridges on the table of the dining room.

While Ettore and Paolo were hiding the weapons and I was cooking eggs in a hurry, Luigi Capriolo arrived.[10] For as long as I had known him—and it was already many years by that time—I had always seen him smiling. He was smiling when, freed from his first period of imprisonment, he announced his upcoming marriage. He was smiling when, after more difficult years in prison, he told me that his marriage had gone up in smoke, but the "work" went on, and he was happy all the same. It was to him that we ran during the most intense periods of anxiety and serenity—at the time of the declaration of war on France, as well as during the time of the German attack on Russia.[11] In his simplicity we felt something solid and constant, and everything about him was absolutely genuine. But on that night of 10 September, he was not smiling when he entered our house. His face, which was not very expressive, was marked by the same serious fatigue that I had seen on the faces of the soldiers in the barracks and on the faces of many whom I met on the road. Profoundly conscious of the political significance of the moment, his mind and body were still suffering from the tragic loss we felt all around us. He agreed with Paolo immediately. While he ate quickly, I heard them talking with expressions and terms that, after a few days, would become part of our daily routine, but that at the moment still sounded new to me, and were accompanied by an obscure menace: "Organize the resistance"…"sabotage"…"armed squads." For now, tomorrow morning they would go together in search of weapons.

As he was leaving, Momi Banfi arrived, exhausted.[12] A member of the military, he had managed to avoid being taken by the Germans. He had not slept or had any peace for three days. He staggered from fatigue. We could not leave him in the house that we were about to abandon, considering the danger, but how could we make him walk the six kilometers to the Vigna? Capriolo said that he would take him to a safe place to sleep, at the house of a companion. That night I saw him smile for the first time. Human empathy, the joy of being able to help someone who was fighting the same battle, even if he had not known him before, restored his optimism and hope. We parted under the glow of that

antifascista, 1919–1940 (Milan: Edizioni Avanti, 1961), Allason revealed the high degree of resistance to fascism in Turin during the 1919–1940 period, long before the *Resistenza* of 1943–1945. In 1934 Allason spent a period of time in prison for her antifascist activities.

[10] Luigi Capriolo had been convicted by the Special Tribunal as a member of the Communist Party. He served as a liaison officer between the Susa Valley and the Lanzo Valley and later as an inspector for the Garibaldini Command in the Cuneese Valley.

[11] Italy declared war on France on 10 June 1940, entering World War II on the side of the Germans. Hitler invaded Russia on 22 June 1941.

[12] Arialdo (Momi) Banfi, a lawyer, was a representative of the Action Party in the first Piedmontese Regional Military Committee.

smile of his. That is how I saw him again in my mind sixteen months later when, in France, in an underground newspaper, I read the news of his horrible end.[13] And that is how I still see him today.

Outdoors, in the street and on the tram, outside life appeared drearily normal. Now, for most people, the resigned, subdued passivity of the Italian people began to replace the incredulous bewilderment and angry rebellion. They had endured the bombings, the fires, the famine. They would also endure the occupation. Deep in their hearts, everyone was certain that they would come out of this; but how, very few knew.

Certainly I did not know. After all, our climb toward the hill in the evening did not represent anything unusual for me. How many times during the periods of bombing had we traveled that road! The eighteenth-century house, guarded by two old cypress trees, was always the same, and we always found the same cordial, serene welcome there.

Only the next morning did I truly begin to become aware of reality when, passing in front of Porta Nuova in a tram, I saw some German soldiers on guard, armed to the teeth, in camouflage uniform with machine guns close at hand.[14] Suddenly the absurd, incredible hope that my heart had nourished in order to protect itself crumpled. The pain was unbearable. I started to cry, and I could not stop. Another woman who had followed me with her eyes also began to cry. A man coughed gruffly and turned his head. Another lowered his head and closed his eyes. "*Mah!*" said the conductor with a sigh.

The morning passed quickly in taking care of small practical matters. Paolo went off with Capriolo. I saw Carlo Galante, who had come from Cuneo, where Galimberti and Bianco had already begun to round up squads of armed men. I saw Grosso, one of our union organizers, who spoke to me of the work he had done that morning and the previous evening to reestablish contacts with the worker groups. I saw Perosino, a young man who had been my student at the Sommeiller [school] that year—it was strange how he had singled me out and had come right toward me. He had two hand grenades in his pocket (two "Balilla" bombs, the first I had seen) and many plans in his head for the organization of young men, surprise actions, etc.[15]

From the despondent weariness I felt around me, from the emptiness where I seemed to have found myself, initiatives and hopes were born. The desire for resistance was taking shape.

---

[13] Capriolo was hanged by the Nazi-Fascists on 3 August 1944.

[14] Porta Nuova is the main train station in Turin.

[15] Carlo Galante Garrone was a magistrate and supporter of the Action Party. Dante Livio Bianco was a lawyer, member of the command of the Italia Libera partisan band, political representative of GL Division I in the Cuneese Valley, and regional commander of the GL formations in the Piedmont region. Grosso was a union organizer for the Action Party.

More than ever I felt that I had to stay in my house, that my instincts did not tell me that I was in danger, and that perhaps my house might be the only meeting place for many people. Nevertheless, I decided that we would leave for Meana in the afternoon. Monday—it was then Saturday—I for one would return. I made an arrangement with the concierge—the valiant Espedita—who, for twenty months, indefatigably, day and night, watched over us and over our house and to whom in large part I believe we owe our surprisingly safe existence. I urged the lawyer Cattaneo, who lived on the ground floor at that time, to move the canary cage out of a specific window sill, in the event of some alarm, so that I would not end up involuntarily in a cage myself.[16]

At the station, among the crowd that looked like the habitual mass of "evacuees," everything was as usual; there were only the Germans on guard, immovable and hostile, as if they were closed off by a magic circle. "What a change from yesterday morning," I heard someone behind me say. I turned around. There were two young men in overalls. Evidently they too had been at the meeting at the Camera del Lavoro, and there was the same pain that we felt in their incredulous eyes.

I saw the saddest dejection, however, in the soldiers whom we found at the station, and especially in Bussoleno when we climbed up the valley again. They were what was left of the Italian Fourth Army, which, after having tried to resist and fight in Moncenisio and Modane (someone had been able to block the Frejus tunnel), found themselves without a leader, and without orders. Abandoned, they now tried to flee the Germans and go back home.[17] After they had endured three years of "national service" without conviction, for two days they had really believed they had to fight. But then they were alone, and increasingly oppressive disillusionment and bitterness had replaced their blaze of heroic enthusiasm. One had begun drinking in order to dull his senses. Another had tried to console himself with the idea that the war was over for him. But their relief and drunkenness tasted of desperation, and sadness without any hope of consolation arose from that spectacle of useless strength and useless pain. As always, in the most tragic moments, alongside the generous goodness of most (in those days thousands of fugitive soldiers were supplied with civilian clothes in the Susa Valley), the stingy selfishness of others was revealed. When the train left the station, the action of someone who, with an old jacket in his hand, tried to bargain with a drunken and half-nude soldier remains in my memory.

When I arrived in Meana, it was like finding a forgotten paradise. Here the dejection had not yet arrived. Among the chestnut trees adorned by the sunset,

[16] The lawyer Giovanni Battista Cattaneo, a tenant in the same building where Ada lived, helped devise a scheme to protect her, and to warn her if the police were in her home or had passed by recently. Cattaneo would place his canary's cage in the window if there were no danger, and hide it if there were danger.

[17] The Frejus tunnel links Italy with France.

the carts came back, laden with straw, and from each house the smoke from the fireplace rose toward the sky. We could hear children playing and animals calling, as if the whole world were at peace.

Paolo slipped away quickly and returned after an hour, his eyes sparkling. With a gesture of triumph—the same gesture with which a few years earlier he had shown me a four-leaf clover or a mushroom he had found—he deposited two hand grenades and a gun on the table. He had been to the nearby crossing keeper's cabin, which the *militi* had abandoned.[18]

Tomorrow, he said, I will go with Gianni to take a tour of the other signal towers.[19] You'll see that we will find a pile of stuff.

I wanted to ask him, "And then? What do you want to do? What do you need to do?" But I did not have the courage. I felt tired, like I was drained. I could not face the situation and make decisions. For one moment more, I wanted to ignore, to forget, to forget and to sleep.

The following morning—it was Sunday—after a night's sleep and the prospect of an entire day of peace, I finally had the free time to think.

I understood, at first somewhat confusedly, that for us a grave and difficult period had begun, when we would have to act and fight ruthlessly and continuously, assuming responsibility and facing every sort of danger.

Personally, none of this surprised me. After all, as a little girl and as an adolescent—and indeed, alas, also as an adult—had not my model been "La piccola vedetta lombarda"?[20] But I was terrified for my son, who had thrown himself into action so decisively.

I tried to talk to him in the afternoon, on the terrace that was dominated by the Rocciamelone, associated with the memory of so many faraway hours of innocent repose and quiet games.[21] But, perhaps in response, Paolo loathed the romantic heroic attachments that were so essential to my character, despite my efforts, through long and painful self-discipline, to control them. There was no need to make decisions, he said. He thought that the situation itself would tell us what had to be done.

Whistling, he slid down from the terrace to the meadow below, and set out toward the railroad. Ettore and I looked at each other. For him everything was so simple. Perhaps he was right. At such times, words and plans were useless. Day by day we would do what had to be done.

---

[18] *Militi* were members of the Milizia Volontaria Sicurezza Nazionale or Mvsn, a military organization of the most fanatical champions of the fascist regime.

[19] Paolo's friend Gianni Jarre.

[20] "La piccola vedetta lombarda" (The Little Lombard Lookout) was one of eleven parts of the book *Cuore* by Edmondo De Amicis, which tells of heroic acts carried out by children.

[21] The Rocciamelone is a mountain peak in the Italian Alps that stands at 3,538 meters.

13 September–16 November 1943

For the entire period of the underground struggle, every evening I wrote, in a tiny note-book, skeletal notes in a cryptic English that was almost unintelligible, which today enables me not only to reconstruct the facts, but also to relive the atmosphere and state of mind of those days.

13 September, Meana. I was getting up (it was still dark and it was pouring) when Anna Jarre came to tell us that in the neighboring town, Chiomonte, the Germans had arrested all the men between the ages of eighteen and sixty-five.[1] I decided to leave anyway. Ettore and Paolo would be on the lookout and, at the first alarm, would make a run for the woods. On the train, some women who were from Chiomonte (there were almost no men) recounted how the measure had been carried out following the ransacking of a military shoe storehouse. A few pairs of shoes were given back, and the men let go almost immediately. All the women who were with me in the train car, and who had one of their men involved in the epi-sode, spoke about it with the euphoria that usually accompanies an escape from danger. No one took the situation very seriously, at best as a brief parenthesis. Everyone said that they had given civilian clothing, help, and comfort to the dis-banded soldiers. Bragging innocently, they competed over who had given the most ("I clothed eight of them!" said one) without being aware of the danger that this represented. Others, who got on at Bussoleno, spoke about partisan bands who must have taken refuge in the Cervetto. I would have to go and see.

In Turin, everything was normal. The canary cage was back in its place, and the house was perfectly quiet. No one, as I had correctly predicted, had come to look for me. I saw Debenedetti, and together we tried to outline a network of contacts.[2] I saw a friend from Savona, whom I put in touch with people from here. I saw one of Ettore's colleagues who wants to "work" with us, and made contacts for him as well. And finally I saw the engineer Carrara, who wants

---

[1] Professor Anna Jarre was in charge of assistance for the Mfgl and a collaborator of the partisans.

[2] Leo Debenedetti was a professor and representative of the Action Party in the first Piedmontese Regional Command.

an important secret meeting with Andreis.[3] In all, I think that my presence in Turin has been useful.

When I got home, I found everything peaceful in Meana as well. There are Germans at the station, but so far you do not see them in the town. Paolo went to Frais, but he only found two or three lost soldiers, and so he decided to go down to the city.

14 September. This evening we carried the weapons that Paolo and Gianni had collected during the last few days to a safe place in a cave. It is a place that the young people of the town used to talk about as if it were a legend. Paolo had searched for and discovered it during the last few months. We explored it together. Its entrance in the side of the mountain was imperceptible, and it opened up into spacious tunnels and grottoes. Unfortunately we were not able to find another way out, which would have made it an ideal hideout, but even as a cul-de-sac, it could serve quite well as a storehouse. We went there in the middle of the night in order not to be seen by anyone. A dim fog veiled the light from the moon.

15 September. This morning Ettore too went down to Turin and returned to work. I thought it would be useful to keep up the semblance of normal life as much as possible.

In the afternoon, according to the agreement we had made before we left each other on the evening of the 10th, we had our first meeting. Silvia, who came from the Pellice Valley, was there.[4] It appeared that things were going well down there, since they had formed Giustizia e Libertà bands. The Waldensian tradition of the valley was useful for the organization of a possible guerrilla war.[5] But something had to be done in the city as well. How, it was not yet clear.

18 September. When I arrived at the station in Turin, I found myself in front of a large portrait of Mussolini on horseback, with *l'esprit* on his cap and his hand raised in the Roman salute.[6] I did not react at all. It counted for so little now, and I think hatred is absolutely unproductive.

---

[3] Enrico Carrara was an engineer.

[4] Dottoressa Silvia Pons, a *staffetta* and organizer of the Mfgl. Although the word *staffetta* is sometimes translated as "courier," this definition does not give a true picture of the activities of these female partisans. Historian Victoria de Grazia called the *staffetta* a "jack-of-all-trades of partisan warfare." She listed some of the duties of a *staffetta*: carrying messages and orders, keeping lists of contacts, preparing safe houses, transporting news pamphlets, and sometimes carrying weapons. Victoria de Grazia, *How Fascism Ruled Women: Italy, 1922–1945* (Berkeley: University of California Press, 1992), 283.

[5] The Protestant Waldensians had a tradition of worshipping in secret through an underground system of contacts in order to avoid persecution.

[6] Mussolini wore a plume on his cap, symbol of an elite military unit.

21 September. This morning we left for the Cervetto with Paolo and Gianni. We did not notice anything in particular, either in Mattie or along the road. When we reached the top of the hill, I left Paolo and Gianni at some distance and went down to the hotel. The precaution was not necessary. Under the pergola, there were two soldiers intent on making a large kite for the innkeeper's little girl. I tried to question them discreetly. Yes, they were in the Italian Fourth Army, they did not want to go with the Germans, they were ready to fight, but were waiting for orders from Badoglio, which they were sure to receive by radio. And their companions? Did they know where they were? No, they really did not know. They had all scattered. It appeared, however, that on the other slope of the valley, they were being rounded up by the thousands. But there is a certain baker, behind the tobacco shop, in Borgone, who had the scoop on everything. I made a mental note of this and returned to the boys, somewhat discouraged, but they thought we should continue climbing to the Balmetta right away. Someone might be there.

In fact there were three others, organized quite nicely in the hideout, much less ignorant, and therefore much less talkative. After a little while, however, they opened up. One, who appeared to be the leader, spoke vaguely of mules that had been requisitioned and of machine guns that had been buried. He gave the impression that they were in contact with someone in Bussoleno. We were not able to get anything specific out of him, but it is certainly important to know that an organization, however rudimentary, exists in the valley. This is what we must achieve.

Having left the Balmetta, we stopped for a moment in a meadow. It was a splendid day and it was hard to believe that we were not simply on an outing. Then we went home through the mountain passes.

That evening the radio announced the liberation of Sardinia and Corsica. We listened to Croce's speech with deep emotion.[7] To think that, if we had gone to Sorrento in July, probably we would have stayed there, and at this moment we would be "liberated" and Paolo would not be in danger. But these are useless thoughts.

23 September. Today I went to the Sommeiller to give exams. This too is part of the strategy of normality. I know perfectly well that almost all of my colleagues are antifascists, but I do not go out of my way to talk with them. I am terrified of useless chatter, more hazardous than dangerous speeches.

It made me laugh to have to give German exams. I protested to no avail that I did not know German. "You will learn more and more by examining," the headmaster had said. Obviously. To avoid any mistakes, however, I passed him. He was a soldier and came from Rodi.[8]

---

[7] Benedetto Croce and his family had been evacuated to the island of Capri.

[8] The Italian army had occupied Rodi Island in Greece.

24 September. On Silvana's bicycle, I went from Susa to Bussoleno, where I did not find anything. But on the road half way between Bussoleno and Bruzolo, right before San Giorio, there was a high-tension pole that had been knocked down, and there were Germans around it busily putting it back upright. My heart began to pound. It seemed that the "rebels" had carried out acts of sabotage here. Animated with renewed hope, I continued my investigations in Bruzolo and Borgone. Pretending I was the grieving sister of someone who was missing, I questioned all the bakers, tobacconists, and everyone I encountered. I did not learn anything, and I was convinced that there was nothing there. Yet even though I turned back, somewhat disappointed, I had become more and more convinced that no partisan bands could be positioned on this arid, exposed slope, without resources. It would be more logical to look for them on the other side, a region rich with woods, *grange*, and pastures.[9]

26 September. Meanwhile we began cautiously to sound out the intentions of the local boys. Today Elso arrived, very eager and enthusiastic.[10] To listen to him, all the boys from Meana are ready to work with us. He rounded up a group at his house, and Paolo and Gianni went to talk with them. It appears that there are several who are serious and trustworthy. The important thing is to have a squad, however limited, as long as it is determined to act and not to wait. Paolo thinks that the most important thing would be to disrupt the railroad, attack the crossing keepers' cabins, and blow up the bridges, basically what we had wanted to do during the forty-five days when, night and day, we heard trains pass, full of Germans coming from France, and we bit our fists with impotent anger. How many times had we walked under the bridge at Arnodera asking ourselves what we should do, but we could not blow it apart with our fingernails. Afterward, luckily, they blocked the Frejus tunnel, but they are already working to restore it. It is essential that the railroad not function.

2 October. Today, in Turin, I finally received some valuable information. Someone told me that Sergio Bellone was in San Giorio.[11] I have a feeling that this might

---

[9] The term *grangia* (pl. *grange*) can be defined as a stone shepherd's hut, typically used seasonally, but it also has a more extensive meaning, depending on the context and the region in question. In some areas, the term *grangia* can mean any temporary or permanent pastoral dwelling for mountain folk who usually live in the towns at the bottom of the valley. In other areas, the term only refers to a place to store grain. In medieval times, the term *grangia* meant granary. The term was later used by Trappist monks who participated in agricultural efforts to increase the productivity of the land. They organized their agricultural property into farms that depended on the monastery, which they named *grange* after the ancient French use of the term.

[10] Elso Pesando was a partisan in the first Meana formations.

[11] The partisan communist Sergio Bellone was a political commissar in the first formations in the Susa Valley, then leader of sabotage activities of the IV Garibaldini Brigade, and then leader of sabotage and countersabotage activities in the Piedmontese Regional Military Command.

be the right course of action. He must be a Communist. He had received a very serious sentence from the Special Tribunal, and got out of prison during the forty-five days. I do not know him, but I met his father at Croce's house. As a gift, he had brought him his book, *La Mignona*, which narrates a medieval legend about San Giorio in particular. Why had I not thought of this before? And yet the pole that had been knocked down in front of the old fortress should have made me aware of it.

This evening, when I arrived, Paolo was not there. Somewhat anxiously I waited for him on the terrace, under a sky full of incredible stars. He arrived at 8:00 p.m., saying that he had been to the Assietta. I did not quite understand what he had been looking for, but he was cheerful and satisfied.

3 October. Yesterday they stopped the train between Meana and Bussoleno and examined everyone's papers. It is becoming difficult for Paolo to travel. I had false papers made for him, but they did not seem very convincing to me. Yet, I could not prevent him from traveling.

4 October. Ormea, the young doctor who gave me injections and whom I discovered afterward was a reliable comrade, brought me to the military hospital where there was an English pilot, whose name was Dennis and who had been wounded during the air raid of 8 August (the one that destroyed my remaining window panes).[12] Since they were taking very good care of him, he was now almost completely healed. In civilian life, he was a journalist. We chatted cordially, and I tried to explain the Italian situation to him. Until he recovers, he can relax in the hospital, where the doctors, nuns, and nurses are being very attentive. Then, we will arrange for his escape, and make sure that he is safe.

There are two other Englishmen, ordinary soldiers, at the hospital. While we were painstakingly trying to make conversation with them (they are from Northumberland and speak in an almost incomprehensible dialect), the Italian orderly arrived with a small saw and a little board and explained to them with gestures that he was making a board for playing checkers. Great signs of joy, absolutely childish, on the part of the English. Then came the other orderly with a map to show them with marks where the Allies had arrived. More expressions of delight. Without knowing a word of each other's languages, they understood one another perfectly.

In the same room with them was a Yugoslavian prisoner who, on the contrary, was much less childish and had a slightly worried look. I told him how

---

[12] Ferdinando Ormea, a medical doctor, helped to organize the expatriation of Allied prisoners. Dennis was a captain in the Royal Air Force.

much we admired their resistance. His brown eyes lit up. "You too will learn," he said, in excellent Italian.

7 October. Things are falling into place, little by little. I was in San Giorio and I found Sergio's mother and father. I was not mistaken. There is a band, and it is clearly on our side, on the northern slope. When I arrived, his father had just been preparing a package of potatoes to bring to the *grangia* where the boys were staying. He recognized me immediately and welcomed me cordially. I understood, even if he did not tell me, that it was Sergio himself who had blown up the famous pole. I asked very few questions, restricting myself to requesting a meeting. They were cautious, but without a trace of secretiveness or fear. They are Communists. "Communists are honest," said Sergio's mother; "We are honest." I said that I had never doubted it, but that even those who were not Communists could be honest too, like me, for example. We ended up laughing together, in perfect harmony. His father seemed to me to be an excellent "quartermaster." His mother was a little high strung. It is not surprising when I think that, having just seen her son after so many years of prison, now she was watching him embark on an even more dangerous adventure. I embraced her wholeheartedly.

I will return the following week. I will meet Sergio, or they will tell me where I can find him.

8 October. I went to the parish priest's house. He is a capable young man, whom I already knew, all caught up in his "mission" and perfectly trustworthy. We sized up the young men of the town. Basically we could count on all of them, albeit to varying extents. He declared that he was willing to work with us, and expressed himself about many things in terms similar to those used by Sergio's parents. The coincidence was not accidental. Obviously the problems are the same, from whatever point of view they are considered— as long as a person is honest. I understood what Sergio's mother meant by her declaration of honesty, something very different than the conventional meaning of the word. Today someone is "honest" if he is willing to face death to remain faithful to his beliefs. It is marvelous how at this moment the idea is the same for the priest as for the Communist. Perhaps there has never been such unity in Italy. If only it would last through the trial—and beyond.

The parish priest advised me to look for Agostino Roglio, who enjoyed a certain prestige among the young men of the town.[13] And this evening I did so. He agreed to assemble the young men and organize them. Finally, there are some foundations.

---

[13] Agostino Roglio was a teacher and organizer of the first partisan bands in Meana.

13 October. Italy declared war on Germany. Now we are cobelligerents with the Allies. But the news did not make any impression on me. For us there is no difference. Perhaps it will have some importance for those who are waiting for orders from Badoglio (although by now they have returned home peacefully), but certainly not for our native mountain folk, nor for the workers of Turin. War, we are the ones who will wage it, our war—and the chrisms of a discredited authority, which no one believes in any more, are of little importance to us.[14]

18 October. I was at Castagnone's house to collect Issue Number 5 of the underground newspaper *L'Italia Libera* (Free Italy).[15] I like this typographer, whose eyes glow with resourceful goodness and who prints underground newspapers with such cheerful aplomb and without the least concern. Perhaps, like me, he too depends on the benevolent affection of a concierge and of his neighbors. I always see personal rancor at the root of every denunciation. When a person has no enemies, the danger is much less.

19 October. I was in San Giorio, but unfortunately Sergio's father had been arrested the other day. The denunciation came from Turin. The entire town, loyal, kept quiet. An evacuee stupidly pointed out his house. The old man did not have time to escape, and they brought him to Turin. His personal position does not seem serious, but certainly they will hold him as a hostage in the hope of getting his son. His mother, who was very upset the other day, was, by contrast, very quiet today. She had not forgotten the meeting. I will see Sergio or his cousin one morning next week in the Cervetto. It is more essential than ever to be discreet. In homage to such discretion, I chose a *nom de guerre*: Maria Salvi. But I doubt that I will have the chance to use it. What good is it since everyone knows me? Furthermore, if I say my real name, all suspicion disappears. My true identity even has its advantages from the point of view of the police.[16]

20 October. Paolo went with Gianni and two other friends to examine the Comba Scura bridge. It appears that it is the ideal bridge to blow up because, since it is constructed over a very narrow gully, at the opening of two tunnels, it will be quite difficult to rebuild it. At the present time, the matter of bridges and viaducts is especially important in the valley.

---

[14] Holy chrism is made of olive oil mixed with balsam and is used in sacraments of the Catholic Church.

[15] *L'Italia Libera* was the newspaper of the Action Party.

[16] Partisans often took battle names or *nome di battaglia* to disguise their identity.

23 October. I was not able to return to Meana for several days because work in the city had increased. There are always people to feed and put up for the night (by now everyone is convinced that my house is safe), and there is typing to do, and material to bring to and collect from the typographer. There is always unpleasant news as well. Grosso was arrested in a *trattoria* and I had to go to the owner to make her talk, but it seems his position is not serious. On the other hand, the situation has worsened for the English officer at the hospital, who, now that he is healed, will probably be handed over to the Germans. Ormea is planning to help him escape. Fred Fiorio gave me the key to one of his apartments to settle him in temporarily.[17] This morning I went to his house to get it. Fred had been outside all night with a device for carrying out an attack. He said he would send me a railroad worker who wants to blow up a bridge near Susa.

25 October. Today it poured, nonstop. I saw Ormea, who told me about the Englishman's lucky escape. There had been no need for Fred's apartment. Dennis is perfectly safe at the home of a good family who is looking after him lovingly. I will go to find him in a few days.

Fred's railroad worker, whose name is Della Valle, came to look for me.[18] Next week he will go to blow up the little bridge of the Morelli.[19] It is a modest undertaking, but it will be good experience. He will go with his comrades to Meana, where I will guide him. In the next few days I will study the safest and shortest way.

26 October. This morning Paolo and I were in the Cervetto. There was a dense fog that lifted later, allowing a faint, misty sun to filter through. I found Sergio's envoy. He will meet me tomorrow with Ugo, his cousin, who appears to have command of a group of some importance.[20]

27 October. In Mattie I met Ugo, whom I quickly recognized because of his red hair. We chatted for about two hours, and were in perfect agreement. Essentially there was a group in the surrounding area connected with other groups in the Lower Valley. In the Middle and Upper Valleys, in contrast, there was absolutely nothing. This is where we need to work. We laid the groundwork for a good relationship, and we will do something together soon. So, from a military point of view, the work is sketched out. We still need to get in touch with

---

[17] Fred Fiorio was a lawyer and the first commander of a civilian squad of the Action Party in Turin. He was deported and died in Germany.

[18] A partisan in the Susa Valley, Della Valle was killed by the Fascists in November 1943.

[19] A village in the Armirolo Valley.

[20] Ugo Berga, a student and a political commissar of the 106th Garibaldini Brigade of the Susa Valley.

possible politically oriented individuals in Susa to create a kind of Committee of National Liberation there.

31 October. Today they came to tell me that there were spies in Meana, and they told me precisely who they were. I remained skeptical, and tried to calm down those who were suspicious. Nothing is more dangerous to a person's state of mind than the phrase "dàgli all'untore."[21] Even those who were the most hot-headed Fascists yesterday may have changed their minds today or, if nothing else, have kept quiet. In my opinion, there are no spies here. I do not feel them in the air. It is simply a matter of being careful. But we need to avoid creating them—the spies—with our very suspicion.

This evening we heard Omodeo's speech at the inauguration of the University of Naples.[22] It seems like a dream, but it gives us courage.

2 November. Ugo did not waste any time. Today he came to our house to plan a strike. It seems that there are weapons hidden in Frais. Tomorrow morning he will go there with Paolo. Meanwhile we gave him some of our hand grenades, which will be useful to him. While we were talking, Cesare arrived.[23] At first I was a bit reluctant to bring him up to date, but when he began to talk of bands, requisitions, and strikes, discretion seemed pointless to me. Therefore we spoke openly. He will help us in the zone around Oulx, which is the worst in the valley because of its fascist constituents. Thus a new field of activity is opening up.

3 November. This morning, according to the agreements we made with Ugo, Gianni went to Villar Dora, where apparently the command of the Lower Valley is located. Paolo, on the other hand, went up to Frais with some others, but around one o'clock, he came back in a hurry to ask for help from Ettore and from as many others as he could find. They went back up to Frais together. The weapons were there, and they hid them in a safe place for the time being. To carry them away, however, they would need a vehicle or a much greater number of people.

---

[21] Literally "give him to the poisoner" or "give him to the hangman," the expression "dàgli all'untore" has come to mean "kill him." Ada is concerned about those ready to jump to the worst of conclusions about other people.

[22] Adolfo Omodeo, an ardent antifascist, was named the head of the University of Naples after 25 July 1943. He wrote for Benedetto Croce's journal *La Critica*. He was also one of the leading representatives of the Action Party on the Cln of Naples.

[23] Cesare Alvazzi was a student and detachment commander in the Autonomous forces in the Chisone and Susa Valleys, and later became a liaison officer with the Allied Forces. Alessio Alvazzi, Cesare's father, was an appelate court advisor.

In the afternoon, I made one last excursion as far as the Morelli to final-
ize the route. Everything was ready. This evening, Della Valle and his friends
should have arrived on the last train. They were to stop at my house, and then
I was to accompany them to the bridge. I spoke about things in general terms
with Mario Cordola, my landlord. I know that he is completely trustworthy,
and therefore that I can tell him where things stand. I cannot bring armed
people into the house without telling him anything. Instead of raising objections, however, with great simplicity he offered to help us.

I had just finished conversing with Mario when I heard a cry and commotion
in the surrounding fields. It was a neighbor who had lost a sheep in the nearby
fields. Half the town disappeared into the fields to help him find it. It scared me
to death that they might see my friends arrive. Usually there is no one in these
parts at this hour. We too joined in the search. After a little while the stupid
sheep was finally found in a nearby field, and everything was quiet again.

But no one arrived on the last train. I stayed up late, thinking that they
would arrive by some other means, but in vain. Let's hope that it is a question
of a misunderstanding or a postponement, and that nothing bad has happened
to anyone.

4 November. We spent the afternoon in Susa, in Teta's store.[24] Discreetly
I brought her up to date about several matters. Her store would be an excellent
meeting place for a variety of activities. If we need it, she will give us a cart for
transporting weapons.

5 November. I went to Giorgio Agosti's courtroom. The coolness with which this
young judge does the most dangerous things is extraordinary. His office is frequented pretty much like my house, and I think that it would be an excellent
storehouse for newspapers and perhaps for weapons as well. He has a sense
of level-headedness that gives me a feeling of security. We can count on him
for small matters as well as important ones. His slightly ironic manner is perfect for avoiding any form of excitement. I met Sandro Trinch, who will be the
political commissar for the Susa Valley, at his house.[25] It appears that there is
little or nothing of the Action Party in Susa, however. Nevertheless, he gave me
useful information.

The Russians have retaken Kiev.

---

[24] The store owned by Celestina Roglio (Teta), Paolo's former governess and a partisan
collaborator.

[25] Sandro Trinch was a lawyer who became commander of the civilian squads in the Susa
Valley.

7 November. A fruitful day. I went to look for a certain woman, one of Trinch's clients, who lives near the station. In a manner that was a bit vague, I convinced her to keep a package of documents for me that I was afraid to keep at home, and even more afraid to keep in Turin, and that on the other hand would be completely safe at her house. Then, toward evening, I went down to Susa, and I went to look for a certain Barberis, whom Gianni had mentioned to me.[26] He was not home, but his wife was there, a gracious little woman, with whom I got along immediately. Gianni's report was accurate: Barberis, who is employed in Turin, is in contact with the politically oriented individuals in Susa. His wife works with him. When I was about to leave, he himself arrived and, after I brought him up to date, he accompanied me almost as far as Meana. It seems that there are no members of the Action Party in Susa. He, Barberis, is a Socialist. We roughed out some areas of common ground, and we will work on these. After supper, a meeting in the house with Agostino and Gianni.[27]

It was windy for the entire day and the dry leaves flew about, falling from the trees like they had gone mad.

9 November. For the first time after the forty-five days, Galimberti, Bianco, and Scamuzzi reappeared. [28] They are in the Cuneese Valley where they are doing splendid work. Mario Andreis was visibly moved when he saw them again. For a moment I wanted to go with them, but I realize that my place is here.

At noon there was an alarm, but by now only a few people go down to the shelters. A sort of indifference has developed, which appears incredible after last year's terror. Life ceases at the sound of the siren, trams stop, stores close, but the people just look up in the air. Today it is sunny, and everyone has gone into their gardens to enjoy it, like a vacation.

12 November. Today, I went with Ettore to find the English officer that Ormea had helped to escape from the hospital. He is in a house on the hillside, and there are two other prisoners with him. The woman who is hosting them is making them comfortable and feeding them butter and jam, which frankly seems a bit much to me. Ettore photographed them so that we could obtain false identification cards for them and try to get them to go to Switzerland, where they will be so much better off. The officer really wanted to have his picture taken with Ormea and me. I signaled to Ettore and he understood. Without saying anything about it, he pretended to take the picture. Afterward

---

[26] Luigi Barberis was a clerk and representative of the regional Cln of the Susa Valley.

[27] Gianni Jarre was a student and organizer of the first partisan bands in the Susa valley.

[28] Leandro Scamuzzi, a businessman and member of the command of the "Italia Libera" partisan band, later became political commissar of the II Sector and ultimately political commissar for the II and X GL Divisions.

we will say that it did not come out. It does not seem to me to be the right moment for saving keepsakes. But evidently these friends of ours have strange ideas regarding the situation.

13 November. Fred has been arrested. That is why we were not able to find him for the past several days, and why I did not learn anything about Della Valle. Perhaps he too was arrested?

14 November. Early in the morning—we had gotten up a short time before—Sergio Bellone arrived. I had never met him, but I recognized him immediately. A handsome, distinguished, and sincere face, and a candid and precise manner of speaking. He too—I quickly realized—was obsessed with bridges, but he has the advantage over us in that he is highly competent in the field of explosives. We studied the most important bridges in the valley at length. Up there, in Villar Dora, they were planning a big attack. It appears that we can remove the explosives without danger to Villarfocchiardo. It is a question of deciding whether to blow up the Comba Scura bridge or the Aquila bridge, opposite Exilles. Tomorrow they will go to investigate the matter and decide. I will have to find Della Valle (if he has not been arrested) and warn him so that he does not try something that by now will be pointless. Instead, I will try to get him and his men to participate in a new attack for which we will need a lot of people.

I was discussing these things when Barberis suddenly burst in, out of breath, to notify me that his friends from Susa, the politically oriented individuals he had mentioned to me, were about to arrive. In fact, a few minutes later, looking out the window, we saw a strange cortège coming up the road, ten or twelve people who tried to stroll along casually as if they were not together, but nevertheless managed to be quite a conspicuous group. Although apparently they had not done so on purpose, all of them were dressed somberly in black (only one, who was younger, had on a bright windbreaker) and all of them had strange physical anomalies: one had a bandage over his eye, another a big tumor on his forehead, and a third the beginning of a goiter. They were walking up slowly. One stopped to gaze at the scenery, another bent over to look for something (mushrooms or violets?) in the dry leaves on the side of the street. Even the children who were playing on the path interrupted their game and stared open-mouthed at them. Certainly behind every window in the small town there was someone who noticed, astonished and worried. If they were the infamous, rumored spies, we would be in a fix, but luckily they were not.

Observing the strange procession, Sergio and I exchanged a glance. We did not know whether to laugh or cry. Ettore, with his usual common sense, went to meet them to get them to come in quickly, preventing any further buffoonery and keeping the dog from barking at them furiously. Finally they were all here in the house, "collected" if nothing else. I breathed a sigh of relief. We introduced ourselves. Fortunately, Sergio had told me his *nom de guerre*: Guido Reni.[29] What there was in common between the methodical engineer and the cultivated painter I just do not see, but someone who has 100,000 lire on his head cannot go around using his own name.

We sat around the table. Everyone was coughing because one was smoking a pipe filled with absolutely putrid herbs. All of a sudden the one with the tumor on his forehead got up and began solemnly: "Here we are all reunited after, for twenty years, the tombstone of fascism..." etc. etc.

Out of the corner of my eye I saw that Sergio, who was seated near me, was about to burst out laughing. I gave him a discreet punch that brought him back to seriousness. Why mortify that sincere man? Who knows with what effort he had put together that speech, and for how long he had been waiting for the occasion to give it? So we let him finish, limiting ourselves to nodding our approval. But as soon as he finished, before someone else had a mind to respond in the same tone, Sergio began to talk. He formulated the question of the underground organization in the valley in a manner so clear and precise I was positively in awe of him. He summarized everything in a few points and proceeded to repeat them, schematically, simply. I sensed that beneath his youthful enthusiasm there must be a preparedness that was not his alone. For the first time during those months I felt a strength that was unrelenting, and it was our strength.

At the beginning the good men who had come together were a bit obstinate. They had come to make nostalgic speeches, to nurture comforting hopes, and to move each other by saying certain words and phrases. Evidently, the visit to me must have been essentially a sentimental pilgrimage. Instead, here was a young madman who calmly but relentlessly placed specific responsibilities before them: one, two, three....

But nothing convinces and dominates like clarity, and after a while they were all in agreement and repeated the things that Sergio was able to drive into their heads. It was really lucky that, by pure chance, he was at my house this morning. Otherwise, in all probability, I would have let myself be overcome by the magnificent speeches and the meeting would have been concluded in a plethora of noble sentiments. Instead some essential points were clarified, and I learned what to do for the next time.

At the end, Barberis, turning to the young man in the windbreaker, said with a mysterious air: Did you bring what you were supposed to bring? To which the other, half timid and half insecure, did not respond. But, when Barberis repeated the question, he finally decided to pull a kind of short black cord, a little longer than his palm, out of his inside pocket. Then I remembered having

---

[29] The Italian Baroque painter Guido Reni was influenced by Raphael.

said to Barberis that we needed a detonating fuse in order to activate the explosive, and he had decided to procure it for me voluntarily.

This time I was not quick enough to stop Sergio's hilarity. "Ha! Ha!" he started laughing loudly, with a large irresistible smile. "Ha! Ha! Why, don't you know that it takes meters? What do you want to blow up with that tiny little thing?"

I tried to minimize the harshness of his candor, saying that, after all, the important thing was to begin. Even that little piece could be used for something. Besides, just like he had found that one, would he not be able to find more in the same way? The young boy promised, reassured, and I noted with relief that there was not a shadow of resentment in him. The meeting closed on a tone of general satisfaction. Only Barberis, who is intelligent and sensible, told me he was a bit mortified: "Perhaps I did the wrong thing in bringing them. They are not anything extraordinary, but there is no one else for now." I encouraged him too. "You did very well. We must work with what we have, and the meeting was very useful."

So they left, with the same caginess as conspirators in an operetta. Gianni, who was arriving from the opposite direction and saw the group descending, hesitated a moment before coming up, also thinking that something had happened. Instead he found us very cheerful, intent on talking about the strange visit, and he too was won over by Sergio immediately.

I promptly prepared a nutritious meal, even if it was a bit heavy: *polenta*, potatoes, and chestnuts. We continued to converse. We arranged immediate matters, and we spoke about others: common friends, ideas, books, and short-term and long-term hopes for our country.

In the afternoon Cesare arrived, and then Teta. They too were perfectly at ease with one another. This communal spirit, which puts everyone on the same level despite different surroundings, mentality, and interests, seems to me to be one of the most positive aspects of today's experience.

16 November. I was not able to find Della Valle, although I did something rash to try to track him down, looking for him in places where my presence could not pass unobserved. Either they had arrested him too or, after Fred's arrest, he had to make himself scarce. Let's hope for the second hypothesis. But even news from other parts gives the impression that a wave of arrests has been unfolding.

Last night, wanting to warn Sergio not to count on Della Valle, I left on the first train and stopped at Condove. I thought I would deliver my message quickly and, around an hour later, take the last train back to Meana. Instead the train arrived late, my address was far from the station, and it took some effort to find him in the pitch darkness. Even though I ran like crazy, I arrived at the grade crossing as the train was already whistling in the distance. Discouraged,

I turned back. I have always felt humiliated when I miss a train, as if I had suffered a personal affront.

When they saw me return, the friends with whom I had left the message welcomed me with affectionate hospitality, fed me, and comforted me. Sergio arrived after dinner. In the morning, he had gone to inspect the bridges with Paolo and Gianni, and they had decided on the Aquila bridge. The attack will be carried out on Thursday. That same evening a pick-up truck will remove the explosive (the T$_4$) from Villarfocchiardo, and will bring it to Exilles along with a certain number of men.[30] Simultaneously Paolo will guide another group of men from Bussoleno through the mountains so that they can join the others.

"Then?" I asked instinctively.

"Then what? asked Sergio.

"What will Paolo do?"

"He will turn back, unless he has to participate in the attack."

I had the feeling that my heart had stopped in my chest, and I asked timidly:

"Can't I come too?"

"Ha! Ha!" laughed Sergio loudly. "What for? To attend the show?"

I did not blame him for his rudeness. I realized he was right. I cannot carry heavy loads. I know how to run fast, but certainly not as fast as the boys. There are other things that I can do; not these, even if I would have liked to very much. For these matters, Paolo will do.

I swallowed hard and gulped down the little glass of *grappa* that our host had offered us.[31]

"*Brava!*" laughed Sergio with admiration. He began to talk again, and he told us about Don Foglia, the chaplain of the "rebels," the young, extraordinary priest who entered a church dressed like a priest and came out of the sacristy dressed like a butcher and who, with the most unusual disguises, often went through the entire valley on his trusty bicycle, making contacts, encouraging, and enlivening—indefatigable.

I listened, while watching our host's baby—a boy only a few years old—sleeping peacefully on the sofa in the pleasant warmth of the kitchen. Why, why could my child not be like this one? Why was he so much bigger?

---

[30] The Italians called the powerful but safe and inexpensive explosive cyclotrimethylene-trinitramine "T4." The British called it RDX (Research Department Explosive or Royal Demolition Explosive). Georg Friedrich Henning of Germany patented this explosive in 1898, but it was not used until World War II.

[31] *Grappa* is a potent liqueur that often serves as an after dinner drink.

Later one of Sergio's cousins came and brought me to her house to sleep. In the morning I returned to Turin, taught at Boselli, and saw the usual crowd of people.[32] Finally, in the evening, I was indescribably relieved to find Paolo still in Meana, because I thought he had already left. He too talked with me enthusiastically about Don Foglia, related the adventures of the inspection of the bridges (Volante, surprised by soldiers on guard duty, had wriggled out of difficulty cleverly by dropping his trousers hurriedly and pretending he was attending to a need of nature), and he gave me details regarding the program for the next few days.[33] He will go to Mattie to meet Ugo's men, whom he will guide through the woods, avoiding the towns. They will spend the night in Losa or in Frais. The next day they will arrive at a point above Exilles, where Don Foglia will take responsibility for the men in order to bring them to the bridge. Paolo will turn back. He would like to participate in the strike, but thinks that it will not be possible. Since he will be arranging for the transport of the famous weapons from Frais to Susa at the same time, he will be needed here.

I helped him prepare his knapsack. He will leave tomorrow morning.

---

[32] The school where Ada taught was the Scuola tecnico-commerciale Paolo Boselli in Turin.

[33] Army officer Guido Volante helped to organize the first partisan bands in the Susa Valley. He also organized Action Party civilian squads.

17–23 November 1943

At this point I found a gap in my notes. The anguish of those days was so great that I did not even have the strength to jot down my usual remarks. But the same anguish engraved every detail in my memory, and on my nerves. That is why it is possible for me today, at a distance of more than four years, when I think about those days again, to relive them hour-by-hour.

I remember perfectly that, during the morning of 17 November—it was a Wednesday—while leaving for Turin, when I said goodbye to Paolo I felt like I was being physically torn apart. I was able to get control of myself and, for the entire day, while thinking about him constantly, I remained calm. I taught school, typed, and met people, as usual.

But the next morning, when I woke up, I saw that it was snowing heavily. The sudden change in the weather worried me tremendously (the day before it was perfectly clear), because it increased the difficulty of the mission. All the same, I did a bunch of things. I asked around to find a typographer who would print *La Riscossa Italiana* (the newspaper of the Turinese Cln) and was able to find someone who agreed to do the typesetting.[1] I tried to tone down the impact of a violent debate between two of our friends. I saw Penati with Braccini, who agreed to assume the central command of our Piedmontese GL formations. And I reached the station just in time to take the train, which was already in motion.[2] In the cattle car, in the dark, there were people who were singing. An insane anxiety took possession of me. If only Paolo had returned. I dreamed of finding him in the peaceful house, listening to him tell how it had gone, and finally relieving the anguish of those two days.

---

[1] "Riscossa" means "revival" or "comeback," but "alla riscossa" means "revenge."

[2] Many cities in the north, including Turin, had their own Cln or Committee of National Liberation. Fausto Penati was a university professor and representative of the Action Party in the municipal Cln.

At the station it was Gianni who was waiting for us. "And Paolo?" I asked immediately. "He has not returned yet," he responded. While he climbed up the dark road, beneath the snow, he recounted the story.

Wednesday morning, they had gone together to meet Ugo's men and had found them at the Mulino del Diavolo—about twenty men armed to the teeth. Some of them looked suspicious, and began immediately to protest and complain about their troubles. Together they had gone up toward Losa, avoiding the town, until they found Lieutenant Ferrero, who had come up from Susa with another group and the vehicles for transporting the weapons.[3] There they split up. Gianni joined Ferrero and his men. Paolo went ahead with the others. The sudden snowfall had undoubtedly complicated things and made the trip longer. According to Gianni, this was what brought about the delay.

I wanted to believe him. This was how it must have been. It was a simple delay. He could arrive any minute. Perhaps he had arrived while we were climbing up, and we would find him at home. But the house was dark and empty. Then I lost heart, dismayed, without even the strength to help Ettore, who busied himself with lighting the fire. My boy! I looked at his things all around, and pined as if I would never see him again.

Now, as I think about it, I understand how my despair could seem excessive, compared to the much more serious agonies that followed afterward. But it was the first time I was aware that he was in such serious danger and I was not with him. Not knowing where he was, and where I could imagine he was, distressed me more than anything else. Was he still up in the mountains? Had he gone down into the valley? Had he left the others and tried to turn back alone? Or had he stayed to participate in the strike? It was supposed to happen during that night, according to the plan, but hadn't the snow prevented it?

I was obsessed with the most terrible and absurd possibilities. Still, after a while, I pulled myself together, braced myself, and tried to eat, read, and even sleep. Every once in a while the dog barked. I ran outside onto the balcony, full of anxiety and hope, but there was nothing but darkness, darkness and the snow that fell relentlessly.

Day finally came, ashen and somber. It was still snowing, with no sign of ending soon.

I left a note on the table: "Dear Paolo, if you arrive before me, look in the cupboard for a piece of roast *loca*" (goose). (From the time when he was small, Paolo had called *l'oca* "la loca", *l'ombrellino* (the umbrella) "il lombrellino", il Mar Jonio (the Ionian Sea) "il Mar Marionio"). I will return tonight. Many kisses. Mi."[4] I left with a strange sensation of emptiness, in my mind and in my heart.In

---

[3] Lieutenant Ferrero, or Vittorio Morone, was a professor and commander of the partisan forces in Susa.

[4] Essentially the young Paolo had made the article (il, la, l') part of the noun. Paolo called his mother "Mi."

Turin I continued to move, act, and speak, as if in a dream. In the afternoon, while Sandro Galante was at my house, a strange individual I saw through the peephole, who was leaning against the wall on the staircase landing, his eyes fixed on my door, frightened me.[5] Who could it be? Why didn't he go away? The most plausible response was that he was a policeman. Perhaps there were others downstairs also. But why didn't he come in? What were they waiting for?

I collected the things I had in the house that would arouse suspicion—a few newspapers, a notebook of notes, and some false identity cards. But I hated to destroy them. What if the alarm were unfounded?

Courageously, Sandro decided to leave, taking them away. I noted with relief that the little fellow did not follow him, but remained at his post. After a few minutes the concierge, who had spoken with Sandro, came to reassure me. The little fellow was some fool who was waiting for a neighbor, who lived across from me. In fact, a little while later, when this person arrived, he went into the house with him.

Then I continued to see people. At the end of the day, someone came to warn me that a friend who was associated with Trinch was in danger. I just had time to dash to this person's office to warn him, so I had to run for the train again. In the car, which was unusually crowded, I fell into a kind of unconsciousness where, at intervals, a violent stab of pain surfaced.

When we arrived at Meana, we had a hard time reaching the house, so high was the snow on the road. Again the house was empty. There was my note on the table and "la loca" in the cupboard. I was so desperately tired that I did not react. It seemed that this empty and absurd state of anxiety would continue forever. The comforting hypotheses fell apart, one by one. The bridge had not been blown up. There would have been news of it on the wires. It was not possible that, given his experience and knowledge of the mountains, Paolo would not have been able to turn back, even if the snow were high. Evidently he had remained with the others. But what were they doing? Had they been discovered? Had they been captured? What had happened while they were trying to flee?

Later Gianni came, and even he was not able to explain the delay.

We decided that the next day, if Paolo did not arrive during the night, we would go to Exilles to search for news. The decision gave me some peace and I was able to sleep. It had stopped snowing, and this seemed to be a good omen.

But the next day—it was Saturday—it snowed again. I was so exhausted that Ettore did not dare leave me and, instead of going to Turin to work, he decided to come with us. At Salbertrand, while we were getting off the train, Gianni whispered in my ear: "That's Don Foglia!" I saw a tall, thin young man with a

---

[5] Alessandro (Sandro) Galante Garone was a magistrate and representative of the Action Party on the Piedmontese Regional Cln.

curiously Etruscan profile under his beret, armed with a pair of skis. Discreetly we followed him outside the station and for a stretch of the path. When we were almost outside the town, we approached him and Gianni, who had already met him, asked him about Paolo. "I do not know," Don Foglia responded, shaking his head. "He must have remained with those good-for-nothings who preferred to stay in Frais instead of going down to carry out the strike."

I clutched at Ettore and felt like I was going to go out of my mind. Either I did not know my son, or Paolo could not have stayed in Frais. If he had not gone down to Exilles, he would have returned home. A jumble of crazy possibilities flashed through my mind: he had frozen to death, an avalanche had swept him away, he had tried to force the "good-for-nothings" to go down, and they had killed him.

"But…" Don Foglia continued, after he looked at me carefully, evidently struck by the resemblance, "Is Paolo that boy who was with you the other day at the Comba Scura bridge?"

"Yes," said Gianni. "Yes…yes," I said too.

"Then he is here with us. He has been an excellent guide, and has arrived with a group of men."

My God! Then he was alive and not very far away. I closed my eyes. There was no more snow around, but flowering meadows under an all blue sky.

"Will we be able," I asked timidly, "will we be able to see him for a moment?"

"Better not," said Don Foglia reluctantly. "Every movement arouses curiosity and awakens suspicion. We have already waited for too long, and the strike can only be carried out tonight."

He explained. The unexpected snow had prevented them from transporting the explosive in the truck easily, according to plan. The project, no longer viable, had to be modified. That evening, the men would arrive on the last train, each one carrying a suitcase with about twenty kilograms of explosives. The others, Paolo among them, would come down from the *grangia* where they were now, a short distance from the railway station. Together they would prepare the explosive, and light the fuse. Then, with the greatest speed, they would disperse. If everything went well, the explosion would occur around midnight, and at dawn Paolo should be home. I was so happy that I did not even feel sadness at the thought of not being able to see him, even though he was so close by. We said goodbye to Don Foglia and returned to the station. But the train would not depart before five in the afternoon, and it was not advisable to stay at an inn in the town, where inevitably our presence would be observed. Therefore we decided to go on foot as far as Oulx, to Cesare's house, and then take the train from there.

We set out in the snow that continued to fall, mercilessly. The local road, even though we had traveled it so many times, was unrecognizable. We advanced slowly, trying to while away the dreariness of the road with chatter. The joy of having found Paolo had rendered me so euphoric that I did not keep quiet for a minute. We reached the Ventoux bridge a little after 11:00 a.m.[6] It was early and, instead of immediately cutting across the town, we decided to go around up to the bridge of the Beaume, and we went through the tunnel under the mountain. It was a great relief to walk for a moment on the dry ground without feeling it snow on us. My poor fur coat was literally soaked, and Ettore and Gianni were not any better off than I. The tunnel was deserted. (Who went out in such weather?) We took advantage of it to examine it in depth. There were four blast holes, which were open—good to know for when it was opportune to block the road in addition to the railroad. We sat in the last one and lit a cigarette. Whether it was the physical comfort of finding ourselves in the shelter for a moment or the effect of my optimistic chatter, the fact remains that at that moment all three of us felt absolutely happy. We told each other so, half shy and half amazed. To look at things objectively, there truly was no reason for happiness, but that is precisely what permits us to experience this gush of sudden joy that does not have roots in anything external, but simply in ourselves. It is all the more vivid when life is most intense. I felt moments of the most perfect serenity—satisfaction, completeness, harmony —precisely during moments of the greatest danger. It is like when waters flow with a normal rhythm, they polish the stones that make up the bottom, dulling them. Only when a storm uncovers them do these stones, still quivering, pick up and reflect glittering flashes of the most vivid light.

But these are ramblings of today. That day, seated in the blast hole, we did not make so many remarks. We were happy, and that was that. We looked at the future and the world with optimistic serenity.

Yet we still had to move. We reluctantly left the shelter that had seemed so welcoming to us. Almost at the exit of the tunnel, we found another opening that brought us down to a spacious cave. There must have been a guard post there, because the frames of the "bunk beds," a broken chair, and even a box spring were still there. We could see the traces of a machine gun emplacement that dominated the bridge and the road—good to know this also.[7] Unfortunately there were not any weapons nor anything useful, only a bunch

---

[6] There is now a hydroelectric plant in the Susa Valley called Pont Ventoux, but I believe Ada is referring to the Ventoux bridge over the Dora river.

[7] An emplacement is a prepared position from which a heavy gun or guns are fired.

of rubber hoses and gas masks, with which Ettore filled his knapsack, considering that he could use them for one of his complicated and mysterious gadgets.

Finally, we went out again in the snow. The wind was picking up too, frigid and a portent of more snow. We crossed the bridge with difficulty and arrived at Oulx. The wind was not as strong among the houses, and people were going back and forth on the road (perhaps there had been a market), at least enough to keep our presence from attracting notice. We took advantage of this to pass in front of the fascist headquarters—a real fortress with barbed wire, sacks of sand, and pointed machine-guns. Then we went to Cesare's house.

It was the first time that we had gone into this house, which then became, in the following months, an invaluable fulcrum. Its extraordinarily comfortable atmosphere struck me right away. People and things have the air of being perfectly "in place." Everything had a certain noble style, which came from a long tradition—not heroic, but uninterrupted—of exercising the most time-honored virtues. The positive value of this tradition shone out against the backdrop of general confusion. That house, with its lovely old furniture, tin plates, and paintings, and that entire family, linked by a profound tenderness, appeared—at that time of improvised houses and scattered families—to be an incredible oasis.

The welcome we received—even though we were almost strangers—warmed our hearts. We were Cesare's friends and that was enough. I told a white lie—which was more or less plausible—about the shoes that I had gone to buy at Salbertrand. They believed it, or at least they had the good manners to pretend to believe. "And Paolo?" asked Cesare. "He stayed home because he has a little cold," I answered.

When we left, it was snowing so heavily that I could not see out of the train window. When we reached the condemned bridge, Gianni signaled to me with his head, and I recited a prayer silently.

At the station in Meana, there was so much snow that we almost were not able to get off the train. At home, we downed a mouthful in a hurry. Then Ettore and Gianni left in the direction of Frais to see if the "good-for-nothings" were still there, but they returned after two hours. It was impossible to advance with so much snow. If they had continued, perhaps they would have reached Frais at noon on the next day. It was better to wait for Paolo to return with precise news. If only they had all left and there was no longer anyone at Frais.

The last train passed, whistling. According to plan, it should have brought the men with the suitcases of explosives. One hour later they should have gone down to Oulx, taken another hour or two to prepare, and the explosion should have taken place. Would we be able to hear the strike? Ettore thought so, unless the snow had suffocated it completely.

We poked the fire and put on a pan of potatoes and another of chestnuts, the standard foods of the period. Paolo would probably arrive with someone else. As soon as they arrived, I would make the *polenta*.

With my ears pricked and my soul torn apart, I sat near the fire and corrected proofs. The hours passed, but we did not hear anything. Two o'clock, three o'clock, four o'clock. I had finished correcting the proofs and read a thriller. The potatoes were cooked, and the chestnuts too. The snow had changed into a relentless gray rain. In the absolute silence we could hear the slow drip from the gutters. Ettore fell asleep with his head on the table.

Again the questions and the possible scenarios followed each other in my mind. Had they made the strike? Was it successful? Had they been discovered first? Had they been captured afterward?

At seven o'clock, exhausted and losing hope, I threw myself on the bed, while a weak light made its way among the clouds.

At nine o'clock, I woke up at the dog's barking. I rushed onto the balcony. Someone was climbing through the meadow, a man I did not recognize. But the dog, Tabui, recognized him, because he had begun to bark and was going to meet him, wagging his tail. All of a sudden the stranger raised his hand in a gesture of greeting and said, "*Ciau, mi*" (Hi, Mi). It was Paolo, so worn out by fatigue that I had not recognized his face.

I did not have the strength to go and meet him: I waited for him at the door, motionless, and after a minute I felt him in my arms, and my joy was so great that I finally shed the tears that I had been able to hold back all that time.

Only when he had removed his soaking wet clothing, put on dry clothes, and sat next to the stove that Ettore had lit again hurriedly, did he begin to tell the story.

At the beginning, everything had gone extremely well. On Wednesday evening they had arrived at Losa where they had spent the night, but the following morning the unexpected snow had complicated things. Advancing had become much more difficult and, when they arrived at Frais, some of the men (Don Foglia's "good-for-nothings" that later became Gianni's chaps "who did not have a very reassuring appearance") had refused to continue, deciding to return to Bussoleno the next day. The discussion with the men, and the increased difficulty of the journey, did mean that they had reached the place for the rendezvous late. Don Foglia was no longer there, but they met him going down to a *grangia* farther below, along with Carli, Volante, Ratti, Guido Garosci, and some others.[8] They had remained there waiting for the truck that, naturally, had not

---

[8] Carlo Carli, second lieutenant on reserve and commander of the partisan formations of the San Giorio-Chianoc zone, was killed in an ambush on 21 January 1944 and decorated with the Silver Medal for Military Valor. S.P.E. lieutenant Giancarlo Ratti was a partisan in the first formations in the Susa Valley and led the Young Town American military mission. Guido Garosci was a student in the Artillery Academy, and a partisan in the first formations in the Susa Valley. Then he joined the information service in Liguria, and participated in the Young Town mission along with his mother, "Aunt" Lina, a *staffetta* and Action Party collaborator.

arrived. The following morning Don Foglia had gone down to Villar Dora to receive instructions and had returned for the meeting on Saturday morning, when we had met him, with the plan that he had explained to us. For all of Friday and Saturday the others had remained at a *grangia* higher up. There was so much snow that they had to shovel snow off the road in order to climb up there.

On Saturday evening, as soon as night fell, they moved to the railroad station. The train had arrived with the men and the explosive, but when they counted, they found one missing—and what was more, he was the least trustworthy person. Where could he have stopped? They had to hurry, before they were caught in the act.

Under the pouring rain the work began feverishly, directed by Sergio. Paolo, placed on guard at the head of the bridge, had his own work to do, first with two railroad men, who quickly declared themselves to be loyal, and, what was more, even offered to help (one was Carletto Bertrand, who later would become our valuable travel companion), and then with a strange, terrorized little fellow whom he had difficulty restraining so he would not run, shouting, to warn the entire town.[9] "I have eight children!" he shrieked, wriggling. "Be quiet, and no one will harm either you or them," responded Paolo scornfully, putting his gun under his nose. He was quiet for a minute, but as soon as the barrel of the gun was lowered, he began to shriek again and try to flee. This went on until the signal came that the work was finished, and the little fellow, set free, fled with startling speed, his long cloak fluttering comically, giving him the appearance of a large, clumsy bird.

But when the time came to light the fuse, the technicians had qualms about doing it. It would be impossible to disperse quickly up through the mountains— as they had first thought—because the snow prevented any rapid movement. They would have to race through the tunnel toward Gravere, more than two kilometers long. They could not run the risk that the explosion would occur while the men were still in the tunnel. They had to give them the time to go through it; therefore, they needed a longer fuse. A piece of fuse was attached, but it must have been defective, or perhaps it was not attached properly. The fact remains that it did not function.

They went through the tunnel hastily. Then they slowed up and stopped, waiting. Forty minutes passed, but they did not hear anything. After a period of anxious waiting, reality gained the upper hand. The fuse had not functioned. The strike had failed. One of them gave way to expressions of impotent anger. Another wanted to turn back, to try again, but it was not possible. By now the little fellow had warned the town, and perhaps the missing man had been

[9] Carlo Bertrand (Carletto) was a railroad worker and partisan in the IV Alpine Division of GL in the Susa Valley.

found. They had to give up and leave. For now, this is how it had gone. The experience would be useful for another time.

It was five o'clock in the morning. Soon it would be day. They had to leave in a hurry. Sad, exhausted (they had been in the rain for twelve hours, without food or rest) they set out to return. They tried the way through the mountain, which the snow had rendered impassable, but without success. There was nothing to do but to follow the local road. They ran into two policemen, looked at them, saw that they were armed, and continued on without saying anything.

At Gravere, one group stopped in a stable. Others made for Bussoleno. From Susa, Paolo had climbed up to Meana through the short cut.

As he finished telling the story, he lowered his head and suddenly fell asleep. With a sense of painful gratitude, I watched his face, which was so young, profoundly marked by that night of fatigue, anxiety, and disappointment. I had him back again. I had him next to me. But for how long? With lucid certainty, I felt that this was only the beginning.

Later, it stopped raining, and around noon, a pale ray of sunshine made its way out. Ettore went down to the station to renew his season ticket and heard people talking about the failed strike. Naturally the attempt had been discovered. Later Anna Jarre came to tell me that they were even talking about it in town, and that someone had mentioned Paolo and Gianni's names. We decided that it was better to leave for a few days, and to let the reverberations fade away. Then we could return. Meanwhile, there were also things to do in Turin.

24 November 1943–23 March 1944

24 November, Turin. Yesterday and today, Paolo and Gianni have been on the move continuously, first to transport the proofs and then the copies of *La Riscossa Italiana*. In the end, in order to do it more quickly, Paolo went to E.I.A.R. to borrow a delivery van.[1] With it full of newspapers, he went across the city cheerfully.

Someone came to ask for help for a "rebel" from the zone of Almese, who was gravely ill with peritonitis. I ran to Penati's house. He was able to find a car to use either to go see or send for a trustworthy doctor. Despite his impeccable elegance and his magnificent cats, which are undeniably bourgeois, Penati is turning out to be really quite capable.

Today I was at Caffé Rosa, where Barberis introduced me to a Socialist whose name he did not tell me, but who evidently was important, at least to him, and who wanted to come to Susa on Sunday for a meeting of the antifascist parties. But they are really strange, these Socialists. I do not know why, but it seems to me that they have come out of an old reader, and that, on the whole, they have remained in the era of *Cuore*.[2] Honest, courageous, trustworthy, even intelligent sometimes, but archaic. I sense quite a different tone among the Communists, who all have their roots in the reality of today, and whose actions are very effective, quite a different tone among the members of the Action Party, courageously projected toward the future, and even among the Christian Democrats, at least for the few with whom I am acquainted, whose tradition, if nothing else, is not so limited. These good Socialists give me the impression of a fine piece from the nineteenth century that was put away carefully in naphthalene through the First World War, fascism, and this Second World War. Will

---

[1] Ettore worked as an engineer at the E.I.A.R. (Ente Italiano Audizioni Radiofoniche) plant in Turin.

[2] Ada is most likely referring to *Cuore* by Edmondo de Amicis, written in 1886 and a young people's classic used in the schools. The patriotism in the story reflected the values of the newly unified Italy.

they come out now and breathe new air and shake [the dust] off their backs, or will they remain preserved forever?

26 November. Today a strange sort of railroad worker came to my house, a certain De Stefani. A Southerner by origin, as we could hear unmistakably in his accent, he has an excellent knowledge of the entire Susa-Bardonecchia line, and has supporters throughout the entire valley. For every town I mentioned, he responded invariably, "I have a cow there." I do not know how many cows he had. He even had a contact in San Damiano d'Asti, but there, instead of a cow, it appears that he had a wife. Nevertheless, he will be very useful. Having been evacuated to Bardonecchia, he goes back and forth almost every day. Clearly he knows what and who will be necessary to block the Frejus tunnel once more. I will certainly stay in touch with him, but I did not completely understand him yet. He must have something "up his sleeve," as the English say. He will return tomorrow with a friend that he wants me to meet.

27 November. In fact he did come, with a strange little chap whose head was as shiny as a billiard ball, whom he held in the highest regard. Then I understood everything. They were Masons, and they had been making overtures to see if the Action Party would welcome them as a group. I confess that it really made me laugh. Was it possible that Masons still existed? Now these men were really archaic. What is more, they take themselves so seriously, saying "my venerable," "my brother." Idiotic. The world sure progresses slowly.

Nevertheless, I showed neither surprise nor amusement, taking their proposal into serious consideration. I would speak with the "leaders." (I said it exactly like that, even though I felt like laughing, but I could not treat them as inferiors.) I thought that it would be difficult to come to an agreement for the group, but probably single individuals would be welcome. (Everything goes into the soup, right?) In fact, when I spoke with the "leaders" about them, Mario had approved of my response. "It is better that they not be seen, however," he had hastened to add. "Keep in touch with them, and you deal with them."

"Very well. Thanks."

Later Libois came, a Christian Democrat that I have known for twenty years and who now represents his party in the underground Cln.[3] He came on behalf of the Cln to propose that I work with a women's organization whose goal was to engage women in the underground struggle. I confess that, after the suffragist enthusiasm of my faraway adolescence, I had no longer concerned myself with women's issues. Did a woman question really exist? Women should be given the vote, and they will be given it—it is only logical. As for the rest, I think

---

[3] Eugenio Libois was an attorney and representative of the Christian Democratic Party in the Piedmontese Regional Cln.

that today's problems—peace, liberty, and justice—touch men and women in the same way. Perhaps not recognizing the problem was my own deficiency. Nevertheless, it seemed that I was the least suited to undertake such a task. Undoubtedly, I would have refused if, for some obscure political reason, Mario had not said that I had to accept. So I obeyed agreeably.

28 November. Today is Sunday. It has been a quiet day, as if we lived during normal times.

Only one visit this morning—Sandro Delmastro, a dear young man whom Paolo met during the few days when he was in the Pellice Valley this autumn, and who is now involved in organizing the citizen squads.[4] He did not come for political reasons, but simply to introduce me to his fiancée, Ester, a beautiful brown-haired girl with a sweet, serene, and intelligent appearance.[5] It pleased me to see them together. Sometimes we also need relationships that are purely human.

The afternoon went by peacefully. Paolo showed me his stereoscopes from Paris and I read Paul Fort to him.[6] How far away all this seems! The stereoscopes, made by his uncle, are from the beginning of the twentieth century, but perhaps is it not also the civilization that we loved that has remained in our hearts like an incurable nostalgia? Did not all this die, die forever, in June of 1940, die because it had to die?[7]

30 November. Unexpected events. At eleven o'clock they informed me that Valle, the legendary head of the "rebels" in the Lower Susa Valley, was ambushed on the road between Sant'Antonino and Condove, and they do not know if he has been captured or killed, together with Felice Cima, "Barba," and someone else.[8] But at 11:30 a.m., there he was, accompanied by Trinch. Valle himself! The car they were in had been stopped—evidently after they were informed on—and the others had been killed. He had been able to save himself by jumping into the Dora river, swimming, and reaching the other bank unharmed, notwithstanding the furious gunfire aimed at him. (His overcoat marked their target at many intervals). Then, having cleaned up and dried himself off at a friend's house, he had taken the train and arrived in Turin without a problem.

---

[4] Sandro Delmastro had his doctorate in chemistry. He was an officer in the first GL formations in the Pellice Valley, and then commander of the citizen squads of the Action Party in Turin. He was captured by the Fascists in Cuneo and killed on 5 April 1944.

[5] Ester Valabrega became a partisan *staffetta.*

[6] Paul Fort was a French poet associated with the Symbolist movement. A stereoscope is an optical instrument that allows one to see drawings and photographs in relief.

[7] Italy entered World War II on the side of Germany on 10 June 1940.

[8] Felice Cima was a student. "Barba" (Marcello Albertazzi) was a worker. Both died in an ambush on 27 November 2013.

His absolute lack of rhetoric struck me. He told me about the terrible adventure with the composed, detached tone with which a banker might describe a disaster on the Stock Exchange. Only when he talked about his fallen friends did he show emotion for a moment. He is a handsome young man with an agile and alert physique, and many of those gifts of which an adventurer or hero is made. He seems to be one of those people for whom today's situation can bring out his best qualities.

1 December. The strikes continued, one after the other. Today they arrested Debenedetti. It appears that, while they were taking him to fascist headquarters in a tram, he was able to get rid of a notebook containing some notes that might arouse suspicion. For now there is no other news, and we are worried about him.

At noon, while Galimberti, Ormea, and Momigliano were at my house, the alarm sounded.[9] Naturally no one moved, but at a certain point the house had quaked terribly, and I, who was in the entrance hall, was thrown against the bookcase. The bomb had fallen nearby, on Via Confienza. I thought about how ironic it would be if, in the midst of so many different dangers, we had been killed stupidly, like rats under the debris.

2 December. Debenedetti escaped. They had beaten him, taken all of his money (it appears that unfortunately he had a lot, and not only his own), and then shut him up in a room with another poor wretch who was shattered by the thrashing. At a certain point, driven by the desire to look for help for the poor fellow, who was moaning, he went near the door—and found it open. It was around six o'clock in the morning. He went down the stairs, ran into a woman who was washing the floor and said "good morning" to her, continued to go down, pressed his hat well down over his head to hide his swollen eye, and passed in front of the sentinel with a fine Roman salute, to which the sentry responded by standing at attention. How did it happen? Who did they think he was? No one knows. He forced himself to walk slowly until he turned the corner. Then he wanted to run and catch a tram, but he no longer had a cent in his pocket. Little by little, tediously, cautiously, he reached the house of a friend.

At least this is how they told it to me. He stayed out of sight for several days, as a precaution, but it is a relief to know that he is out.

3 December. A tedious and difficult day, filled with misfortunes: missed appointments, delays, etc. To top it all off, it rained. But something brightened my day immensely. This morning Lisetta told me, in her usual monotone: "Did you

[9] Franco Momigliano (Mumo), who had his doctorate in law, was a partisan commander and union organizer of the Action Party.

know, Vittorio is my fiancé?" "Oh, really?" I said, without making anything of it, thinking that it was one of many identification card tricks, etc. I thought about it momentarily, and then did not think about it anymore. But in the afternoon, during a quiet moment, Vittorio said to me: "Did you know that Lisetta and I are engaged?" Then I understood, and I felt my eyes fill with tears and my heart swell with joy. What a magnificent thing is a love that is born like this, among the dangers, despite the anguish that oppresses us and the tragedies that surround us. I think that, no matter what happens, everything will go well for them now. They cannot fail to live their most magnificent hour in its fullness. I think that this affirmation of faith, of *life*, is a good omen for all of us. I have always loved Lisetta, from the day when I first met her at Elena's house, with her air of a somewhat wicked little angel, and underneath, her totally healthy and energetic enthusiasm.[10] I do not know Vittorio as well. Except for a fleeting encounter in a conference room many years before, I can say that I have known him since 3 September (the day of the landing in Calabria), when he came to my house, having just returned from his long imprisonment. I remember how I had been so struck by his sense of fatigue and disorientation that I forced him to retire to the balcony or to the entrance hall every once in a while, since he could not bear the conversations and discussions, which were new for him. Then with what simplicity and courage had he resumed the struggle again, notwithstanding his particularly dangerous situation, overcoming the need—which would have been most natural—for a period of peace and respite. I believe that I will grow to love him as well. I think that these two, besides loving each other as man and woman, will be good for each other because of their complementary qualities.

Yes, every now and then, there is something truly wonderful.

6 December. A long conversation today between Vittorio and Braccini. From the moment when he accepted the command of GL bands in Piedmont, this university professor, new to politics and to the underground (I believe that I saw him for the first time on 9 or 10 September), has turned out to be a leader who is effective, scrupulous, courageous, and discreet at the same time. Moreover, his remarkable human empathy and his zest for life win everyone over. If circumstances were different, perhaps he would have continued to study his animals, teach, give exams, and take care of his family, without even suspecting that he had the stuff of a conspirator, and perhaps of a hero. It is strange that there are men whose qualities shape history, and others for whom history creates qualities and virtues.

Sergio came to summon Paolo so that he would go with him to Comba Scura tomorrow, to study another bridge, and recover from the unsuccessful destruction of the Aquila bridge, whose failure he has not yet gotten over—and

---

[10] Elena Croce, Benedetto Croce's oldest daughter, who moved to Turin after her marriage.

understandably so! The next day they will stop at Martinetto, near San Giorio, for the ceremony to take the oath of the "partisans." (It appears that this is the term that has been settled upon to define those who up until then were called "rebels" or "patriots.") I asked, "Will you return for sure the day after tomorrow?" "The day after tomorrow, or in three or four days," Sergio answered, laughing as usual. "And if, while we are there, it occurs to us to do something great?" I ended up laughing too. If I cannot laugh at these matters, I will end up by going crazy. In the evening, before going to bed, Paolo read me Basile's delightful story: the story of Ninnillo and Nennella.[11]

7 December. I expected anxiety and anguish, and instead by evening Paolo had already come home. When he finished the inspection at Comba Scura, there was a message to take to Turin. Therefore, he had given up the ceremony in Martinetto and had gone down to take the message. I experienced a joy that was absolutely out of proportion. Every time Paolo returns, I feel what those who are condemned to death must feel when they are granted a stay of execution—an almost physical relief, and the desire to make the most of each hour and each minute.

8 December. I did something really careless today. I wanted Dennis, the English officer who had escaped from the hospital, to meet Braccini. I arranged the matter with Ormea, and then I notified Braccini about it by telephone. Naturally I did not tell him what it was about. I only asked him to come to my house at six. But a person does not make such a dangerous appointment that might arouse suspicion by telephone. I repented afterward, but it was already too late. If I canceled the meeting, there was the risk of causing more trouble. Therefore I was worried and nervous all day long. Around the appointed hour Lisetta and Vittorio arrived, probably wanting to relax in the warmth and have a friendly chat. If they are going to be able to make the most of this vagabond honeymoon without repose, by the simple fact of being together, sometimes they need a little pleasant warmth, an illusion of home and hearth. My damaged house, full of people, is perhaps the only place where they can have a little break. This evening, however, I sent them away, even if it made my heart ache. If something unfortunate happened, I did not want them to be there too.

Instead it all went well. First Ormea arrived, with Dennis and Maurizio, the nephew of the remarkable woman who had sheltered him, and then Braccini. After the initial formalities, the discussion began. It was a question of convincing Dennis to take moral command, so to speak, of the English ex-prisoners presently in Piedmont, or in the partisan formations, who were either lodged with

---

[11] The story of Ninnillo and Nennella is one of Giambattista Basile's fifty folk tales in *The Pentamerone*, written between 1634 and 1636.

the farmers in the country or were guests in private homes, and whose situation is probably very comfortable but still precarious and dangerous for them and for others. It is a question of taking a kind of census of them and then of sending them to Switzerland a few at a time. (It appears that it is not terribly dangerous.) In the meantime, however, it is good to bring them together, keep them united, and give them the impression that they are regimented in an organization that, although it can provide them with security and advantages, also imposes a certain line of conduct. Dennis would be very good at the hub of this organization, both because of his rank (he is a major) and because of his training and character. But it was not easy to convince him. The matter was complicated by the fact that Braccini does not understand English and Dennis does not understand Italian. I had to act as interpreter. But most of all it was complicated by his typically English slowness and pedantry. He wanted to know everything, in the most minute detail, even that which we could not tell him because we did not know ourselves. I translated Braccini's answers for him, which, in my opinion, were most comprehensive. "Hmm..." said Dennis with his classic British stutter. "I see...but" and he gave a string of objections, for the most part of an official nature. In the end, he was convinced. We drew up an order of business on the spot, which Dennis signed with the *nom de guerre* of Alexander, notifying the scattered Englishmen that we were thinking of them and we would see that they were taken to Switzerland. We will think about making it reach groups as well as individuals.

Then Dennis left with his bodyguard, on a bicycle, the way he had come. Braccini stayed a moment longer to wipe the perspiration off his brow. So did I.

9 December. Today an amusing telephone call between Braccini and me.

"Do you know, *signora*, I found another dog of the same breed as the one you had me see yesterday evening."
"Oh, did you?"
"It would be interesting if we met, all the more because mine has to leave quickly, for a warmer climate. (It was not difficult to understand that it was a question of another Englishman, who was getting ready to cross the lines toward the South.) Don't you agree?"
"Yes, certainly, we will arrange it for tomorrow (namely, according to the agreement we made yesterday, at eight thirty in the morning at the market where I go shopping before going to school.) By the way, did you see the horses I sent you?"
"Which ones? The ones from last week?"
"No, another two horses."

And so forth. I wondered what a possible—but not likely—listener would think of such a telephone call. Basically he had not said anything specific. After all,

Braccini had called me from the Veterinary Institute. Besides, why could I not work with horses and dogs?

10 December. Today a communist woman came to my house to talk to me about the women's organization with which I was supposed to work. She is unpretentious and nice and calls herself Rosetta. The name of the organization is the "Gruppi di difesa della donna e per l'assistenza ai combattenti della libertà."[12] I do not like it. In the first place, it is too long, and furthermore, why "defense" of women and "assistance," etc.? Wouldn't it be simpler to say "volunteers for liberty" for women as well? Nevertheless, I read the rough draft of a leaflet that the Groups would pass out, and the tone seemed appropriate to me. In fact, it did not address women's rights, as the word "defense" might suggest. Instead, it tried to explain the significance of our war to ordinary women and how, as women, they could work with us. The tone, which was a bit mundane, did not lack some effectiveness, however. I began to understand what "work among women" might mean today. It is a question of speaking a language that would best appeal to women's qualities because, while affirming a theoretical equality, it was necessary to recognize the existence of profound differences that create diverse sensitivities, interests, and impulses.

A socialist woman, a woman from the Liberal Party, and a Christian Democratic woman should work with us also, but at the moment there still aren't any. We will begin. In the meantime, I will try to mobilize the women I know and convince them to make socks and clothing for the partisans. Nothing convinces someone of the goodness of a cause more than working for it. A woman who has been indifferent up until now but who has made a pair of socks for the boys in the mountains—it will not be difficult to convince her to do this—will be committed and bound to her battle and will be predisposed to face much more serious responsibilities tomorrow.

12 December. It is Sunday again, and again it has been a miraculously quiet day. I darned socks and began to reread *Energie Nove*.[13] Vittorio would like me to write a brief pamphlet on Piero like the one that Franco Venturi wrote about Rosselli.[14] I hesitated a great deal, because speaking about Piero was extremely

[12] Rosetta (Maria Negarville) was a representative of the Communist Party in the Gddd. A literal translation of the name of the organization would be "Groups for the defense of women and for assistance to the freedom fighters."

[13] When she was sixteen, Ada had accepted Piero Gobetti's offer to contribute articles to the student periodical *Energie Nove*, an effort that soon led to their romance and eventual marriage. *Energie Nove* became the first of three journals edited and published by Piero, followed by *La Rivoluzione Liberale* and *Il Baretti*. The first issue of *Energie Nove* came out on 1 November 1918.

[14] The antifascist leader Carlo Rosselli (1899–1937) had contributed to Gobetti's *La Rivoluzione Liberale*. He intervened to help fight totalitarianism in Spain during the Spanish Civil War, crying "today in Spain, tomorrow in Italy." He helped to found the antifascist newspaper *Non Mollare* in

difficult for me. Then I decided to accept, seeing that no one could write it with better understanding, since it was simply a matter of presentation and publication. In addition, it pleased and moved me to reread today those pages that were distant in time, but that had never seemed so close and so current.

13 December. Terrible news. Della Valle has been killed. This is why we did not hear anything more about him. He was murdered a week ago, in an atrocious manner, in the neighborhood of Almese, while he tried to carry out an act of sabotage. I only saw him once, but I could not tear his face and its expression from my mind. It appears that he has left a wife and a daughter.

14 December. Today a ban on driving cars in the Susa Valley appeared in the newspaper. The matter is inconvenient, but in some way it makes us proud, serving almost as an official recognition of the activities of the partisan bands. Today Ugo arrived as well. The German-fascist pressure is becoming stronger and stronger in the Valley and they had to abandon the most convenient bases, which would become too exposed and dangerous with the snow. They are thinking about organizing the winter activities along two lines: one squad of skiers that will maintain contacts high up in the mountains, and a squad of saboteurs, residing in Turin, that will carry out their strikes in the Lower Valley. At this time, the entire General Staff is in Turin, intent on the work of reorganization. Too bad. Everything was going so well, even if things arose spontaneously, without being too organized. Now we are passing into a new phase, and every development has its demands.

16 December. This evening Braccini brought me his "dog," which I introduced to mine. His name is Johnny and he told us about a myriad of romantic adventures: arrests, escapes, shipwrecks, and so on and so forth. He did not convince me, and his English also left me somewhat perplexed, but Dennis did not raise any objections and, as far as pronunciation is concerned, he knew much more than I did. Now Johnny is going to the South, but before he leaves he will provide us with contacts on the Swiss border. In his opinion, the crossing is very easy. Let's hope so. Undoubtedly the meeting was useful. Nevertheless, I will be relieved when he has left. Of all those whom I have met in these past months, Johnny is perhaps the first who has aroused a sense of suspicion in me. I do not believe he is a spy, but simply an adventurer, whose daredevil nature, useful at certain times, can be dangerous at others. Seeing him next to Johnny, I appreciated our Dennis, with his slowness, pedantry, and scrupulous British honesty.

17 December. Today was my Saint's Day. It was also my mother's. At my house we used to have big celebrations. From morning on, good wishes, flowers, and gifts began to arrive. In the evening there was a party. This is how the cycle of Christmas holidays began.[15]

How far away all this seems! It is almost as if it belongs to a world that has disappeared forever. Sometimes I wonder what my father would think if he could see me today, doing what I am doing, under conditions so different from those he had dreamed about for me. Even if sometimes I feel a desperate nostalgia for all this dead past, perhaps it is better that it fade away in time.

18 December. Today, to rid me of nostalgic childish musings, there was a string of alarms. It appears that the Tribunal, a safe hideout up until now, is in danger. Momigliano warned us of rumors that indicated our house would be marked. As usual, I did not believe the rumors very much. Nevertheless, Ettore finally decided to bury the famous gun, which he found on 10 September, and which up until now had been leaning against the wall of the cellar. He had thought about giving it away. Someone had even proposed bringing it to Meana in a stovepipe, but basically burying it had been simpler. It could also be useful here.

To regain a bit of serenity, I reread Piero's essay on Alfieri and his "Matteotti."[16]

20 December. After so many days of rain, the sun returned today and it seemed like a day of spring. Then Sergio arrived, all upset because the reorganization of the Valley had somewhat disturbed his plans. Only when I got him to talk about his "strikes" did he calm down. "When the high-tension poles explode, it is like a fireworks spectacle," he said. "You should see the magnificent circles of light—yellow, blue, and green—a marvel!" He laughed loudly, happy like a little boy.

23 December. Ormea and I accompanied Carlo Mussa to see Braccini at the Veterinary Institute.[17] He will work on transporting prisoners to Switzerland. He understands English, which is indispensable, he understands Russian,

Florence. Carlo Rosselli and his brother Nello were assassinated on 9 June 1937 by the *cagoule*, an extreme right wing French group promised weapons by the Fascists in return for the murder.

[15] In Italy, many individuals celebrate not only their birthday but also their name day, the feast day of the saint for whom they were named. Celebrations on one's name day are often as important as those on one's birthday; 17 December was the feast of the Prophet Daniel and Ada's name day. It was also the feast of Saint Olympias, and therefore also the name day of Ada's mother, Olimpia Biacchi. Ada's birthday was 23 July.

[16] The Italian writer, dramatist, and poet Vittorio Alfieri inspired Italians to work toward the movement for unification, or Risorgimento, in the nineteenth century. The murder of socialist leader Giacomo Matteotti by fascist gangsters on 10 June 1924 exemplified the brutality of the Fascists against their opponents. Piero Gobetti's article, entitled "Matteotti," appeared on page 103 of the 1 July 1924 issue of *La Rivoluzione Liberale*.

[17] Carlo Mussa Ivaldi was a brigade commander in the formations in the Pellice Valley and later commander of the Mobile Medical Operations Group.

which could be useful to him, and he has physical courage and a flair for organization and command. Ormea, with his air of pretending to be a fool, is able to do things with an incredible audacity about which others would not even dare to think. (For example, had he not schemed to have me leave the hospital arm-in-arm with Dennis, under the eyes of the orderlies and the guards? I would have done it too, given that it was something I valued, and probably it would have gone very well, had I not been forbidden from doing so in order to save myself for other less amusing tasks!) Entrusted to the two of them, with the help of the faithful Maurizio, the work had to go well. Braccini too showed that he was satisfied with the arrangement.

28 December. Today Paolo turned eighteen years old. Though impressive, this is not very old for what he must face. Sometimes he seems very young to me, and sometimes he seems like a man.

Parri came in the afternoon. I had not seen him since June of '42, that is, since prehistoric times. Now he is the commander of all of the GL forces of Northern Italy. Still the same head of white hair, the same composed manner of speaking that is a bit labored, the same very sweet appearance, and still tired. He works too much. He has always worked too much.[18]

Unfortunately I could only stay with him for a little while. People continued to arrive, so I had to ignore his presence, and I had my hands full listening to everyone and sending everyone away. He spoke at length with Vittorio and Braccini about military matters. On the whole it is better that I was not there to listen. Perhaps I could resist torture. (I do not know because I never tried it.) But who could assure me that I would not talk while in a delirium or under the influence of a drug? When it is not indispensable, I prefer not to know.

29 December. Tonight they blew up the bridge at Arnodera. Sergio did it after all. I bet he's satisfied. I too am satisfied. Now the traffic will be interrupted for several months. Surveillance will be made more arduous, and working more difficult, but we will work all the same. Yes, it truly was a magnificent thing. It is too bad that we could not have been there too!

31 December, Meana. We arrived here this evening. After the last repeated attacks, the line is under high surveillance. At all the crossing keepers' cabins, which were formerly deserted, there are now Russian prisoners: Russian traitors and White Russians.[19] (Who knows if we will be able to "put them to work"? After all, what

---

[18] Ferruccio Parri was a professor and commander of all of the GL formations. A member of the Action Party, Parri became prime minister of Italy at the close of the war, to be replaced within six months by Christian Democrat Alcide De Gasperi.

[19] White Russians were counterrevolutionaries who fought against the Bolsheviks.

does it matter to them?) On the train, people told terrifying stories of their violence, greed, and lechery. But all is quiet in Meana and, although there are many people at the station, they have not yet committed any particular atrocity.

So here we are, waiting for the New Year. The stove is lit and there is a pleasant warmth. A distant date is engraved on the chimney: 31 December 1934. At that time we came to enjoy ourselves, and Paolo was so happy to find so much snow. I can see him sleeping, so small in the improvised little bed in this very room, with his little white wool cap with a tassel. He was a child then, a happy child, who dreamed about toys, the little playhouse, the mountains, and skis. Now I cannot do anything more for him, or practically anything. He must solve his problems by himself, and he knows how to solve them. I can only try not to stifle his initiative, and his vital force. I will try hard never to do it.

1 January 1944. We went toward Arnodera to see the bridge that had been blown up. Sergio was right to be proud of his work, and the Germans around here, according to what I was told, justifiably defined the act of sabotage as a masterpiece. Out of five pillars, three were completely destroyed and two reduced to the bare minimum. We could not get near them because there were a number of Germans around—we call them *cruchi* here—who must be arranging transport for passengers, but for the moment we stayed to enjoy the sun. What a small world it is! One day a farmer from Cantalupo heard himself addressed by a *cruco* in genuine Meanese.[20] How could it be? He was the son of a man from Meana who had moved to Alto Adige and then learned German. These things happen— things that would not be strange at all if men were not so crazy as to wage war.

2 January. Today we were in Oulx at the home of Cesare, with whom Paolo had agreed to go to the abandoned military base of Monte Pramans one of these days, where it appears that there are explosives. I realized that he had a fairly specific plan regarding actions for the future, but faint-heartedly I preferred not to talk to him about them. When we returned, Ettore and Paolo performed experiments with the ballistite samples Cesare had provided. They seemed interested and satisfied, but the horrible smell has always given me a headache.

6 January, Turin. Three days in Turin. The usual comings and goings, alarms, and bad news. The relative peace of the last few days seems like almost an unfair privilege.

Zama was killed in a skirmish in the Pellice Valley.[21] I do not know him, but I have heard a lot about him. He is South American, a native of Ecuador I believe, a member of the Foreign Legion who, having parachuted into Italy during the

---

[20] *Cruco* (or the plural, *cruchi*) was a derogatory term for "German(s)."
[21] Eduardo Zapata (Zama) was commander of the 15th Garibaldi Brigade.

height of fascism, was discovered and captured, and was about to be killed the very morning of 25 July. Naturally he was able to escape and, after 8 September, he joined our partisan bands in the Pellice Valley, where it appears that he has carried out activities of an extraordinary nature. At the news of his death, the reaction of Mussa, who knew him, struck me profoundly. I can see that, besides courage, he also possesses very human qualities and is capable of making friends.

More bad news. Valle has been arrested, in the Lanzo Valley, it appears, where he was transferred. They do not have definite news. I am worried, but I have the feeling that he will be able to escape. He seems to be one of those who always escape.

Today Vittorio and Lisetta were here all day long. It is Epiphany and I would have liked to make a nice *focaccia*, but I did not know what to make it with, and I had to be satisfied with making a pumpkin cake that Lisetta loathed. I consoled her with a pot of fruit-malt that she was crazy about.

Toward evening, Braccini came and stayed to talk for a long time. Paolo explained to him his plan for the exploration of the forts in the Upper Susa Valley. After this preparatory work, it would be necessary to create small groups of *paesani* in every center, especially in those areas farthest from the railroad and closer to the border, and, together with these individuals, to seize the forts, temporarily and in random fashion. This plan should open up plenty of prospects and Braccini demonstrated a lively interest.

9 January, Meana. Paolo left this morning for the planned trip to the Pramans. I stayed at home for the entire day reading *La Rivoluzione Liberale*, and diligently making notes.[22] Then, when evening fell, I put on an old pair of pants, turned my fur coat inside out so it would seem like some kind of an overcoat in the dark, and threw an ugly hat on my head. I would have challenged anyone who did not take me for a man. I went down to Susa with a nice jam-jar of glue to affix the leaflets of the Cln that urged the young men who were born in 1925 not to present themselves for the draft.

There was a beautiful moon, which helped me some and troubled me some. I truly did a fine job, I will say without false modesty. I affixed placards everywhere, from the door of the church to the door of the brothel.[23] I put one on the

---

[22] In *La Rivoluzione Liberale* Piero Gobetti advanced his belief that Italian liberalism had failed to create a stable social order. For Gobetti, liberalism was not a form of state; liberalism meant the exercise of human freedom through political struggle. After the occupation of the factories in Turin in 1920, Gobetti insisted that the working class had to have a role in the "liberal renewal of Italian political life." The first issue of *La Rivoluzione Liberale* came out on 12 February 1922. An edict of 27 October 1925 demanded that Piero stop its publication, and another in November 1925 ordered him to cease all editorial activity.

[23] State-controlled houses of prostitution were legal in Italy until 1958, when the Merlin Law (named after socialist leader Lina Merlin) abolished them.

wall of the home of Barberis, who probably will wonder who on earth was there. I lost a little time pasting another on the wall of the hotel where the Germans are staying and which is frequented by the few young men from around here who are collaborators, because there is always someone who is going in or out. In the end, I succeeded. Then I returned easily to Meana without being harmed, other than getting the lining of the fur coat dirty with glue. I confess that I had a very good time. If only all underground work were like this!

10 January, Turin. Today, two pieces of very good news. Valle has not been arrested or, as I predicted, he has been able to escape. Anyway, he is out. And Zama is not dead. After being left for dead in the straw of a manger on a farm and having ingested a good dose of morphine for the purpose of ending it more quickly, he heard the Germans arrive. They did not see him, however, even though they sat down right over the manger. After a while, the Germans left. Seeing that he had not died, but on the contrary was feeling better, when the road was free Zama dragged himself out to look for help. Now, for all practical purposes, he is out of danger. It seems like a tale, and instead it is the truth. It was Giorgio who gave me the news, with a satisfaction that was not very well disguised by the cynicism with which he defends himself. He concluded, "Tell Mussa and you will make him happy. He cared about him so much." I told him right away. His joy was as ardent as his pain had been before.

This evening Paolo arrived from Oulx, relaxed and satisfied. There are cannons on the Pramans, which he photographed, and a large amount of ballistite. One of these days he will organize an expedition to go and get them.

After dinner, I went to the Canelli Hotel—the headquarters of the Socialists during the forty-five days, which inexplicably stands fast, like my house— where Passoni gave me a nice packet of francs (those of the Italian Fourth Army), which I found a way to have changed into lire.[24] I did not think that I would also be a currency exchange agent. Today I am content, and everything seems magnificent.

11 January. I went to the Canelli Hotel early in the morning to bring the lire I had in exchange for the francs. (I had never seen so much money at one time—an entire suitcase full of thousand lire notes!). There I found Cirenei, the lawyer, who was a friend of Marchisio and Zino.[25] He spoke mysteriously of important things. It was a question of making the Cln of Northern Italy

---

[24] Pier Luigi Passoni was an accountant.

[25] Cirenei was a member of the Cln of Liguria. Lino Marchisio was a doctor, and Mario Zino was a professor. Both men were representatives of the Action Party in Genoa.

recognized by the government of Southern Italy. That way it could enact laws, issue decrees, coin money, etc. Yet what real value would this recognition have?

Then, for the entire day, various people came and went continuously. Mario Andreis returned safe and sound from Rome, where he had gone on a mission. It is a great help to have him here again. He grumbles and scolds, but he acts, and gives us a feeling of security.

12 January. A day of alarms.

I had just come back from shopping (and from putting various leaflets in the shopping baskets of the women at the market at the same time) when I received a strange telephone call from Ettore. From his office he told me that "Aunt Ada was sick." It is a prearranged phrase by which I understood that there was something wrong. Without thinking much about it, I hurried toward E.I.A.R., but I could not get there because the surrounding streets were all blocked. They were having a "roundup." (It is the first time I had heard this term.) They are denying access to a block of houses and are searching the houses one by one, looking for weapons, draft evaders, and outlaws. If they do it in Via Fabro, we are in a fix.[26] I ran to the house, chased everyone away, and tried to hide the material and newspapers as best I could. What if some sticky situation came up for Ettore and they came to search? Instead nothing happened, and after a while Ettore returned home easily. It is truly lucky that E.I.A.R. is a state utility and its engineers are almost "taboo." They even have permission to go out after curfew, which can be very useful.

Around one o'clock in the afternoon, however, there was another alarm. Vittorio had an appointment on Via Roma with a Communist from the Cln, with whom he then had to go to a certain place. This place was in a neighborhood that would be "rounded up" in the afternoon. Therefore we had to prevent him from going. I too went to the appointment, attracted Vittorio's attention, explained the situation to him, and had them come...to my house. The situation might seem absurd, but there was not much choice. Besides, it went well.

The two men left after a little while and I was getting ready to make soup when Ormea arrived to tell me something. Then after around half an hour he returned to warn me that, in his opinion, the house was under surveillance, because there was a fellow in the garden who looked suspicious, etc., etc. After a moment, there came Mussa with the same impressions. I did not want to believe them, and I chased both of them out, but perhaps they were right. It would be better for us to leave for a few days. Tomorrow morning I will notify my friends and in the evening we will leave for Meana. If it is not too late. But worrying does not serve any purpose.

---

[26] Ada's house was located at 6 Via Fabro.

20 January. I spent several days in Meana with weather that was unusually mild and almost like spring. I stayed in the sun and Paolo and Graziella [Cordola] gathered the first primroses. I worked on *La Rivoluzione Liberale* and I thought about the women. Major events—the discovery of a nice piece of fuse in an abandoned sentry box in the lime pit, and a trip to Oulx to make arrangements with Cesare.

This morning, Paolo and Gianni left for the Chaberton and I returned to Turin. Evidently the suspension of all activity had been useful. The faithful Espedita, everlastingly on the lookout, no longer noticed anything suspicious.

On the other hand, there was bad news concerning Ormea, Johnny, and the others. It appears that they were captured in a town near the Swiss border. Last week, they let around seventy people go through. They probably exaggerated the number. It would not surprise me if it had been Johnny who was guilty of some stupid recklessness. Nevertheless there is no precise news, but I am convinced that Ormea will be able to escape.

21 January, Meana. Today, in school, at the "Principe di Piemonte" I received a circular during class in which they asked all the professors to declare whether they had sons who were born in 1925, and if so, whether they had presented themselves for the draft. I went directly to the headmaster—who is an annoying stuffed shirt, full of his own authority, but whom I do not think is a bad soul—and said to him simply: "I know I am speaking with a gentleman. I have a son who was born in 1925 and he has not presented himself."

He raised his eyes, evidently impressed and surprised. (In fact, it is clear that he did not know who I was. I was a teacher in his school and that was it.) "Where is he?" he asked. Certainly I could not tell him this, even if I believed him to be basically a good man. "I do not know," I answered, staring at him until he had to lower his eyes. He was fiddling with the papers, but I saw that his hand was trembling. "Indeed," he said after a minute. "It will still be necessary to say something to the superintendent. We could say, for example, that your son was in Southern Italy when it was invaded and that you have not heard anything more about him." "Certainly," I answered, "say it just like that. Thanks." I went away. I absolutely did not think I would find him helpful. He was filled with apprehension, yes, but gifted with some inventiveness. As for the rest, apart from the headmaster, I did not dislike the atmosphere of this school. During the last few days the upper classes were reduced considerably. The boys of draft age have disappeared, one after the other. I have the impression that not even one has presented himself.

This evening, when I arrived here in Meana, I found Paolo. From the last turn in the road, I saw a thread of light coming out from the window of the kitchen, and my heart began to beat as if it were going to explode. He had returned, happy and satisfied, burned by the wind and the sun. The trip to the Chaberton had gone very well. They went up to the top, saw what interested them, and met trustworthy people in Fénils whom they could use for references, footholds, or an eventual group, local or from the outside. Naturally, they had had plenty of dramatic episodes. On the trip there, Gianni slipped, hanging by only a ski pole on the frozen snow, and Paolo had his hands full helping him to pull himself up without falling himself. The first night they slept at the "Quajé," which the good local guides define as a "comfortable *grangia*," but which is in realty nothing but a few stones and a few boards, where it is not possible either to take shelter or to light a fire. Although they were well-clad, they suffered terrible cold nonetheless. The next night they decided instead to stay in a military barracks that was in good condition, on the same hill. They tried to light the fire but, since there was no chimney, the smoke almost asphyxiated them, and therefore they ended up sleeping out in the open. Considering that the Colle is 2,600 meters high and that we are in the so-called days of the "merla," it was quite a feat.[27] Unfortunately, Gianni, who was outside the longest, got frostbite on the thumb of one hand, which still hurts. The greatest danger occurred on the return trip, however. While they were crossing the bridge at Arnodera, two soldiers pounced on them, evidently struck by their knapsacks and tired faces, sunburned and with long beards. Fortunately they were equipped with a permission slip from the Military Hospital supplied by the incomparable Ormea. Seeing so many stamps, signatures, and writings in German, the two soldiers, while they were not very convinced, had to let them go.

This too is over. And it went well.

24 January, Turin. This evening, in Meana, while we were waiting for the train, we were struck by the unusual activity of a German noncommissioned officer who was loading steel beams that were intended for the reconstruction of the bridge at Arnodera. He seemed like one obsessed: he ran, pulled, lifted, pushed, and carried with a mechanical persistence and an almost fanatical zeal. His frenzy was all the more remarkable when contrasted with the evidently purposeful slowness and reluctance of the Italian railroad workers. At a certain point, when they had to lift a weight, he was on one side, and there were four men on the other. Still he was the one who did the most. He exhibited neither arrogance nor violence, but only a surprising, almost desperate seriousness. I could not believe it. The Germans that I see working around here are in most cases almost as worn out as our men. Then someone explained. It appears that his superiors promised the noncommissioned officer that they would send him home with one month's leave if he could put up a makeshift bridge in a short

---

[27] The expression "giorni della merla" or "days of the blackbird" means the three coldest days of the year. According to legend, a beautiful white dove was so cold that it sat on a chimney to keep warm, and the soot from the chimney turned it into a blackbird.

time that would make it possible to avoid the transfer. Poor thing, he got all excited, worked, and devoted himself to doing it. I feel sorry for him, but I truly hope he does not succeed, or else we are back to the beginning, and will have to think about blowing up another bridge. When I arrived home I heard from a very worried Espedita the news that probably tomorrow *rastrelleranno* (they will carry out a roundup) in our neighborhood.[28] And I was the one who had made Paolo come down to Turin this very evening! Early tomorrow morning (usually the roundups begin around ten o'clock) I will send him to someone's house, in an area that is relatively safe because it has already been searched. There is nothing in the house that will arouse suspicion.

25 January. At seven o'clock, Ettore awakened me, saying: "They are already here. They are quicker than we are." Pricking up my ears, I heard the sound of whistles and voices with a Southern accent in the street. "But no," I answered with my usual morning foolishness (and not just morning), "they are Southerners." "Exactly," said Ettore. Looking out the window through the shutters, he added: "They have blocked Via Juvara." Even though I did not want to, I too had to acknowledge it. At the corner of Via Juvara and Via Fabro, there was a group of soldiers with machine guns. They whistled cheerfully and chatted among themselves. At almost the same time, there came Espedita, who was very scared, to tell me that they had begun to search the house. "But the road toward Piazza Arbarello is still open," she said. "If Paolo hurries, perhaps he will be able to slip away." The relaxed foolhardiness that surely some benevolent deity favors me at times when I am in a pinch made me reject the suggestion. If they caught him while he was trying to escape, it would be worse. "Then," I said, shrugging my shoulders absurdly, with all evidence to the contrary, "it is also possible that they will not come here."

Nevertheless, we had to awaken Paolo, who was still sleeping. "Wake up, it's the roundup. It would be better if you got dressed."

"Yes," said Paolo, miscalculating, no less stolid and foolhardy than I, "but first I want to take a bath." It was natural that he wanted to, after the trip to the Chaberton, and I did not dare to contradict him.

He had just gone into the bathroom when they rang at the door. I ran to open it. They were two classic policemen, similar in every way to those with whom, long ago, I had acquired a certain unpleasant familiarity. I quickly realized that it would not be difficult to manipulate them. Ettore, who turned up, brought one of them into his little room, terrorizing him with its prohibitive disorder. I brought the other into the study.

---

[28] The verb "rastrellare" literally means "to rake" or "to comb". Here, Espedita used the verb to warn Ada of a roundup.

"Just books in there?" he asked, nodding at the bookshelves.

"Just books."

"Have you read all of them?"

"Not really," I answered, laughing, and the visit continued on this friendly tone. In the little room near the kitchen there were several suitcases, usually used for transporting underground newspapers, which seemed to interest him very much, but naturally there was nothing inside.

"Empty," he commented, with sarcasm perceptible only to me, as I saw him close them again with a disappointed air. In the dining room, I saw him cast a suspicious glance toward the built-in cupboard, which was locked.

"Do you want me to open it?" I said, jiggling a bunch of keys. "It contains provisions."

"No, no," protested the policeman, thinking that I was worried about food rationing. "Who doesn't have provisions? Certainly we cannot die of hunger."

When I popped out into the hallway, I saw Ettore who, after having shown the other policeman Paolo's room, saying "bedroom," he flung open the door of the bathroom, announcing nonchalantly, "Here is the bathroom."

"Very good," said the policeman, as if he was visiting an apartment to rent, and turning around, he came back, without even going in. The bathtub was not near the door. Consequently he had not even seen that there was someone in it.

"Nothing?" he asked his colleague, when he met him in the hallway.

"Nothing," answered the other. They went away, saying goodbye courteously. Left alone, relieved, and wanting very much to laugh, we wondered if we should thank the stupidity of the policemen, or Ettore's impassivity, or the foolhardy indifference of Paolo and me. Again I was convinced that I should pay attention to my instincts, which were not likely to be wrong. The fact that someone who tried to escape from the neighbor's front door (as Paolo could have done) had been stopped, questioned, and taken away, confirmed it for me.

Still, I was somewhat worried about the cellar. When the search of the entire apartment building was over, however, one of the policemen, probably the chief, asked the concierge if there was something or someone that should be brought to his attention.

"Certainly not," Espedita had said, with an offended air. "Only honest, peaceful people live here."

"Have you found anything suspicious at all?

"No, but even if there were something, we did not see it," answered the policeman.

"Do you want to go into the cellar?" Espedita followed up, encouraged by this affirmation.

"No," answered the policeman, "it is really not necessary, but if the Germans or anyone else come to ask, say that we searched everywhere." They went away, with their devotees. Great Italian People!

In the afternoon, Mumo brought me a "woman" who was all set to work with "women." Her name is Ada, like mine, but she calls herself Adriana.[29] We chatted for a long time, and not only about women, about which, by the way, we agreed quite quickly. She is a beautiful girl, with her blue eyes often opened wide in an expression of comic amazement, and a manner of speaking that is half mincing and half witty. She agreed to write the pamphlet for the women that I should have written, and I was really relieved.

27 January. Mario Lamberti arrived.[30] Of all of Piero's friends he is perhaps the most profoundly intelligent, the most sensitive, and the one to whom I often felt the closest. It is too bad that his health only permits him sporadic activity, without ever allowing him to express the best of himself. Yet, despite his physical limitations, what persistence he has for wanting to act and to work! I remember his trips to Turin and Meana, in 1928 and 1929, when he still believed that we must and could produce something like *La Rivoluzione Liberale* clandestinely—his efforts, enthusiasm, and pain. I remember how, when he saw that by then this effort was fruitless, during respites from his illness he began to study economics and prepare himself for "afterward." There would be months, and sometimes years, when we did not see each other, not even exchanging a postcard. Then we would meet each other, and it was as if we had left each other the previous day. This is the sign of true friendship.

Today he has come to Turin to stay. He wants to earn his living and, at the same time, he wants to work with us. His decision, if it makes me happy on the one hand—both because we will have him nearby and also because he exhibits an adventurous and juvenile vitality that cannot but please me—it worries me on the other. Given the condition of his health, he is often used to living in a convalescent home, with all the comforts. Will he be able to adapt to a life of work and exertion?

I immediately had him talk with Mario Andreis and Peccei, who proposed to him that he work on developing the economic theory of the Action Party in detail. Hearing me extol Lamberti's economic training, his studies at the best German, English, and American universities, and the esteem that Einaudi has for him, Peccei winked as if he had been offered a good bargain.[31]

---

[29] Ada Della Torre (Adriana), a professor, partisan *staffetta*, and eventual organizer of the Mfgl.

[30] Mario Lamberti was an economist and a collaborator of Piero Gobetti's *La Rivoluzione Liberale* and on the *Rivista Economica*. He was an inspector for the GL Command in the Susa Valley.

[31] Senator Luigi Einaudi.

Lamberti said he would think about the suggestion. He is full of enthusiasm at the thought of being useful, and of working with us, but he does not want to be paid for this work. He would rather look for work at Fiat, where he has acquaintances. I understand him perfectly and I do not blame him, even if I would prefer that he work for us exclusively.

30 January, Meana. Today, with Ettore, Paolo, and Gianni, I went beyond Arnodera, beyond Refornetto, and up to the top of Olmo. It was a marvelous day and I picked a lovely bunch of primroses.

The purpose of the walk was an inspection of the fort situated above the small town of Olmo. At a certain point, having left the two boys on the lookout as they explored a certain cave dug out of the side of the mountain, Ettore and I went down to the little town, and then set out on foot toward the fort. We found barbed wire, but it was so low that we could climb over it very easily, and a sign that prohibited passage, but it was so high and so badly damaged by foul weather that we could very easily not have read it. So we went forward on up to the storehouse. Through its windows—closed by grilles, but certainly not impenetrable—we were able to make a rapid inventory of the drawers of bullets and hand grenades contained in it. After having seen what we were interested in, we continued on and climbed up to the top, in order to then descend on the other side. In my opinion, we should always take a complete tour of interesting places. While we were looking for where to pass through the barbed wire, which was not so low here, some man with a dog came toward us. Ettore squeezed my arm, and he maintains that he said, "It's a soldier." Fortunately, I did not hear him. I responded tenderly to his squeeze, while thinking that this man with the gun and dog would never go hunting in the area around the fort. In the meantime, I made affectionate teasing gestures in the direction of the animal who, contrary to what usually occurred, did not respond to me. Meanwhile the man had reached us. "Your papers," he said. At least Ettore maintained that this was so, but I did not even hear this, evidently having been made deaf by the usual protector deity. Displaying the most radiant of my smiles, I asked the soldier, whom I continued to regard as a kindly hunter friend, "Can we climb down on this side? Which way do we go?" Evidently my foolish cheerfulness, my bunch of primroses, and our air of lovers who were a bit elderly disarmed the guard at the fort, who pointed out the best way, and even helped us cross over the barbed wire.

Only when we were outside of the little town did I become aware of reality. Mentally I gave thanks that Paolo and Gianni had not been with us.

4 February. This evening, when I arrived, I found Paolo, who had come back from a two-day trip in the Bousson Valley with Gianni. They slept in an abandoned *carabinieri* barracks, right on the border.[32] They found a large amount

---

[32] The *carabinieri* were Italian gendarmes.

of weapons, which we would have to arrange to have carted off, and many interesting documents—armaments treaties, reproductions of passports from every country, and lists of suspicious people not to let expatriate. They also made useful contacts in the neighboring towns.

7 February. Yesterday morning, taking advantage of the fact that it was Sunday, when no one was working, we paid a visit to the bottom of a nearby lime pit. There are tunnels that could serve as excellent antiaircraft shelters and storehouses. There is also the possibility of carting off some explosives when we want to do so. Unfortunately it is dynamite—not very effective and dangerous, especially with the cold. In the afternoon, we went down to Susa, where I finally met the famous Lieutenant Ferrero, who it appears commands several groups and to whom we could perhaps entrust the command of our formations in this zone. Since we were scarcely able to talk with him, he promised that he would come to my house in Meana today. So today we waited for him all day long, until we decided to leave for Turin without seeing him.

9 February, Turin. Called by telephone, I went to the superintendent's office, somewhat anticipating and somewhat fearing what awaited me. To my great satisfaction, the superintendent received me immediately, with a courtesy that was almost effusive. "I am happy to meet you, dear *signora*. What can I do for you?

"If you are waiting for me to talk, you are in for a surprise," I said to myself, and I responded sweetly: "I really do not know. It is you who had me summoned."

"Of course, of course…" and he browsed through his papers in the meantime. "It is about your son, it appears. You do not know where he is?"

"No," I responded tersely.

"Oh, poor *signora*, poor *signora*, how well I understand. He is in Southern Italy, according to what they tell me, is that not true?"

At this point I felt that, as much as it disgusted me, I could not but play along with his game. Taking advantage of our relationship with Gliozzi, a native of Calabria, I fabricated a more or less believable white lie.[33]

"Sure, sure," confirmed the superintendent. "Would you by any chance have a letter from your son from this town before the invasion?[34] Or perhaps a simple postcard…."

"I can look," I said, without compromising myself.

---

[33] Mario Gliozzi was a professor of mathematics and member of the Cln for the schools in Piedmont.

[34] The Allied landing.

"Here, here, look. It is quite all right. So many ugly things! Sons separated from their mothers! This poor country of ours, invaded on all sides, torn by discord...."

I looked at him. Was he taking me for a ride or was he serious?

He was serious, and his eyes were glistening with emotion. He said more things of the same nature, and he accompanied me respectfully as far as the door.

When I went outside, I could not help but think, for the second time in a little more than a week—Great Italian people!

Yet sometimes I wondered up to what point all this is human understanding and adaptability, and up to what point foolishness and a "could not care less attitude" instead.

Mumo and Adriana slept at my house and we worked until three o'clock in the morning, correcting and completing the pamphlet for the women, which seems to me to have gone quite well.

20 February, Meana. This morning we left for Oulx, the three of us with Gianni and one his young friends, Pillo, who will work with us.[35]

Great excitement on the train. The newspaper carried the news of the death penalty for young men born in 1925 who opposed the draft, and who did not present themselves before the end of the month. The news is certainly grave. Even if my usual optimism tells me that it is above all a question of an intimidating measure that will be difficult to implement, we cannot fail to take account of it. Intimidation can reach a certain point and then become actual enforcement. If, as I hoped, the young men continued not to present them-selves, the reaction could become bloody. Certainly I do not know up to what point Gianni and Paolo will be able to move about freely, even in Meana, and if Paolo will be able to go back and forth between Meana and Turin.

At Oulx we met Cesare, who gave us the appropriate directions. We went along peacefully in front of the soldiers' barracks and the German command, looking like Sunday day-trippers, and we crossed the bridge of the Beaume. Then, at the foot of the ascent, we separated. Paolo and Gianni went up toward the Pramans, Cesare returned home, and the two of us went with Pillo along the road to Bardonecchia. I wanted to feel Pillo out a bit. I questioned him for a long time and I immediately felt a motherly tenderness for him. Even if he was still a bit immature, he appeared to me to be surprisingly well-focused. I felt a burning generosity in him, and a capacity for sacrifice without reserve. I think he could work with Mumo in distributing the press. Even though he is also of

[35] Paolo Spriano or "Pillo" was a student and organizer of the partisan bands in the Susa Valley. He later became a well-known historian of Italian Communism.

the '25 generation, he was declared temporarily unfit at his military examination, and therefore for now has some protection that is, unfortunately, relative and temporary.

Then we too moved toward the Pramans and we climbed a bit to meet the two boys. We stopped at a group of deserted *grange*. The sun was hot and the dry grasses of the meadow emitted a perfume that, mixed with that of the pine trees, gave the illusion of the sea coast. After a while, there came Paolo and Gianni, tired, loaded down, and satisfied. With his natural enthusiasm, Pillo wanted to carry one of the two sacks full of ballistite. Ettore took the other. So we returned happily to Meana.

At home, near the fire, a long conversation with Paolo, who was very excited. The threat of the death penalty, even if it terrified him, opened new avenues for him. He is convinced that many young men, faced with danger, will go to enlarge the partisan ranks. Some of them could be used to form small flying squads brought in from the outside that could work to continuously sabotage and harass the German and Republican forces in the Susa Valley.[36] It is not possible to create a zone that is entirely partisan in the Susa Valley, like they did in the Cuneese Valley, Pellice Valley, and elsewhere. So far the Susa Valley, with its railroads, streets that are suitable for vehicles, and valleys leading to France, has been too important for the Germans to abandon it. At this time it appears that there are more than 3,000 Germans in the Susa Valley, in addition to the Republicans. Here there can only be guerilla forces, in the true sense of the term—nothing bureaucratic or cumbersome, but small, nimble groups who can move easily and are experts in sabotage, and who are brave and absolutely trustworthy. Such individuals are not found locally. The higher up you go, the more slowly the tide of the war of liberation arrives, almost obeying a law of physics. The inhabitants will give their complicity, support, and help, but we should not expect initiative from them. For this one needs people from the outside. Paolo thinks that, between him and Gianni, they can organize the thing. He has in mind several young men from Turin who could join them. He is also thinking of Franco Dusi and, naturally, of Cesare. Later, when work in the city becomes dangerous for him, Pillo could come also.[37] I have never seen Paolo so optimistic and talkative. Evidently, he has a specific plan that has been well developed during these months of contacts and exploration. Now that the snow has disappeared, the good weather will make his work easier, the supplying of provisions will be less difficult, and the fact that he gets along so well with Gianni will guarantee essential organizational unity.

[36] Flying squads were from other areas and could move from one place to another. Republicans were those loyal to the Republic of Salò.

[37] Franco Dusi was a medical student and an officer in the GL formations in the Cuneese Valley. He was shot on 9 October 1944.

While we were chatting, Ettore prepared an explosive mechanism with an old tin can, with which he will try an experiment tomorrow by blowing up a high-tension pole.

21 February. We were waiting for Gianni and Pillo to go with them to carry out the experiment in sabotage. Instead, for the time being, only Pillo came. Gianni's father had arrived from Turin, evidently frightened by the news of the death penalty. It appears that he wants to make him go to Switzerland. Naturally Gianni does not want to go, but will he be able to resist?

Paolo decided that the two of us would go to blow up the pole. Therefore, we left for the Colle Montabone, which sits above the railroad. I remained on top to stand guard, and he went down toward the railroad with his shopping bag, which contained the ballistite, iron wire, and fuse, in short, everything "necessary," skipping like he was going for mushrooms. There was a huge sun and a great silence all around. At a certain point on the railroad, two Germans appeared with a big pot, probably ordered to bring the mess rations to those who were on guard at the crossing keeper's cabin beyond the tunnel. But Paolo had already vanished. Surely he had seen them before I did. After a while, when the Germans had disappeared, I saw him maneuver near a big pole, and then disappear again. After a few minutes, we could hear an explosion, similar to an explosion of a mine, which the surrounding mountains echoed, magnifying it. Then after an interval that seemed eternal to me, there was Paolo, still with the shopping bag on his arm and a look that was half disappointed and half annoyed. The ballistite had exploded, as I had well heard, but the pole remained hardly damaged, rather than collapsing. "It appears that we need more. Or we need to bury it. I will ask Sergio," he concluded.

At home we waited for Gianni and Pillo. Gianni was embarrassed, and torn. He did not have the courage to rebel against his father, and he did not know how to refute his reasons, or how to resist the tears of his mother. This evening he too will go down to Turin. In a week he will go into Switzerland through a passage in the Susa Valley.

Paolo did not say a word, but I saw him become pale, and I understood that it was a grave blow for him—a blow similar to the one he had experienced on 10 September when he saw Turin surrender to the Germans without resisting.

Not even I, however, knew how to say something meaningful. In good conscience, I could not urge the son to rebel against his father, a fine person and motivated by the best of intentions. I would have been able to do it if he had tried to convince him to present himself to the Germans, but basically he only sought to save him, and from his point of view perhaps he is right. Even I, in spite of everything, will breathe a sigh of relief when I know that Gianni is safe. You do not find many boys like him. Perhaps it is our duty to preserve them for tomorrow.

24 February. Sorrow. Paolo's disappointment and the downfall of his plans for the Susa Valley, weigh heavily on me as well. It is not by any means worth thinking that he could carry out alone a program that was already out of proportion for the strength of two. Moreover, it is not easy to find someone who could replace Gianni in intelligence, courage, dependability, and knowledge of the mountains. Above all, no one has participated in the creation of the project, and knows the intricacies, possibilities, and dangers like he does.

Having abandoned the work in the Upper Valley, Paolo had to go away. It is absurd for him to remain in Meana (where he would not remain without doing anything anyway) and even more so that he travel back and forth between Meana and Turin. I spoke with my friends and everyone thinks that he would do well to join one of our formations. Even he agreed, although he was not very enthusiastic. But he understands that it is necessary and perhaps the new experience is also tempting. Some want him to go into the Cuneese Valley, where our partisan bands are better organized, but he prefers the Pellice Valley, perhaps because it is closer to the Susa Valley, where he might be able to make brief visits to keep in touch. It also gives me a greater sense of security. He will leave at the beginning of March.

28 February. Final days in Meana with Paolo, but the thought of the imminent parting kept me from enjoying the sweetness. Moreover, the weather has changed and it has been drizzling for two days. Today it even snowed a little.

This morning we buried the sacks of explosives in the stone pit by the cave. I tried to engrave the exact point on my mind so that, when it is necessary, I can find it again. This evening we unearthed the revolver (the 6.35 mm inherited from his uncle) that Paolo will bring with him into the Germanasca Valley.

During this time Ettore is busy preparing a minuscule gadget that, scattered on the street (possibly in the middle of the cow dung) will make the automobile tires have a blowout. I do not understand how it works but I like it. It is bloodless and very useful at the same time.

1 March, Turin. This morning, as soon as I arrived in Turin, there was Gigliola, radiant, with a magnificent revolver that had belonged to a German orderly.[38] Yesterday evening, in the restaurant where she was eating with Franco, a German officer hung his cloak on a clothes peg, with a belt and the revolver attached. Gigliola covered it with hers. Then, just as she was leaving, she took the revolver from the scabbard, slipped it into her purse, closed the case again, and went away peacefully. I advised her not to be seen again in that restaurant, at least for a few days, but this is precisely the kind of work for which Gigliola is best suited, with her abundant natural courage and her girlish pranks. There

---

[38] Gigliola Spinelli was a commander of the citizen squads of the Action Party.

are other young women of her character, even if they are not exactly like her. Why could they not do this type of work systematically, in crowded trams, for example, when it is dark? I would like to try it myself one of these evenings.

2 March. I accompanied Paolo into the Germanasca Valley.

Before he left, he told me: "Calm down. It's nothing dramatic." In fact there really was nothing dramatic.

The trip went very well—as far as Pinerolo by train, then on a smaller train to Perosa. When we arrived down below, we asked discreetly which was the road for the Germanasca. Everyone gave us directions enthusiastically, with an air of cheerful complicity, as if they were saying, "Oh, we know very well where you are going!" While on the one hand this made me laugh, on the other hand it worried me. A woman, who was from the Veneto, set out right by our side and accompanied us, while praising the life that they led in the Gianna: "You are going to the Gianna, right? (How could we tell her no?) My son is there too. They are doing very well. They even have an accordion!"

"Then they are all set," I thought. Taking advantage of her loquaciousness, I asked her if there was some way to avoid doing the sixteen or seventeen kilometers of road on foot.

"At one time there was a mail coach, but it does not operate any more now," she answered. "You can utilize the talc-graphite truck that goes up and down, or some private wagon. For example, there's the cart that belongs to the courier from Perrero. Hey!" She made a sign with her arm toward a little old man who was starting up an old, dilapidated gig on which there was already a lot of luggage and a girl with an enormous suitcase. The old man stopped his horse and waited for us to approach.

"Can you take along a boy and his mother? They are going to the partisans."

"Get on," said the old man, with a large wave of his whip.

"Thank you, and goodbye," I hardly had time to yell to the woman, while the carriage moved, jolting.

While we were leaving the town, I saw two armed young men in one of the last shops, with camouflage jackets.

"Are they Germans?" I asked Paolo, bringing my hand instinctively to my breast, where I had hidden the revolver.

"Not at all," laughed Paolo. "They are partisans."

In fact I had noticed something atypical about their dress. It made a real impression on me to see them move around armed, freely. What if this truly was the Promised Land? And I was worried about leaving Paolo here!

In the meantime the horse, trotting very gently, advanced forward into the valley, which was becoming more and more narrow, with sharp and hidden turns. It was sunny, but in the areas that were in the shadows, it was terribly cold. I understood how they could keep such a valley defended, and I consoled myself, thinking that it would be easy to prevent access to enemies. The old man was not talkative and neither was the girl. She said only that she was returning home after having worked as a servant. "You want to see the partisans, huh? You like handsome boys!" said the old man in patois, shaking the whip.

In Perrero, the gig stopped. We continued on foot until we found a talc-graphite truck that brought us as far as the turn for Maniglia. Then we continued, in the company of a girl, a sister of a partisan, who came from Barge and was a *staffetta*. At noon we were in Pomeifré, a little group of houses in the shadow of the mountain, from which began the short cut for the Gianna. "You will be there in half an hour," said the girl.

For the entire trip along the valley, I was struck by the atmosphere of normality and peaceful security. No one was hiding, and no one was afraid. So this is freedom.

Relaxed work and tranquility also dominated the Gianna. A big building created for the personnel of the talc-graphite plant was now occupied by the Partisan Command. With its many windows thrown wide open to the sun, and with its tanned young men with arms or torso bare, who moved through the space in front and on the terraces, it seemed like a convalescent home or a big hotel, and war and danger seemed farther and farther away.

The commander, Roberto Malan, welcomed us cordially.[39] "I think I will send you to Praly," he said to Paolo, "to be a political commissar with Emanuele.[40] The commissar," he hastened to add, "is a partisan like the others, who does everything that the others do. In addition, he tries to politically educate the more and more numerous recruits who continue to pour in."

At that moment Zama arrived, the extraordinary South American I had heard about who has died and been resurrected several times. His "worn out" appearance struck me, while I knew that he had to be very young. He had come to notify Roberto that on that evening an important strike on the R.I.V. would be carried out, and that therefore he needed to go down into the valley immediately to make the final arrangements.[41]

"Do you want me to take you down?" he offered politely. "Let's go on my motorcycle, you, Roberto, and I, as far as Pomeifré. There we will take a car." I said that I would go down on foot. Two people on a motorcycle, given the icy

---

[39] Roberto Malan was reserve officer and commander of the V Alpine GL Division.

[40] Emanuele Artom, a student and political commissar of the GL formations in the Germanasca Valley and an Italian Jew, was captured and killed by the Nazi-Fascists on 7 April 1944.

[41] The R.I.V. plant, founded in 1906 by Roberto Incerti in Villar Perosa, specialized in the manufacture of ball bearings.

road, seem to me to be a more than enough of a load. On the other hand, if I dash down by the short cut, I will arrive in Pomeifré before them. There I will gladly take advantage of the car.

I said goodbye to Paolo, without much distress. It was all so peaceful, safe, and serene. I ran down in the midst of the snow, repeating to myself: "You see? You worry too much!" As I had predicted, I arrived at Pomeifré before the motorcycle. I sat to wait on the embankment of the bridge. The banks of the stream were still covered with ice but, in the places where the sun shone, there were already trees covered with buds. "Spring is returning!" I hummed to myself. I wanted to feel happy at any cost.

After a while I saw the motorcycle arrive, but Zama was alone. Roberto had had a spill a few meters before. I was glad that I had not shared his fate. When I saw him arrive, shaking the snow off his back, I set out with him below while Zama prepared the car. If we meet each other again, fine, but I do not want to run the risk of missing the small train to Perosa.

On the way, Roberto indicated the points of interest and turns: "Here we have a machine gun, there a guard post, here a look out." Listening to him convinced me all the more of what I had thought on the trip there, that the configuration of the valley was such that it was enough to reinforce the natural defenses in order to render it nearly impregnable.

Soon Zama reached us with the car that left me off at Perosa one hour before the departure of the small train. I went into a cafe and pastry shop and ordered ersatz coffee.[42] The owner, who had seen me pass by with Paolo in the morning, treated me with affectionate cordiality. "Was that handsome young man your son? Oh, you will see that he will be just fine!" She showed me her children, a boy and a girl, four and six years old, and very good-looking.

"Now everything is going well, because the partisans are here," she said. "Before, when the Germans were here, I lived in continual fear. Let's hope they do not return!"

"Let's hope not!" I echoed with all my heart.

At the appointed hour I took the little train, and then the train at Pinerolo. When I arrived home, I found Ettore, who was making other strange, diabolical devices with Giancarlo Scala and Volante. Tomorrow, normal life resumes.[43]

8 March. The daily routine continues, if you can call routine a life so devoid of orderliness and full of the unexpected—people of every kind, men and women, young and old, Turinese and foreigners, soldiers and politicians, partisans, trade unionists, and organizers.

---

[42] Ersatz coffee was a coffee substitute during World War II.

[43] Giancarlo Scala had his doctorate in law, was a member of the Piedmont Military Committee of the Action Party, and later was commander of the GL citizen squads of Turin.

I introduced Pillo to Mumo. They hit it off at once, and Pillo began to work with his characteristic zeal.

Sergio brought me one of his precious typescripts that I named the "Manual of a Saboteur," which in essence reflects his expertise and seems extraordinarily useful. I will make some copies of it.

Saturday and Sunday we were in Meana and in Susa. I saw Lieutenant Ferrero who, while raising many objections, ended up accepting the command of the GL formations in the Middle Valley. We were at Barberis' house, where one of his uncles was staying, one of those old Socialists whose defenseless candor moves me. They are the kind who, if you feel they are opportunists, you do not feel very sorry for them, but when, like this man, they are completely unselfish, you cannot but appreciate them, and their very obsolescence is comforting.

In Meana I began to write the pamphlet on Piero.

The first blossoms are sprouting on the trees.

10 March. Yesterday Lisetta and I carried out an amusing venture.

For several days, following the decree about the death penalty, an increase in those who presented themselves for the draft took place (which fortunately was minimal). We had to encourage the young men and make them understand that, if they presented themselves believing they were saving themselves for the time being, they were really putting themselves in a bogus position that did not decrease their danger now in any way, and would become more serious later on. It is sad to have to emphasize this practical and utilitarian side of the matter, but propaganda is useful, especially for those who do not have solid moral principles. Moreover, what can we expect from these young men who grew up during fascism, without teachers and without guidance, when they were not lucky enough to belong to a family or environment that was politically sound? Therefore we made a little flyer along these lines that seemed quite good to me, and we passed it out by the usual methods. But Lisetta thought that we should distribute it directly at the exits of the secondary schools, especially the technical ones, and at the administration building for the military. After a preliminary visit to the military administration building, we had to abandon that idea. There is too much surveillance and, what is more, someone who gets as far as the military administration building will not easily let himself be convinced to turn back by an anonymous piece of paper. This left the schools, and we decided to do the two principal ones today: the "Pierino Delpiano" where I would go, and the "Principe di Piemonte" where Lisetta would go, since I teach there. Therefore we left around five o'clock (classes end at half past five), Lisetta by bicycle, with a handkerchief on her head to cover her blond hair, which is too recognizable, and I on the tram, with an old hat that I have not worn in years. I arrived in view of the "Delpiano" when the students began to exit. I waited for the oldest to leave, and then I approached coolly and distributed the leaflets to them, saying: "Read it carefully. It is something that will interest you." When I saw that they were beginning to read, discuss, form a group, and summon each other, I went away quickly and jumped on a tram on Via Rossini. Relieved, I found Lisetta at my house. It had gone well for her too, and she appeared satisfied. This morning at the "Principe di Piemonte" the boys spoke excitedly about the little leaflets brought by the "girl." At the "Delpiano" it appears that they put one up in the hallway right away.

This evening I helped Sandro Delmastro write a plan of action for the citizen squads. Tomorrow I am going to the Germanasca to find Paolo. At the same time, I will take advantage of the opportunity to bring some newspapers up there.

13 March. Having learned from previous experience, no sooner had I arrived with Ettore in Perosa on Saturday morning than I set out immediately toward the Germanasca, in the hopes of finding transportation. In fact, a talc-graphite truck took us, but left us on the road for Maniglia this time as well. ("These are the talc trucks," Ettore commented, seeing them all covered with white powder. "Who knows if we will also see the graphite trucks covered with black powder?") We continued on foot, until we found a checkpoint that was not there two weeks ago. Undoubtedly we would have had to provide explanations if Roberto had not arrived and immediately let us pass. There had been some alarms, he said, and they had to take precautions.

At Pomeifré we met Paolo, with his old, threadbare raincoat and a long beard, but who seemed to me to be the most elegant young man on earth. Having exchanged some small talk with his companions, we set out along the road, and we sat in the sun on the edge of the river. We had so many things to tell each other.

He told me about his experiences. He had not gone to Praly; on the contrary, even Emanuele had returned from there. Up to now they did not have specific responsibilities. They did a little of everything, and especially acted as storehouse keepers, but in the coming week he will go down to Perrero, where he will work at the auto center. Then he narrated an amusing episode. The very night of his arrival, there had been the famous strike against the R.I.V., where the sabotage of irreplaceable machinery—everyone said with pride— had been better than a bombardment. Having finished the task of sabotage, they carried away what might be useful: boxes of provisions, sacks of flour, etc. Among other things, they had dragged back a very heavy box with immense difficulty. At the time when they took it, one of them had broken the cover in one place and felt carefully under the packing. "Bottles!" he had said, satisfied, feeling something hard and round under his hand. But when, having unwrapped it completely, they opened the box, anxious to brag about how they had happily succeeded in the enterprise, they found a marble bust of Senator Agnelli instead.[44]

The other episode was less pleasant. Some man had arrived with whom Zama had accounts to settle. (It appears that he had been the source of all of Zama's previous troubles.) Evidently, he had come to spy, and perhaps with worse intentions, too, because they had found a loaded revolver on him, with a round in the barrel. Zama had him shot. While Paolo told the story, I observed his face with some anxiety, fearing that I would find satisfaction or indifference there. Instead, he said, with restrained discretion: "It made a certain impression on me." I let out my breath. It can be necessary to kill, but troublesome if we find it simple and natural.

We had dinner at the little inn at Pomeifré where we could not spend the night as I had hoped, however, because Bertolone the engineer, director of the R.I.V. plant, who had been taken away the night of the strike and held as hostage until management could agree to certain requests from the partisans, occupied the only available room.[45] I saw him leave with a book under his arm, and he did not seem at all unhappy to me, even if they had confiscated his shoes and he had to walk in slippers.

After dinner we sat in a thicket, which naturally was still barren, and where I tried to mend Paolo's raincoat as best I could. Later we stopped on the embankment of a bridge at the turn for Massello, and I drew Paolo's attention to the magnificent "sheets" of water on the river, similar to those in the area around Meana and Pollone where, as a little boy, he used to go to swim with Croce's girls during the warm, peaceful summers.

At five o'clock, the children of Pomeifré got out of school, filling the valley with noises and games. The sense of absolute normality and serenity that exists in these towns struck me, like it had the time before.

Then Paolo returned to the Gianna and we went down to Perrero. There were a lot of cars going back and forth on the road, and we found two trucks that had returned from a strike in the piazza of Perrero. The boys looked excited and satisfied.

Then we went to sleep, in peace. It seemed impossible not to wake up with a start at every rumble of a motor, and at every horn of an automobile, thinking instead, with deep satisfaction: "They are ours." For months, I should say for years, I had not felt a similar sense of relaxation from tension. I slept peacefully, but was awakened by the wind, which had become very strong. I thought regretfully that perhaps it would impede the "action" that was expected for that night, but I fell back to sleep immediately.

[44] Senator Giovanni Agnelli was the president of R.I.V. Agnelli later founded the Fabbrica Italiana Automobili Torino or Fiat automobile company.

[45] Pietro Bertolone, managing director of the R.I.V. plant.

The next morning I left for the Gianna, chatting pleasantly with Ettore. We stopped for a moment to observe an abandoned military stable, which they will probably make into a storehouse for the cars. We were at the Gianna around 10:00 a.m. and, having met Paolo, I left to converse and debate with a group of his friends. The discussion was not very different from many held in my house in these last few years, but the sense of an experience that had been lived sustained it, transforming hopes and aspirations into reality. Then, after dinner in the big refectory, Zama told us about some of his extraordinary adventures, and Ettore found a way to make himself useful fixing a radio. Meanwhile Bianca, a young communist friend of Alberto Salmoni, and Frida Malan, Roberto's sister, arrived.[46] They brought books for the library in the Gianna, but unfortunately they also brought the news that Willy Jervis had been taken while he was going down to the Pellice Valley by motorcycle. It appears that he was carrying explosives, letters, and documents that might draw suspicion.[47]

On the return trip, I stopped at the hotel in Perrero to wait for Roberto, who was supposed to give me a letter for Turin. The owner was reading the Bible, and this gave me a sense of security and peace. Meanwhile Frida spoke with me at length regarding the woman question, about which she has ideas that are certainly original. Then, with the letter and instructions, we left.

---

[46] A communist Party activist and organizer of the Gddd, Bianca Guidetti Serra became a distinguished attorney, brought the first case for equal pay for equal work to civil court in Turin, and was a member of the Turin City Council. She served for many years as president of the Centro studi Piero Gobetti in Turin as well. In her book *Compagne: Testimonianze di partecipazione politica femminile* (Turin: Giulio Einaudi, 1977), Guidetti Serra presented testimonies of fifty-one working women (factory workers, dressmakers, embroiderers, shop-girls, and clerks) who became active in the Gddd, most of whom were Communists. She practiced law until 2001. Most recently, she wrote her autobiography, *Bianca la rossa* (Turin: Einaudi, 2009), with Santina Mobiglia. Frida Malan was a teacher and inspector for the Piedmontese Regional GL Command. She later worked with Ada Gobetti to form the Mfgl, and co-edited with Ada the clandestine newspaper *La Nuova Realtà* [The New Reality] beginning in February 1945. Malan later served on the Turin City Council and as president of the Regional Commission for Equal Opportunity in Piedmont. Participating in the *Resistenza* helped Malan choose her life's goals, one of which was "to study the laws in every field that prohibited women from doing so many things." See Frida Malan, "La donna nella Resistenza," in *Aspetti dell'attività femminile in Piemonte negli ultimi cento anni: 1861–1961* (Turin: Comitato Associazioni Femminili Torinesi, 1963). In an interview on 16 November 2000, Malan told me that her time in the *Resistenza* was the most important in her life and that her tombstone would bear the words *Partigiana combattente*. She died in Turin in February 2002. Alberto Salmoni had his doctorate in chemistry, was a partisan in the formations in the Pellice, Germanasca, and Chisone Valleys, and was commander of the "F. Dusi Column" of the IV Alpine Division of GL.

[47] Guglielmo (Willy) Jervis was an engineer and member of the Piedmontese Military Committee of the Action Party. The Germans killed him on 5 August 1944. He was decorated with the gold medal for military valor.

This evening Cesare came. I had to tell him all the details about the trip, the partisans, and Paolo. He listened with visible envy, while I thought with melancholy: "Never fear, you too will ending up going there. It will not end first, unfortunately!"

14 March. Today Mumo arrived with somewhat worrisome news. It appears that the Germanasca is in a state of alarm. It seems impossible. Sunday everything appeared to be so peaceful! Perhaps the situation is related to the arrest of Jervis, whose situation seems rather serious. Come to think of it, the checkpoint and the informer were quite clear signs. With his usual composure, Giorgio reassured me. Nevertheless, Mumo will go up there tomorrow and, if something has happened, he will certainly be a tremendous help to Roberto. We will miss him here, however. Pillo will feel it most of all because he too has become fond of him in these last few days. Leo Diena, who already has some work experience, will take his place.[48]

20 March. I was in Meana. I worked on the pamphlet about Piero, and I saw Barberis and Lieutenant Ferrero, who accepted the command. Let's hope he works out. While returning on the train, I thought that I could have been very good at being "political commissar" for the GL formations in the Susa Valley. Without false modesty, I feel that I could do it very well. But I think it is useless for me to speak about it with my friends and to solicit the "responsibility," because I would find it difficult to convince myself to do it. The important thing is that I "function" as political commissar. Certainly official recognition would serve to consolidate my authority. Yet during such times, weak is the authority that needs sanctions that are more or less official. If I am able to do my job well, I will obtain all the authority that the most bureaucratic chrisms could give me.

When I arrived in Turin, I found a brief letter from Paolo—which was delivered by way of Giorgio—and which consoled and reassured me. Leo Diena, who had come to sleep at our house and who had a pair of new shoes made of "patent leather" that were furnished by the indomitable Giorgio, was there. I was so relieved and happy, and Leo is always so amusing that we laughed all evening long.

23 March. A woman from the Liberal Party, Irma, also showed up, who placed at our disposal her semi-bombed-out apartment where we had our first meeting today. In addition to Irma and Rosetta, whom I already knew, there were also Bianca, and Noela Ricci, the sister of a one of Giorgio's colleagues at

---

[48] Leo Diena was a student and organizer of the Action Party.

court—beautiful, courageous, intelligent, and blessed with two nice sisters who were ready to work.[49] The Gruppi di difesa were taking shape and becoming a reality.

Since during this time the Fascists were conducting a campaign to force state teachers to pledge their loyalty to the Republic of Salò, we deemed it necessary to give the impression that we were fighting against the threat with contradictory propaganda. Evidently it is a matter of pure stupidity and a desire to annoy on the part of the fascist hierarchy. I believe that the oath of the teachers matters quite little to the Germans. If no one responds, the thing will fail by itself, but there is the danger that a certain number of teachers will rush to do it because of this stupid "excessive cowardice" so typical of the Italians of our time. Therefore, we must encourage those who are uncertain, and scare the timid with counterthreats. We made a leaflet and enclosed it in envelopes with the letterhead of various publishing houses, addressing them to the teachers of the schools in Turin, the majority of whom were women. We already had proof that the leaflets were received and had some impact. With a suitcase full of these leaflets, Pillo left for Casale and Alessandria, where, relying on some of his acquaintances, he will see that they are delivered to the teachers in the area.

I received news today that Gianni has arrived in Switzerland safe and sound, and I was very relieved.

Alarming news, albeit confusing and contradictory, arrived from the Germanasca. It appears that the valley has been attacked, but we do not know the outcome. Tomorrow we will go and see.

---

[49] Irma Zampini was a representative of the Liberal Party in the Gddd. Noela Ricci was the wife of Aldo Visalberghi, a professor and chief of staff for the Piedmontese Regional GL Command. She later helped to organize the Mfgl.

24 March–1 April 1944

Now, when I think about it again, I realize how great my anxiety was at the time, even if, as can be seen from my diary, I tried in every way to curb and contain it.

I was not able to sleep at night any more. Perhaps this explains why, on the morning of Saturday, 25 March, while the alarm clock rang repeatedly, I woke up one hour after the train had left. Not even Ettore woke up, which was even more unusual.

The only thing we could do was to take the next train. I was very upset. I was thinking about Paolo, who perhaps had come to meet us and had become frustrated when he did not see us arrive, and felt profoundly unhappy. Not even for a moment did it enter my mind that something serious had happened. On the contrary, to overcome my bad mood, during the trip I forced myself to correct some notes for the pamphlet about Piero that I was writing at the time.

But in Pinerolo there was no connection for the little train for Perosa. We had to wait for two hours. An air of anxious sadness surrounded us. The news, while still uncertain, was very pessimistic nonetheless. The Germans had attacked the Germanasca and Chisone Valleys in force. They had gone up with a truck, radio, and weapons of every kind, even a canon. "But they will not be able to reach the Gianna," I said to Ettore to console myself. "They will have stopped them on the road. They will have blown up the bridges, and blocked the roads." I remembered Roberto's words: "Here a machine gun, there a look out...."

To overcome my anxiety, which I felt becoming stronger and stronger, and to do something useful at the same time, I went to look for a colleague, a teacher in a school in Pinerolo, whom I knew was in contact with our people, and I interested her in the Gruppi di difesa.

The conductor of the little train, which we finally boarded, gave us disastrous news. By now the Germans dominated the entire valley. They had arrived in Praly. "And the partisans?" I asked with a lump in my throat. "Dead, vanished," he answered. "But didn't they defend themselves?" "Yes, they fought," he answered, "but they were taken by surprise, betrayed, who knows?" He shrugged his shoulders while he punched the tickets. There was in him, as in all the others that I saw around, a dumbfounded, disoriented sadness. The parenthesis of liberty had been too inebriating and too short. Therefore the reawakening and disillusionment were all the more bitter. As for me, fortunately by now my anguish had reached the point where it was transformed into obtuse, if still sad, indifference.

In Perosa, the German display of forces was truly impressive: bunches of soldiers around, with camouflage jackets like those that our men wore, but how different! In the piazza there were fully functioning kitchens, a cart with a radio with antennae mounted on it, even an armored vehicle and a long cannon pointed toward the Germanasca. *L'Unità* and *L'Italia Libera*—which I had brought and posted two weeks ago—hung in shreds on the walls from which they had been torn.[1] The people of the place moved about through their daily chores with the somber, implacable bitterness that I had seen on the faces of the Turinese on 10 September.

"What should we do?" asked Ettore, uncertain.

"Let's keep going!" I begged.

I thought that if I were able to find the woman from the Veneto who had a son at the Gianna again, perhaps I would have some news, but I knew too little about her. While I asked in the neighboring houses, I was not able to track her down.

Yet we set out nonetheless. In Perrero perhaps they would know something more. Perhaps we would be able to continue.

In the valley, full of sunlight, there was an aura of death. No more of the serene, almost festive, rhythm that I had noticed there the other times. Here and there you could see black ruins on the sides of the mountain, some of which were still smoking. *Grange* were burned because of complicity with the partisans, as a reprisal. The military trucks that continuously ran up and down, loaded with heavily armed Germans, were the only sign of activity. All of a sudden we realized that it would have been better if we had ridden ourselves of the damaging documents that we were carrying with us. We did not have many newspapers because Giorgio wisely advised us not to bring much, given the rumors that were circulating. Ettore had a set of Piero's books in his knapsack (for the library at the Gianna), which basically did not seem to me to be very dangerous. In contrast, I carried in my blouse several letters that it would have been more prudent to destroy. Therefore, we retreated behind some rocks and burned them, while we thought of a possible alibi in case we were asked where we were going. Ettore could say that he was going there to fix a radio. Given their mentality, perhaps the Germans would not have noted the absurdity of going there at such a time. But whose radio? The pharmacist's, perhaps, or the town doctor's? Would that be sufficient information? There was a pharmacy in

---

[1] *L'Unità* was the newspaper of the Italian Communist Party.

Perrero (I had noticed it in passing), and almost certainly a town doctor as well. The doctor probably had a radio and, if they questioned him, he certainly would have gone along with it. In the worst-case scenario, we could always say that we had bad directions. So we agreed on this version.

As soon as we returned to the local road, we ran into a small group of boys who were going down toward Perosa.

"What happened farther up?" I asked plainly.

The tallest looked us squarely in the face with distrust and did not answer. I also remember that at that moment I felt a sense of pain at the thought of the impressions that the cruel and unnatural circumstances would leave on these children. The others were more talkative.

"They have arrived as far as the bottom of the valley," said a small lad, evidently proud of being so well informed.

"Are you sure?" I asked. "Then we cannot go to Praly?"

"Oh, no. They blew up the bridge at Pomeifré and there are Germans on guard."

Ettore and I exchanged a forlorn look. Then it was useless to keep going.

"And the partisans?" I asked again.

"They hid up in the mountains and caves," answered the child.

"No, that is not true, we do not know that," interrupted the tallest with a tone of admonishing prudence. "We cannot see them anymore. That's all."

"Didn't they fight?"

"They fought, and how!" said the little one. "They even shot down an airplane! There is a dead one a little farther up."

I grasped Ettore's arm, feeling like I was going to go crazy.

"We are leaving," said the boys. "Good day."

"Good day," answered Ettore. Then he turned to me, comforting and compassionate. "Oh no, come now! What are you thinking?"

"Let's go!" I was hardly able to utter, imploring.

We continued. There were no longer mountains and meadows around us, but only a gelid and empty abyss. This must be hell, I thought.

At a short distance from Pomaretto, we saw a group of women stopped at the edge of the road, one of whom had a baby who was sleeping in a pram. From their demeanor and the expression on their faces, we realized that he must be in this spot. In fact, in the brief stretch of meadow, between the road and the cliff of the mountain, partially hidden by a bunch of stones, the partisan who had been killed lay motionless on the ground.

No, it was not Paolo, even if we could not make out his face, which was bent backward. But I did not feel any sense of relief. An unbearable pain ran right through me at the sight of that stripped and lacerated young flesh, as if it had been my own flesh, that of my son. I have never felt so strongly as in that moment the deep, instinctive maternal solidarity that makes every woman feel that every son of every other woman is her own son.

It was the first time that I had come visually and physically into contact with the cruel reality of the massacre. During the bombardments, circumstances had spared me the sight of human victims. There was an enormous difference between seeing and hearing a story, despite the greatest wealth of details. Even if we could be moved emotionally—because of the implications and their human significance— when faced with the broken trees and the houses in ruins, nothing, not even the destruction of the most gigantic edifices and the most famous works of art, is even remotely comparable to the stifling of a single, small, insignificant human life.

It seemed that I would never be able to smile again, that I would never be able to listen with gratitude to the laughter of Paolo and his friends. When the order of the universe is turned upside down, we can no longer even believe in the reality of the sun.

I began to cry, to sob hard, without being able to stop, finally spilling the tears that had been falling in drops in my heart during that eternal, timeless morning.

The women looked at me, astonished. There was pain in their eyes as well, but, after two days, the rush of pity had eased a bit.

"Did you know him?" they asked.

I shook my head, not able to speak. Then they began to tell the story, alternating, like in a chorus:

"His name was Davide."

"He is from Pramollo."

"He has a father, a mother, and a sister."

"He stayed behind when the order came to retreat."

"He wanted to blow up the cliff to block the road."

"They caught him while he was going down."

"They fired at him immediately, and then they beat him severely with their guns."

"The Germans have prohibited us from touching him."

"We are here so as not to leave him alone."

"They notified his father and his mother."

"They will be here soon."

Poor little Davide. He was one of those brave sentinels on which the defense of the valley had seemed to me to be so well established. The inevitable defeat was not his fault, but that of the invincible forces. He had done his duty. Until the end. And he had been killed.

Little by little, my sobs abated. I tried to cover the lifeless, mortal remains, understanding the value of certain ritual gestures, even if I realized their impotent futility. We said goodbye to the women and started to head back. I do not know what I would have done if I did not have Ettore nearby. Perhaps I would have run screaming against the first Germans that I found. Perhaps I would have let myself fall on the ground waiting for a truck to run me over. I do not know.

While we were walking, I saw through my tears that the first violets were sprouting timidly in the meadows. "Why," I said almost shouting, "are violets still sprouting on this earth? What are they good for?"

After a few hundred meters, a little girl arrived running through the nearby meadow, and with little cries of joy, began to gather the violets, a little girl four or five years old, with little blond braids, very much like Graziella. "There," Ettore told me then, "see why the violets are sprouting. So that the Graziellas of the whole world can gather them and be happy."

As always, in his simplicity he had found the right response. I looked at the little girl and learned that I could still smile.

What should we do now? At this point it no longer made sense to go up and down through the valley. We would not learn anything more. Nor could we abandon the search, return to Turin, and stay there, waiting and overcome by extreme anguish.

"Don't you think that Giorgio will know something?" said Ettore.

I clung to this idea like an anchor of salvation. Certainly Giorgio knew. In Torre Pellice, there was, so to speak, the Central Command for all the valleys. There they probably were aware of the movements of the partisan troops that had to retreat. It was impossible that they would not have news. We would go down to Pinerolo and go back up to Torre Pellice the same evening. The plan, precise and feasible, restored my composure somewhat.

An old man appeared in the window of a house along the road, with worried and anxious eyes.

"Well?" he asked. Perhaps he had seen us go up in the morning and was hoping to hear some news from us. Perhaps he too had a son among the partisans. Nevertheless, "our men" were up there.

We shrugged our shoulders, extending our arms with a forlorn gesture. The old man withdrew, sighing profoundly. I heard him say something in patois to an old woman whose white head went by for a moment.

It was almost four o'clock when we reached the entrance to Perosa. The little train did not leave before six. In order not to attract too much notice, we decided to delay a bit on the little piazza in front of a Waldensian temple not too far away. There was a bench, in the shadow of some apple trees covered with snow-white flowers. On the façade of the temple was written, "I am the resurrection and the life." A sense of peace seemed to emanate from those words, the same peace, serene and inescapable, greater than any anguish and any pain, that seemed to radiate from the austere line of mountains behind which the sun was setting. Certainly, I thought, for those who believed literally in those words, everything was simpler and consolation easier. Perhaps young Davide believed in them, if he had not been estranged from the faith that his parents had handed down to him along with his biblical name. Certainly his mother believed in them. What sustained those who had fought and died in that valley, in Italy, in the world, if not faith in something greater than their individual, temporary life—something that some call God and others homeland, and others liberty and social justice and democracy—but that was still fundamentally something for which we could sacrifice our own mortal life because there was in it a certain eternal resurrection? "I am the resurrection and the life."

In my handbag I felt the sheaf of notes on which I had worked in the morning, on the train. Piero's life. Were not those ideas for which he had given his life, with such ruthless awareness and with a sacrifice that was only apparently arid, reborn today, after so many years of subterranean ferment, in the ardor of our battle? Had not young Davide, perhaps without knowing it, died for them?

I opened my notes and began to work.

At Pinerolo, it was not easy to take the train for Torre Pellice. It was Saturday, and all of the evacuees had gone home. With effort, we were able to claw our way up onto the footboard of a cattle car, clinging to the bar, but after a moment they made us get off, saying that they had to attach other cars. We waited patiently. In a while we could see a postal wagon advance on the rails. We rushed on it in hordes and had difficulty getting on. No, we could not stay there either. Again they made us get off. The situation repeated itself many times. In the end, we were able to squeeze into an enormous throng in a car. I held my breath as much as I could. At least there I did not have any trouble standing up. Finally the train left. The travelers began to chat. The usual themes resounded incessantly in their conversation—Germans, partisans, roundup, sabotage. But I did not want to listen. I did not want to think. I busied myself looking for the little shoe that a baby had lost in the crowd, and that the mother was not able to find in the dark.

When we got off at the station of Torre Pellice, we were in pitch darkness. I had been in Torre many times when I was a little girl, with my father, and I remembered his tidy and somewhat melancholy appearance, typical of small, provincial Switzerland.[2] But now, in the darkness, I was not able to find my

---

[2] Ada's father, Giacomo Prospero, had emigrated from Switzerland to Turin.

way. There was almost no one on the roads. All the travelers had run home as soon as possible. We ran into one soldier. The blackout, scrupulously observed, only let rare threads of light filter out. Finally a woman appeared whom we asked where Signora Rollier was, at whose house I knew that Giorgio's family lived. The woman gave us a complicated explanation, pointing to one area. We headed in that direction, but quite soon we were in front of a row of little houses that were all the same. Then the road ended and we could not make out anything else. By the light of a flashlight, I read on the door of one of the little houses: "Professor Pons." Perhaps it was a relative of Silvia, certainly a Waldensian. We rang the bell discreetly. Professor Pons was not a relative of Silvia, but was very courteous. He slipped on his overcoat and came to accompany us up to the right street. After a few minutes, we knocked on the Rolliers' door and, to my great relief, it was Rita herself who came to open it for me.[3] I told her briefly what had happened and the reason for our visit. Practical and intelligent, she did not digress into questions, but quickly had Giorgio summoned, and in the meantime gave us something to eat. Only then did we realize that we had not eaten anything during the entire day. The physical well-being produced by the food, warmth, and light, and the relief of finding ourselves among friendly faces, gave me a momentary feeling of euphoria. When Giorgio arrived, I welcomed him, joking, "I beg you, do not say that it is a nice surprise. We really can do without that." Giorgio tried to reassure me. He did not know anything precise, but he thought that the next day he would have some news. As to what happened to them, the boys had retreated into the mountains, on the slopes of the Pellice and Chisone Valleys. Perhaps they had tried the crossing, or perhaps they had found refuge in the talc mines. We should not worry excessively, however. He had not heard mention either of massacres or of mass shootings. They are things that we learn about right away and, furthermore, that we have the tendency to exaggerate rather than to play down. Given my state of mind at that moment, his arguments seemed persuasive to me, and I wanted to feel comforted. We spoke about other things, I played with the children, and I turned the pages of an album of Babar. (How Paolo had laughed one time, having heard on the radio a broadcast of *France Libre*, in which they narrated the adventures of *Babar, éléphant français libre*.)[4] Then Giorgio and his wife brought us to sleep at their house, which was not too far away. But when they left us, that feigned serenity, which had sustained me up until then, fell, and I wondered how I would make it until morning. Fortunately there were books in the room. I took one and read it doggedly, without stopping, as if I had

---

[3] Rita Rollier was the wife of Mario Alberto Rollier, a university professor and organizer of the Action Party and the European Federalist Movement.

[4] Jean de Brunhof's stories about Babar the elephant, first published in 1931, became a French children's classic. *France Libre* was the name of the radio broadcast of liberated (free) France.

swallowed a drug. It was *Golden Apples* by Rawlings, but notwithstanding my remarkable memory, I did not remember a word of it.[5] It was not reading, but a mechanical process of stupor and misery. Toward dawn, I fell asleep.

The next day was like a period of suspension, a wait filled with anxiety, where only the affectionate attentiveness of our friends kept us from going crazy.

Ettore fixed clocks and other gadgets and took pictures of Aldo, Giorgio's son, who was then about eight months old. I remember when Giorgio had announced his birth during the Badoglio period: "My son was born during fascism, but he only lived fifty days in slavery." It seemed a good omen then, as if the baby truly brought with him a promise of liberty.

In the morning I had a long, exhaustive conversation with Giorgio about a number of things. In Turin we always saw each other on the run and there was not time. I do not mean time to talk in depth, but not even time to mention everything that was happening. I remember that at a certain point he showed me the photograph of a baby.

"Do you know him?"

"Of course," I answered quickly, surprised. It was a picture of Piero, the son of Elena Croce and Raimondo Craveri. A few days before, Giorgio explained, a certain man, who had parachuted from the South, had gone to his house with a radio station to organize attacks for our formations. This certain man said he was sent by Raimondo, who had organized an entire set of attacks. As a sign of recognition, he had the photograph of the baby. Giorgio believed him right away, a little because the parachutist, whose name was Marcello [De Leva], inspired confidence, and a little because he had seen in the photograph of the baby a marked resemblance to his grandfather, the philosopher. Nevertheless, my confirmation made him even more certain. If the thing really works, it will be a very big help to us. It made me happy to learn that Raimondo was working actively, but, looking at Piero's little face, I could not help thinking with anguish in my heart of Elena's pain, because she was separated from her children, who had remained with their grandmother in Parella.

Later, Giorgio accompanied us on a stretch of road toward Colombier, the small town where Lisetta's mother and father had taken refuge. It was a pleasant little road, on the side of the hill, through meadows and trees in bloom. Like the other day, the radiant, serene sweetness of nature seemed as if it were mocking us indifferently. All of a sudden Giorgio said, "I am fed up," with an exasperation that was unusual for him. "I am weary of this blue sky, sun, and flowers. What I dream about now is an ugly cafe, filled with stink and noise, with smoke and electric light." I understood him very well. Sometimes I too felt this nostalgia for city life, even in its less attractive aspects, because it was normal life.

---

[5] The novel *Golden Apples* (1935) by Marjorie Kinnan Rawlings.

Lisetta and her family gave us a friendly, hearty welcome. I was happy to see her father again, whom I had only met during the Badoglio period, when he had just gotten out of long years in prison. Now, hidden in a little house in the woods, he was working on the compilation of one of his scientific works.

Later we went to the home of Rita, who had gathered together a certain group of women of the town, friends of hers. I spoke with them about work among the women, but found them unenthusiastic and slightly distrustful. I could not blame them, thinking of the reaction I had the first time they talked to me about such matters. Intelligent and learned women, who had exceptional education and experience, have difficulty understanding the instinctive solidarity of ordinary women, as women and as mothers. Yet I thought that I could foster the idea of liberation among the women, based precisely upon this solidarity and upon this consciousness of their strength and their power, which was just barely awakened, like the great movements that had turned the world upside down and were capable of changing the face of the earth. I tried to explain my ideas to them, which were still quite vague to me, attempting to compensate for the lack of clarity with the enthusiasm of someone who believes in a new path, even if she is still searching for it with difficulty.

There was news, but it was not certain or precise. There were friends, inhabitants of the Germanasca, who came to relate what they had seen in the final hours before the arrival of the Germans, or what they had heard said by others. From the Command, however, directly from the partisans, there was nothing. It appears that a group had retreated on Monte San Giuliano, between the Germanasca and Pellice Valleys. From someone else we learned almost with certainty that they had traveled toward Massello. Instinctively, I immediately focused on this last idea. Massello was on the slope opposite the Chisone Valley. A person could pass from the Chisone Valley to the Susa Valley. If Paolo were safe, he had certainly gone to that side.

We decided that the next morning—by now there were no more trains—we would go to Massello.

Once again, the next morning—it was Monday—we went down to Pinerolo on a train that was unusually crowded. Again we went up to Perosa on the little train. The Germans were not moving around as much, which made us think that the roundup had just ended. Again we set out toward Perrero. On the faces of those we encountered there was the same air of stupor, half incredulous and half sad. The cadaver of the young partisan was no longer there (undoubtedly his relatives had come to take it), and we did not see anyone around. We stopped for a moment. Ettore constructed a rough cross with two branches and we planted it on the place where he had fallen. I decorated it with a pine branch and some flowers—traditional gestures toward which an almost ancestral impulse thrusts us, even if we sense their tragic uselessness.

There were various checkpoints. They asked Ettore for his papers and seemed satisfied. As for me, they just made me open my handbag. What we were doing and where we were going evidently did not interest them, because they did not ask us anything.

Nevertheless, we still went up to the doctor's in Perrero. It was always better to create an alibi for ourselves, and above all we hoped to have some news. The doctor was not there. His wife, who was very courteous, told us what she knew. She said that a group had traveled toward Massello. There was her brother-in-law, Ciccio, the Paltrinieri brothers, and others whom I did not know.[6] She did not know Paolo, so she could not tell me if he was with them. They had not automatically shot and massacred them, but they had captured an organizer who was quite an old man, a certain Lombardini, and some others about whom she did not know anything precise.[7] The Germans had burned some *grange*, as a reprisal, and it appeared that now they were getting ready to blow up the principal hotel that had been the seat of the Partisan Command. She told us to speak to the Protestant minister in Massello for news.

While we were leaving the town, we passed in front of the little hotel where we had slept two weeks before. The Germans were going back and forth, intent on performing various tasks. The owner, with her face closed and hard, was washing in the fountain. She nodded to us, but we did not dare to stop and talk with her. We passed in front of the stable. The door had been clumsily enlarged to let the trucks pass through when it had been transformed into a garage by the partisans. At various points the wall was removed and broken. Collisions of vehicles driven by an inexpert hand (perhaps Paolo's), or signs of firearms?

At the turn for Massello, with a pang in my heart, I looked at the "sheets" of the river that I had contemplated with Paolo the last time. As we proceeded into the valley, the signs of destruction and of the battle became more evident. A big bridge had been blown up. We could not resist an almost professional curiosity regarding the quality and quantity of explosive used. We found some automobiles, abandoned and smashed to pieces. Evidently, not being able to take them with them, the partisans, retreating, had rendered them unserviceable. We noticed others in the river, ruined.

The road went up into the valley along the mountain stream that, swollen from the first thaw, broke foaming against the rocks at the bottom. The hot southern sun brought a strong odor of resin from the pinewoods around us. The physical relief of walking, and the illusion of getting closer to Paolo, gave me

---

[6] Ciccio Quattrini was a partisan in the V Alpine Division. Marcello and Antonio Paltrinieri were students and partisans in the formations in the Germanasca Valley.

[7] Jacopo Lombardini was a teacher and a partisan in the GL formations in the Pellice Valley. He was deported and died in Germany on 24 April 1945.

some serenity. All of a sudden I heard the song of a cuckoo in the distance, the first of the year. This too seemed to be a good omen.

After the destroyed bridge, we did not encounter a living soul for the entire trip, except for a mountaineer who suddenly came out of the woods to ask us if it were true that they had taken Lombardini. At our affirmative response, he exhibited such simple and profound sadness that it made me understand how much Lombardini—whom I did not know and who died more than a year later in a concentration camp—had been loved and admired by this population.

In Massello it was not difficult for us to find the pastor's house. But his daughter, Speranza, did not give us very reassuring news. Yes, the night before a group of partisans coming from Perrero had indeed passed through Massello. Naturally she did not know Paolo, and I did not know how to describe him. "He has the face of baby," I began, but then I did not know how to go on. "Tall like me, dark-haired," continued Ettore. Tall? Dark? Suddenly I realized that I would have said "small, blond" instead. The image I had inside me at that moment was that of a small boy dressed in red, his head covered with blond curls, who ran in a green field blooming with daisies.

I interrupted, "Where did they go?"

The girl resumed her story. They arrived the first night, famished. It seemed that they had been saved by a miracle, and that the Germans were still pursuing them. She and her family had given them something to eat. Then they left right away for the mountains. If they could, one of them would return in the night to get more food.

"You do not know where they went? You cannot tell us? Isn't there someone, experienced, who can accompany us?"

The girl shook her head. Impossible. The Germans had looked for them for the entire day, combing the surrounding mountains. At various times airplanes had come down low, firing with machine guns. She made us see that going to them was the equivalent of giving the enemies directions and a guide.

I could not say she was wrong, even if I felt all my hopes dashed. "Did they tell you if they were trying to go to the Chisone Valley?" I asked.

"No," answered the girl, "they only said that, if they could, they would come back here tonight."

We decided that we would spend the night at the only little hotel. If someone arrived, they would come to notify us, and we would be able to speak directly with him. It was the only thing to do.

When we left, while it was not yet five o'clock, the sun was already hidden behind the mountains. An icy wind descended from the gully. The little hollow, which had seemed to be a peaceful oasis full of sunlight when I arrived, now seemed like a scene of empty desolation. I looked at the mountains that enclosed the valley, bare and still covered with snow up high, illuminated with the final, tarrying streak of sunlight. Everything seemed so peaceful up there.

But the girl had said, "They fired all day long." I thought of our boys, tired, famished, threatened, and pursued on every side, like hunted beasts. The optimism that had sustained me for the whole day seemed childish, absurd. For a moment I thought I would go crazy.

Deprived of every human hope, I sought help, as I did two days earlier, in the awareness of an inevitable, supreme, and ideal eternity. Did not Piero's essay on Matteotti end by saying: "The generation that we must create is precisely this: of volunteers for death, in order to give back to the working classes the liberty that has been lost"? Were not perhaps these "volunteers for death" the boys who fought their desperate battle on these mountains? Was there not a higher, more equitable justice in the fact that in this generation that Piero had wanted to create, through his work and by his example, there was his own son, animated by the same spirit? Again I said to myself, even if it had been possible, I would have never tried to hold Paolo back, to keep him safe. Everyone carries within himself a destiny, not ordered by the stars, but determined by the innate qualities of the individual. The greatest crime against life is to deny these qualities through weakness or fear. Even during his brief existence, Piero had fulfilled his destiny, performed his duty, and spoken his words. Paolo is just on the threshold of life, like a fruit that is not yet ripe, bursting to overflowing with promise. Only the imperfection of our sight demands appreciable and concrete results as proof. There are actions that seem outwardly and rationally futile, which instead have an inevitable and profound significance.

There was no glint of human consolation in these thoughts. They were like the arid, inhospitable reef to which the shipwrecked person clings while its ruggedness wounds him and does not grant repose. I do not want to, I cannot, be shipwrecked. Even in my anguish, therefore, I was able to reach some sad equilibrium.

It was too early to go to the hotel. In the meantime we had to invent a believable story, because it was neither the season nor the time when regular tourists would arrive in this isolated village. We headed toward Balsiglia. By following this road we would arrive at the Colle del Pis, which led to the Chisone Valley. More than two centuries before, the persecuted Waldensians had fled through this mountain pass, and then returned home (*La Glorieuse Rentrée* of 1689).[8] Evidently places, like people, have their destiny.

We sat for a long time near the bank of the stream, absentmindedly observing two little boys who were fishing. Then, wearisomely, sadly, we turned back.

---

[8] In 1685, the Edict of Nantes was revoked and the Protestant Waldensians were driven out of the valleys of Piedmont. In what became known as the Glorious Return of 1689, a group of Waldensians ferried across Lake Geneva, marched through the Alps, and returned triumphantly to their valleys despite the hostile French Savoyard troops that occupied the territory.

See http://www.fondazionevaldese.org/en/percorsi/guardia04.php.

We told a more or less acceptable story to the owner of the little hotel—who did not ask us many questions anyway—which had to do with one of my sisters, who was a friend of Speranza.[9] While I forced myself to swallow a little soup, the little boys whom we had seen fishing in the stream near Balsiglia arrived. A strange little old man was with them, who suggested that we share a meal together. The boys would put in the fish, he would contribute two loaves of bread, and the owner would furnish the wine and a salad made of onions. In a moment, the little room was filled with movement and noise. In the meantime, they cooked the fish, ate, drank, and narrated episodes and stories about fishing. Only once did one of the boys begin to speak about the Germans and the partisans, but the others let the conversation drop immediately. Soon more people arrived and everyone began to sing together, strange songs that we did not know, in Italian, but with the strong accent of those who lived in the valley.

Was it incomprehension? Indifference? No. They had hoped, fought, suffered, and risked with the partisans. They would do it again, when it was necessary. Indeed it was the breath of relief that they drew by distancing themselves from the immediate danger, the vital, instinctive breath that permits man to survive the worst tragedies. They enjoyed the elementary and fundamental things of human existence—fire, food, and song—almost as if they had a new, more alluring flavor.

At a certain point, we went to sleep. The room opened directly onto the stream, which filled it with a din. I knew that Ettore, who was already falling asleep, would certainly awaken if Speranza came to call us. Fatigue and suffering plunged me into a deep sleep.

When I awakened, it was bright daylight, and the asthmatic rhythm of a mill accompanied the roar of the stream. They had not come to call us. Therefore no one had come down. Good sign or bad sign?

In either case, we decided to return to Turin. By this time remaining in the valley no longer made sense. We went to say goodbye to Speranza, and we went down again along the road, between the stream and the pine trees. Again we saw the cars that were smashed to pieces, the destroyed bridge, and the "sheets" of water. In Perrero there was no one in front of the hotel, and we went in for a moment to speak with the owner. She remembered Paolo very well: "He was here a moment before the Germans arrived. Then I did not see him any more." "Did they capture anyone?" "Yes, it appears that they took that tall, blond boy named Giorgio." I thought of Giorgio Diena (but fortunately it was not true).[10] The doctor's wife, to whom we brought the most recent news, directed us to a teacher who seemed to be in contact with a group of partisans

[9] Ada had no sister. She was an only child.

[10] Giorgio Diena, an Italian Jew, was a student and organizer of the underground press for the Action Party. He was also a partisan in the Pellice, Chisone, and Germanasca Valleys.

who had taken refuge in a cave not too far away. The teacher, a woman who was already middle-aged, with a lovely, serene face under her white hair, indeed gave us good news about some of the boys, and among them specifically about Giorgio Diena, who miraculously had not been captured. She had an enthusiastic and fierce zeal that made me sorry that I could not stop to chat and discuss things with her.

In Perosa, where we arrived around noon, the rhythm of coming and going and surveillance was even slower than the previous day. If the Germans would go away, the partisans could show up again, a little at a time. We went to eat in a trattoria. There were Germans there too—handsome, cheerful blond boys. Divested of the divisions, of the hated symbols, how were they different from our boys? I thought that if it had been one of them in place of young Davide, I would have felt the same rebellion and the same pain. I remembered the sentiments of an old woman from Meana who had a son in Africa during the war: "I pray for him and I pray for all of them. For all of them. Even for the others." They were others for her, not enemies, simply other sons of other mothers. It was the universal and eternal consciousness of solidarity that unites all mothers.

In Pinerolo, I bought two thrillers that I read on the train until it got dark. In Turin, no news. Again I was tormented by uncertainty and emptiness.

There is no time worse than when a person is awakened from the restful unconsciousness of sleep with a feeling of anxious, unrelenting sorrow. The next morning—Wednesday—I had been wondering how I would have the strength to begin a new day when Ettore, who had gone to the door, came in excitedly, saying, "He has arrived! He is in Meana!" He handed me a note.

Yes, it was his handwriting, Paolo's horrible handwriting, for all that my eyes, dim with tears, permitted me to perceive. He had arrived in Meana the day before, with Alberto and another two individuals. The bearer of the note would give me the details. He was waiting for me in the evening with "something to eat." For a moment I had a strong sensation of giddiness, as if I had gulped down a glass of brandy. Then I threw on some clothing, and rushed to the home of the "bearer of the note," Luigi. Never did a human being seem more like a heavenly messenger, but despite my elation, I understood that, even if he were an angel in the flesh, he still needed to have breakfast. I hastened to prepare it for him, while I listened to him tell the story. Meanwhile Giorgio arrived, who was happy about the news, but he was worried about Mumo, about whom he still had not heard anything. He looked after Luigi right away, and saw to it that he would be sent to another formation.

For the entire morning there was a continuous commotion. I had been away from Turin for four days and naturally a lot of things were behind schedule. Around one o'clock, Mumo arrived, tired, with a long beard and his old raincoat torn, but he was alive and free. I threw my arms around his neck with the feeling that joy, at times, like sadness, could be too much. "What an extraordinary thing!" he was saying to me in the meantime. "What a stupendous thing!" He had saved himself by the skin of his teeth, thanks to his knowledge of the mountains. He was with a group that had been discovered at San Giuliano. The Germans had followed them. Gustavo Malan and Emanuele, among others, had been with him.[11] At a certain point, he let himself slide along a wall of rock that ended in a big drop. He could not find the others any more. He thought that Gustavo had hidden, but he had the feeling that Emanuele had been captured. (Unfortunately it turned out to be true.) With a shudder, I thought about his face and eyes, which were so grievously and typically Jewish.

In the afternoon I saw a lot of people, including Pillo, who, satisfied, told me about his efforts regarding the teachers at Casale and Alessandria (even cited by the *Popolo di Alessandria*, the most zealous fascist newspaper in Piedmont). At 6:00 p.m. I left with Ettore and Bianca, whom I had notified that morning.

In Meana, while climbing up by the road, I wondered if the reassuring streak of light would appear at the usual bend, and I saw a shadow come to meet me, right in front of the willow tree of Villa Carlotta. "Paolo," I said. I opened my arms, without the strength to say more.

Only when we were in the house could I see his face. All three of them—he, Alberto, and young Gigi, whom I had not yet met—seemed extraordinarily handsome, like they were glowing.[12] The sun of the high mountains had tanned them, and a day of rest had outlined their features. Or perhaps it was my joy, and my feeling that it was a miracle, that made them so handsome in my eyes.

While they ate the provisions that I had procured with so much difficulty, they recounted the story briefly, disconnectedly, as it had happened.

The quiet, normal life that I had so appreciated in the Germanasca had been unexpectedly interrupted two days after my last visit. The Fascists had occupied Perosa, thus blocking the valley, and quite soon they had begun to run short of food. Therefore the partisans had tried to retake Perosa. There had been a battle, but the Fascists had received reinforcements, including some tanks, and it had been necessary to retreat. Then, after a few days, the Germans had come, and there had been negotiations, which naturally our forces had rejected. On Thursday, they had been warned that the Germans were about to arrive in Perrero. Immediately they had taken steps to burn the list of names, records, and documents that might arouse suspicion. They had tried to put aside some provisions, to carry off all the weapons, and destroy the motor vehicles or render them unserviceable—until someone had run to warn them that trucks with Germans were about to enter the town. Then they

[11] Gustavo Malan, a student and a partisan in the V Alpine GL Division, was the director of the underground newspaper *Il Pioniere*.

[12] Gigi Scanferlato was a factory worker and a partisan in the Germanasca and Pinerolo formations.

had all left, some toward the Gianna, some toward Massello, and some toward Maniglia, with cars loaded with weapons and goods. With his usual, incredible optimism, Paolo had attempted to jump on the last car. They were still in view, before the turn, when a German tank had appeared on the road and had fired at them, but without hitting them. Then they had overturned the car, sending it to break into pieces at the bottom, and they had proceeded with difficulty, in close order and carrying the enormous loads, for the entire night. They had wandered through the mountains for three days. They did not know from what part the Germans would arrive, and they had lived in a state of constant alarm. All of a sudden they had seen a long column come up that someone thought were Germans, and that instead had turned out to be partisans who had come up from another area. An airplane had swooped down to fire at them with a machine gun, but they had been able to hide. At a certain point, they were stuck in the middle of two attacks, when the Germans had even searched the Borsetto Valley, where Marcellin was located with his men, chasing the lines in retreat. They were not very cold because the weather was particularly mild and pleasant. Instead they were hungry, and Paolo said laughing that when he looked at the cow dung at points where there was no snow, after everything, he might have even tried to eat it.

Finally on Monday morning they had crossed the Passo Cristofe, facing the Chisone Valley. It was as if they were before an innocent, silent paradise. There was no roundup there. Even if he did not tell me, I was certain that Paolo had felt his heart beating when, from the other part of the valley, he saw the familiar and friendly lines of the Assietta chain again.

Here they split up. Zama and some others headed toward Sestrières, where two of them had a house. Instead Paolo, Alberto, Luigi, and Gigi had come down as far as Laux, and had hidden the weapons carefully in the area around the lake. While they were crossing the town, a little man popped out of his house and came toward them: "If you are hungry, boys, take it." From under his coat he brought forth a big loaf of bread. Then he had run away, disappearing into the darkness.

Everything seemed quiet. Therefore they decided to go to Usseaux to Madame Belléard's house. We used to stop there during our summer outings in the Chisone Valley, and Paolo was certain that even now they would be welcome. To pass from Laux to Usseaux, however, they had to cross the local road, no more than a few hundred meters away. When they were about to come out into the road, they saw a car appear. They remained motionless, with their hearts in their throats. The car seemed to slow down, and then it picked up speed, continued, and disappeared.

Madame Belléard welcomed them cordially, and gave them food and rest. When they finished the meal, they went to sleep in the *grange* of the Pian dell'Alpe. When it was day, they climbed up to the Colle delle Finestre; in the evening they arrived "home." The next day Luigi, who was the oldest and therefore the least likely to arouse suspicion, came down to notify us.

It was late when we finished chatting, asking, and responding. We got dressed for bed as best we could. I kept Paolo nearby. He told me so many more things, about the battle of Perosa, during which they had fired without ever seeing anyone (I do not know why, but it made me think, proportions aside, of the Battle of Waterloo, as *La Chartreuse de Parme* had described it), about when he had crossed the bridge near Pomaretto, beset by the rounds of mortar fire, about the people who came outside to offer them cigarettes and, again, about the little man from Laux who had given them bread ("What good people!" I said many times), and then about when, during the machine gun fire from the air, they had piled in a heap against the trees, one on top of the other, and he had felt Alberto's heart beat very hard next to his own.[13]

Then he fell asleep. I listened to his breathing for a long time, and the calm beating of his heart. I did not even know how to be happy any more. I thought about the others about whom we have not yet heard anything, and about their mothers. This miraculous nearness to my son seemed to me a privilege for which sooner or later I would have to atone.

---

[13] *La Chartreuse de Parme* is a novel by Stendhal.

2 April–25 June 1944

2 April, Meana. A day of peace, which was incredible and impossible after the torment and anxiety of the past several days.

Thursday morning, Alberto came down to Turin with Bianca, Ettore, and me. I was a bit worried about his too unmistakably "partisan" appearance but, having shaved and traded his knapsack for an old suitcase, he stood out much less. Then in Turin, in order to leave the station, which is always the critical point, Bianca took him under her arm on one side while I talked with him animatedly on the other. It went well. When I saw him on the tram with Bianca, I breathed easy momentarily.

Then I began to run like someone possessed. After several days of absence there were thousands of people to see and thousands of things to do.

Nada announced to me that the leaflet for the women was ready.[1] Where should we bring it? I thought that I should take advantage of Irma's offer and leave it at her house. I accompanied him there with a heavy suitcase. But after he left, when Irma and I opened it in order to place the leaflets in an armoire, we saw that they still had to be folded into sixteenths. Therefore, I decided to proceed immediately with the operation, and Irma wanted to help me. While she worked, she confided in me and told me that she was happy to be able to do something, and make herself useful. I believe that there had not been too many problems in her life before: a good husband, a wonderful place to live, new clothes, and some nice country holidays. Now her entire world is in ruins. Her husband is a prisoner, her lodgings damaged, and all the rest seems to have lost its flavor. But it is to her credit that, in order to escape her problems, she seeks comfort in work for the common cause.

At home, I saw the mother of Giorgio and Paolo Diena, among others. They took her husband away because he is Jewish. It gave me immeasurable pain. She too was an ordinary woman, like Irma. I remember when I met her, in Meana— her little house, her attractive, healthy children, her joy in making fruit jam for

---

[1] Nada was Franco Venturi.

the winter and organizing little trips in the car with her small family. She did not have worries, or heroic aspirations. Now everything has fallen apart. She has neither house nor husband nor children any longer. Everyone is scattered, in constant, impending danger. What is most heart rending is her desire to be strong at any cost. "I am happy that the boys are in the mountains. They must continue to fight," she repeated often with a trembling voice. I wonder how long she will be able to endure all these things that are so much bigger than she is.

In the evening, in Meana, again I found Paolo and Gigi, a nice communist boy, loyal to Zama, and a former typographer—down-to-earth, frank, and genuine, with that even-tempered, human seriousness that children of the poor often have. He has no father, his mother is a concierge, and his sister works as a seamstress. He worked as a typographer and liked his work. He will go back to doing it when it is all over. He likes to ride his bicycle, and his greatest aspiration is to participate in some bicycle race. For him the partisan war is an inevitable reality, like the draft would be during normal times. The risks and dangers are a normal part of it, and we should not worry about them too much. He has no worries or problems, but is all alive with a charming normality.

The next morning, I accompanied him to Turin. When I saw him enter the front gate of his house, I felt a moment of happiness at the thought that a few minutes later, his mother—who had been notified of his return the previous day—would have the joy of feeling him in her arms.

Then for the entire day, several men and women came. In the evening I returned to Meana with Cesare, who really wanted to see Paolo again and hear him tell about his adventures.

Today has been a divine day. It was sunny and windy. We went with Paolo along the lane that led to Arnodera, against the clean background of the Denti d'Ambin, among the briars that were beginning to be covered in white, and meadows that were dotted with yellow and violet.[2] The chestnut and walnut trees were still bare, but there was in the little gorge, along the stream, a birch tree covered with new leaves of a tender green, quivering in the sun. This very young tree inspired me like a consolation and a promise.

4 April, Turin. They arrested all of the members of the Military Command of the military formations in Piedmont while they were going to a meeting in the sacristy of San Giovanni. They had papers, documents, and money with them. Their position is very serious. They have put together a type of trial. They have condemned them to death, evidently to give an intimidating example. They are still hoping to obtain a pardon, and a delay that would make it possible for them to be saved somehow. But there is little hope. Their friends, whom I saw

---

[2] Literally, the teeth of Ambin, the Denti d'Ambin is an elegant rocky ridge broken into three principle "teeth" that are very arid. See http://www.altox.it/ValsusaAlpinismo/dentiambin.htm.

today, are literally undone. All those who have been arrested have conducted themselves magnificently. Upon hearing the sentence, General Perotti had given the attention order and cried: "Long live Italy!" Giorgio attended the trial and was able to embrace Braccini.

I have been thinking about Braccini most of all, because he is the only one I knew. For the entire day it was as if I were obsessed by his voice: "*Signora*, how is your dog?" I realized how strong was the bond that drew us together. Yet, before 10 September, I did not know him. He was not an old antifascist, sustained by a long tradition, reinforced by years of faith and underground work. He was a new man who understood the significance of the hour in which he lived, and threw himself into the battle with an intact treasure of courage and energy. Perhaps this is why his devotion had so much more value. It is not possible that the extraordinary human richness, because of which he was immediately able to create a close rapport as soon as he spoke to someone, can be destroyed.

5 April. They shot them this morning at dawn, in Martinetto. A frustrated desire to fight that bordered on fury shook me, and I understood what it meant to "vindicate our dead."

Today Lisetta, Vittorio, Mario, and Lea were at my house for a long time.[3] After such blows, we feel the need to stay close to each other in order to survive, and to resist.

The mother of the Diena brothers came again. Her husband is in Bolzano, from where it appears that they will take him to Germany. Someone told her that Emanuele Artom had been killed, after horrible torture. While I had forced myself to be calm for the entire day, I had a violent onset of rebellion. Is there no limit to cruelty and grief?

6 April. There is no limit. The strikes followed one after the other, unrelentingly. Sandro Delmastro has been killed.

Reckoning that he was in danger after the arrest of Braccini, with whom he was continually in contact, his friends decided to send him into the Cuneese for a while, near our partisan bands. They stopped him at a checkpoint, were not convinced by his documents, and made him get into a truck to take him to Cuneo. They stopped a moment at the entrance to the city and Sandro jumped out, hoping to flee. A volley of machine-gun fire brought him down.

Atrocious. Even more atrocious than the death of Braccini and the others, who at least were able to oppose the sentence with their brave dignity, judging the judges with their very conduct, and even more atrocious perhaps than the terrible

---

[3] Lea Andreis, wife of Mario Andreis, was a painter.

death of Emanuele, who had been able to rise to martyrdom above his prison warders. Such a death is absurd, without meaning, and without consolation, as if, in addition to his life, even the right to die well had been taken from him.

After I thought about it clearly, perhaps instead this death devoid of any rhetoric and any possible glorification is exactly the one that Sandro, who was so unpretentious, modest, and averse to gestures of any kind, would have chosen for himself, if he could. Sandro did not belong to my generation, where we dreamed— and still often dream—of dying with a bullet in our forehead, wrapped in a flag. He belonged to that generation of "volunteers for death" envisioned by Piero, who face their destiny, whatever it is, in its tragic aridity, without the need to embellish it, or cover it with heroic airs. They are more like heroes because they do not want to be one. They do not even know that they are one.

I am thinking about Ester's agony. I remember when they came here together, happy and in love. I also remember the last time I saw him. By chance, we happened to be at a tram stop and, in homage to the rules of the underground, we pretended that we did not know each other, limiting ourselves to a little wink and a rapid smile. During the trip on the tram, I observed him as if he had been some stranger. He had a long beard, and the collar of his raincoat was torn. At that time, I had come from a meeting with an industrialist with whom I maintained certain contacts. I could not help but notice his handsome white silk shirt that had been freshly ironed, and the perfect fold of his pants. The contrast between his elegant sense of well-being and Sandro's tired and worn-out appearance—which mirrors the appearance of the majority of our friends— struck me with a sense of sad injustice. At a certain point he got off, throwing a glance of goodbye at me, and my eyes had followed him with a maternal tenderness, full of hope and promise. He would not always be like this. One day even he would have a happy life, a house, and neat clothes. . . . Instead, I did not see him again. I will always remember him like he was the last time I saw him, with the simple indifference of an anonymous hero.

7 April. I was at Irma's house, where we laid the groundwork for the regular delivery of packages to the political prisoners in Turin, of which there are around a thousand and who will starve if they do not receive anything from the outside. Irma offered to bake cakes. Starting tomorrow she will prepare food for a group of Frenchmen who are in bad shape, since they do not have relatives here. The blond Paola Jarre will be in charge of taking the packages to the prisons. I think that on many occasions her lovely, radiant face will be useful for placating any *cerbero*.[4]

---

[4] Paola Jarre, a collaborator of the partisans, was in charge of assistance for the Mfgl. A *cerbero* was an especially vicious guard whose name derived from Cerberus, the beast from Greek mythology who had three heads and guarded the entrance to the underworld.

Before leaving, having collected from Castagnone the leaflets on the killings that had taken place, I took a few and posted them in various trains stopped at the station, which were still almost empty. I spread others on the train, and stuffed them into purses and pockets during the trip. With Cesare's help, I left still others in the station at Bussoleno during the stop.

9 April, Meana. It is Easter, but there is no peace in the world. There is sun, the poppies are beginning to show their first tender leaves, and the surrounding fields are filled with violets and daisies, but it is as if there is a veil of imperceptible sadness over everything, which makes the sun pallid and fades the most vivid colors.

Today, we spoke with Paolo for a long time about the Germanasca. Notwithstanding some positive aspects, basically the experience has not convinced him. In his opinion, the occupation of entire areas, if it can be necessary and at times even useful, is not a real partisan war. The euphoric enthusiasm of liberty that has been won is followed quite soon by the indifference of routine. It is natural to let oneself go, relax the tension, and delude oneself that the dream can endure. When inevitably, due to circumstances, the awakening comes, disoriented despair follows the enthusiasm, not only for the partisans, but also for the civilian population that is following their adventures and their destiny. According to him, the partisan war must not be abandoned nor become routine. If, on the other hand, it must by necessity form part of an overall plan, it must always be based on the initiative from which it was originally born, and never bureaucratized. The partisan army must never be a good or bad copy of a regular army, but must be born spontaneously of the conscious will of the people. For him today great actions are not conceivable or desirable. It is best to restrict oneself to the constant work of disturbance, sabotage, and active resistance. It is necessary to give young people the sense that they are responsible for every action that they believe should be undertaken, big or small, not to offer new formulas or new frameworks they can slip into more or less comfortably once again.

Seeing that circumstances had brought him back to us, Paolo, at least for now, did not want to abandon the Susa Valley again, which, since it is of vital importance for the Germans, presents the ideal conditions for a guerilla war as he conceives of it. For now he will go with Ugo, who reestablished his group above Mattie. Who knows if later, with some good contacts, he will not be able to carry out his old plan for flying squads in the Upper Valley. I am aware that, beneath his apparent indifference, he is very tenacious in his views, and I believe that, sooner or later, he will be able to translate them into reality.

14 April, Turin. Even the very young Franco Dusi, who, out of excessive prudence, had tried up until now to stay out of the game, appeared today in the clothing of a combatant. Through the Ricci girls, he came into contact with the underground movement and now works with our formations in the Canavese with the enthusiasm and momentum of his high-spirited, exuberant nature.[5] Even if I would have preferred not to think of him in danger, primarily because of his mother, I am really happy for him. No consideration of any kind must be allowed to diminish or take away from the young people the spontaneous flowering of joyous enthusiasm that is their "first love," whether it be for a woman, a country, an idea, or perhaps for all of these things together. I read in Franco's eyes that he is now living this marvelous and incomparable hour.

17 April, Meana. They killed Walter Fontan, the young native of Exilles, who had great courage and intelligence, and who was also trying to organize a group of partisans in the Upper Valley.[6] Most recently, he devoted himself to helping the groups of White Russians on guard at many points of the railroad to escape in the mountains—weapons, equipment, and everything. Up until now it was going well for him, but the other night one of the Russians betrayed him. He had gone down to the crossing keeper's cabin with some companions to bring him with them. Walter called to him, according to their agreement: "Ivan! Ivan!" When he did not receive a response, he entered the crossing keeper's cabin, and a volley of machine-gun fire brought him down.

It has rained nonstop for two days. Today Paolo went to the Cervetto to make arrangements with Ugo. He will go up there next Monday, but he will continue to remain in touch with Susa. There are some good boys with Ugo at the Cervetto, including two of his former schoolmates, Trattenero and Daví, one of whom had been taken by the Fascists and cruelly beaten before coming into the mountains, but he knew how to resist and keep quiet.[7] There are also two Englishmen and several Russians. The Englishmen are honest and highly disciplined, but slow and a bit crafty. One of them, whose name is Andrew, wounds himself somewhere every time he polishes his gun. Today he punctured his foot. "You are stupid," Ugo told him. "Not stupid, unlucky," answered Andrew, unmoved. Instead, the Russians are undisciplined but courageous and audacious to the point of foolishness. Everything goes well until they find something to drink. If they drink, they quickly want to start firing, which is not always opportune or convenient. One sleeps continually with his head on the T_4 case for fear that someone will make off with it. Another arrived today with a hand grenade he got from somewhere and, with the air of one who wants

---

[5] In addition to Noela Ricci, the other two sisters were Lisa and Nenne. These two were students and *staffette* in the citizen squads.

[6] Walter Fontan was a student and organizer of a partisan band in the Upper Susa Valley.

[7] Carlo Trattenero was a medical student and partisan in the Garibaldini formations in the area of San Giorio in the Susa Valley. He was killed by the Fascists in the autumn of 1944. Fulvio Daví was a partisan in the formations in the Susa Valley.

to perform a fine prank, placed it on the lit stove, around which his companions had gathered.

19 April. Yesterday, in Turin, the Civil Engineers took care of fixing the windows. It is advantageous, because this way at least we will be able to open and close them, even with the plywood. They asked me if I had other damages that needed repair. I would have liked the two tottering walls repaired, but how can I place the workers, whom I do not know, in my house for the time necessary to redo the walls, with the continual comings and goings in the house? Therefore, the walls are still unsafe. When this is all over, we will think about having them repaired.

The absolute indifference that I have for my house today is strange. Even though I have never been very much of a housewife, at one time I cared about it a little. I remember the kind *choc* (shock), quickly tempered when I found the books intact, that I felt when I returned from the cellar after the raid of 8 December. We found the doors and windows wrecked, the windowpanes broken, and everything turned upside down. Instead today nothing matters to me anymore. If they told me that within a moment the house would blow up in the air, I would hasten to leave, without remorse, with a little parcel of indispensable objects, and naturally the useful documents, and perhaps the gun buried in the cellar. Today I think that all of the objects to which I attributed a value yesterday—the beautiful Baccarat crystal from my father, the tablecloths embroidered by my mother, even Piero's precious library—no longer have any significance in this struggle that is relentless and total. Today the *impedimenta* are no longer the usable rubbish of tradition, but real and true *impedimenta* in the etymological sense of the word.[8]

25 April, Turin. Today, a little after noon, there was a bombardment at the Aeronautica, with the consequent stopping of the trams, missed appointments, crossed wires, etc.[9] In addition, around 2:00 p.m., there was a kind of thunderstorm. I had school at 2:30, and at 2:25, I was able to jump onto the first tram that came back into service. When I went to get the ticket, I realized that I had forgotten my change purse. Who did I see get on right at that moment and come near the conductor but Duccio Galimberti, whom I had not seen at least since last October, who had been wounded in a skirmish where he fought like a lion, and who now had taken Braccini's place in Turin. He had grown a splendid beard, but I recognized him right away just the same. With the greatest naturalness I said to him, "Please, can you give me a lira?" I saw him raise his eyes, surprised by the request and the hushed tone, but since he recognized me, he

[8] *Impedimenta*: obstacles.
[9] The Aeronautica was the Fiat factory that made airplanes.

paid without batting an eyelash. The ticket taker, who was not very convinced, continued to look me squarely in the face. "What impudence," he seemed to think, "What a technique for 'pinching'. Yet to look at her, she did not seem to be one of those."[10] When he saw me get off, he followed me with a perplexed and frustrated look, while Duccio remained in his seat, unmoved.

28 April. The other day Mumo left for Milan. Yesterday Vittorio moved there too. These moves are undoubtedly useful for security and organizational efficiency, but we will miss them a lot here.[11]

Today, when I returned home, I found Giorgio, Trinch, and Pinella, the legendary Pinella, Livio Bianco's wife, about whom I had heard so much.[12] She is a tiny little woman (smaller than me, I think), with a head of curly blond hair and bright eyes that are perennially opened wide. Before the war, she had the most placid bourgeois life imaginable. Today she has revealed extraordinary qualities of activity, courage, and initiative. She talked animatedly with Giorgio, who did not want her to go to Livio's in the Cuneese, for fear that they would recognize her and stop her. "No, no, they will not recognize me, I am sure of it. I will put a handkerchief on my head," she said, her face hardening in a decisive and obstinate expression similar to that of Bette Davis. With a rush of sympathy, I, who had never seen her before, felt instantly certain that she would continue into the valley and that nothing untoward would happen to her at all. How could things not go well for such a little woman?

But there came Leo Diena, with the news of Pillo's probable arrest. They were at the corner of a main street, at one of their usual rendezvous on the fly, their purses filled with newspapers. Suddenly two individuals came near them and stopped Pillo while Leo was able to get away. Since he had not showed up any more in any of his usual addresses, they must have arrested him. Giorgio decided that it was necessary to take all the things that would arouse suspicion. With his usual practical promptness, he filled two heavy suitcases with papers and newspapers and took them away, removing the others as well.

29 April, Meana. I received news about Pillo. He is at the Nuove.[13] They beat him, but not much. We know that he conducted himself well and that, as a whole, the situation is not very serious. I quickly cooked a cake that Paola Jarre would take to him tomorrow with some other things.

---

[10] The ticket taker probably thought she was a prostitute because she was asking for money.

[11] Both Vittorio Foa and Franco Momigliano were Italian Jews, so their situation was especially precarious.

[12] Pinella Bianco, Dante Livio Bianco's wife, was a partisan the I Alpine GL Division.

[13] The Nuove was Turin's main prison from 1870 to 1986.

Tonight, coming to Meana, I ran into Paolo, who had left Bussoleno, after having accompanied a team to the Cervetto (the Winchester Team), which had parachuted from Southern Italy with a radio transmitter, to take part in the guerrilla war and organize strikes.[14] There were three Italians: Giulio, Franco (whom we will call *il Dinamitardo* to distinguish him from many other Francos), and the radio operator, Mario.[15] Lieutenant Ferrero entrusted them to Paolo, who would take them around in search of places that were better adapted to strikes, and would organize acts of sabotage with them for which they had particular ways and means.

1 May, Turin. Today Zama arrived, who had come down from Sestrières, where he had remained up until now, and who would be able to join some other formation, or better yet, return to the South. Given the condition of his health, it would be better to find him a position that does not make excessive demands on him, and that does not consume the rest of his strength. I will talk about it with Giorgio. But today, seeing him here, Zama made a peculiar impression on me. While he was up there in the Germanasca, he had an energetic and decisive air, that of a leader. This morning he seemed like a wounded little boy, and his expression, rather than being authoritative, was imploring. I notice that this happens often to men who are considered to be "action men." The atmosphere in which they live, and the activities they perform, determine and modify their mental attitude, while men that we might call "men of thought" are almost always the same in whatever circumstances they find themselves.

Around one o'clock, we went to find Giancarlo Scala, who is staying in an isolated little villa near Borgo San Paolo, with Marisa and Volante.[16] I gave them a terrible scare because I dispensed with the traditional ringing of the doorbell, but I promised that I would not do it again. We spoke about several things, and about some devices that Ettore was contriving to derail the trains. Then Marisa offered me a cake prepared by some monks who sympathized with us. Being there in the garden, eating the cake and taking in the spring sun, it seemed like a feast day. "We are celebrating the first of May," Marisa said. Already. Today is the first of May. The day does not hold many memories for me. When the feast was still celebrated, before fascism, I was a baby. My father closed the store, and I was a little afraid. I remember once, much later, Capriolo told me

---

[14] The Winchester Team was named after the famous rifle made by Oliver Fisher Winchester and the Winchester Repeating Arms Company.

[15] Franco *il Dinamitardo* (Franco the dynamiter) was Federico Tessiore, an officer in the army and vice captain of the English Winchester Mission. Giulio Debenedetti was a businessman and head of the Winchester Mission. Lidio Baracchini (*Mario radiotelegrafista*) was a wireless operator for the Winchester Mission.

[16] Marisa Scala was a laundress and a *staffetta* in the citizen squads of the Action Party. Borgo San Paolo was a working-class neighborhood of Turin.

that even under fascist rule, when he was not in prison, on the first of May he went with other friends to take a walk in the hills and there they sang the "International." The story left me strangely moved.

5 May, Meana. Mumo has been arrested. Almost immediately after his arrival in Milan, he ran into a spy on the street that the partisans had captured in the Germanasca, an unfortunate fellow that anyone would have wanted to shoot, and that Mumo set free instead. Evidently he did not merit this indulgence because, seeing his liberator in Milan, he followed him, denounced him, and had him arrested. Now Mumo is in the San Vittore and his situation appears serious.[17]

I went to Castagnone's on the run to collect a certain number of false identification cards, which Ettore will prepare, with stamps furnished by Giorgio, step by step.

In Meana I found Paolo, who had returned from Exilles where he had gone with some others to come to the aid of a person who was being tyrannized by the local Fascists, and where he met the family and friends of Walter Fontan.

14 May. Today, finally, I was able to have an exhaustive talk with Lieutenant Ferrero. I had to speak with him about many things, above all about Marcellin, who, as far as we knew, had hidden with his men in the Chisone Valley after the roundup in the Germanasca. Left without connections with the Central Command and without money, he would not be able to wait around. All those who have come into contact with him have judged him to be a man of first order, with organizational capacity, courage, seriousness, and influence over his men. Since the Chisone Valley is on the other side of the Colle delle Finestre, it seems logical to go there to look for him, hear about his plans and needs, help him to overcome the difficult period, and formulate a common plan with him. Paolo can go. I can also do it, if he prefers, or we could both go, but Ferrero assured me that he had already organized the meeting, and it would take place in a week.

15 May. This morning, on the train, I met Cesare, his two hands bandaged and his face riddled with little holes, who was going to get himself taken care of at the hospital. His father, who accompanied him, was furious. "He is no longer a baby," he said. "At his age he should understand that he must not touch contrivances that he does not recognize. Instead he goes fishing in the Dora, finds a kind of bomb, amuses himself with it, and lets it go off in his hand." Meanwhile the son looked at him with an expression that said, "Tell it just like that and it is better. If I look like I'm stupid, it does not matter." In fact that is not how it happened, as I learned quickly, and as he explained to me as soon as we were able to

---

[17] The San Vittore is Milan's oldest prison.

talk alone. He had not gone fishing in the Dora, but to the top of the Pramans, with his faithful and courageous friend Guido the carpenter, to salvage the detonators from some missiles used for German hand grenades. While he was dismantling them, one went off. Essentially it had been a real miracle that, instead of the tip of a finger, it had not taken away his head and his hands and had not blinded him. Guido helped him and bandaged him as well as he could, but after the shock and loss of blood, returning from up there had not been an easy thing. At Oulx, everyone had believed this story of the Dora, even the doctors. They gave vent to scolding him, which irritated him on the one hand and amused him on the other. That they would believe a bewildered young boy in the town is undoubtedly very useful. Now he is worried because he will not be able to do anything for several weeks. I, on the other hand, am concerned that they take good care of him and that the incident not leave permanent scars.

This evening, when I returned to Meana, Mario Cordola warned me that they were preparing a reassessment of those born in 1925 who had evaded the draft. The matter is entrusted to the *Municipio* and therefore will not be carried out with much seriousness, but who can be sure that a squad of soldiers will not come to inspect for the occasion.[18] It is better that Paolo disappear for a few days, for the safety of the house as well. He has decided that he will leave for Turin with me tomorrow. Let's hope that it will not be like falling out of the frying pan into the fire.

18 May, Turin. He did not fall into the fire, but only just by a thread. Yesterday we went down to the station to depart, but the train arrived almost an hour late. At Chiomonte they searched it from top to bottom, and several people who did not have their papers in order were stopped. Paolo has a false identification card that says that he was born in 1926, but the risk is always there. At Bussoleno we noticed a great commotion. There was a roundup there also, and an inspection of who gets on and who gets off, but they did not get on the train, and I truly do not know why. Instead Barberis got on, having emerged unharmed from the roundup with the news that they had stopped Ferrero. It was a disaster because I had arranged a meeting for him with Duccio and Valle to discuss the GL activity in the valley, in light of the general action. I had to go to the meeting alone and give them the necessary information, in anticipation of the meeting with Ferrero, which I hope will be soon.

21 May. Today I finally was able to arrange the meeting at my house. They had a long talk (Sergio was there too), clarifying many points and arranging many things. I insisted on the liaison with Marcellin, delayed by this week's round-ups. Paolo explained his ideas on the organization of the Upper Valley.

---

[18] The *Municipio* is the city hall.

When they left, a violent storm erupted. We took advantage of it to try an experiment that we had been thinking about for a long time. From the balcony of our dining room a person can easily pass onto the balcony of the house next door, which is also vacant and bomb-damaged. It is a question of knowing if, once inside, they can get out through the door that opens onto the stairs, and then go down onto Via Assarotti. In the event of a visit by the police during the night, I could delay the police officers while Ettore and Paolo get to safety. But we had never dared to try it for fear of attracting attention. Certainly this evening, during the storm, no one would be on the balcony or on the street. Ettore and Paolo crossed over and, by the light of a flashlight, they went through the neighbors' flat, making sure that the door that opens onto the stairs opens from the inside. Eventually it can be a way of escape, but let's hope that we will not need it. My house is very useful as long as it does not "burn" (even this term is new).[19] Once the police set foot in here, even if they do not pick up anyone, the address will no longer be useful.

23 May, Meana. Paolo wanted to return to Meana, convinced that if he took advantage of the state of mind created by the recent roundup, the local people, who up until now had confined themselves to a purely passive resistance, could be persuaded to become more active. He was right.

This evening, as soon as we arrived, we saw Daniele from Campo del Carro arrive, a strange fellow with a magnificent boxer's physique, and an unusual manner of speaking, often flowered with biblical expressions.[20] (He defined the confusion and disorder as "a Babylonia.") During the threat of the roundup, he had retreated with a group of other young men to some isolated farms. Now they wanted to establish themselves as a regular squad, and they asked for instructions about this. Paolo went to them immediately and returned satisfied. They are adequately organized and there is an ex-sergeant among them, Alessio, who has some experience in military organization. For provisions, which are always the most serious problem, they have the support of their families. Now we must figure out how to use them.

26 May. Paolo ran a serious risk again today, from which he was saved almost by accident. While he was going down to Susa by the usual shortcut, at a certain point he found it blocked by barbed wire. Instead of jumping it in one jump, even though he was in a hurry and already late, suspicious and cautious, he got ready

---

[19] During the *Resistenza*, the underground term "burned" meant places that could no longer be used because they had been discovered by the enemy, that is, by the Nazi-Fascists. Ada Marchesini Gobetti and Goffredo Fofi, *Diario partigiano* (Turin: Einaudi, 1972), 212 n. 1.

[20] Daniele Benetto was a farmer and a partisan in the IV Alpine Division of GL in the Susa Valley.

to turn back and take another road. When he returned, they told him that the Germans had mined and closed the path in the vicinity of the railroad, but did not take the trouble to put up any warning sign. A little twelve-year-old girl, less cautious than Paolo, had jumped over the barbed wire and was wounded extremely badly. She was transported to the hospital in Susa and died a few hours later.

1 June. The new month begins with good news—Pillo is free. By dint of his playing dumb, the police were convinced to have little to do with a mere pawn who did not have any important contacts. The one who knew everything was that fellow who was with him at the time of the arrest. Naturally he did not know who he was. He had met him in some cafe. For several days the policemen accompanied him to the cafe and stayed to play billiards with him, waiting for the mysterious individual, who of course never came. Finally today, while pretending to go to the toilet, Pillo was able to sneak away, leaving the policeman in the lurch. Then, making sure that he was not being followed, he went to notify Anna Jarre. Then he left for Milan, where no one knows him. It is a story that seems unbelievable, like many of the things that are happening today.

4 June. Last night Paolo left with some members of the group from Susa to go to the Chaberton to pick up weapons and tools.

This morning there were two long alarms, one at ten o'clock and the other at noon. We saw the airplanes distinctly, and heard very loud bangs from the direction of Bardonecchia.

In the afternoon I went to look for Daniele at his house and met his mother and his sister Elena, a strong and decisive girl who studied to be a nurse and is ready to work with us.[21]

At home, Teta was at my house with the news that they had bombed Oulx. (This is where the bangs had come from.) Moreover, she had seen several trucks loaded with Fascists headed for the Upper Valley. I hardly had time to worry when Paolo arrived.

He had escaped by a miracle this time too. The expedition had gone well. On the way back, when they arrived in the vicinity of Oulx, the others had gone around the town. Instead he had crossed it, wanting to meet with Cesare and deliver some things to him. At the last turn, he saw in front of him an armored vehicle with a group of Fascists who, having planted a machine gun in the middle of the street, were preparing to stop the passersby. There was no longer time to slip away. If they stopped him with what he had in his knapsack, it would be a disaster. Since he could not do anything else, he continued to walk casually,

---

[21] Elena Benetto was a farmer and a partisan *staffetta*.

without quickening his step. The soldiers had let him pass, stopping the one who came immediately after him instead, as if a cloud had hidden him from their eyes. (Sometimes I think this cloud really exists.) Then, as soon as possible, he got out of circulation and, crossing streams, walls, and private courtyards, and in the end even the Dora, he reached Cesare, and then the station, where he nonchalantly took the train. For this is the absurdity of the situation these days—that in one place a person risks his skin and finds himself in bedlam, while a few steps farther away, he is perfectly safe. The bombardment—evidently directed at the Ventoux bridge—had not done serious damage, but had frightened the population terribly and the evacuees most of all.

Later, while listening to the English radio, we received the news of the liberation of Rome. This is truly a comfort. I am thinking about my friends from there and, with disconsolate anguish, of Leone Ginzburg, who did not live to see this day. I am also thinking about new prospects that are opening up for us. At first, I did not believe that it would be so long. Now sometimes it seems instead that this situation will never end.

6 June. Things are coming to a head. While I was at home this morning in Turin, for lack of another headquarters that was safer, preparing the packages of newspapers to distribute with Paola Bologna, Maria Daviso, and the Ricci sisters, Ettore arrived saying, "They have landed." "Who?" I asked stupidly. "The Allies. In Normandy." "Oh, really?" I responded with indifference. I had too much to do. Or perhaps I had not understood correctly. It was not the time to become excited, and to let others get excited, perhaps in vain.[22]

Only when I was outside with my purse full of little packages to distribute, and I had time to think about his words again imperturbably, did I realize that perhaps the matter was really important. Everyone with whom I spoke and to whom I delivered the newspapers, as well as the friends I met by chance, had heard the news and were elated about it. I even seemed to discern a sense of satisfaction and relief on the faces of people I did not know in the street and on the tram.

In the afternoon there was a meeting of the Gruppi di difesa, which for some time had been meeting at the home of Medea Molinari, the Socialist, in her house near the hillside. But we were hardly able to talk about anything but the landing.[23] Medea's father, an old antifascist, offered us a bottle of white wine and wanted us to toast the next victory. "It is the end," he said, moved, his eyes shining.

---

[22] Paola Bologna was a journalist, a collaborator of the Action Party, and an organizer of the Mfgl. Maria Daviso di Charvensod was a lecturer in history and an organizer of the Mfgl.

[23] Medea Molinari was a civil servant and representative of the Socialist Party in the Gruppi di difesa della donna.

When I arrived in Meana this evening, I found Paolo very excited. He was at the radio all day long and was able to tell me the particulars. It is the very opening of that second front that we were awaiting for so long, and it appears that it was carried out with gigantic vessels and with an extraordinary technical efficiency.

Yes, by now it is useless to try to deny its importance. It is a decisive event. It is certainly the beginning of the end, if not exactly the end. Yet it is strange how I do not feel profoundly and intimately touched. Perhaps it is because I am too occupied with innumerable little daily tasks that make it impossible for me to see the whole picture. Today, meeting with a new person prepared to work with us counts more for me than the movements of an immense army that is far away. Moreover, I cannot forget that inevitably every large scale action of war is accompanied by destruction and massacre.

8 June. When I went down to Susa with Paolo, I met Franco *il Dinamitardo* and Mario the radio operator at Ferrero's house. They too were very excited about the immediate repercussions of the landing on our work.

Today we need to make "Giuseppe" function (the radio transmitter has been so named). Located up until now in the sacristy of a church in Susa, it has not yet been able to get through to the base in Bari. I proposed bringing it to Meana, where we might mount an antenna and also have the services of Ettore, whose intuition as regards apparatuses is at times like that of a miracle worker.

In fact they brought the station up in the afternoon, but every attempt was fruitless. They tried the most diverse and extensive antennae. (For the entire day Paolo climbed the poplars around the house stretching wires. I wonder what the women who were grazing the goats in the neighboring meadows were thinking.) They repeated the call again and again, until late into the night. The base did not respond. Ettore thinks that it is too far up in the mountains. In any case we will need to bring "Giuseppe" back to Turin, and from there to some town in the neighboring hills.

We will try again the day after tomorrow; if even this is unsuccessful, we will proceed with the transfer, which Ettore could carry out very well. Furnished with a pass from E.I.A.R., who would suspect him if he were carrying a radio device?

9 June, Turin. A day that made my head spin. I calculated that today fifty-four people passed through my house. Sometimes I wonder if my trusting to instinct and Espedita's surveillance and our neighbors' benevolence does not border upon foolishness. Then I tell myself that it would be difficult to replace the reference point represented by my house.

Today, for example, a character arrived who called himself Albertino, a very brave young man who helped several friends escape from prison in conditions that were downright rocambolesque.[24] I recognized him immediately because his hair is bleached and he walks with a cane, pretending to be lame. I told him that, if I were a policeman, his appearance would strike me. But he says he had made too many blunders to go about with his natural features, and that this way he feels a bit protected. And if it is a question of his state of mind, evidently there is nothing to say to him.

Ester who, instead of lapsing into self-pity, is working more actively than ever, has immediately settled him into a house that will serve him and various other "clandestines."

14 June. Yesterday, Ettore and I worked all evening to prepare identification cards and false papers. I specialized in imitating the signature of Giuglini on Fiat work documents, and it seems to me that I really succeeded quite well.[25] In the meantime I thought with some apprehension of Paolo, who nowadays continues to run from Susa to Daniele's group, moving around easily under the nose of the Germans and transporting the strangest things: letters, money, explosives, and machine guns.

Today, bad news. The head of the other team who parachuted with the Winchester Team and settled in the Pellice Valley was killed. Now we have to go and collect his apparatus, which, it appears, was able to make the connection. Franco *il Dinamitardo* wants to send us a girl whom he considers to be less suspicious. We will see.

In the afternoon, at Medea's house, we discussed the newspaper of the Gruppi di difesa for a long time. It will be called *Noi Donne* (We Women). I am not really enthusiastic about the name, but I accepted it all the same when they told me that before now it had been the name of a women's newspaper in Spain, during the revolution, and in France.

16 June. Today, with a proud and satisfied air, Franco Venturi brought me the first issue of *Nuovi Quaderni di Giustizia e Libertà*, so well done, so well edited, so magnificent even typographically speaking that it will represent an incomparable record in the domain of the underground press.[26] Franco's almost boyish joy increased and certainly brightened our pleasure in seeing the "notebooks" in their new appearance. (How could I not think of those published in France that Rosselli had given me when I went to Paris, and that were passed from

[24] Giorgio Latis (Albertino) was an accountant and an inspector of the GL Command. He was shot by the Fascists on 27 April 1945. Rocambolesque is an adjective meaning essentially "over the top," like the character Rocambole in the crime novels of the French writer Pierre Alexis Ponson du Terrail.

[25] Ubaldo Giuglini was in charge of personnel and legal matters at Fiat.

[26] Edited by Franco Venturi, *Nuovi Quaderni di Giustizia e Libertà* (New Notebooks of Justice and Liberty) was printed illegally in Piedmont.

hand to hand in Italy, giving everyone a sense of continuity and promise?) We had to celebrate the event in some way. Maria arrived with cherries from the Borello that served as a modest and symbolic toast.

19 June, Meana. Finally we went with Ferrero into the Chisone Valley, but we did not find Marcellin. Instead we found Giorgio Diena, who occupied the barracks on the lake at Laux with a group of men. I would have liked to scour the valley, perhaps for two or three days, and find Marcellin at any cost, but it appears that no one really knows where he is, and there is the risk of losing a lot of time. Giorgio came to an agreement with us: he would tell Marcellin (whom they call Bluter here) about our visit and will work on arranging a meeting for us, perhaps at the Colle delle Finestre, which it seams they intend to occupy. We in the Susa Valley can send some men up there too. I think that meeting to establish a functional collaboration is more urgent than ever. The formations in the Chisone Valley—which are "autonomous" and therefore connected with the Liberal Party—occupy the entire Valley, from Fenestrelle to Sestrières, and seem well organized.

At Laux we ate with the boys and the atmosphere did not seem much different than that of the Gianna. The extraordinary variety of weapons and clothing of these partisans struck me: jackets, shirts, and very strange headgear of various colors. One, with a yellow tassel in his hair as long as a girl's, played the harmonica. Another two amused themselves by fishing in the lake. One was bound "to the stake" for I do not know what deficiency. There were even two fascist prisoners, who did not look very unhappy, employed for cleaning the tables. In all there was an air of almost playful serenity. Again, like in the Germanasca, I felt an inebriating sense of liberty, and I wished that at least for them it would last a long time, as long as possible.

After the meal, it began to rain. We made the crossing in the rain in the midst of flowering rhododendron bushes. The journey there and back in one day is quite exhausting. Tonight I must admit that I am bushed.

20 June, Turin. Again I saw Pillo, who had calmly come to Turin to take an examination at the university. These are things that can be understood only in Italy. Of course it seems incredible that someone who has escaped from prison can turn up at an examination, naturally with his personal particulars. Only someone who lives in a world of chaotic disorder, of compartments completely sealed off from one another and ruled by chance, like we do today, would think of it. I did not dare dissuade him, but I insisted that, after he took the exam, he go away quickly, if only to prepare for another one. I think that now he should come into the mountains, if his physical condition permits.

Other very good news. Mumo and Carlo Mussa, who it appears were up to all kinds of mischief, were freed somewhat like in a novel. Carlo's brother Angelo, who resembles him a lot but has a calmer manner, told me this evening.[27] For some time it would be better if both he and Mumo remain somewhat distant from each other in order not to run the risk of being captured again.

23 June. At the meeting of the Gruppi di difesa we divided the city into five neighborhoods. The assistance work has now acquired sizeable dimensions and division is inevitable. One group of women will preside over each neighborhood (possibly one per party), and will make sure that aid is distributed to the families of political prisoners, deportees, and partisans, with money furnished by the Cln. It is a delicate job because we must find these families and approach them without arousing their suspicions, and without creating trouble for them. It is an activity that requires the qualities of readiness and insight. For my part, up until now the women to whom I entrusted this responsibility have functioned very well. I hope that, with the expansion of the work and therefore with the increase in the number of people employed, the standard will not be lowered.

25 June, Meana. For several days I had the impression that something was being planned in the valley. I do not know whether it is good or bad, or whether it is on our part or on the part of the enemy. I do not have any actual fact to justify my feelings. I simply sense it in the air. Perhaps the person who can give me some hint is Ferrero, who is more difficult to find than ever. Today I went with Paolo to Susa twice to look for him. We had just returned, late in the evening, when one of Daniele's boys arrived to tell us that Bluter will be at the Colle delle Finestre tomorrow. Ettore ran to Susa to notify Ferrero that finally they had found him. He will go up tomorrow morning and is counting on finding Paolo up there. Instead I will stay home to receive I do not know what message from the Lower Valley.

---

[27] Angelo Mussa Ivaldi (Lino) was a commander of the GL formations in the IV Zone, then commander of the II GL Division Group and later a member of the general staff of the VIII zone.

On September 9, the day after the announcement of the armistice between the Badoglio government and the Allies, Germany sent additional forces across the Italian border and occupied all of northern and central Italy, including Rome and extending almost as far south as Naples. German forces amounted to eighteen divisions by the beginning of October. Those who chose to resist the German occupation needed means to defend themselves. Here the young student Paolo Spriano (Pillo), Ada Gobetti's son Paolo Gobetti, Paolo's friend Gianni Jarre, and Ada Gobetti paused after collecting weapons from blockhouses in the Susa Valley, located in the Piedmont region west of Turin. *Courtesy of Archivio fotografico Centro studi Piero Gobetti*

On New Year's Eve 1944, Ada left for France with a group of partisans. They climbed
across the Alps through the Passo dell'Orso and carried important documents
to the French and Allied commands in Grenoble, which had been liberated a few
months before. Six members of this group are pictured here: Alberto Salmoni, Ada
Gobetti, her son Paolo Gobetti, Virgilio Corallo, Bruno Salmoni, and Eraldo Corallo.
Alberto Salmoni, an Italian Jew who managed to escape arrest, was a chemist and
commander of the Franco Dusi column of the IV Alpine Giustizia e Libertà Division,
the noncommunist antifascist movement to which Ada also belonged. His brother,
Bruno, a surgeon, had been held in prison but managed to get out. Once he reached
France, he would work in a French hospital until he could be taken to Southern Italy,
where he would enlist in the Liberation Army as a doctor. The Corallo brothers, who
were mountaineers, guides, and carriers, possessed skills that would be useful for
the transport of weapons that they hoped to obtain in France and carry back to
Italy. Ettore Marchesini, Ada's second husband, and Paolo Spriano also went on the
mission. Spriano later became a historian and wrote a five-colume history of the Pci.
Courtesy of Archivio fotografico Centro studi Piero Gobetti

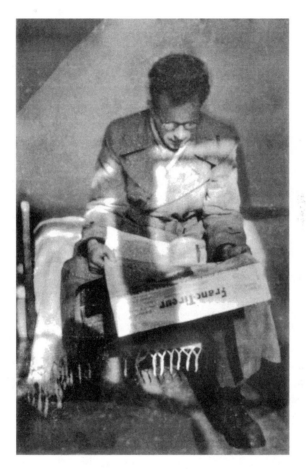

In the winter of 1944–45, the group of partisans
with whom Ada traveled to France in order to hand
over important documents to the Allied commands
arrived at their destination of Grenoble, France, where
they stayed for a month. Ettore Marchesini is reading
the French underground newspaper *Franc-Tireur*, the
publication of the *franc-tireur* resistance group in Lyon.
Courtesy of Archivio fotografico Centro studi Piero Gobetti

Ada and Paolo Gobetti after their return from France in the winter of 1945. Paolo is wearing the jacket of a *maquis*. Literally meaning "underbrush," the term *maquis* was used to refer to a French partisan during the French Resistance. *Courtesy of Archivio fotografico Centro studi Piero Gobetti*

Partisan *staffette* at the Borello, the villa of Maria Daviso that served as one of the headquarters of the Giustizia e Libertà forces in Turin. Maria Daviso is the first on the left. The fifth from the left is Vera Marchesini, Ettore's niece. A *staffetta* (plural *staffette*) was a female member of a partisan brigade who transported messages, made contacts, or carried arms, among many other duties. *Courtesy of Archivio fotografico Centro studi Piero Gobetti*

During the Liberation of Turin in April 1945, Italians greeted the partisans on Piazza Albarello at the Corner of Via Fabro in Turin. Ada Gobetti's home at 6 Via Fabro had long been a meeting place for antifascists and, during the German occupation, it became a safe haven for resisters. *Courtesy of Archivio fotografico Centro studi Piero Gobetti*

Ada Gobetti with the partisans of the Stellina Brigade immediately after the Liberation of Turin, April 1945. Aldo Laghi (Giulio Bolaffi) is to her right and Captain Angelini (Angelo Andreis) is to her left. Laghi commanded the entire IV Alpine Giustizia e Libertà (GL) Division, in which Ada played a leadership role, and Captain Angelini was Laghi's chief of staff. The IV Alpine GL Division had approximately seven hundred men by the latter part of 1944, approximately 7.5 percent of all the GL formations in the Piedmont region. *Courtesy of Archivio fotografico Centro studi Piero Gobetti*

26 June–4 July 1944

My impression was not wrong: difficult, eventful days were being organized for the valley.

The morning of 26 June, Paolo left around 5:00 a.m. for the Colle delle Finestre, where he was to meet with Ferrero and Marcellin. Around one hour later, Ettore went down to the station, but returned in a little while because the train had not left. They were talking vaguely about bridges being blown up, occupation, and roundups. After a while he went down for the second train, but even that one did not depart. The traffic was interrupted. Putting together the various rumors, he was able to learn that the partisans (evidently the Garibaldini from the Lower and Middle Valleys) had attacked Bussoleno in force, and had blown up the railroad bridge under the nose of the Germans. We climbed on the *truc*, the hillock that is behind the house, and from above we saw the bridge that was blocked. Noises, explosions, and machine gun shots came from the valley.

Indescribable anxiety took hold of me at the thought of being so close to the battle and not being able to do anything, because I really could not do anything. I could not go down before Paolo and Ferrero returned. If I went there to look for them, I risked not encountering them.

Therefore I waited, nervously. Paolo returned around five o'clock in the afternoon. He had found Marcellin's men at the Colle, but not Marcellin or Ferrero. Naturally he did not know anything about Bussoleno. All three of us decided to go down to Susa immediately. At the station, someone warned us that the Germans had arrived in Susa in force, and that they were taking all the men between fifteen and sixty years of age. We went down just the same, all eyes and ears, trusting that the Germans did not know the shortcut (which turned out to be true).

A little before the end of the path, we left Paolo waiting (at the first alarm, he could fling himself into the vineyards) and we entered the town. At the turn, I went a few steps ahead of Ettore, and it was a wise thing because suddenly I found myself in front of a group of Germans who were fanning out as they advanced, stopping all of the men. I brought my hands behind my back and made an expressive gesture with them, which Ettore certainly understood because, instead of emerging onto the main road, he made a run for a nearby alley.

Thanking my innate qualities as a woman, as I had many other times, I passed easily amidst the Germans and reached Teta's store. The atmosphere of the small town was somber and heavy because of the roundups. The streets were almost deserted, and there were only women on them. Behind the walls, behind the closed windows, we could feel hatred and fear. I listened to the latest news from Teta, and with great care I made a trip to the home of Ferrero— whom for this once I was happy not to find there, and where I learned from his wife that he had gotten to safety in time—and I returned to the main road to see the Germans move toward Meana, having finished the roundup in Susa. I entered the shortcut running, picked up Ettore and Paolo in two different places, and together we hurried to return to Meana to announce the imminent arrival of the Germans. The townspeople welcomed the warning with gratitude, and immediately undertook their safety measures, but some of the summer vacationers responded, with a somewhat offended air, that neither they nor their sons were criminals, that they had their papers in order, and that they were not afraid of either the Germans or the Fascists. "We are not partisans, not us," a woman told me with a tone of importance. Without commenting, I left her with her illusions.

We had just arrived at home when a young boy came running to warn us that the Germans were at the station, and that they had already arrested several people. Immediately Ettore, Paolo, and Mario Cordola set out up through the woods toward the Golvet, a rise of some distance, beyond the road, where there are two *grange*. After a moment Dralin, Mario's father, followed them. He was lame and no longer young, but unlike the good women who were summer vacationers, he was not convinced of the lawfulness of the invaders, and he preferred not to run the risk of being captured.[1]

I think that there was no longer one man in the entire small town, except for Berto, who is eight years old, and old Tanin, who is decrepit and virtually powerless. In the houses, ostensibly wide open, the women did their housework, waiting for the visit from the Germans. But the Germans, surely deeming it more prudent to stop for the night in the vicinity of the station, did not come.

Night fell and it began to rain. Before it was completely dark, Esterina and I left for the Golvet with something to eat.[2] We arrived drenched with water and sweat. We found the men settled in one of the *grange*, where there was even a bit of straw. On the return trip, Paolo came down with us, which was

[1] Pietro Cordola (Dralin) was the owner of the house in Meana where Ada lived.

[2] Esterina Cordola, Mario's wife, was a farmer and knitter. Graziella was their daughter.

an advantage because it was pitch dark and the path was not very well marked in certain places. At home I helped Paolo pull out the revolver and bombs that were buried under the terrace. It was past 2:00 a.m. when, with the new load, he left again.

Fatigue and anxiety plunged me into an impenetrable sleep, without stirring, from which Esterina came to shake me around 7:00 a.m. with the announcement that the Germans were about to arrive. In fact they arrived soon after, fully armed. Some of them surrounded the house and four climbed up, but either they were not really serious, or they did not find anything that aroused their suspicions, because they went through in a few minutes. Naturally the various radio devices, the batteries, and Ettore's instruments did not fail to invite their curiosity, but when I explained to them, in my elementary German, that my husband was employed at the *Rundfunk*, they seemed satisfied.[3]

A half hour later, we saw an unhappy cortège pass in front of our house. In front and in back, heavily armed Germans, and in the middle, those who had been "rounded up," loaded with boxes of munitions. Not one from Meana. All summer vacationers, of various types and ages, from a very grown up little boy of fourteen to an old professor with a beard. They had taken all those who had let themselves be found, indiscriminately, without any regard for profession or social position or age. There were also the two sons (ages sixteen and seventeen) of the woman who had looked so sure of her own respectability the night before. While feeling pain over it, I could not help but hope that at least the lesson might serve to help her understand things better.

I made a run to Susa, but without success; there was the same uncertain atmosphere of bitterness and fear. The trains were not running, and it was as if the small town were isolated. Truckloads of Germans continued to arrive and proceed up through the valley, cautiously staying on the major roads. Those who were rounded up had been locked in the rooms of the school.

Having returned to Meana, I went up to Golvet with dinner, Esterina, and faithful Tabui. The men were doing very well and had constructed a kind of lookout, conveniently shielded, where they took turns being on guard and watching the movements of the enemy. It had stopped raining and all of a sudden the sun came out. I lay down on the grass near Paolo and fell asleep. When I woke up, it was still sunny and Ettore said, laughing: "Stay there, both of you. I want to take a color photograph of you. We will call it 'partisan woman and child'." In fact he did take it. Aside from my sleepy appearance and my torn dress, it is a very beautiful photograph.

On the way down, Esterina and I found everything quiet. The Germans had gone away, and the men were still up in the woods. Those who had been

---

[3] *Rundfunk* literally means radio, but in this case Ada means the radio plant, E.I.A.R.

rounded up were brought to Susa, except for two or three of the oldest that they had released. Old Dralin, who had come with us (at the same time making use of the occasion to take up a bag of grass for the rabbits), decided that he was no longer in danger and returned home.

The next morning, the 28th, I went down to Susa, passing through Arnodera. Isolated and away from the big roads, it had not received the visit from the Germans, so life went on, peaceful and normal. But just before I entered Susa, I saw a big crowd of Germans, determined to empty a house of its furniture and household goods. "What happened?" I asked a woman who, with a baby in her arms, was watching with an air of somber bitterness. "They found weapons. Now they are emptying the house and then they will burn it." "And the people?" "They were able to escape, but now they are taking all their things. By dint of hard work, they had just been able to buy new furniture." An old man near them shook his head with hatred. "Damn them!" he said, spitting. The violence used on the property and on the "things" that had a human value for them, representing years of work and sacrifice, offended them. Seeing the sanctity of the house violated and its contents displayed before everyone's eyes wounded them personally.

In Susa, there was a crowd of women around the school—wives, mothers, and sisters—who tried in vain to move the guards, Italians, to pity, and to persuade them to bring food and messages to their men. Suddenly a German officer came outside; evidently annoyed by the crowd, he gave orders to make it clear out. "Go, go away, you cannot do anything here," said the Italian soldiers, with a conciliatory tone, trying to push away the women who, with the passive stubbornness of the hopeless, were determined not to move. Raus! Raus! shouted two Germans subsequently, jumping out with rifles in their hands. In a few minutes they drove off the women, hitting them blindly with the butts of their rifles. While they carried out the brutal act, their faces did not express any brutality: they were impassible, soulless. In their ruthless gestures, there was neither fury nor cruelty, but something frighteningly mechanical.

While I went away along with the women, a little fellow, whom I had often seen on the train, came near me saying: "Now they will take them to Germany." A woman that I knew by sight, passing next to me, touched me with her elbow and whispered to me: "Don't talk to that one. He is a spy." A spy? I looked at the little fellow who meanwhile continued talking, repeating rumors that he had heard and absorbed. He was small, very dark, and a Southerner, as we could hear from his accent, different in his manner of speaking and appearance from those from the town. This is probably why they distrusted him. Whether or not he was a spy, I felt really sorry for him. To the mountain folk from here, closed, silent, and shy by temperament, his Southern verbosity, perhaps benevolent and perhaps shallow, must have appeared incomprehensible, like the rigid expressionlessness of the Germans had appeared to me. Nothing, not even the pain of the wives and mothers, not even the pathetic impotence of the population, defenseless before the armed injustice, seemed as dangerous and grievous as this incomprehension, creator of hatred.

The next morning, the 29th, while I was going down to Susa, this time by the main road, as I neared the town, I met groups of women who were crying. As soon as I saw one that I knew, I asked her what had happened. "They took them away. They will take them to Germany," she responded. After two days of waiting, in which the families had alternatively agonized, hoped, and prayed, those who had been rounded up had been loaded onto trucks and taken away. The trucks had left just then. Neither the woman who was talking with me nor those who were with her had anyone among the deported, almost all strangers. Their men were in the mountains. Yet they were crying. In these tears every difference, antagonism, and suspicion faded away. I too cried with them, ashamed that I had thought, two days before, that the mother whose two sons had been taken away had basically deserved the lesson. With their charitable tears, these ordinary women had taught me that there is something deeper than the canons of justice.

Susa seemed like a house where a serious disaster had occurred. When the transport and the funeral ceremonies were over, indispensable daily tasks were taken up again wearily. We could see men on the streets again, and the stores began to reopen. I looked for Ferrero in vain. He was not there, and did not even leave me a message.

When I went back up to Meana, I found Ettore and Paolo at home. Even Mario Cordola had returned. They had seen the trucks depart from above, and they had realized that the roundup was over. We outlined our plans right away. Paolo observed that the roundup must have driven a number of young men to take refuge in the mountains. Therefore it was a good time to form squads in the Upper Valley. It was even more urgent than ever that he get in touch with Marcellin who, since he occupied the adjacent valley, which was free for now, could represent a secure hideout for our partisan bands. Therefore we decided that we could go to the Chisone Valley in search of Marcellin the following day. Only after we found him would we go down to Oulx where, relying on Cesare, we would be able to begin our work.

Never did the Colle delle Finestre—where, because of its position as a narrow mountain pass, the clouds that rise up from both valleys cross almost continuously—seem so radiant with sun, sky, and flowers as on that morning of 30 June. At the summit of the climb, above the pink flowering rhododendrons, the stocky lines of the eighteenth-century fort, forlorn in its anachronism and impotence, stood out against the bright blue like the profile of an enchanted castle.

At Colletto we found Mario and two groups of Meanese partisans among whom a slight disagreement had emerged, but whom we pacified quickly with the promise of a definite arrangement. On the other hand, a little farther ahead, at Casette, we were welcomed by Daniele's group which, having already been established before the roundup and having overcome the first phase of confusion, was functioning properly by now.

While we continued to climb, suddenly, at the foot of the last and steepest climb, we saw two armed partisans on guard—those of Marcellin. They occupied the fort and their commander, Dema, had us visit the defenses, which were excellent in relation to the ordinary partisan standard (they even had a 20 mm antiaircraft gun), but insufficient against an attack in force with motorized means of transport.[4] Two individuals from the Caucasus—some of those who had escaped from the railroad—gave me their photographs so that I could procure documents for them, although in reality I did not know how they would be able to move around, even if they were furnished with excellent documents, given that they did not know one word of Italian.

Then we began our descent hurriedly and soon we were in Pourrières, where there was a checkpoint. They did not know us and did not want to let us pass. One of Dema's men arrived just in time, who not only vouched for us but also accompanied us up to Pragelato, where he left us in the arms of the *carabinieri* on duty. Suspicious and rigid, as suits the guardians of order even if they are in the service of unlawful forces, these men asked us a bunch of questions to which I must say we responded in a manner that was rather evasive, but that evidently sufficed to convince them. They also invited us to stay for supper with them, but we preferred to go to the hotel across the street, the Frezet, where we would also be able to sleep. The Command was in the neighboring hamlet, Les Granges, at the Hotel Passet, but Marcellin was on an inspection tour, and would not return until late in the evening.

While we were eating, I explained some of my worries to Ettore and Paolo. How would Marcellin receive us? After all, he did not know us at all, and we had neither documents nor credentials. What if he had us put into a concentration camp? We had one right there in front of us, in the Grande Albergo Albergian, and the prisoners ("suspicious people," said the owner of the Frezet vaguely) were unperturbedly playing *bocce* in the courtyard.[5] They seemed like they were doing very well—they were certainly better off than we were in the Susa Valley and even in the city—but we had not come this far for a rest and a vacation. Even without going this far, Marcellin might not take us seriously, and might send us back without a specific agreement. The step that we were taking toward him had the character of an individual, more familiar initiative. From what we had seen up until now—checkpoints, *carabinieri*, and commands—everything in the Chisone Valley happened according to regular, almost legal, formalities.

---

[4] Dema was a partisan in the formations in the Chisone Valley.
[5] *Bocce* is a game similar to lawn bowling.

"In short, when we are finally able to meet Marcellin, I do not really know what we will tell him," I concluded.

"Oh," said Paolo with a bit of humor, "We will tell him 'Good evening, *Signor* Marcellin.'" Then the rest will happen by itself.

Instead it was not "good evening," but "good morning, *Signor* Marcellin," which we probably said to him when we finally found him the next morning, but in reality I do not remember, because the understanding between us was instantaneous, complete, and cordial. I can still see the typical room of a hotel in the mountains, with geraniums in the window and the antique dark mahogany sideboard, where the owner introduced us and where he promptly joined us. I can still smell the scent of old furniture and a rustic kitchen, strangely fused with the vague odor of a barracks (leather and sweat) that always accompanies the presence of soldiers, of whatever nationality and class they happen to be. Finally there he was before us, the notorious and so much sought after Bluter-Marcellin! A mask of anxious energy gave his face of a mountain dweller, framed by the typical partisan goatee, an expression so much more mature and adult than his age warranted. Besides his native virtues of resistance and courage, two qualities of his were valuable: a certain *savoir faire*, a capacity and adaptability for relationships with people of every class, perhaps due to his experience as a ski instructor; and a respect—rigid perhaps, but not completely useless—for the traditional laws of military organization, this due to his experience as a sergeant major in the regular army. Here was the secret of his hold over the men, and of his success. If he had possessed only audacity and courage, that is, if he had been purely a hero, he would have dragged behind him a small group of fanatics. But the mass of regular partisans—thrust into the underground by an instinct for self-defense rather than by a purely heroic imperative—and the Alpine population would have subconsciously distrusted him and would not have supported and followed him. If he had possessed only good social skills and the qualities of accommodating opportunism, it would have not meant anything to the healthily unrefined hearts of his mountain folk. With only his military spirit, he would have enchanted the *carabinieri* and the career officers who followed him, but he would not have appealed to the brave aspirations and spirit of adventure of those who had abandoned factory or office or school to come to fight among the mountains. The lucky combination, the right balance of these qualities that only seemed contradictory, made him a protagonist adapted to this war of ours, where the heroic initiative that gave strength to a few was for many still accompanied by nostalgia for the past, suspicion, and fear of the future.

My earlier worries dissipated quickly. Marcellin did not ask for credentials; nor did he want to know from whom or how our initiative had been authorized. We came from the adjacent valley, which was the fulcrum of every one of our possible actions or of those of the enemy because of its strategic importance, to propose collaboration and to ask for and offer help. His expert instincts told him that we were not troublemakers. Our conversation proved to him that we knew the places, men, and situation well. Therefore, why not speak freely? Why not lay down the basis for working together? Papers in hand, we drafted a network of contacts between the two valleys, and a regular system of notices and information that, at the right moment, would enable us to carry out actions together. We arranged a meeting with the representatives of the neighboring Pellice Valley, with whom to discuss, on a general level, the possible creation of a single division.

At noon, we were at table with quite a few people. There was Major Serafino, a genuinely honest and capable kind of soldier who immediately gave us the impression of a courageous and sensible gentleman; a French *maquisard* who had come to arrange a liaison; a marvelous desperado who called himself "Lupo," head of a company of saboteurs and full of ardor and soul; and several others.[6] We talked about various things and also about the radio. Having learned about Ettore's expertise, Marcellin asked him to look at one of their transmitters, which, like ours, did not function, even though it had ample range with respect to antennae, etc. Better still, why would it not be possible to set up a partisan radio station straight away that would transmit news, notices, various programs, etc., throughout the valley and even beyond? We decided that, since he did not have specific responsibilities in Turin for the moment, Ettore would remain in the Chisone Valley for this purpose.

In the evening we made the final agreements with Marcellin. He also furnished me with a pass, signed "Bluter" and duly stamped, which proved to be very useful in his zone. Then I had my work cut out for myself in studying and enciphering the names and addresses of all kinds of individuals to whom many people asked us to bring news. The owner of the Hotel Passet made me a clever little sack to hang from my belt in which to hide letters and documents. The morning of 2 July, which was radiant like the preceding ones, found Paolo and me traveling to the Susa Valley through the Colle di Costa Piana. I remember a marvelous flowering of red poppies at the beginning of the climb, and a little stream among the pebbles farther up in the shadow of the pine trees, in which I would have gladly taken a bath. Around ten o'clock, we began our descent on the other side along an alternating succession of meadows and larch trees. Everything seemed quiet. A woman with a baby in her arms who was grazing goats confirmed for us that there were no alarms for the moment.

---

[6] Ettore Serafino was a major in the army and commander of the Monte Albergian Brigade of the Chisone Valley. "Lupo" was a partisan in the formations in the Chisone Valley. A *maquisard* was a member of the French Resistance.

At Villa Clotès, we saw a group of armed men arrive, but our fear only lasted for a minute because we quickly realized they were partisans from the Chisone Valley, whom I had to let see the pass from Marcellin.

When we went down to Oulx, I found only Cesare's mother and little brother. Cesare had gone into the mountains with the other young men of the town on the day of the roundup. What had first been a phenomenon of individual and isolated heroism was transformed, with the incitement of danger, into a mass movement. Naturally the movement was directed toward the nearby Chisone Valley, which presented relative guarantees of safety and organization. Cesare was with the group at the Colle Triplex.

While we climbed back up, I heard shooting in the vicinity of Sauze and, crossing the hamlet, I ran into a Republican officer who was wounded and being carried in the arms of his soldiers. Evidently there was a skirmish with the partisan patrol we met before. Relieved, I saw that the Republicans (around a dozen in all) were hurrying to leave, frightened. Taking advantage of the momentary security, we climbed back up to Villa Clotès calmly.

Paolo had made friends with the owner of the hotel, she too the mother of a partisan. When he heard the news, he decided that the next morning he would join Cesare at the Triplex in order to learn about his intentions and plans. The owner of the hotel offered us a room where we could sleep, and wanted at any cost to prepare dinner for us on the veranda—crowded during other summers and during the ski season and, naturally, deserted now. Night fell sweetly on the valley, while the last sun lagged on the summits of the mountains before us. Suddenly I seemed to be on the veranda of Croce's house in Meana, during the tranquil summer evenings, and to see, next to Paolo's face, the thoughtful faces of the girls, to hear again the quick-witted voice of the Senator, and to feel the warm hospitality of their house once more. I felt a sorrowful nostalgia for this past, which seemed so far away now. I told this to Paolo. "Who knows?" he answered with a pensive air. "It may be that next year at this time we will all be around the long table at Pollone again." I understood that, even if in a different manner and to a different degree, he too felt the same nostalgia.

The next morning, 3 July, dawned without sunlight. I saw Paolo disappear into the fog, attached to the tail of a mule that was bringing provisions to the partisans at the Triplex, and went down toward the valley. Several times I was forced to show my pass to groups of partisans that emerged unexpectedly in the fog. I went down by the local road and, walking quickly, began the distance of twenty-five kilometers that separated me from Susa. A dense, annoying drizzle fell, and the main road was absolutely deserted. I did not encounter anyone until Exilles, save for a drenched old beggar benumbed with cold, who asked me for some lire to get himself a *gôlà* (swig) of something hot. A little before Chiomonte, I met a farmer who was no longer young with his daughter and a cart loaded with straw. We walked a piece of the road together, commenting on the events of the past few days. At a certain point, we heard the sound of a car that was approaching. Immediately the man threw himself into the woods that skirted the road and disappeared. His daughter shook her head with disgusted bitterness. "Like a delinquent," she said, "and yet he never did anything wrong. But the Germans are taking all the men. In Chiomonte they took away seventy-year-old men and even a lame shoemaker." The German automobile passed near us without stopping. The girl with the cart paused to wait for her father. I rapidly started on my way again under the rain that was becoming more and more intense.

Chiomonte: Germans in all the hotels, a fleet of cars, field kitchens, and the movement of troops.

Gravere: Fascist Command, flags with swastikas, black pennants with *fasces*.[7] Evidently they had no intention of going away. They seemed ready to stay. (In fact they did remain up until the end.) I made a mental note of the symbols, signs, and numbers on the German motor vehicles, in order to report them to Turin.

It was around one o'clock when I arrived in Susa, tired, soaked, and piteously hungry. I went immediately to the house of Ferrero, who was not there, but whose wife promised me an appointment for the afternoon. Then to the store of Teta who, seeing me arrive, raised her arms to the sky and said *povra dona* (poor woman) with the same tone as the one with which she used to welcome Paolo when he was a little boy, saying *por cit* (poor child) when he returned after having fallen into a stream or after some other misadventure. She did not ask me where I had been, nor what I had been doing, but she put me to bed like she would have a baby, and brought me something to eat. Then she said to me: "Now sleep. I will come to wake you up at five o'clock."

When she awakened me, it had stopped raining and a ray of sunlight filtered through the white curtains. For a moment I thought I was still dreaming. Those white curtains were the same ones that I had in my room when Paolo was born—which were then given to Teta when she was married—and I instinctively looked to the right, where the little cradle with the blue wool cover would have been. But the cradle was not there. Instead there was Teta, with a cup of hot tea and my clothes, dried, mended, and ironed.

Then Ferrero's sister-in-law accompanied me through out-of-the-way alleys, up to the borders of the inhabited area, in the vicinity of the church of San Francesco, stopped at a little door at the corner of a long wall, and knocked conventionally. For the second time that afternoon I thought I was dreaming. The little room that opened before me, flooded with sunlight, was a painter's studio. Many paintings, almost all landscapes, were hung on the walls. There was

---

[7] An ancient Roman symbol of power, the *fasces* were a bundle of sticks bound to an ax.

an easel, a desk piled high with papers, and a bookcase full of books. From the little sofa at the end of the room Ferrero stood up to come to meet me, but the person who had opened the door was a priest, with an intelligent and kindly face under his white hair. I realized that it had to be Don Rescalli, the painter-priest from Susa, whom Elena Croce had told me about once, and immediately I also became aware of the church where the radio transmitter must have been hidden. That peaceful room, filled with beautiful things, where everything spoke of contemplation, of placid and serene work, was so unbelievable that I had to make an effort to bring myself back to the reality of the moment. Don Rescalli disappeared discreetly, and with a few words I brought Ferrero up to date about what we had done and about new possibilities for action. He approved of my initiative, and he spoke to me somewhat mysteriously about some partisan bands that, having come from the Lanzo Valley under the command of a rich gentleman who called himself Laghi, were settled on the slope of the Rocciamelone and toward whom recently, as everywhere, a large influx of local young people had made their way. I insisted on precise information. I wanted to make a complete report for Turin and convince someone, possibly Duccio, to come and get a sense of the situation, which seemed stagnant when it should have been dynamic and active.

Meanwhile Don Rescalli returned, accompanied by a delightful old woman (I do not know if she was a neighbor or a relative) who brought in her cloth purse a thermos full of tea and homemade biscuits. With a sense of relief, I enjoyed the sojourn in that comfortable and relaxing atmosphere, the lovely old furniture, old porcelain cups, and little silver teaspoons with which they offered me tea—while blaming myself for the weakness. In the meantime I said to myself: "My God! How comfortable all this is! I always thought I did not really care about such things. Is it possible that my instincts can be so bourgeois?"

Almost unconsciously, I began to speak with Don Rescalli about painting and pictures. I felt so good that I did not want to leave. When I finally decided to move, the hour of the curfew had already passed. Don Rescalli pointed out to me a lane through which I could reach the shortcut before long. Half an hour later I was in Meana. I found everything quiet at home. Esterina gave me the news. They had no longer seen either Germans or Fascists, life had become normal again, almost all of the evacuees had returned to Turin, evidently less afraid of the bombing than of the roundups, and the majority of the young people from the town were in the mountains.

I spent the evening and part of the night writing a long report for the Turin Command about the situation in the [Susa] Valley, and about the contacts in the Chisone Valley. The next morning, 4 July, I left as usual on the train that had to some extent begun to operate again. A little before Bussoleno, however, we were forced to get off for the transfer. On the ruins of the bridge that had been destroyed ("Good work!" I thought, looking at the fragments of the big, shattered pillars) they had thrown up a makeshift bridge made of boards and ropes. They had not repaired the sides, but it was wide enough so that we could proceed, one at a time, without danger. But the passengers of the train—or rather the female passengers, since there was not even one man—while crossing it, lapsed into thousands of little gestures and small cries of feigned fear. These little actions, these mincing little cries had irritated me greatly several times before on the train, when well-built girls who were big and fat like grenadiers pretended that they were afraid, and squeezed together giggling at the sight of a minuscule little soldier, armed with an almost harmless, old model rifle.[8] These manifestations of fear atavistically justified by the desire to provoke and attract masculine protection, and that now can only arouse the silent contempt of the Germans who were present, unmoved, at the transfer, filled me with cold, invincible fury. I had in front of me a woman around my age who stopped, uncertain and afraid. "I can't, I feel giddy," she wailed, shaking her hands. "Move forward or I will throw you over!" I told her brutally, with a low and cruel voice, and I felt capable of doing it. Terrified, the woman went ahead and naturally reached the other side without the least incident. Of those who came behind, no one cried any more. Yet today, when I think about the episode again, I blush with shame, not for the act in itself, harmless and maybe even useful had it been carried out with instructive detachment, but for the state of mind that had inspired it. Nothing can ever justify brutality. That a reasonably civilized person like me could behave in that way reveals up to what point the climate of war and violence can invert behavior, values, and customs.

When the transfer was over, we got back on in a cattle car. As soon as we arrived at the station in Bussoleno, however, a German made us clear out of it with the violent scream of *Raus!* Evidently the train was not going to continue. While I looked around and noted that in the station and on the trains one could no longer see an Italian railway worker, my eyes fell on a familiar face that struck me because I did not expect it. Lamberti! With his usual pensive and distracted air, a little knapsack on his back, and an umbrella suspended on his arm.[9]

"What are you doing here?" I asked, approaching him.

The blue eyes behind his glasses lit up with joy. "I came to look for you," he said.

I realized then that my prolonged absence from Turin had worried our friends. Vague and imprecise news had arrived from the Valley that of course was exaggerated. They had not heard anything more about us. Lamberti had offered to

---

[8] A grenadier is a very big rat-tail fish with a large head.

[9] Cesare Alvazzi told me that most partisans carried an umbrella along with their raincoats and their guns. Cesare Alvazzi, interview by author, Susa, Italy, 11 November 2001.

come and look for us. He was the most suitable because he was the least reckless and his papers were in order. Having arrived the night before, he had slept in Bussoleno, and now he was looking for a way to get to Meana. At worst he would have done the road on foot.

With a few words I brought him up to date on the situation, and told him what we had done. Now it was no longer a question of going to Meana, but rather to Turin. The train was not going to continue. We had to start out on foot, hoping to find some lucky transportation or a train in some station farther ahead.

We began with a group of other people who had the same plan. The unusual adventure had excited Lamberti a little, and he continued to chat animatedly, telling me about *Il diario del bastone e della carota*, which he had read recently.[10]

At a certain point I said to him, "Why don't we address each other with *tu*? We have known each other for twenty years and it is absurd that we address each other with this eighteenth-century *lei* while people that hardly know each other use *tu*. Not to mention that, in any emergency, it is always better to pass for relatives."[11]

Lamberti blushed intensely. He said I was right, and that he would try, but it would be tremendously difficult for him.

We talked pleasantly and reached Sant'Antonino, where there was a rumor that perhaps after an hour a train would depart for Turin. I was starving and I told Lamberti who, while he seemed surprised to hear it, gladly helped me look for something to eat.

Then we waited at the station of Sant'Antonino for a long time, taking turns reading a cloak-and-dagger novel that Lamberti had brought with him. Finally, toward one o'clock in the afternoon, a supplies train brought us as far as Collegno, where we took the Rivoli tram.

Turin made a strange impression on me, as if I had been gone for months. The house was empty and, as far as Espedita knew, nothing special had happened in my absence. I quickly notified Giorgio of my arrival, and began to think about the following day's work.

---

[10] Most likely she meant Benito Mussolini's *Il tempo del bastone e della carota, storia di un anno (ottobre 1942–settembre 1943)* (The time of the carrot and the stick, the story of a year, October 1942–September 1943), supplement to the *Corriere della Sera*, 1944.

[11] Lamberti was used to addressing Ada with the formal *lei* rather than the familiar *tu* that was used between close friends and relatives.

5 July–14 November 1944

5 July, Turin. The weariness of resuming the rhythm of meetings and underground life again after so many days of different activities. For the entire morning I ran around bringing messages that had been entrusted to me in the Chisone Valley. Everywhere I was rewarded by the flash of joy with which—after the first moment of distrust had passed—the news was received. Then in the early hours of the afternoon, in Piazza Rayneri, I met with Giorgio, Nada, and Sandro. The day before yesterday Pinella and Alda had been arrested.[1] Luckily they let them go almost immediately, but the house on Via Amedeo Peyron will not be useful as an address for quite a while, and work will become more and more difficult. We spoke about the Susa Valley and about the Chisone Valley, and we will talk about them again tomorrow in a more appropriately military light.

Later I went to Medea's house for a meeting of the Gruppi di difesa. Among other things, we talked about organizing a mail service between the partisans and their families, an idea prompted by the trial run that I had happily carried out. With a numbering system and codes on the part of the "postmen," the matter does not present much danger.

6 July. A meeting today with Giorgio, Bellone, Galimberti, and Valle, who had read my report. I was pleased to see that they were beginning to become interested in the Susa Valley. Someone will come as soon as possible. At home, after a flurry of women and various personalities, I saw Franco *il Dinamitardo*, who also wants to come to the Chisone Valley.

13 July. During an alarm, in the underground passage, in the corner where my uncle was developing photographs, we showed a roll of film that had reached Nada by way of Switzerland containing a reproduction of French underground

---

[1] Alda Bianco Frascarolo was the fiancée and later the wife of Alberto Bianco, a partisan in the I Alpine GL Division.

newspapers—*Franc-Tireur, Combat*, etc. Nada was exultant because it would be useful for *Il Partigiano Alpino*.[2] It made me emotional to see this tangible sign that they were fighting a battle elsewhere too, with the same spirit as ours.

16 July, Pragelato. Yesterday morning, Ettore and I climbed over the Colle again. We passed the checkpoint at Pourrières without any more hitches, and we climbed back up along the valley, with numerous stops, bringing letters and messages to several places. A little before Pragelato, in a meadow near some abandoned military barracks, we found Paolo with Franco *il Dinamitardo*, Mario the radio operator, Doctor Menzio, who was connected with the Winchester Team, Alberto Salmoni, and some others.[3] They were doing drills. They were all in excellent spirits, as always happens during good times in the partisan zones, and we engaged in good-humored chatter.

At the Hotel Passet, Marcellin was happy to see us again, and he duly appreciated the money that I had been able to bring to him. Major Tonino, formerly of the Germanasca, who gave me the impression that he was serious and capable, is here with him now.[4] We conversed for a long time, examining the local situation diligently. He too sees the necessity for a single command that includes the Pellice, Germanasca, Chisone, and Susa Valleys. He thinks it will be possible to convince Marcellin of the idea, and considers that a visit from Galimberti will be useful for such a purpose. I will try to arrange it.

At dinner, I met Tullio Giordana, a colonel in the Royal Italian Army and director of the *Gazzetta del Popolo* during the forty-five days.[5] He cornered me and detained me there for a long time, inquiring about the authors of various articles in the *Quaderni di Giustizia e Libertà* that had impressed him very much. He is convinced that, when the war is over, he will acquire the directorship of the newspaper again. (Who knows? It might happen exactly like that.) He is already worried about securing staff members who are on the ball. He made a strange impression on me. He is a capable man, not devoid of sensitivity, and of proven antifascist faith and indisputable honesty and courage, but his mentality is completely one of "yesterday." For him winning this war means to return to the Badoglian intermezzo or, even better, to the pre-fascism of 1922. For us it is something else.

This morning I was awakened by the bells that were ringing in the holiday. When I went to the window, I saw Franco *il Dinamitardo*, who was going to mass

[2] *Franc-Tireur* was published by the *franc-tireur* resistance group of Lyon beginning in December 1941. *Combat* was the newspaper of the Mouvement de libération française (French liberation movement). *Il Partigiano Alpino* was the name of the Piedmontese edition of *L'Italia Libera*.

[3] Paolo Menzio was a doctor and member of the English Winchester mission.

[4] Antonio Guermani (Tonino) was a reserve commander of the IV Partisan Zone of the Piedmont region.

[5] Tullio Giordana was also an inspector of the Autonomous forces in the Chisone Valley.

dressed smartly, with a hat and gloves in his hand. It is his theory that a person must dress in a way that does not draw attention, and therefore he crosses the mountains in walking shoes. Certainly this morning, on the steps of the church, he has the very appearance of a leisurely bourgeois summer vacationer in holiday dress, but since this year there are no bourgeois summer vacationers, I wonder if he, in his city outfit, is not more conspicuous than the others in knitted garments and climbing boots.

Taking advantage of the radiant day and of the surrounding tranquility, I went with Paolo along the bank of a brook, and there I began to jot down the *Manifesto del Movimento Femminile G.L.* that Mario Andreis commissioned.[6] I will try to do my best even if I am not good at things like this.

At noon, at table, Marcellin had a worried look, and he was listening distractedly to Franco's long dissertations on the best methods for guerrilla warfare. Later, he explained to me that he was not paying attention to Franco, not because he was tired of his discourses ("But he certainly talks a lot," he said to me), but because he was thinking about news he had received from Fenestrelle, where there was a little skirmish with the Fascists. In fact, a little while later news arrived that someone had been wounded. Paolo Menzio left quickly on his bicycle with surgical instruments, hoping to find faster transportation along the road.

This evening, another long conversation with Tonino. He was enthusiastic about my idea concerning the mail, and he took it upon himself to organize the collection of it in the Valley. Every week either Bianca or I will see to picking it up, and we will take care of distributing it in the city. In the meantime, I collected the usual series of assorted messages. Tomorrow I will make the crossing again alone, because Ettore and Paolo are staying here. Notwithstanding my protests, Marcellin gave an order to a young man to take me as far as Pourrières by motorcycle. At least this way I will avoid the ten kilometers on the main road.

19 July, Turin. Here I am in Turin, at my house, contradicting every rule of conspiratorial prudence. It seems like a miracle after the many problematic adventures of the past few days.

---

[6] The Mfgl would include women from Ada's own Action Party and also a number of Communists, Socialists, and other supporters. According to one report, they wanted to "gather together all those women who" were convinced by the "arduous present circumstances of the necessity to no longer remain outside of the social and political life of the country in the future, but to participate in it actively." They hoped "for the advent of a new society for Italy through a democratic revolution" where the "requirement for liberty" would be "accompanied by claims to social justice." See "Relazione sui Gruppi femminili 'Giustizia e Libertà'," [1944?], Istituto Piemontese per la Storia della Resistenza e della Società contemporanea 'Giorgio Agosti', Cartella Partito d'Azione, PA /ag1/g.

The morning of Monday the 17th (which therefore was really only the day before yesterday, but it seems like an eternity had passed since then), I had gone to the Command, to the Hotel Passet, and waited for the motorcyclist who was supposed to take me to Pourrières. It was 6:00 a.m. and the sun was already high in the sky, but everything was silent, and no one else was around. Seated on a curbstone and waiting, I thought about the *Manifesto*. After a while the owner of the hotel, who was going down to the garden to pick spinach, appeared, She did not know who the young man was who was supposed to come to get me, and neither did I.

At 7:00 a.m., by which time I was about to set out on foot, I heard the telephone ringing inside, followed by animated conversation and a great commotion. When I went into the hotel to inquire, I met a young man with a look that was half sleepy and half upset, who gave me the news. They were warning from Sestrières that the Fascists had attacked the base at the Triplex, and they were now "overflowing" up through the valley. He said it just like that. Although the situation was not very cheerful, I could not help but smile. He spoke as if he were writing a scholastic composition. For the moment it was the news that "overflowed." In a few minutes, one person after the other, everyone from the Command came outside. I must say that no one else, except for the young man, who was evidently surprised in his sleep, gave the slightest sign of panic. On the contrary, Marcellin appeared somewhat skeptical regarding the gravity of the situation. He tried at once to get in touch with Sestrières, but they did not answer the telephone. Nevertheless, he gave appropriate and necessary orders for the counteroffensive, the defense, and the eventual retreat at once. "What should I do?" I asked, putting myself immediately under his orders. Marcellin smiled: "Notify your friends at the Frezet and then come back here. It is good that you did not leave. If you are able to pass by there later, you will be able to bring the news to the Susa Valley and to Turin. We might need help."

I ran to the Frezet, where everyone was still sleeping peacefully. I delivered the news, yet without accentuating it with a catastrophic tone. They got dressed in a flash, and a few minutes later we moved together toward the Hotel Passet. Franco had an idea. If the Fascists were going down into the Chisone Valley toward the Triplex, they were evidently coming from the Susa Valley. A series of acts of sabotage to the railroads and to the road in the Susa Valley would draw the attention and the forces of the enemy over there, thus relaxing the pressure on the Chisone Valley.

Meanwhile at the Hotel Passet the mobilization was proceeding in a rapid, orderly, and precise manner. Serafino had left for the Triplex. Tonino gathered the troops for a possible retreat into the Troncea Valley. Good Giordana was waiting undaunted, with a club in his hand and a blanket rolled up on his shoulders, more touching and anachronistic than ever. Standing on the doorstep, from time to time biting into a sandwich that the provident owner of the hotel had squeezed into his hand, Marcellin made all the arrangements, with the unruffled confidence of a person who expects the worst and knows his business. He needs to empty the storehouses of provisions and clothing, collect the documents in order to destroy them at the last minute, put the weapons and munitions in a safe place, and evacuate the prisoners to a peaceful location. He had been able to get in touch by telephone with the Upper Valley. They were fighting at the Triplex, but for now no one else had "overflowed" along the road yet. Franco's idea seemed excellent to him. If we are able to pass by there, he said, it would be the best help we could give him. He would send a squad of well-armed men with us, with two machine guns, so that they could carry out some ambush along the road.

We left immediately. Near La Rua we met the line of prisoners who had just been moved along the Troncea Valley. At Pourrières we began the climb along the meadows flowered with golden arnica, always on the alert in case we ever saw anything suspicious, but everything seemed calm. Having begun the descent around 2:00 p.m., we made a stop at Casette, where the Meanese squad was. They decided to send some men with us, so that they could form two squads, one for the sabotage of the poles, the other for attacks on German vehicles on the road. A certain Willy, who once belonged to the partisan bands in Bussoleno, who had damaged a hand in a fight, and who had some experience with sabotage, would command them.[7] While the men were getting ready, I saw the sister of a partisan, who was up there for the seasonal pasturage, arrive. She lived in Les Granges and knew the Croces well. She welcomed me and wanted to offer me milk that was just drawn. She conjured up past times and figures and showed me a little puppy that was born in those days and baptized "Partigian."

Quite soon we got on the road again and we reached the vicinity of Meana toward sunset. Then we split up. One group went with Franco and Paolo to lie in wait along the road to Gravere and look for a place suitable for the ambush that would be carried out during the night. The others encamped in the vicinity of Fontanino. When it was dark, Alberto would accompany them straight home, where they were able to rest in the hayloft. Then at a given signal they would go to replace the others in the ambush, who consequently had their turn to rest. Ettore and I went straight home to prepare something to eat for everyone. A young partisan came with us who was not feeling very well, who in theory was supposed to help us look for provisions.

But a surprise was waiting for us at home. The day before, one of my brothers-in-laws had come, Mario told me. From the description I understood that it was Mario Gliozzi, who had left a calling card.[8] The card was cryptic: Aunt

---

[7] "Willy" was a detachment commander in the IV Alpine Division of GL. No last name was given.

[8] Mario Gliozzi was the husband of Ettore's sister, Ada (Dadi) Marchesini.

Ada was sick, it said, but it was not necessary to go and see her because her sickness was contagious. Something must have happened in Turin, and we should not go home. This was clear.

I kept from worrying by starting the potatoes and the *polenta* cooking, and by talking with the young partisan, whose name was Sergio. He was eighteen years old, but was absolutely a baby. He talked with me for a long time about his mother and sisters, who were inhabitants of the Germanasca, with a nostalgia that contrasted strangely with the vainglorious tone in which he recounted, by stages, some warlike episode. He must have caught cold and had a stomach ache. I gave him something hot, and made him lie down in Paolo's bed. When I returned, with one more blanket, he was already asleep, but when I leaned over him to cover him, he sat up unexpectedly and put his arms around my neck. "Good night, Sergio," I said to him, kissing him on his forehead. For a moment I remained near him, caressing his hair with sad tenderness, and thinking about so many things: about his mother, who perhaps at that moment, in her distant isolated cottage, was watching the sun set, wondering where her child was; about Paolo, who was exposed to every sort of danger on the street that was becoming dark; and about the cruelty of this war that even puts children at risk—those who know why they are fighting, like Paolo, and those who do not know, like little Sergio.

Evening fell and the squad from Fontanino arrived. They ate, and then settled down to sleep, some (those who came in) in the house, and the others in the hayloft. But I did not sleep. I felt completely responsible for the house, for Mario, and for the boys. I jumped at every sound of a car in the valley, and I went to the window to watch when Tabui barked.

Around 3:00 a.m., Paolo arrived to awaken the men to change places with the other squad. I gave those who were leaving a kind of hot coffee, and I watched them disappear into the night. I did not awaken Sergio, who was sleeping peacefully, with his face relaxed. It mattered little that it was his turn. The day after he would be more rested. He did not wake up until around 6:00 a.m., when I was getting ready to leave. "I am fine," he said with a satisfied air. "Really, I am fine." I explained to him what he should do later and I left him with Ettore. (As soon as the sun rose the others had hidden scrupulously in the nearby woods.) But before I left, he wanted at any cost to give me two minuscule skeins of wool that his mother had given him for mending his socks. "I will not have much use for them. You can use them," he said somewhat uneasily. I did not have the heart to refuse him, and I left with a lump of emotion in my throat.

When I got on the train, I realized something terrible. I had changed in a hurry, almost in the dark, limiting myself to washing my hands and the tip of my nose. I realized now that my ankles, visible with my sandals, had a black circle of dirt at the point where the shoes that I had worn during the entire previous day ended. It mattered little to me that I gave the impression of someone filthy, but I would not have wanted these revealing signs to make anyone suspicious. When we were in the tunnel, I tried, with my hand wet with saliva, to remove the worst of it. At home, in Turin, I would take a bath, but then I realized that I could not go home. What had happened, and where should I go to find out? To Mario Gliozzi's house? To Giorgio, at the courthouse?

I arrived in Turin undecided, and I was relieved to see Mario Marchesini, who was waiting for me at the station and who gave me the news immediately.[9] It was a question of an alarm that was not very serious. They had gone to ask the concierge for me, who had intelligently notified Mario immediately. There had been police officers in the garden for two days, on the lookout. Fortunately, no one else who would put us at risk had come. They had not gone up to search, and no others were arrested. I calmed down, but it was evident that the most rudimentary prudence prohibited me from going home. I looked at my dirty feet woefully. "Come to wash at my house," said Mario. I accepted with gratitude.

Refreshed and clean again, I went to the courthouse and informed Giorgio of the latest news. Then I finished several things. How stressful it would be not to have a point of reference, a *house*, even though it is always filled with people and in perpetual danger! For the first time, I reflected on what must have been the hardship and suffering of so many of our friends who did not have a permanent house, and who wandered everlastingly from one place to the other. I thought about Lisetta and Vittorio most of all. When I finished my errands, I went to sit down on a bench in the garden in Piazza Solferino and wait for Giorgio. I must have had the appearance of a derelict because he said to me when he arrived: "Poor thing, you look like a *little orphan girl*." Wise and thorough as usual, he had prudently gone to learn about the situation at my house. No one else was there and it appeared that it was no longer being watched. "Oh!" I said, imploringly "Give me permission to go home, just for a moment. I will not sleep there: this evening I will return to Meana. Just for about an hour. I will be careful." Giorgio is truly very intelligent. He did not theorize and he did not talk to me about responsibility, as I somewhat expected. He simply said: "Go there, but be careful: the important thing is that the usual comings and goings not start again for several days, and that no one else go. Remember to go to Valle's house today at 4:00 p.m. You will find Duccio there."

Instead of crossing the garden, I went toward the house from the side on Via Assarotti. According to our agreement, the good lawyer Cattaneo had exposed the canary cage, but in the garden, which was flooded with scorching sunlight, there was no one else. Even if I admitted they were still watching, certainly at that hour the policemen had gone inside to rest. When she saw me, Espedita raised her arms to the sky, protesting, but I reassured her. I would only stay for

---

[9] Mario Marchesini, an engineer, was Ettore's brother.

a minute and no one else would come. I was sure that, as long as I stayed there, she would not stop keeping guard for a minute. When I entered my house, I felt an indescribable relief, as if the old furniture that had been around me since birth, the books collected and saved with sacrifice and love, and the same windows that had been repaired as best we could, gave me a sense of security and comfort. Suddenly I realized that I was desperately tired, and I remembered that I had been on my feet practically since dawn of the previous day. I threw myself on the bed and slept.

I woke up just in time to run to the meeting at Valle's house. Duccio was there and also Paolo Greco, the Liberal Party representative on the Cln.[10] Duccio, who had decided to work in the Susa and Chisone Valleys, was also ready to come to Marcellin's immediately. Unfortunately, I could not bring him there, with the roundup in progress. But we could go to Susa and talk with Ferrero if we were able to find him. The proposal was accepted. Duccio had a car, with "iron clad" documents, and we left almost immediately.

In a little more than an hour we arrived in Susa and found Ferrero, with whom we chatted for a long time. We talked about the relationship with Marcellin, and agreed that we would go to his house all together, as soon as they heard from him.

When the most important discussions were over, I left Duccio and Greco with Ferrero, and ran to Meana somewhat nervously. What had they done? What did they plan to do?

At home Ettore, who was alone, was cooking mushrooms that he had found in the woods. Paolo had gone with entire groups to blow up the railroad poles in the vicinity of Campo del Carro. Would he return? Yes, right after the attempt, which should take place as soon as it was dark, he would come to get his knapsack. Then they would all leave again for the Chisone Valley.

I ate the mushrooms in a stew while I told Ettore about the events of the day. Suddenly I heard a roar, a din that made the house shake. The poles must have been blown up. A quarter of an hour later Paolo arrived, very satisfied. It was the first important act of sabotage that he had directed alone, and he was happy that everything had been carried out to perfection. His companions had stopped to take a break in the woods near Soffiso. He planned to meet them right away. Instead, while I put out something that I had prepared for him in a hurry, he put his head on the table and fell asleep. He too had not slept since dawn the day before. I let him sleep, like I had done the night before with little Sergio. When he woke up, the others had already left. He would go to join them before dawn, with Ettore. If everything went well, they would stop in the

[10] Paolo Greco was a university professor and representative of the Liberal Party on the Piedmontese Regional Cln.

Chisone Valley to finish the work that had been begun. Otherwise, they would return to Casette, to Daniele's house.

I searched my house thoroughly to see if there were any weapons or objects left that would put us at risk. It was after midnight when I finally went to bed. I woke up at dawn. I thought I heard a whistle. When I went to the window cautiously, I saw on the road, emerging from the low fog of the morning, a figure that seemed to have the shape of a Russian. What if they had already arrived? What if we had waited too long? But an instant later, when I could see better, I saw that the supposed Russian was a Meanese who had come to water his field, and who was whistling to call his dog.

Ettore and Paolo left. I did a little cleaning. There was some need for it after two days of traffic and going back and forth. I put everything in order, trying to give the impression that it was a harmless apartment belonging to bourgeois evacuees. Then, around 8:00 a.m., I went down to Susa and, having made the final agreements with Ferrero, I left in a car with Duccio and Greco.

When we approached Avigliana, Duccio proposed, "Why don't we make a quick visit to Giaveno and look for Teppati to hear how our local squads are doing?[11] This way we will have a total picture of the entire valley." The proposal was approved and, when we reached the grade crossing, we made a detour toward the lakes. A German came out from the checkpoint. (I confess that I feel a deep sense of satisfaction every time I pass by here and read the words *Achtung! Banden Gebiet! Banden Gefahr!* [Attention! Bandit territory. Danger, bandits].) Evidently he was reassured by the nice car and the composed and trustworthy appearance of the occupants (I am speaking of Duccio and Greco, not about myself, naturally, because I tried to make myself as small as possible). He did not even want to see our papers, limiting himself to asking with deference, "Organisation Todt?"[12] "No," answered Duccio, laughing sardonically in his beard. "Not Todt. Committee." At which the German stood at attention and let us pass with a soldierly, deferential salute. As soon as we had departed, we laughed heartily. "It is always best to tell the truth," joked Duccio, and he added quickly "We are lost the day we no longer know how to laugh."

Neither Teppati nor his wife, the invaluable Mimí, with whom I would have gladly spoken about her work among the women, was at Giaveno.[13] "They should have come," a neighbor explained to us after an initial moment of evasive reserve. "But today the train from Turin did not arrive. There is no electricity." (With a glimmer of remorse I thought about the poles that had been blown up last night.) We could have gone higher up in search of Nicoletta and

---

[11] Guido Teppati was a notary and organizer of the Action Party in the Sangone Valley.

[12] Organisation Todt (OT) was a Nazi construction and engineering group that used men and boys from Nazi-occupied countries as slave labor.

[13] Mimí Teppati was an organizer of the Gruppi di difesa and of the Mfgl in the Sangone Valley.

Usseglio.[14] But there was a roundup in progress, and it did not seem prudent to insist. Therefore around 11:00 a.m. we went into Turin again, and I got out of the car near Porta Susa.

The day continued very intensely with meetings, trips, and discussions. By now my house is perfectly quiet, but it is better that it not be frequented for several days yet. I will be the person who will have to race around more than ever. Meanwhile tonight I will sleep in my house, which will be a real rest.

22 July, Meana. Paolo returned from the Chisone Valley with good news. The attack had been driven back and the Fascists had been chased away from the Triplex. The zone is still free and life has become normal again. Ettore stayed to finish putting up the station. Marcellin is waiting for Duccio, whom I plan on accompanying the day after tomorrow.

They killed Sibille, Laghi's intendant.[15] He was returning from Urbiano when the Germans stopped him. His papers were in order but, when they were searching him, they found a revolver on him and they killed him immediately.

26 July. The other evening, I met Duccio and Ferrua (in place of Greco) at Collegno, and we arrived together in Meana happily, where we spent the night.[16]

Yesterday morning, at 5:00 a.m., we left for the Colle. The first stop was Casette, where Duccio, in his capacity as head of all the Piedmontese GL formations, reviewed our partisans who, under the direction of the new commander, Martino, had made great progress in terms of organization.[17] But the squad of Czechs who climbed into the mountains from the crossing keepers' cabins of the railroad station where the Germans had put them on guard made the most extraordinary impression. Ferrero had truly done his job well. The Czechs came up without thinking twice, bringing all of their equipment, uniforms, weapons, blankets, curtains, and small pots. They put up their curtains here, and they keep everything in perfect order: very shiny small pots, uniforms well cleaned, weapons perfectly polished. They form a group by themselves with a real leader, and they are organized and disciplined. ("They wash their feet every day," one of our partisans from the Susa Valley whispered to me with a tone

[14] Giulio Nicoletta had a doctorate in law and was commander of the Sergio De Vitis Division in the Sangone Valley. Guido Usseglio was a university professor and organizer of the partisan bands in the Sangone Valley and later commander of the Campana Division.

[15] Tullio Sibille was a worker and an intendant in the IV Alpine Division of GL. An intendant is a high-ranking official or administrator.

[16] Giovanni Gonella (Ferrua) was an industrialist and a staff officer in the IV Partisan Zone, and later commander of the 41st Unified Division.

[17] Beppe Cimaz (Martino) was a land surveyor and commander of a detachment of the IV Alpine Division of GL in the Cenischia Valley.

that was either of complaint or of admiration, I did not know.) We also saw the machine gun emplacements, which were very well concealed.

Around 11:00 a.m., another brief stop at the Colle. A visit to the Fort and a cordial welcome from Dema. Then we set out for the descent, and at 1:00 p.m. we were at the Hotel Passet. They were all there: Marcellin, Giordana, Tonino, and Serafino, in a euphoric state of mind due to their recent victory. Ettore, very satisfied with his work, was also there. The transmitter functions and can be heard throughout the valley under the name of "Radio General Perotti." It appears that it can also be heard outside the valley, even in the vicinity of Genoa.

Right after dinner, we retired to Marcellin's office and began to discuss the points of the agreement. The discussion lasted until seven in the evening. It took all of Duccio's diplomacy and spirit and patience to succeed in putting together the essential points, but in the end we succeeded. It is truly an excellent thing, and an important step toward the unified Command, which I believe we must achieve before the end.

After supper, more talk to draw up the agreement. Then Duccio left again with Martino for the Susa Valley, since he had to be in Turin again today. We listened to the radio broadcast, with the news, some records that were found in a neighboring villa, and a piece of poetry by Major Serafino on the battle of the Triplex, in which Mario Costa, the son of the dialectal poet, had died.[18] Then Alberto brought me to the Frezet on the crossbar of his bicycle. I was lucky because I was so tired that I could no longer stand up.

Today we completed the crossing, and tomorrow Ettore and I would go down to Turin.

28 July, Turin. For two days there were almost continuous alarms with the consequent stopping of the trams and the need to do very long stretches on foot. I think I covered around ten kilometers.

I saw a number of women of the Gruppi di difesa at Medea's house and of the Gruppi GL at Paola Bologna's. I was at Anita Rho's house, where I found Frida and we talked and discussed.[19] At the house of Costanza Costantino, my former colleague and now a collaborator, I met Natalia Momo, a charming teacher who will work with us.[20] Angelo Mussa introduced me to a girl who was employed by Microtecnica, who seemed very energetic and decisive. Barberis introduced me to a girl full of good will who was my student at Savigliano. Certainly I would have been much less tired if I could have made all these girls come to my house, instead of running to four places in the city. By now everything is quiet and

---

[18] Nino Costa (1886–1945) wrote poetry in the Piedmontese dialect.

[19] Anita Rho was a writer and collaborator of the Mfgl.

[20] Costanza Costantino was a professor and organizer of the Mfgl. Natalia Momo was a teacher and organizer of the Mfgl.

I think that, within a few days, the house will begin to function again as an address.

31 July, Meana. Yesterday morning, when I arrived, I did not find Paolo. There was the atmosphere of a roundup in the air. He had gone to Mario's house to sleep in a hayloft of the Cordolas where, in the event of an alarm, it would be easier to flee through the tangle of the roofs than from our house, which was isolated and capable of being surrounded.

In the afternoon, a visit from a company of Fascists, who were coming up from the main road singing and who then set up camp in the piazza right in front of Teta's store, confirmed for me that the rumors and impressions had not been unfounded.

Today I pushed myself to go on patrol as far as Chiomonte, which was also full of Germans and Fascists and dominated by an atmosphere of fear and anguish.

It is obvious that they are preparing a big roundup, much more extensive than that which had taken place in the month of June. Evidently the nucleus and objective will be the Chisone Valley, not the Susa Valley, where the partisans do not have visible bases and are difficult to locate. Here, primarily, where we are, there will be reprisals whose purpose is terror and intimidation, but the bulk of the German and Fascist forces undoubtedly will be inclined to pour into the Chisone Valley. It is a question of hindering them and holding them here as long as possible.

This evening we had a long meeting with Ferrero, who has a lot to do these days. The project will be grandiose: make all of the Czechs who are now on guard at the railroad go into the mountains; at the same time, blow up various bridges, in a way that will make the passage of trains on the railroad and trucks on the main road impossible, and perform other acts of sabotage on the road to Moncenisio as well. (Laghi's squads should consider this.) Certainly, if the plan succeeds, the roundup in the Chisone Valley will be markedly delayed and obstructed. At least they could not arrive from the Susa Valley. But it is not easy to synchronize all these different actions.

1 August, Turin. Today, at Frida's house, with some others, we planned a newspaper for the Mfgl. If Silva Pons gets involved, she will make it something splendid. After a long discussion, we decided on the title *La Nuova Realtà*. The new reality is exactly what all men and women want to create for tomorrow. But will we succeed?

3 August. Going back and forth to Meana is beginning to become a complicated matter. Yesterday evening, after we left at 5:00 p.m. in a cattle car that was incredibly crowded, we had an alarm at Avigliana, the fifth of the day, which meant getting off the train and scattering into the nearby fields. At Sant'Antonino, it meant getting off and transferring on foot for quite a stretch. There was a very long stop at Borgone, and finally we arrived at Meana at 10:00 p.m. Five hours to travel fifty kilometers.

At home, Paolo was not there. He arrived a little while later and told me the latest news. Yesterday evening the partisans had gone down to help the Czechs escape from the crossing keeper's cabin between Mattie and Meana. After a feigned exchange of shots, the Czechs were supposed to leave, bringing weapons and baggage with them. Instead —be it chance or espionage —at the right moment a German armored train that had been traveling on the line for several days arrived. The endeavor had come to nothing because they could not attack an armored train with ordinary guns. Now they will try to attack it another way, with explosives.

The atmosphere of an imminent roundup is becoming more and more intense in the town, and the partisans are taking precautions. Today Paolo and Willy went to the *Municipio*—where naturally they are all in agreement—to arrange things so that the ration cards will not be taken away from the partisans and their families. While they were there, they looked out the little balcony, having heard the sound of a car, and they saw a truck loaded with Germans wearing camouflage helmets and uniforms. Escape among the vineyards, alarm at strategic points, but the Germans had simply taken the wrong turn. They wanted to go to Salbertrand. Had they known it in time, they could have attacked them as soon as they were outside the town and taken them, their weapons, their car, and everything. Instead they left immediately, before it was possible to assemble the people necessary for the action.

4 August. After a day filled with misunderstandings and anxiety and a somewhat unpleasant trip with a transfer in the rain, when I arrived here I found Paolo, who had just returned from Susa, where he had seen Sergio and where he had had his hair cut. (Paolo always does something of this kind during peak times: he takes a bath, has his hair cut, washes his feet. I do not know whether it is stupidity or cleanliness or superstition.) The news that he brought was not encouraging. By this time the roundup was practically under way, and for the moment our plan had to be suspended. The Germans and Fascists had beaten us to the punch. Now it is a question of reducing the damages to the minimum, so that we can begin again as soon as possible. Our group of partisans has received the orders to disband so that they can find the gap in the enemy forces. If they all stick to the orders that were given, I do not believe that we will have many losses here. But what will happen in the Chisone Valley?

5 August. Willy awakened me at 6:00 a.m. with bad news. At the first light of dawn, a small group of partisans, while imprudently running along the main road of Colletto, came to the attention of a truck of Germans that was going up toward the Colle, and became the object of a violent exchange of shots. A certain Durbiano, a native of Santa Petronilla, was quite seriously wounded.[21] His companions were able to carry him to safety as far as a *grangia* that was relatively safe, but he had lost a lot of blood and had to be cared for.

I rushed to Susa immediately, to the hospital, where Doctor Raimondi, who had heard about the case, gave me the instructions and items necessary for the wounded boy.[22] After this emergency first aid we will see what can be done. If they can transport him with certain safety measures as far as the main road, they can send an ambulance to get him tomorrow, and once he is in the hospital, he will be safe.

At home I found Elena, who was waiting for me. I gave her the items and repeated the explanations, and she left immediately.

Around 1:00 p.m. Mario Cordola arrived, upset. While he was going down to Colletto, the Germans had fired at him. He saved himself by a miracle, throwing himself on the ground and dragging himself for a long stretch through the wooded area.

For the entire day the town remained as if suspended in an anguished wait. The young men were all away, or on the lookout. The women, old people, and children were taking care of the animals, keeping house, or tending the garden. A little more than a month has passed since the roundup of the end of June, but the atmosphere is completely different. Before, there was a sense of disoriented surprise in most people, as if they were faced with one of the most distressing and tragic aspects of the war. Now instead there is the consciousness of a battle that we must fight at any cost and that, even if it is lost today, will be victorious tomorrow. This month of partisan war, which has been lived actively even if partially and clandestinely, has served as the political education of these mountain folk and has been of more use than years of speeches, schooling, and theories. After the episode at the end of June, the fearful evacuees from the city went away. The people from around here did not have any doubt as to which road to follow. Even the least intelligent, even those who had been Fascists, perhaps in good faith, even those who at first had been signaled out to me as spies, have taken their place and performed their duty with courageous simplicity. In the waiting of today there is neither excitement nor anxiety, but a kind of forlorn sobriety. Before, all the men of every age were afraid of being sent to Germany. Today the young people know that, if they are captured, as partisans, they will be shot immediately. The masses and crowds have become an army.

---

[21] Vittorio Durbiano was a partisan in the IV Alpine Division of GL. He was hanged in Santa Petronilla on 7 August 1944.

[22] Carlo Raimondi was a doctor in the hospital in Susa.

6 August. Again this morning it was Willy who awakened me with news about the wounded boy. He was not worse. On the contrary, he had regained a bit of strength and, aided by his companions, he felt like going to the main road to be put into the ambulance. The Germans were no longer at Colletto, so they could carry out the transfer with some security. Therefore I rushed to Susa, where I arranged everything with Doctor Raimondi, who proved to be quite practical and courageous. But, while we were preparing things as best we could, a big disaster occurred in the meantime.

For several days I had heard from our partisans about a certain priest, I do not know if he came from Susa or Meana or where, who hung out with them and who was often with them. In fact the matter had not worried me. I do not have a particular aversion to priests, who are conducting themselves very well today. It is enough to think about Don Foglia, and also about the parish priest of Meana, who have rendered excellent services. But today this young, ignorant priest acted foolishly. I am convinced that he acted in good faith, but good faith, in my opinion, does not justify idiocy. After he had taken care of the wounded boy for the entire night, this morning, while I went down to Susa, he convinced him that it would be better to hand himself over to the Germans. He thought he would put things straight by telling a German captain who was a friend of his that this one was not a partisan, but an innocent shepherd boy who had been wounded accidentally. The boy and his companions, with the credulous optimism of the inexperienced, let themselves be convinced, and the naïve priest immediately ran to call the Germans. While I was climbing back up, a truck was coming to get the wounded boy, whom his companions, following the suggestions of the priest, had accompanied and piously placed in a little abandoned chapel. If we had known it in time, we would have been able to attack the truck and carry the boy away, but when Willy and I found out about it, they had already been in Susa for a quite some time. It was enough to make me furious. In all probability by this time the wounded boy would have been in the hospital, virtually safe. Instead he is in the hands of the Germans. I do not have any illusions. I do not believe that they will be *dupes* (fooled) regarding the lie that was concocted by the priest, nor moved by the innocent shepherd boy (of draft age) and by his devotion to the Madonna, in whose chapel they had found him. Now the boy runs the risk of being shot.

In the afternoon, while we gave Willy and Anna Jarre further details about the matter, a little boy arrived, running, to warn us that the Germans were coming. Ettore, Mario, Paolo, and Willy went away, and I remained with Anna and Esterina. But nothing happened. After about an hour, the men returned. From the Truc they had seen a truck of Germans or Fascists arrive at Campo del Carro, and leave from there a little more than a half hour later.[23] They had

---

[23] Here I believe that Ada means the Truc Peyron, which stands at 3,189 meters and is in the Susa Valley, rather than the little hillock behind her home.

noticed strange movements, and a gathering and dispersing of people in the vicinity of the *Municipio*. What had happened?

Unfortunately we did not have to wait long to find out. The Fascists had brought with them on the truck the young Tremaiore, a partisan from the Chisone Valley who had come to find his family, who lived in the vicinity of Lower Meana. I do not know how they captured him. The fact remains that that they hung him on the balcony of the *Municipio*.[24] Then they went away immediately, leaving a squad to be on guard and, with the most serious threats, prohibiting the townspeople from touching the cadaver in the meantime.

The news struck me like a heavy blow. Even without seeing him, I felt the same fury and anguish I had felt in the Germanasca before the inanimate body of young Davide. Fury, anguish, and pity. For him, for his family, and for his very assassins, who were driven by today's brutal obscuration of morality to commit a crime for which they would not be forgiven. As I had then, I felt the need to do something—useless, childish, but nevertheless with meaning in my heart, some homage to the aura of civility and gentility that seems erased from the world today, but to which we must return all the same if we wish to continue to live on a human plane.

Once night fell and Paolo and Mario, out of prudence, had gone to sleep somewhere, I left for Campo del Carro. All the doors of the small town were closed and the lights put out. An unspoken feeling of grief lies everywhere. In the vicinity of the turn for the *Chiesa* (church), suddenly I heard a shuffling of feet of men and animals. I hid behind a hedge. It was the *Alpini* from Monte Rosa, with mules and pack trains, returning from Colletto, where probably they had gone to lend the Germans a hand with the roundup.[25] One of them stopped near the hedge behind which I was hiding and lit a cigarette. In the quick light of the match, I saw his young face, tired and lifeless. Never as in that moment did I feel the cruel and wretched absurdity of being so close and so similar, and at the same time so much of an enemy.

Scaling the gate, I entered the garden of a villa and picked a big bunch of flowers from the abandoned flower beds. Then I crossed Campo del Carro, it too mute and deserted like the other small towns. The moon had not yet come out, and the darkness aided me. But, while I silently neared the *Municipio*, I heard voices in the meadow before me. I stopped to listen. The person who was speaking was from the Veneto. Therefore the people who were watching over the dead boy were not from the town, but probably Fascists on guard, because no one

[24] Stefano Tremaiore, a partisan in the Chisone Valley, was hanged in Meana on 6 August 1944.

[25] The 4th Italian "Monte Rosa" Alpine Division was a military division of the Republic of Salò that aided the Germans. It was formed on 1 January 1944. See www.divisionealpinamonterosa. org.

approached. Walking bent over in the shadow, I turned behind the building of the *Municipio* and then, almost creeping, I passed in front. I saw the shape of the one who had been hanged, and with my hands I lightly touched his feet, which were in big mountain boots. (Strange, I thought, that they had not taken them off!) I deposited the bunch of useless flowers on the steps under him, and I lingered, with a rapid caress of his cold, rigid hand. Then I went away without stooping over any more. By now I had done what I had wanted to do, and it no longer mattered if they stopped me. I was armed only with my sad humanity, with the anguish that filled my heart, and with the irrepressible tears that ran from my eyes, flooding my face. What could they do to me? Whatever they did to me, what did it matter?

But no one saw me, or if they saw me, they did not say anything. Slowly I returned home under the stars, in the midst of a silence that was so absolute that I thought I could hear the beating of my heart.

What will happen tomorrow?

7 August. The sun set after having shone on the world and in the sky for the entire day, unperturbed and indifferent, and countless stars proliferated. But darts of smoke are still rising from the isolated, destroyed cottages, with sudden eruptions of sparks. Dense clouds of smoke wither the green foliage of the trees, and the stagnant, acrid odor of fire lingers everywhere. An unnatural silence weighs down on everything, which the sudden crackling of flames, the wail from an animal, and the cry of a baby interrupt at times, making our hearts race. The town, wounded and lacerated, does not sleep. Like a sick person after a serious crisis, it dozes for a moment, but its distressed limbs are still ridden with painful trembling.

I looked around. My house was intact. Paintings and photographs of happy times hung on the walls. There were books and flowers. I still do not know how to explain the miracle.

Yesterday evening, after I returned from Campo, I fell into a heavy sleep from which, at the first light of dawn, the sound of a car that stopped in front of our house awakened me with a start. I ran to the window and peeped out cautiously, but not so cautiously, however, that the Fascists, with whom the truck was loaded, did not notice me. I drew back immediately, but one of them was already climbing the stairs. Preferring not to let him enter the house, I went to meet him on the balcony. "Where is the little town of Serrette?" he asked briskly. Someone must have reported that there was a group of partisans in the vicinity of Serrette. In fact, Daniele's group had been there for some time, but by now the group had been on the move for quite a while and there was no longer anyone there. I preferred, however, to assume the most dazed and frightened appearance possible, fearing that, if I appeared practical and quick, they would load me on their truck and force me to be their guide, which had happened to others. "It must be over there, to the right, then turn left. No, no, I am mistaken, straight ahead to the right, but on the other hand no, perhaps it is really to the left. You understand, I am an evacuee and do not get around much...." In the meantime I smiled, with such an idiotic air that he left, shrugging his shoulders, and the truck went away in the wrong direction.

I returned home. Ettore, feeling me move, had awakened. I urged him to get up quickly and go down to the station immediately. If he were able to take the train, it would be so much the better. At least he would be safe.

He had been gone for a short time when Mario and Paolo arrived. They too had heard the truck and considered it more prudent to go away. While they were making a little breakfast in a hurry, a truck appeared at the bend, this time loaded with Germans. Mario slipped away quickly among the bean plants, and Paolo joined him with a jump down from the terrace, and in an instant they disappeared behind the willow trees. Just in time, since the Germans, who had gotten out of the car, had blocked the road, placing a machine gun there, and it would have no longer been possible to leave the house without being seen.

Nevertheless for the moment they did not come into the house. They encircled the Cordolas' house, and I saw them enter several doorways and look out several balconies. Since I did not have anything to do, I decided, with strange logic, to go get some milk. Even Borgata Cantalupo was full of Germans. At the house where they give me the milk, the two able-bodied men had disappeared. ("Just in time," Lena whispered to me while she filled the bottle.) A German was trying to subdue, with a piece of chocolate, little Maddalena, who, in the arms of her mother, looked at him, half distrustful and half afraid. While I turned back, I found a group of four, heavily armed, who asked me if this was the way to go to the quarry. What the deuce! Exactly the area where Paolo, Mario, and who knows how many others had headed. "No," I said, shaking my head, "to go to the quarry you go down." Meanwhile I smiled, cordial and persuasive, inviting them with my hand to enter a footpath that, skirting the bottom of the cave, disappears in the woods toward Susa. Convinced, they walked by way of the footpath, they too thanking me and smiling.

When I arrived home with the precious bottle, I found Esterina waiting for me at the door, worried. "They went upstairs," she told me in a hurry. "They did not find anything here, but they have been upstairs for a while and they have not left." Meanwhile Graziella caressed Dionigi the cat, who was meowing pitifully. As I learned later on, the Germans, whom he had attacked ferociously, had hurled him down from the balcony.

Still brandishing the bottle of milk, I climbed the stairs and entered the house, decisive. There was some disorder in the kitchen. I passed into the next room, Paolo's room, where five or six Germans were flinging the papers on the desk into the air.

"What is it? What happened?" I asked in German with a surprised and slightly irritated tone. All of a sudden, the Germans turned around. Evidently my appearance, somewhere between mountain folk and city dweller, my bottle of milk, my German, and my tone baffled them a bit.

"Who are they?" one of them asked me, putting a photograph of me with Ettore and Paolo under my nose.

"That's me with my husband," I answered.

"This one?" insisted another, putting a finger on Paolo's smiling face.

"One of my nephews."

"Where is he?"

"I do not know. He is a soldier. I have not seen him for two years."

"And your husband?"

"He went to Turin to work. He is employed."

"There is no one else here?"

"No one, as you can see," I answered.

In my heart I blessed the unusual laziness that had made me not make the bed immediately, according to my good habits. Evidently two people had slept in that unmade bed, and Paolo's bed, a divan covered with multicolored pillows, gave the impression, which was true, that no one had slept in it.

Meanwhile another German came out from my bedroom, holding in his hand this little notebook where day after day, systematically, I have noted my memoirs.

"What is this?" he asked.

"My diary," I responded serenely.

"Why is it written in English?"

"I am a language teacher. I am practicing," I answered.

"Ah!" said the German.

After he threw the little notebook on the table, he went out on the balcony. But another was still lingering around a battery that Ettore had left to charge. "My husband is an engineer at the Radio," I said.[26] "This is his work." Somewhat relieved and confused, the Germans went away, saying goodbye courteously. I accompanied them up to the stairs and I saw that, before leaving, one of them traced the letter K on the wall with chalk. What did it mean? *Kaputt?*

---

[26] E.I.A.R.

When I went back to the kitchen, I saw my little purse that I had left unattended on the table even though it contained five thousand lire, which I had withdrawn the other day from the bank. The little purse was open, but the five thousand lire, which were very visible, had not been taken. Nothing else had been taken away, except for the key to the house in Turin, which, however, I found a little while later on the window of the adjacent room. Evidently they had thought that it served to open who-knows-what secret repository. Instead, they had found everything thrown wide open.

On the table of Paolo's room, next to the little notebook of my recollections and the photograph that they had shown me, there was another little notebook where Paolo had diligently noted, during Badoglio's forty-five days, the title and date of the semi-clandestine journals that had come out then, and which he had subsequently forgotten at the bottom of a drawer. There were also the photographs of the two deserters from the Caucasus, in uniform, with their names written on the back in Cyrillic characters. What would I have said if they had asked me for explanations? On the other hand, had they seen it? Had they understood? Or had they not wanted to understand?

But an even greater surprise was waiting for me in the bedroom. In the armoire, I had a certain number of articles of military clothing that were useful when someone arrived who had to change clothes, and that I thought I could justify as some old clothing of my husband's or even my father's. Now the Germans had taken them out and thrown them in the middle of the floor, without asking me anything. But, on reflection, fear shot through my heart when, while picking up a pair of pants to put them back in their place, I saw a Sten cartridge fall from one of the two pockets.[27]

I was congratulating myself about the good fortune that had not made it jump out one moment sooner when a young boy arrived, panting, to warn us that they had decided to burn all of the houses in the town. At the small town of Traverse they had already begun. Marcella's house was in flames. She did not even have time to take out the mattresses.

Immediately Esterina began to take out the linens and dismantle the knitting machine that was her craft and her livelihood. I too thought that I should try to save something: winter clothing, shoes, and blankets for now. Wisely, in the morning before leaving, Ettore hurriedly hid in his knapsack an embroidered dinner service, an antique family heirloom that we had brought to Meana to save it from the bombardments. I made big parcels that I threw down from the terrace and then dragged into the nearby woods. I had in my hands the voluminous manuscripts of my translation of Bacon's *Essays* and

---

[27] The Sten was a type of submachine gun produced by the British in 1940.

of the Senior-Tocqueville correspondence.[28] With what anxiety had I tried, around two years before, to bring them to safety so that they would not be lost. They represented the result of months of work, research, and effort. But today I abandoned them without remorse. "They are not good for anything," I thought. "If we come out of all this, I will do other things. What does it matter to me?" Better to save a pair of wool socks, even though they are mended, a can of meat, or a can of condensed milk! How our scale of values has changed in these months! Yesterday the fruit of my intellectual work seemed important and precious. Today the things that count are those that serve the basic needs of life, to ward off the cold and save us from hunger.

While we piled our bundles in the shadow of the poplars, a sudden flicker arose from the nearby Villa Favaro, the last house in the village before ours. Perhaps it would be our turn next.

Graziella's terrorized pain stirred an anguish full of rebellion in me. She ran back and forth sobbing loudly and carrying little childish objects: the cover of a pan, a basket of thread, a bunch of fake flowers, and an oleograph of the Madonna, which she placed on the mattresses as if she had to protect them. She screamed, crying: "Mamma, I do not want them to burn our house. Mamma, let's say the rosary, Mamma, let's pray to the Madonna not to let them burn our house!" Her little universe was crumbling among the crackling of the flames, the clouds of smoke that were rising from the neighboring houses, and the desperate bellowing of the animals that the Germans had taken away from the stables. Alternatively she invoked the Madonna and her Mamma, the only powers she had learned to know and from whom instinct and education had accustomed her to solicit comfort and aid.

I have never been able to stand the exhibition of pain in children, which seems to me to be the most atrocious injustice, the most unpardonable offense. I stopped attending to things and held the little girl next to me. I tried to console her, interest her in what Tabui and Dionigi were doing, and make her laugh. Quite soon I had the consolation of seeing the little face, which had seemed mature and hardened a few minutes before, break into an amused smile, while the darting, curious interest in everything typical of children emerged again in her eyes filled with tears.

The houses around us were burning, but up to now ours was still intact, and for every minute that passed the possibility of escaping it seemed greater to me. Graziella, who was calmed down by now, played at swaddling the cat to make it sleep, when a car driven by a German stopped in front of our house. A light

---

[28] The *Essays* of Sir Francis Bacon (1561–1626) and the correspondence between Alexis de Tocqueville and Nassau William Senior that took place between 1834 and 1859. Ada translated and published Bacon's *Essays* in 1948. Francesco Bacone, *Saggi*, traduzione e prefazione di Ada Prospero (Turin: F. De Silva, 1948.)

of terror reappeared in the little girl's eyes, and she began to cry again. But the German, a sergeant, having gotten out of the car, which was loaded with furniture and linens that had been removed from several villas that afterward had broken out in flames, simply asked to take a drink and wash in our fountain. I took advantage of the situation to ask him if he would burn our house, too. "No," he said looking at the sign made with chalk. "K means that everything is all right. Those to be burned are marked with an F: *Feuer* (fire)." In order to become fully convinced of it, I gave the good news to Esterina and Graziella, who had approached us in the meantime, shaken by new sobs again. "What is the matter with the little girl?" asked the German. "Why is she crying?" "She is afraid, what do you think she is?" I asked somewhat aggressively. "Does it seem to you that these are spectacles suited to children?" I added, pointing out the columns of smoke and fire that were rising around us. The German became serious. The face of a man, tired and desperately sad, suddenly appeared under his rigid mask. "Damn the war!" he said in a low voice. "I too have children. I have been at war for four years. But I hate these things. It is those who command who give the orders. They are evil, evil." He repeated *schlecht, schlecht* (bad, bad) several times with an intense expression of rebellion and disgust. Then he passed his hand over Graziella's blond hair. She did not pull away, but smiled at him, reassured, while he sat on the steps of the stairs in a posture of profound sadness. It was past noon and I thought of offering him something to eat, a little soup, some fruit. He did not want to accept. "I have to go," he said getting up. "Stay a little longer," I implored. "As long as you are here, I think nothing will happen." In fact several cars had passed, and several groups of Germans who, seeing the sergeant seated on the steps, had gone ahead without stopping. At my plea, he went back to sitting down without answering, but he did not talk any more. The cold, impassive, lifeless mask had descended on his human face again.

At a certain point a soldier came to call him. "Now there is no more danger. We are going away," he said. He got back into the car, and he left again without a glance, without a goodbye.

After a while I went to take a walk around the villages close by. The Germans had really gone, leaving the town to summarily heal its wounds.

From a first approximate calculation, it seems that around seventy houses were burned, without being preselected, indiscriminately. That there were no spies in the town, as I had upheld, was demonstrated by the fact that not one house of a partisan had been touched. First they had burned the uninhabited houses that had been abandoned by the evacuees, after having emptied them of their contents, then those of the townspeople, here and there, capriciously, by chance. They had not found anything anywhere to justify the reprisal, which evidently had the simple goal of pillage and terrorism. In some places the Germans were brutal and ruthless, and would not let the terrorized women take anything away. One drove his sadism to the point of throwing into the flames a sack of meager scraps that an old woman had been able to drag out with difficulty. In other places, they had robbed what happened to be at hand, money and gold objects. In others still they were polite and lenient, as in my house. But even those who had not had their houses burned were devastated by the loss of the animals. The Germans had taken away all of them, cows, sheep, and mules, with difficulty, with force, because they did not want to go. They are animals who understand, *cônôscente* as they say here, attached to the owner who shares his stable and his labor with them in a brotherly way. Some turned back, despite the beatings, bellowing desperately, with an anguish that was almost human. The Cordolas' Martin, who was more than eighteen years old, succeeded twice in breaking the rope with which they dragged him, and in turning back, running, neighing, but they took him away all the same.[29] While Dralin told the story, his eyes filled with tears.

At Gran Borgata, Olimpia and her family were trying to put out the fire in a wing of their house, in order to save the main part. I too held the hose that drew water from the nearby stream. Suddenly, on the street above, I saw Ettore appear, with his knapsack on his shoulders. I blinked my eyes, thinking I was dreaming. Then I thought that, having heard the news about what had happened in Meana, worried about us, he had turned back, perhaps on foot. "What are you doing here?" I confronted him. "Why have you come back?" "I have not come back," he answered with his usual composure, "because I never left."

In the morning, at the station, they had stopped him together with about a dozen other departing travelers and, forming them into columns with the cows and the mules, they had brought them to Campo del Carro. They had passed in front of the *Municipio*, and they had seen the one who was hanged still hanging, with the bunch of flowers at his feet that no one had the courage to remove. Then they had shut all of them in the courtyard of a house to examine their papers and their gear. Ettore's papers are exemplary. "What do you have in your knapsack?" they asked while they opened it. "Dirty laundry," answered Ettore. "Lovely dirty laundry," commented the German, unfolding my mother's beautiful embroidered tablecloths, but then they shoved them back into the knapsack, and did not say anything more.

Then a sergeant approached Ettore (my husband's appearance is reassuring to everyone, even the Germans) to entrust him with the charge of accompanying a small herd of animals up to the station. But seeing that a mountain dweller, who was among those who were stopped with him, had winked, Ettore was able to get out of the task with the pretext, which was very true, that he had no experience with animals. The mountain dweller then offered himself enthusiastically. Yes, he had experience with animals, so much so that, yelling,

---

[29] Martin was a mule.

clamoring, and feigning the greatest zeal, he was able to scatter them into the surrounding woods before they reached their destination. I think that these are the only animals remaining in the entire town.

When he was finally released, he was about to set out toward the house when he saw Willy arriving between two Germans. "Leave him with me, I will watch this one," said a Fascist, taking him into his custody. The words were not very promising, but for the moment the one who had pronounced them confined himself to having the prisoner sit down on the steps of the tobacco shop. Ettore had left him there, after having furnished him with cigarettes.

At home, we found Paolo and Mario. From the height of the Truc they had seen the houses burning and the animals being taken away. (Paolo told me afterward about the anguish of Mario, who had raised his arms to the heavens, with a gesture of impotent anger, crying "Have mercy! Have mercy!") Then they had climbed up to the Montabone, where they had seen the Germans leaving, and returned home.

They had just finished telling the story when Willy appeared. Even he had been able to get away. Taking advantage of the momentary absentmindedness of his guardian, he had entered the store of the tobacconist, then gone through to the back room, and then out into the courtyard, from there into the fields, and onto a deserted street. No one had run after him.

Relieved of worry for him as well, we, all together, had that half hour of euphoria that always follows an escape from danger. Later I went down to Cantalupo, which had remained miraculously unharmed, perhaps because of all of the villages it is the one that looks the poorest, and which does not offer an opportunity for any spoils. Filomena accompanied me onto her threshing floor, where she showed me, from above, the houses that were burning below, near the station. She was crying, even if her house, even if her family were all safe. As at other times before, I had the profound sense of a fundamental fraternity.

9 August. After the preposterous blazing sun of the other day, it has been raining nonstop for two days, and the dense rain is raging on the barren ruins.

The Germans returned two times, not to carry out general actions but with the specific purpose of taking away someone who evidently had been denounced. Therefore spies do exist, but not here in Susa, and they do not know my family or me. The men who were arrested—who probably will be brought to Germany—are not partisans but poor, harmless people, among whom is a widower, the father of five children. Evidently it is a question of a private vendetta.

The young boy who was wounded, who had been handed over to the Germans by the priest, was hung yesterday from the balcony of his house in Santa Petronilla. The voluntary surrender and his physical condition did not matter. The brutes had not spared him, but while he was dying, he cried: "Long live the partisans!" The foolish priest has disappeared. If he holds his life dear, he will not be seen again in these parts.

Today I was in Susa, where, however, I was not able to find Ferrero. The Germans have gone away. The roundup is over. There is no precise news from the Chisone Valley yet, but it appears that there was a huge amount of damage there also.

Now it will be necessary to take an approximate census of those who suffered damages in Meana, and then provide some help, however modest, to those who are in the worst shape.

When I returned from Susa, I found a girl at my house, a cousin of Walter Fontan, who calls herself Walter too, a sort of showy beauty, with long, windswept hair and polished nails the color of blood. Yet she had both good will and courage. It was she who had helped almost all the Russians and Czechs escape from the railroad station.

Today the radio said that the Allies have liberated Florence.

11 August. They hanged Jervis. They arrested him in the Germanasca during the first days of March. Since that time there was a constant alternating of highs and lows, anguish and hope. At various times they had announced the imminent shooting. Then it appeared that they would free him, exchange him. Our men did everything they could to save him. But it was useless. They had killed him with some others. Nearby, on the ground, they found a page of his Bible on which at the last minute he had written words of comfort, incitement, and faith. Giorgio has been profoundly struck by it. "In addition to the rest, for me he has also been a friend," he told me, and his voice, usually so firm and ironic, was trembling. I do not know his wife, but I know that she is a strong and intelligent woman. He had three children.

Today I received news of Marisa Scala's arrest. It appears that already for some time now they have kept watch on her and followed her. Since she has come to my house several times, we cannot rule this out as a reason for the visit of the police a few days ago. Now she is in Via Asti.[30]

This evening, when I arrived in Meana, Paolo and Cesare came to meet me on the shortcut, having arrived today after an adventurous flight from the Chisone Valley. The roundup had been severe and crushing even if not particularly brutal, more like a real and true war than a "manhunt." Then there were the reprisals against the civilian population. The partisans, those that could, scattered here and there, in compliance with guerrilla tactics. Marcellin, with a good part of his men and weapons, has retreated into the Troncea Valley, where the Germans are still hot on his heels with nonstop raids. They put the

[30] The Nazi-Fascists transformed the prison on Via Asti into a place for interrogation and torture.

dogs into action, and it is these that they fear the most. Cesare, who is at the Triplex, has come up with others who have stopped at various places in the valley. He preferred not to go down to Oulx, where everyone knows him. He arrived here by way of Frais (where, half dressed as a soldier, he passed near a company of Fascists who did not say anything to him), safe and sound and just a little hungry.

13 August. Finally Maddalena succeeded in having me meet with Laghi.[31] We had a long meeting yesterday, in a wooded area near Urbiano Superiore. He seems to be a capable man, even if he has a healthy (!), very bourgeois fear of the word "politics." I do not believe that he understands the fundamental motives of our war, and our ideals horrify him. Nevertheless he fights the war and pays generously with his person (and also with his purse). Basically he has no liability other than being Jewish and, like thousands of others, he could have very well hidden in some cozy little corner, something that his money would have amply facilitated. Instead, he preferred to throw himself into the fray and organize a group of partisans in the Lanzo Valley. He resisted the roundups, passed by here with his men, and got a new group together. He goes on, and does not give up. All this renders him profoundly respectable. But he let off a lot of steam against Ferrero overtly, accusing him of having left him without money and without connections. I do not want to formulate rash judgments, but I am afraid that, for the most part, he is right. I promised him that from now on I would be in contact with him directly, and that as soon as possible I would bring Valle or someone else up in order to determine the position of his group within the general framework of the Piedmontese Regional Military Command.

At first he seemed a bit suspicious. "I do not want to be involved in politics," he continued to protest. I explained to him that in fact taking part in the GL formations did not signify joining a political party, either for himself or for his men. In the end he seemed convinced, and lapsed into confidences and sentiment. He recalled old memories and showed me a picture of his two children, who were very good-looking. The little girl's name was Stellina, and he wanted to name his formation "Stellina." "I would like to keep the name," he told me. I reassured him. Why change it? "Stellina," beyond being dear to him, is a name with good fortune. I left him reassured and convinced.[32]

[31] Maddalena Dufour was a laundress and a partisan *staffetta*.

[32] The Stellina Brigade formed part of the IV Alpine GL Division, which had approximately seven hundred men by the latter part of 1944, about 7.5 percent of all the GL formations in the region. See *Report on Conditions in Enemy-Occupied Italy*, no. 36 (27 January 1945); Italian Theatre Headquarters Psychological Warfare Branch, Unit 12, APO 512, Secret "D" Section, Occupied Italy; declassified; RG 331, 10,000/125; National Archive II, College Park, Maryland. The word "stellina" means "little star," and is also a term of endearment.

15 August. This morning Radio London gave us the news of the landing in Provence.

I do not want to attach too much importance to the matter, but certainly the battle, and with it the liberation, is approaching. What if it truly is the end? What if we do not have to face another winter of occupation?

We must calm down. We must not get our hopes up too much. The events of war do not depend on us. Rather, let's think about what we must do here. No matter how it goes, the most difficult, the hardest, has yet to come.

17 August. Yesterday, in Turin, seven alarms, and long trips, too many to count. I found Alberto Salmoni, he too having returned adventurously from the Chisone Valley. Even Bianca had her turn at a great adventure. When she went to Fenestrelle to see him, she had found herself in the midst of the roundup. In order to justify her presence and keep them from arresting her, the owner of the hotel had her pass for a temporary waitress who had taken over for the season. For three days, that is until they left, poor Bianca had to serve dinner and pour drinks for the Fascists and the Germans. Now Alberto would like to come with us into the Susa Valley.

I found Valle, and reported my meeting with Laghi to him. He will go up the day after tomorrow and I will accompany him to Urbiano.

18 August. This morning the weather was lovely. It was like living in a world that was all green, blue, and gold. On the other hand, from a material point of view, the situation was rather bleak because, since the flour had not arrived, there was not a crumb of bread in the entire town. What was more, there was no electricity. Therefore we had to light the fire and cook potatoes and *polenta* all the time.

Judge Pratis, a colleague of Giorgio and Sandro whose wife was in Susa, came to notify me that Maddalena was arrested, but it also seems that, given the very clever person she is, she already was able to escape.[33]

In the afternoon I went to Urbiano. I wanted to see Laghi, notify him of Valle's arrival, and make the final arrangements. But without Maddalena's valuable help, the matter was quite complicated. Laghi was not at Urbiano. Now he has gone up as far as Braida, a small group of *grange* where a type of headquarters exists, or so it seems. But even there I had to wait a while, because he was interrogating two loose girls, inhabitants of Urbiano suspected of espionage. The mother, who had also been taken away, waited with me, sharing confidences with me in the meantime. In fact her daughters were not spies. They went with the men (she said it just like this), and what was so bad about it? Girls

---

[33] Carlo Enrico Pratis was a magistrate and inspector for the Piedmontese Regional GL Command.

were made for this purpose. First there were the Germans and the Fascists, and they went with them. Now they were very willing to go with the partisans. They really were not doing anything bad.

After a while I saw the two girls arrive, accompanied by two partisans and by Laghi in person. The search that had been carried out at their house in the meantime had produced negative results, and they released them. "They are not spies," commented Laghi, "but girls without principles. Without precise political ideas," he emphasized maliciously.

We spoke briefly. Then two boys accompanied me to Urbiano, teaching me a useful shortcut.

19 August. Willy and Martino, whom I had summoned, arrived early. The representatives of various groups of our partisans met together in a woods that was not too far away. We waited for Valle, who arrived at noon, by car, with Sartirana and Grassini.[34] I already knew that Sartirana, the ex-mayor of Turin, was working with us, but it still made me laugh a little to see him at my house in Meana, in the clothes of a conspirator. Given the hour, despite my misgivings, I invited him to dinner with Grassini. He did not accept, saying that he would stop at La Giaconera, near Borgone, a place that I did not know, but that, so it seems, the gourmets knew. Evidently he made the right decision, because my meal, which ordinarily I put together as best I could, was not anything special, and I had the impression that not even Valle was very satisfied. He lit up for an instant when I announced dessert, but it was my usual dessert, made with a glass of yellow flour, one of white flour, one of milk and one of jam, without eggs and sugar. He ate a slice. "Do you like it?" I asked him. "Oh yes, it is *nutriente* (nutritious)," he answered. He refused to have more.

Then, after dinner, a long conversation with Martino and Willy. It was a question of entrusting the command of the Mattie and Meana groups to Martino, who had proven himself extremely well during the roundup, and who has the necessary experience and authority, while giving Willy the duty of official liaison between the various groups and those of the Command instead.

The Meanese problem was solved with the agreement between Willy and Martino, but the much more serious and difficult problem of the Susa and Moncenisio partisan bands remained. We needed to find a general commander who could not be Ferrero, since by now Laghi refused to have anything to do with him, and who on the other hand is too problematic. Nor could it be Laghi, who could not move from one part of the Valley to another and who, being on the slopes of the Rocciamelone, would find it difficult to remain in contact with the other groups. It was necessary to find a trustworthy person who was

---

[34] Ugo Sartirana, ex-mayor of Turin, and Luigi Grassini, former director of the Agenzia Stefani, both worked together with the partisans.

composed, not too willing to compromise, new, and therefore a stranger to the quarrels that naturally existed among the local groups. Finding him would not be easy. For a long time we racked our brains until Valle thought of one of his acquaintances, the land surveyor Chiapusso, a reserve captain employed at Cotonificio Val Susa who had, according to him, all the necessary qualities. It was a question of finding him and convincing him.[35]

The two of us went down to Susa on Mario's bicycle. After some research, we found the surveyor and explained the situation to him. He did not refuse, even if he did not seem enthusiastic. He explained his family situation, and imposed specific limitations on his possible activities. I liked him precisely for this moderation, this restraint, this not wanting to promise too much. We explained to him that his function would be essentially that of coordinator, and mediator. Martino on one side and Laghi on the other would take care of what is more properly known as action. His responsibility would be to represent an authority that everyone recognizes voluntarily, and that does not irritate anyone. After we clarified the situation, he accepted. At the end of the meeting, he had joined our "staff" with the name "Captain Longo."

Then Valle and I returned to Meana, partly on foot and partly by bicycle, as satisfied as if we had squared the circle. In reality, we had resolved, at least for the moment, a problem that seemed insoluble.

At home, Valle saw still more of our partisans, and conversed with them for a long time. His visit, his words, the sense that he was concerned about them, that an organization existed, and that this organization functioned, reassured, satisfied, and encouraged them.

Then came a long conversation with Paolo and Cesare about the possibility of groups in the Upper Valley. He approved the plan in general, and advised Paolo and Cesare to go into Martino's group for a while, to learn more and to be able to choose the individuals best adapted to the formation of new groups. This is very appropriate because of the fact that their stay here, in this town, can be dangerous, with the incessant movement and coming and going of armed partisans.

After supper, we wrote down and then typed the first report on the situation here for the Turin Command.

20 August. Today the "Stellina Division of Giustizia e Libertà" was born. It was not an easy thing to bring into existence. For around five hours, from eleven o'clock in the morning to four o'clock in the afternoon, Valle and I took turns listening to and countering Laghi, who talked almost uninterruptedly—an outburst against Ferrero, apolitical concerns, declarations of honesty and patriotic conviction, and the recalling of memories. Evidently he likes to hear

---

[35] Cotonificio Val Susa was a textile factory.

himself talk. On the other hand, it is difficult to make him conclude. With admirable patience and diplomacy, Valle succeeded. But there was a moment when I truly believed that he would lose his patience and spoil everything. For my part, since by this time I was beat, I threw myself down on the meadow and closed my eyes. Fortunately, right at that point, I heard shooting from the area of Chianoc. It was a false alarm, but it served to break the spell. A short time later, laboriously, they were able to conclude and even outline the act of incorporation of the division, saving what was important, ceding on the secondary points, and leaving the beloved name of "Stellina" on the formation.

The meeting took place at Braida. There is another base, higher up, at the hamlet of Micoletto, and another, even higher up, at Mompantero Vecchio, a short distance from the Colle della Croce di Ferro. I was able to appreciate the organization, which is fundamentally good, quite a bit better than the other day, when I had arrived in passing. Here we detect the hand of the man of experience, the businessman. An orderly room and an intendant's office, however rudimentary, are there. The rapport with the local organization is excellent, and supplies ensured. They have sufficient bread, flour, meat, and potatoes. The boys are good, nice, and on the whole seem to have affection for Laghi, who treats them with a certain tone that is half gentle and half authoritative, a bit like a parish priest and a bit like a teacher. Certainly it is an unusual formation, different from all the others. Nevertheless, it will be necessary to teach them some politics, a little at a time. Adjusting to the general tone, I said with a mischievous air that I was leaving, as if I was promising sweets to children if they were good, and that the next time I would bring a few newspapers. Laghi did not seem enthusiastic, but he did not dare say no.

When we returned to Meana, more tired from the chatter than from the road, we found the house full of people: Cesare's family, Anna and Paola Jarre, and Ferrero, who, probably having learned of the presence of Valle, just this once had come without making us look for him. This was clearly another delicate operation: explaining the new situation to Ferrero, and making him swallow without too much pouting his demotion from independent leader to being under the orders of "Captain Longo." I confess that I felt faint of heart at the thought of this new battle. I said hurriedly to Valle "I really do not feel like doing this. You attend to it." So in a cowardly way, even if with a very radiant and hospitable smile, I sent them together into my room. I left Cesare in Paolo's room in the arms of his family, and I took refuge in the kitchen to prepare tea with Paolo, Ettore, and the Jarre sisters. When I entered the room where I had left Valle and Ferrero with two propitiatory cups in my hands, I thought I would find them in who knows what state of heated discussion. Instead I saw them thrown across the bed, talking placidly, in a friendly fashion. From the expression on Valle's face I understood that the operation had been accomplished, and the tooth extracted without too much pain. Even if he felt some resentment, Ferrero is too polite to show it openly.

At a certain point, the Jarre girls and Cesare's family left. Instead, Ferrero lingered and seemed to want to stay for dinner. I invited him enthusiastically, knowing quite well how a respite around a table—even one that is not covered with much food—serves to placate spirits and solidify friendships. After a while, Willy and Martino arrived and, in homage to the same considerations, I invited them too. So the eight of us sat for dinner. Certainly it was not a great meal, but everyone was happy just the same. There was an uninterrupted and reciprocal exchange of courtesies and an enthusiastic praising of friends and acquaintances, near and far. Not one criticism, not one bit of gossip. Too good to be true; things that happen only when people have been previously quite well acquainted with one another. Anyhow, it was a true celebration of brotherly love, an orgy of generosity and noble sentiments. And we could not even blame the wine, the great pacifier of discords, because I only offered them fresh water.

Later other partisans, who had not seen Valle yet and wanted to meet him, arrived. Young Walter, who made a certain impression on him, came too.

Only late at night, when everyone had gone away, were we able to summarize the work of the day and congratulate each other. (Evidently the atmosphere of the celebration of brotherly love had affected us too.) Then, becoming sober and serious again, we dashed off the report, and we perfected the act of incorporation of "Stellina," which I will bring to Laghi tomorrow.

21 August. Valle left this morning. Walter arrived almost immediately, very excited. At Campo del Carro, there was a little truck from the Olivero and Fontana transportation firm, which had come to bring back to Turin the belongings of an evacuee, who by now prefers the risk of bombardments to that of retaliatory fire. Why not take the truck? A group of partisans had already gathered, armed, and the matter seemed very easy. I left again immediately with Paolo and Cesare, who returned a little while later. The evacuee had begged them to let him take away his belongings. (He was not a rich gentlemen, but a poor worker, and those few pieces of furniture were all he had.) On the other hand, the driver, showing understanding and sympathy for the partisans, had given them his word that he would return the next day with another truck, not one that had a gazogene converter like this one, but one that ran on gasoline, and was therefore much faster.[36] They had let him leave with this promise.

In the afternoon, I went to Urbiano and handed the act of incorporation over to Laghi. Then when I returned to Susa, I heard them say that the Germans

---

[36] Gasoline was scarce during World War II. A car with a gazogene converter used wood, coal, or some other type of fuel. The car ran by burning wood chips and coal in a water heater.

were establishing a command in Meana, which undoubtedly would make life much more complicated and difficult. If they do it soon enough, however, It appears that the Allies are advancing on all fronts.

23 August, Turin. The victories followed one another, nonstop. Radio London continues to give us good news uninterruptedly, just as the raucous voice of the loudspeakers of the regime used to harass us with a series of dismal news in the summer of 1940. Bordeaux, Bucharest, Grenoble, Paris. I felt my heart swell with a joy that was almost painful at the thought of the liberation of Paris. How I had suffered at her fall! It seemed that an entire world had collapsed. Perhaps it truly had collapsed. Today, liberated Paris cannot and must no longer be the Paris of yesterday, the one in whose intellectual atmosphere we had grown up, the one I had desired so much and loved so nostalgically. What will the Paris, or better yet what will the world, be that will come out of the torment of today?

For the entire night, I stupidly ruminated on these thoughts without being able to close my eyes. I felt an anguish that was almost panic. I am afraid of this tomorrow that will be so different, so hostile perhaps to too many things I had believed in. I understand that it must be so. I am ready to give my life so that it will be so. But will I have the strength to live here, in this "new order" of tomorrow? Will I learn how to remake myself completely—blood, instincts, thoughts, and dreams—so that I will be able to breathe freely in the new atmosphere without feeling like a nostalgic, forlorn survivor?

This morning I prepared clothing for Paolo and Cesare, because they will join Martino's partisan band tomorrow. Then I went down to the station to go to Turin. But the trains did not leave. With the approach of the war's front (for two days we could hear the cannons boom from the other side of the Alps), bombardments of the lines of communication are more and more frequent, and the railroad has ceased to function.

Then I went down to Susa, where I took Silvana's bicycle and left.[37] The alarms followed one another, and the bombardments echoed among the mountains. At Borgone, I had to make a detour because the bridge had been blown up. I saw the holes on the road and in the nearby fields that the bombs had produced. Suddenly the airplanes swooped and the people threw themselves down on the grass to hide. I continued foolishly, unperturbed, without ever getting off the bicycle. As always happens when I do not pay attention to something dangerous, I arrived in Turin unharmed.

26 August, Meana. Pillo, who decided to come into the mountains with us, arrived in Rivoli on the tram, which fortunately is functioning again. Ettore

---

[37] Silvana Roglio, Teta's daughter.

and I followed by bicycle, between an unrelenting alternation of torrents of rain and pale clear spots. From Sant'Antonino on up, we began to encounter trucks loaded with Germans and with French *pétainistes*, evidently fleeing ahead of the pursuit of the Allies.[38] Naturally the situation made me rejoice, but the unusual movement on the main road worried me. I was afraid that surveillance would be increased and that Pillo's youthfulness would make someone suspicious, but no one said anything. Only between Bruzolo and Bussoleno, at the height of the bridge that had been blown up by the partisans, around which there were squads of Germans and Fascists working, did a German noncommissioned officer yell something incomprehensible at us, accompanied by threatening gestures. Perhaps he wanted us to stop and work with them. We continued unmoved, without either speeding up or slowing down and without responding, as if we had not understood that he was talking to us. No one took the trouble to follow us.

Having arrived happily in Meana, we found Paolo and Cesare, who had come down to get weapons and other things. I was happy about it, even if the presence of the three boys in the house was basically not very prudent.

In the afternoon I went to Urbiano with money and letters for Laghi, but I was not able to see him. His group has been attacked by fascist forces (they say there are three hundred men) commanded by Germans. They were fighting in Sevine. To try to reach the place of the battle was useless, and what is more, unwise. Therefore I waited in the vicinity of Urbiano, in anticipation that someone would come down. But I did not see anything. Nevertheless, we could hear shooting from time to time. After a while, having made arrangements with one of Longo's cousins, I decided to return home.

28 August. While I went down to Urbiano twice yesterday, I was not able to learn anything precise. They were saying the strangest, vaguest, and most contradictory things. Everyone was dead, the Fascists had been made prisoners, no one had returned any longer, and the Germans were preparing to send reinforcements. But, I do not know why, I had the impression that things had not gone so badly. In fact this morning Silvio came to my house with excellent news.

On Saturday afternoon a squad of partisans, on guard near Urbiano, had seen the Fascists (around two hundred men under the command of German officers) set out in force up the mountain. They had anticipated them, warning Laghi and the other groups that were higher up. These groups were placed

---

[38] *Pétainistes* were those individuals who were loyal to Marshal Henri-Philippe Pétain, a military and political leader during World War I, who headed the Vichy French government, which collaborated with the Germans during World War II. After the war, Pétain was convicted as a traitor and sentenced to death, a sentence that was commuted to life imprisonment by Charles De Gaulle. Pétain died in 1951.

strategically and were able to surround the enemy, who, without becoming aware of their movements, had established themselves in the Grange Sevine. The partisans were fewer in number than the Fascists, and much more poorly armed. Laghi had sent a *staffetta* to ask the Garibaldini groups from Chianoc for help, but he attacked without waiting for them. The problem consisted of forcing the Fascists to surrender without entering into open battle with them wherein, besides the inferiority of our men, there would have been grave danger to the families of the mountain folk (almost all women and children), whom the Fascists had shut in the *grange* with themselves, and whom they certainly would not have hesitated to use as a defense and a shield. With some shots opportunely fired and some shrewd movements, Laghi was able to make the enemy believe that the attacking forces were much more superior than they were in reality. There were angry negotiations, orders, and counterorders, and dramatic moments, but in the end they obtained the surrender. They only gave a few Germans permission to leave. The Fascists were all taken prisoner. When the Garibaldini arrived, everything was over. They only helped to sort out the prisoners and the weapons. The booty must have been sizeable, and it would be a very good thing if Laghi had given us some automatic weapons, which we lack entirely, and which are indispensable for any isolated attack or act of sabotage.

I wrote to Laghi about this, and I delivered the letter to the very trustworthy Silvio, along with the communications from Turin.[39] Naturally for now the partisans had not returned to their usual bases, but were scattered here and there. It appears that Laghi is in the vicinity of Mompantero Vecchio.

Then I gave a hand to the boys who have been creating a little newspaper for two days (typed, of course) under the title *Tempi Nuovi* (New Times). It gives news of the war and of the partisan situation, and tries to explain, in terms that are simple and accessible, the reasons for the war, and also what must be done tomorrow so that today's sacrifice will not be in vain. In the evening, they posted them in the various villages, and up until now no one has dared to tear them down. This evening I went with Paolo to post them in isolated and forgotten Arnodera as well. Then I went to look for Marcella, whose house and belongings had been burned and who has two small children, and I brought her a little aid from the Gruppi di difesa, which she welcomed with grateful enthusiasm, pointing out to me other houses similar to hers, which I promised to provide for. The lack of any detestable greed on the part of these people was remarkable. They accepted the help with gratitude, but without any obsequiousness, and above all without egotism. They think of others as well. "We were created to help one another," they say.

---

[39] Silvio Verquera worked together with the partisans from Susa.

29 August, Turin. The boys have left, and I prepared for the usual thorough cleaning, right in the midst of which Pratis surprised me, disheveled and dirty, with the latest news. This confirmed the earlier news, which they are already calling "The Battle of the Sevine" in the valley, even if in reality it was not a great battle.

Walter came also to call Ettore, who returned a short while later with an amazing piece of news. The driver from Olivero and Fontana had arrived with the truck that runs on gasoline to hand it over to the partisans. He had kept his promise.

Then, having left by bicycle and having found a train in Condove, we reached Turin without any mishaps.

31 August. Many women, many men. In order not to travel so much on foot, I have resurrected my old bicycle and even use it for Turin, though I do not have permission for it. If they sequester it from me, I will not lose anything important. I found Valle again and, besides giving him the latest news, introduced him to Alberto, who would come into the mountains with us.

1 September, Meana. My use of my bicycle in the city was of short duration. Following an attempt yesterday that someone on a bicycle carried out against a German soldier, bicycle traffic has been prohibited.

Today, Ettore and I had to leave for Meana with Alberto, and since in the best of hypotheses the train would only go as far as Sant'Antonino, we had to take the bicycles. But how to bring them to the station? The only solution was to transport them in a handcart. For this Espedita's father gave us a helping hand.

In Sant'Antonino, when we got off the train, we mounted the bicycles and arrived in Meana, which was already dark. We thought we would find the house empty, and instead there were the boys, in excellent spirits. In agreement with Martino, they had decided to move into the Valley to form the famous local groups there. Cesare knows the individuals from the Susa Valley who had gone with Marcellin, and who now in all probability were prudently hidden at home. Alberto's arrival was welcomed with joy. He too knows Marcellin's men; he was a captain in their formations. His presence will be very useful, not to mention the fact that, since he is a little older than the others (he was born in 1918), he can have the necessary authority over everyone. They continued to make plans for the entire evening.

2 September. Today I accomplished a modest undertaking, which is nonetheless one after my own heart.

This morning Silvio came with a letter from Laghi, who, while he gave me a receipt for the money and letters I had sent to him, communicated to me that he had left a Tommy gun in Braida for our group. Truly we had hoped for more, but a Tommy gun is still valuable. Therefore I decided to go and get it in the afternoon. Bringing it from one place to another in the Valley, through Susa, represented a problem, but I knew that one way or another we would resolve it.

At Braida, which we reached through the pouring rain, there was a group of partisans, created from the most audacious and trustworthy of the entire formation, among whom was the exceptional, honest, and level-headed Carletto from Exilles, and a handsome agreeable fellow with a bandaged head that the others call "Testa 'd gis."[40] They were a bit annoyed by the order to hand over the Tommy gun to me (the almost amorous jealousy that these boys have for their weapons is strange), but when the two of them recognized me as the mother of Paolo—with whom they had participated last autumn in the failed attempt to blow up the bridge at Exilles—and learned that the Tommy gun was for him, the distrust streaked with rancor changed into enthusiastic consensus. If they had dared, perhaps they would have given me something else. Nevertheless, they promised me my own personal revolver.

Meanwhile Ettore dismantled the weapon as best he could, but the barrel was still terribly long and difficult to hide. Luckily, given the rain, I had the famous "Loden" cape on my shoulders, which had been the joy and pride of my adolescence. I could hide the Tommy gun under there, but the cape was short and the bottom stuck out of it. I also had an old cloth purse, which I usually use for shopping. I shoved the bottom in it, thus covering up the part that stuck out from the cape, and as the partisans crossed their fingers, we left.

At the entrance to Susa, I sent Ettore ahead so that he could give me a sign if he saw anything worrisome. I followed him at some distance. We passed in front of the barracks, the cafe full of Germans, and the checkpoints, until we reached the shortcut for Meana with a sigh of relief. I had just gone beyond the turn that then hid me from the eyes of the last Germans on guard when, perhaps because I was anxious to go faster, I slipped in the mud and slid clumsily. The perforated barrel of the Tommy gun came out at least an inch, tearing my precious cape at the shoulder. I looked around. The vineyards were deserted. I could not help but think about what would have happened if I had slipped two minutes before. The boys certainly would not have had their Tommy gun, and it would have been a real shame, given the joy with which they had welcomed it and had begun to clean it and watch over it!

When I got home, I washed off the mud and fixed the Loden garment as best I could. After dinner, they made precise plans. Tomorrow morning, Cesare and Pillo will go to Casette and bring newspapers and other things and make the final arrangements. But Paolo and Alberto will go to conduct an inspection

---

[40] In Piedmontese dialect, "testa 'd gis" means literally "head of plaster," but can be translated as "hard-headed."

along the railroad to look for the most suitable place to derail the military train while it is in transit during the night. After they make the strike, they will head in the direction of the Upper Valley at dawn. Next Saturday one of them will return here to give and receive news, if possible. If not, they will notify us and we will go to meet them.

Overall the news is good. The Allies have broken through the Gothic line.

4 September. Yesterday I went back and forth to Susa several times to do various errands, and when I returned home, I found that the boys had already eaten dinner and Paolo was washing his feet. "Caught in the act!" commented Alberto jokingly.

It had gotten dark by now and soon we left with the new Tommy gun and what was necessary for derailing the train. We did not know exactly at what hour it would pass, but by now it was certain that no more civilian trains would pass by before dawn. We had to make the preparations quickly in order not to miss the strike.

Having reached the point that Paolo and Alberto had chosen the other morning, near Crossing Keeper's Cabin Number 40, Cesare and Pillo stood guard with weapons at the two opposite sides. In the meantime, I kept watch on the path that came out of the woods. The moonlight was splendid, even too splendid for us. The stretch of railroad was isolated between two tunnels and above an escarpment, but at any moment, on one side of the tunnel or the other, a patrol of Germans on an inspection tour could appear. I gave a start more than once when I noticed a shadow, which turned out to be that of a tree moved by the wind, or heard the rustling of a wild animal. After a few minutes, which seemed eternal to me, the work was finished, and I saw Alberto and Paolo approaching, whom Pillo and Cesare joined immediately. Together we withdrew to the shadow of the nearby woods, where we could overlook the street without being seen, in expectation.

We stretched out on the ground. I curled up with Paolo in his long cloak. I felt so secure and happy next to him, and there was a silence in the night that was so sweet that I forgot the anxiety of what was about to happen and I dozed off easily. When I awoke the moon had set and the sky was full of stars. Suddenly I saw one fall, furrowing the sky with a streak of light. I thought of a wish to make: that the strike go well, and that the boys be able to form partisan bands.... Today we can only wish and hope for these little things, specific and immediate. We do not have the courage—perhaps due to a kind of superstition—to hope for big and important things: the end of the war, the safety of people dear to us....

Paolo pulled himself up to sit down (it was his movement that awakened me), and I felt a heightened tension in him. I pricked up my ears too, and seemed to hear something like a roar approaching. "The train?" I asked in a whisper. "No, they are cars," answered Paolo. Meanwhile even the others had moved. The roar of the motors was strong and distinct by now. Prudently we came out at the escarpment. On the street right under us a line of trucks loaded with Germans that had come from Oulx was advancing. Their excited, guttural voices reached us through the nocturnal silence. "They are going away, the Allies are advancing! I said softly with a mixed sense of apprehension and joy. "Um!" said Paolo, dubious.

I looked at my watch. It was two o'clock, and useless for so many of us to remain on guard. Alberto and Paolo would stay. Cesare and Pillo would come home with me and at dawn they would move, with their knapsacks, into the vicinity of Fontanino where, after the train passed, the other two would join them. Together they would leave for the Upper Valley, without returning to the house any more.

I set out through the woods and vineyards with Pillo and Cesare. Suddenly Cesare disappeared, but he rejoined us quickly with his hands filled with bunches of grapes. "They are already ripe!" he said in a tone of boyish satisfaction.

At home, I had just gone to sleep when I awakened all of a sudden. I thought I heard the same strange enemy voices that I had heard a little while ago from the height of the railroad. Had it been a dream? No, because Ettore had heard them too. Without turning on the light, I left the door ajar and peeped prudently. On the meadow in front of the house, dark forms were stirring and sharp orders could be heard, as well as the clamor of weapons and materiel. Evidently it was a question of a company of Germans who must have come to Meana to pitch camp for the night, as they had warned me in Susa in the afternoon. Who could imagine that, with so many places, they would come right under the windows of my house?

The situation was not pleasant. Certainly the Germans had not come for us, but at any moment they could come into the house on any pretext, however innocent. What would happen if they found the two boys with their knapsacks ready, and filled with hand grenades, fuses, and explosives? The most rudimentary prudence forced us to send them away immediately. I awakened them very gently, trying not to frighten them, but they were far from being frightened! They were so profoundly immersed in the blessed sleep of those of their age that it took me a good five minutes to force them to open their eyes and explain to them that they had to leave. Pillo fell back to sleep three times. Cesare began to moan and complain that he had a stomach ache. "You ate too many unripe grapes!" I told him, "but now is not the time to feel sick." Thank God they woke up, got dressed, and took their knapsacks, still with the dreamy, automatic movements of children who were forced to get up earlier than usual, which gave me a feeling of tender pain. Then silently they went out on the terrace, and from there they jumped into the meadow opposite the one where the Germans were. Ettore lowered the four knapsacks and then he too went down with them. "They are too loaded down and too sleepy," he said. "I would rather bring them to safety." He returned quite soon, after having accompanied them to Fontanino, and having left them to continue to sleep in a dismantled *grangia*.

After a few hours, the Germans cleared away the camp and left. What they had come to do, I do not know.

This morning, while I was going down to Susa, I heard the alarm wail and the airplanes buzz. Immediately the German antiaircraft battery, placed near the shortcut, began to shoot furiously. But soon I also heard stronger explosions, very close by. The airplanes were bombing. As soon as the antiaircraft battery quieted for a moment, I got back on the road and, when I reached Susa, the alarm was practically over. It was the first time that they had actually bombed and, after they heard the alarm, the people, accustomed to seeing the airplanes pass without worrying about them, had panicked a little. But the dominant sentiment was bitterness toward the Germans. If there had not been antiaircraft fire, they would not have bombed, they said, and they were not wrong. In reality there was not much damage. The bombs had fallen mostly in the fields. Susa is not an interesting target, being cut off from the principal railroad line of Modane, and its industries (Assa and Cotonificio) serve little purpose for the war.[41]

Then I went down to Braida to the home of Laghi, whom I had not seen since the "Battle of the Sevine," and with him I put together laboriously, with frequent interruptions, a report to bring to Turin. When I was about to leave with the precious booty (around a dozen typed pages), Carletto ran after me to hand over the revolver he had promised me the other day, a Beretta for which, with touching thoughtfulness, they had made a coarse case out of leather.

6 September, Turin. Today, between one trip and another, a strange telephone call from Valle. I ran to the appointment. A friend had warned him that a denunciation regarding my activities in Meana and Susa had arrived at the police headquarters in Vercelli. The person is well informed because in the denunciation it also mentions my relationship with Jarre and Barberis, albeit with misspelled names. I truly do not understand who it could be. Furthermore, why at Vercelli? Had the same denunciation arrived at the police headquarters in Turin? I do not believe so, because probably I would have known. Nevertheless, it is something old, and the alarm does not seem to me to be such that it will constrain me from leaving the house. At worst I will try to have people come as little as possible.

9 September, Meana. This morning I got off the train at Sant'Antonino, where we had to solve a difficult problem. There were four of us: Bianca, Paola Jarre,

---

[41] Assa was a steel mill.

Ettore, and I, and we had only three bicycles. After a careful examination of the situation, Ettore attached his very heavy knapsack onto Paola's shoulders and carried Bianca on the bar of his own bicycle.

The trip was agreeable. Twenty-five kilometers on the bar are not very comfortable, and Bianca tried to soften the improvised seat by adding a pair of pants that she was bringing to Alberto. Thus from time to time Ettore reached out his hand to see if she was still there and said laughing, "I wanted to see if you still had the pants." The sun was hot, which made him sweat profusely. Paola was also sweating, with the heavy knapsack. I, who was carrying only myself and a modest little knapsack, was sweating too. Bianca was not sweaty but sore, but this did not prevent her from keeping herself happy the entire time with little stories and songs.

At home no one was there. Right after dinner, I went down to Susa and back up to Urbiano, but was not able to find Laghi. At Braida they told me that he was at Micoletto. At Micoletto they were expecting him at any moment; he had gone to a meeting with the Garibaldini bands of Chianoc. I waited for him for another two hours, entertaining myself with the boys in the meantime. (There was also a German prisoner, Walter, who seemed very happy to stay with the partisans.) Then I decided to leave and return the next day.

At Susa I went to look for Ferrero, whom I had not seen since the evening of the celebration of brotherly love. By means of the mysterious gestures of his relatives, I think I learned that he had left to carry out the sabotage at the bridge at Villafranca d'Asti, which he had been thinking about for some time.

When I went back up to Meana, with joy and relief I found Paolo and Alberto, satisfied with the work they had accomplished. After they left here, after they had notified Gran Prà, they arrived at the Grange del Seuil, where Cesare was determined to find a certain Carnino, a partisan with him in the Chisone Valley, who had to be the way to find all the others again. Therefore they headed for his *grangia*, where they found his father and mother. They swore that they did not know the young man they were talking about at all; on the contrary, they had never even heard his name. While they were talking like this, they saw several young men approaching, with guns aimed. But quite quickly one of them threw his gun away and hurried to embrace Cesare: it was Carnino himself, the young man that the father and mother said they did not know. The misunderstanding was cleared up quickly. "My" Tommy gun, with which Paolo had decked himself, had made them be mistaken for Fascists who had come to drive out the partisans. Hence the negative responses of the parents, while the young men, who had quickly gone into the garden, got ready to attack the "enemy." When they recognized Cesare and all fear disappeared, everything was immediately "joy and festivity." They offered them something to eat and a place to sleep, and gave them the information they requested. As predicted, the local partisans, when they returned from the Chisone Valley, had hidden their own weapons with jealous care, and were waiting for a good time to reorganize. Therefore they welcomed the idea of constructing a group under the command of Cesare and his friends enthusiastically.

Having gotten off to a good start like this, in the last few days they had truly worked quickly and well. They had found a headquarters in the Gran Bosco between Salbertrand and Oulx, not too comfortable judging from the descriptions, but quite safe. They had personally gone to look for the scattered partisans one by one, and they had reunited and organized them. The group is virtually formed. The weapons are sufficient. Providing foodstuffs, being a matter of local items, does not seem to be difficult. Extensive opportunities for action are opening before them.

10 September. I went to Laghi's with Paolo, who wanted to report to him about the work he had accomplished, and announce the construction of a new group that in all respects must be placed within the "staff" of the division. The visit lasted practically all day. Between one conversation and another, people continued to come: businessmen and directors of the factories of Susa, whom Laghi was able to make help him with the reassuring air of a *persona per bene* (good person). Barberis also came, with whom we discussed the creation of socialist Matteotti partisan groups in the area.[42]

13 September, Turin. Terrible news. Lisetta was taken in Milan by the Koch Band, and she is in the gloomy country cottage at Via Paolo Uccello where so many dreadful things happen.[43] Only two days ago I had received a card in which, with her usual carefree simplicity, she spoke about her life in Milan, the number of cigarettes Vittorio smoked, and the baby she was expecting in three months. Knowing that she is in those hands is frightful.

15 September. News from Lisetta. It appears that up until now they have not done anything serious to her, and that she is behaving stupendously. Despite the threats and the slaps, she did not reveal her own address until she rightly believed that Vittorio had understood, and had gone to a safe place. Nevertheless we do not know what they might do to her from one minute to the next. Certainly it is not a place suitable for a woman in that condition.

---

[42] By 1944, four principal partisan bands existed in the Piedmont region: the Garibaldini (Communists), the Matteotti (Socialists), the Giustizia e Libertà or GL (Actionists), and the Autonomi (usually Christian Democrats or Liberals). These partisan bands tended to occupy different areas, a likely reason for the relative lack of disagreements among the partisan formations. For example, the Garibaldini were active in the Langhe region south of Turin and the Autonomi were prevalent southwest of Turin in the area around the town of Oulx. Three of these four partisan bands existed in the Susa Valley.

[43] La Banda Koch was a specific division of the Republic of Salò that specialized in torture.

In those days knowing she was in danger made me furious, which resulted in increased activity. I cannot say how many people I saw, and how many steps I took.

16 September, Meana. On the train up to Sant'Antonino, with Ettore; then by bicycle up to Urbiano, and from there on foot up to Micoletto. But Laghi was at Mompantero Vecchio. We were already about to get ready to face a long climb when Giôanin, Maddalena's brother, arrived, who, according to the orders he received, sent for Laghi and gave us something to eat in the meantime. This Giôanin, whose age is not easily definable—between thirty and forty years old—has a peculiar face, like the people from the Susa Valley, with rough, pronounced facial features like those of the primitive figures of the crèche scene. The constant, unbroken gestures of his very dark eyes and his large, witty mouth accentuate his marionettelike features. Highly devoted to Laghi, he engaged us in a long conversation about the virtues of the commander. Then, winking cunningly, he told us about several tricks he had played on the Germans with his expression of simpleminded kindness.[44]

Then Laghi arrived, accompanied by Captain Angelini and a lieutenant.[45] I delivered money, letters, and newspapers in abundance to them, and a good number of badges ("So many red ones!" said Laghi, turning up his nose), and we chatted for a long time.

Then, having gone down to Susa, I saw Pratis and Barberis, and we climbed up to Meana in the nightfall. Naturally the house was dark and empty. Everything was in order as I had left it: no unmade beds, dirty kitchen utensils, ashes on the table, or clothing in all the corners. I felt an acute nostalgia for the boys, for their noise and their disorder, and for their blessed dirt. But I consoled myself thinking that I would be with them again tomorrow.

19 September, Turin. The day before yesterday, Sunday, having left Susa around ten in the morning, in the rain, we arrived in Oulx after one o'clock, and it was still raining. It took us around double the calculated time, but the incline of more than five hundred meters is quite difficult for me and, especially on certain stretches near Exilles, I was terribly fatigued. Without the frequent help of Ettore, who gave me benevolent "stimuli" in the form of energetic pushes on my back, and who carried my bicycle on stretches where we were forced to go on foot, I do not know if I would have made it.

Cesare's father came to accompany us as far as Montfol, where the boys were. It was no longer raining, but the sky was still dark and the atmosphere

---

[44] Giôanin (Giovanni Dufour) was a farmer who collaborated with the partisans.

[45] Captain Angelini (Angelo Andreis) was an office worker and chief of staff of the IV Alpine Division of GL.

oppressive and menacing. We had almost arrived when I saw a big bear with a long beard, the hair of a sheep, and a long gun coming to meet us. It was Paolo, whom I almost did not recognize, he was so tanned and seemed so big and bearded. Soon Pillo and Cesare also arrived and, at the end of the climb, in a meadow, there was Alberto, engaged in a discussion with about twenty partisans. The boys quickly brought me up to date on the situation. While they were forming their group, Patria, a young man from Exilles who had been with Marcellin, was doing the same thing.[46] Now his men had come from Sauze to cart off sugar and other foodstuffs and above all wine from the stores. Naturally our boys, who up until now had not carted off anything—not wanting, until it was absolutely indispensable, to burden the civilian population of the area even minimally—had protested and made them restore the sugar and the rest, but they had encountered great resistance regarding the wine. (For these mountain folk, wine is a fundamental necessity.) It is true that it is a question of wine taken from the hotels, and therefore its loss does not affect individual families. But then, our partisans objected, if this wine is confiscated, we who are from the area should take it, not you who come from the outside. And so the animated discussion over this point dragged on. When he saw us, Alberto called Ettore for help, relying on his dignified appearance, on his eyeglasses, and above all on the mysterious authority with which he clothed him, introducing him as an emissary from the "Turin Committee."

We left the two of them in the clutches of the litigants and, guided by Cesare's father, we retired to the shelter of a *grangia* inhabited by people he knew, and who gave us warm milk and the comfort of a nice fire. The son of the owner of the house, Sergino, a young boy with a face that was intelligent and true, showed us his paintings and drawings. From his observations and conversation, I had the impression that the partisan battle was for him—and, let's hope, also for the other children from these mountains—a positive experience. Then I took out the newspapers I had brought, and the badges, which were distributed and welcomed immediately, with childlike festivity.

Then Alberto and Ettore arrived, happy to have resolved the question of the wine to everyone's satisfaction. I noted that Alberto did not have any shoes, and asked him why. He answered that they hurt him (in fact, they were not his, they were Valle's shoes, which, God forgive me, I had given him without even asking permission from the owner, seeing that he needed them) and he had entrusted them to a local shoemaker so that he would enlarge them. Meanwhile he traveled through the woods and fields that were drenched with rain with a pair of big socks, which he defined as *calze di viaggio* (travel socks).

---

[46] Patria was a surveyor and commander of the Autonomous brigade in the Dora Valley.

It had gotten late and begun to rain again. Cesare's father returned to Oulx and we moved toward Sauze, where, at the Savoia Hotel, we could stop and converse easily. Whoever saw us on that mountain path, in the rain, in the impending evening, would have considered us a strange cortège: Ettore and I with our city clothes, Alberto with his "travel socks," Cesare with an old Alpine hat and a long Model '91 gun, Pillo with his torn trousers, limping because of a recent fall, and Paolo with his sheeplike hair and the Tommy gun.

At Sauze, in the cozy, comfortable room of the Savoia, we examined the situation, which looked good and promising, notwithstanding the creation of the so-called competing group, with whom it is simply a question of maintaining a good rapport and organizing common actions. We penned the act of incorporation of the group—consisting of about thirteen points—which I would type in Oulx the next day, and bring to Laghi and the Turin Command.

Right then Radio London gave us excellent news: the liberation of Viareggio and the landing in Holland. Unrestrainedly optimistic, I continued to repeat, "You will see that within two weeks, a month at the most, it will be all over, and you can return home." The boys, even if they were not perfectly convinced, played along with the game. We talked about planning a marvelous Christmas meal, one that would satisfy everyone's tastes. After this parenthesis of hope, I felt sad that the boys, who had all more or less caught cold or suffered from rheumatism, had to take the street up to Montfol again in the rain, and travel for a long time in the dampness of the Gran Bosco, in order to find their "den" again in the dark, which only Paolo would be able to track, thanks to his mysterious sense of direction. Therefore I convinced the owner of the hotel to let them sleep there too. Certainly it gave them great satisfaction to find, after so many days of the den, real beds with clean linens and embroidered pillowcases with very sweet sayings like *Dormi bene* (sleep well), *Sogni d'oro* (dreams of gold), *Angelo mio* (my angel), or *Amore* (love), which naturally, the next morning, bore the imprints of their heads, not entirely clean.

Then yesterday morning, after having had breakfast all together while Radio London broadcast songs (among which were "Amore, amore, amor" and another that had for a refrain "That's love, love, love"), Ettore and I went down to Oulx. The sky was still dark, but for the moment it was not raining. At Oulx, I went to Attorney Odiard's place to type the report: a gorgeous old building, with an austere library full of books with eighteenth-century bindings that, notwithstanding my curiosity and nostalgia, I did not even have time to browse.[47]

When, having finished writing, I returned to Cesare's house, where Ettore was waiting for me, it was almost noon. We left, but just outside of Oulx one of the tires of my bicycle began to go flat. Even though Ettore reinflated it, it

---

[47] Giulio Odiard was an attorney and representative of the Action Party in the Cln of Oulx.

continued to deflate every five minutes, rendering it impossible to go on, so that, after several useless attempts, Ettore carried me on the bar of his bicycle, which he drove with one hand while he towed my bicycle with the other—a very comfortable system of travel and above all very safe on a slope, with brakes that were less than mediocre. At Exilles, notwithstanding our inquiries, we were not able to find either a bicycle repairer or something to eat, nor in Chiomonte, which was chock full of Germans. But there a fellow gave Ettore a small piece of rubber and a little adhesive, with which he began to try to repair the flat tire under a shelter where a German was shaving. I stood next to him to shelter myself (it had begun to rain again in torrents), and in the meantime I looked at the German, who, when he finished shaving, put his razor away, washed the mess tin, and arranged his things with a silent bourgeois orderliness, heedless of the fun some little boys were making of him. Timid at first, then encouraged by his lack of reaction, they grew bolder, becoming obstinate and annoying. "Raus!" the German yelled suddenly with a ferocious voice, and then turned to us laughing. He also had the appearance of an honest man, but I could not return his smile. The children had run away, breaking up, and I felt acute, excessive pain—for their present fear and even more for their subconscious arrogance of a little while before. I thought about Sergino again, and about the other young boys from up there, so openly and simply fraternal with the partisans. I weighed the difference. No, evidently the Occupation was not an educational experience.

As soon as Ettore had finished repairing the tire, we left, but after a few hundred meters—perhaps it was the fault of the adhesive, of the instruments used, or of who knows what other weird contraption—the tire began to deflate, just like before, and we had no other solution but to resume the not-very-satisfying system we had used previously.

It was almost four o'clock when we arrived at Susa, dripping wet, starving, and exhausted. In the always secure haven of Teta's home we found the usual solace. She sent for Pratis and Longo, to whom we handed over the report to bring to Laghi, and to whom I entrusted my bicycle so that they could have it repaired for me.

Around five o'clock we left again. It was no longer raining, the bicycle was running like a charm, and we truly thought that our adventures were over, at least for the day.

But no. At Sant'Antonino, we waited for the train for a long time. The cafe at the station was full of Germans, they too waiting for the train. Evidently they had drunk a little too much of the abominable Marsala—the only drink that was available—and under their usual impassive and mechanically ferocious mask, their intimate, raw humanity made its way. They wanted to fraternize with everyone. They offered their bread and their things. They showed photographs of their wives and children. Since there was someone in the room who played a few notes of a tune on the accordion, they wanted him to play, and they began to dance awkwardly among themselves. At a certain point they even began to sing the "Internazionale." But their gaiety remained without joy, their cordiality without response, as if an invisible barrier of fear and inescapable bitterness kept them isolated.

It was past eight when someone came to notify us that the train would not leave that evening. By now it was too late to reach Turin by bicycle before the curfew, and yet I really did not feel like spending the night in the station in the company of the Germans. Therefore we decided to continue as far as Condove, where we would ask Sergio's parents, who had already welcomed me the year before, for hospitality.

At Condove, we stopped to eat something in an inn where we were obviously the only occasional patrons, and where the owner was in a great hurry to send us away. I do not understand why. We were not even outside the door when we heard the static screeches of a radio with which they were searching for stations. It was the hour for Radio London and they did not want to lose the connection; nor, on the other hand, did they trust listening to it in the presence of two strangers who could be Fascists, *agents provocateurs*, or spies.

Sergio's parents hosted us with simple cordiality. In the morning the odyssey was finally over. It was no longer raining. On the contrary, the sun was just about to come out, and the train brought us punctually to Turin, where I began to see people immediately, among whom was a certain Max, captain of the U.N.P.A., who agreed to represent the Action Party in the Cln of Susa. He seems like a discreet individual, and the U.N.P.A. barracks will be an excellent and safe address.[48]

Good news. Frida, who was arrested in the Pellice Valley and brought to Via Asti, has been freed. To offset this, bad news. They have arrested Marta, the Communist from the Gruppi di difesa.[49]

20 September, Turin. It rained all day, and I did not have a moment of peace.

Among other things I went to the Lancia factory, where an employee who was a native of Urbiano wanted to introduce me to a very important man from whom we hope to obtain some financial assistance. To the extent that the Allies are advancing, the industrialists are becoming afraid and are putting their hands in their purses, and it is not bad to take advantage of it.

---

[48] Franz De Marchi (Max), a businessman and commander of the U.N.P.A. (Unione Nazionale Protezione Antiaerea or National Union for Anti-aircraft Protection) of Susa, worked together with the partisans.

[49] Marta (Teresa Testa) was a tailor and representative of the Communist Party in the Gruppi di difesa.

At home I found Signora Pajetta, whom I had not seen in many years, since the time when she used to bring her little Gaspare to play with Paolo, who was the same age.[50] I remember how Paolo used to laugh at the lively mimicking with which she made certain puppets move to amuse him, and how I admired her for the courage and inexorable vitality that made her so serene, notwithstanding her difficulties, pain, and anxiety for her two sons in prison and exile. She still has the same indomitable vitality today, intact, but a veil of inconsolable sadness has fallen upon the laughter of her keen eyes. Little Gaspare, having grown up under his mother's example, has become a partisan, a hero, and rests forever among the mountains of the Valsesia. His mother, even if she is extraordinarily strong, even if she is supported by a steadfast faith and by her love for her remaining sons, cannot be like she was before. The human simplicity of her sadness, which made us cry when we embraced, has rendered her greater and dearer to me.

She came to speak to me about the Gruppi di difesa. Her instincts told her that there is something that is not right, that there was a misunderstanding and a kind of antagonism between the representatives of the Communist Party and those of the other parties. She paid me the honor of believing me so little sectarian that I would want to resolve this misunderstanding, and she begged me to go to Milan to meet with the Central Committee of Northern Italy of the Gruppi di difesa, convinced that a solution could emanate from clarification and personal understanding. I too am convinced of it. I will speak with my family, and will go to Milan as soon as possible.

23 September, Meana. Now it is already dark when we leave in the morning. This morning I took advantage of it to attach flyers under the porticos and along the main streets, while I went to the station on foot. I got off the train at Sant'Ambrogio, and we continued the trip with Bianca and Anna and Paola Jarre, this time furnished with a bicycle for each.

Great movement in the vicinity of San Giorio—checkpoints, a truck, even a panzer.[51] Evidently there was a roundup in progress. We passed by with the maximum aplomb possible, and meanwhile I thought that it would have been a particular disaster if they had followed me, especially because they would have taken the money I was bringing to Laghi. But as usual, no one said anything to me, and one more time I blessed my insignificant appearance—neither blond nor brown haired, neither tall nor short, neither fat nor thin, neither pretty nor ugly—which let me pass unobserved, and which no one remembers. Later I learned that not everyone had been so fortunate. For example, they had opened the knapsack of one person from Meana and searched the pockets

---

[50] Elvira Pajetta was a teacher and organizer of the Gruppi di difesa in Romagnano Sesia.

[51] The panzer was a type of German tank.

carefully, even concentrating doggedly on an innocent box of ersatz coffee. Who knows what they were looking for?

At the turn for Castel Pietra, a signalman warned us not to go to Susa because they were confiscating all the bicycles. I gave up the quick visit that I intended to make there, and went directly up to Meana.

Alberto, who was about to carry out an explosion in the Chisone Valley, arrived a little after noon. Marcellin has probably gone to France and the valley was practically empty, without partisans and without Germans. Toward evening Paolo arrived, satisfied with the work he had accomplished lately. Leaving Pillo the task of organizing the group in Sauze, he continued to build a network of contacts in the Upper Valley, at Beaulard, at Château, and at Savoulx. He had found trustworthy and decisive individuals, and the construction of a new group is imminent.

Then we listened to a speech by Croce that Radio London was broadcasting from Naples. It was emotional to hear his voice again, with the intonations and accent that could not be mistaken. It was like a voice that came from another planet, from another world. Yet we are separated from each other by not more than a few hundred kilometers. Suddenly I felt acute nostalgia for this past, so recent and yet so far away, when we could find consolation for all the bad things surrounding us in the communion of a tight number of souls who formed a kind of safe and secure "spiritual religious group." What will this spiritual religious group be tomorrow? With what other forces will it be necessary to make agreements or fight?

25 September. Yesterday Paolo and I had one of those small, unbelievable adventures that make me think at times of a cloud of protection truly forming above us that makes us invisible.

Having gone down to Susa to go together to Laghi's, at the turn for Urbiano, unexpectedly we were before a Fascist on guard. It was too late to turn back, and therefore we had no other choice but to continue on, talking animatedly. The Fascist watched us, but seemed not to see us, and we were in the middle of a roundup. It must have begun right then. (That is why the people we met while we were walking down had not warned us.) They must have been the same forces we met the day before in the vicinity of San Giorio. It was a roundup on a grand scale—loaded carts and trucks continued to arrive, groups of Fascists were already bedding down in the surrounding fields, and others, with their machine guns, were setting out toward the town.

Our position was critical. We could not think of being able to reach Laghi, who certainly would not be found in his usual locations. In order to leave, we would have to pass by the guard post again, and nothing would prevent them from stopping us this time. On the other hand, we could not continue to stay there, in the way, Paolo with his face of "1925," and me with my purse (the usual shopping purse) filled with so many precious and interesting little things. Just in the nick of time I saw a girl from Urbiano, the sister of a partisan, with a basket strapped to her shoulders and the most innocent and "local" appearance that you could imagine. In a loud voice she invited us to gather grapes in her vineyard nearby. Joking and promising a bunch of grapes to the Fascists as well when she returned, she brought us to safety through the vineyard. She gave us the news. As soon as they sighted the Fascists, the *staffette* had run to warn the partisans, who certainly had gone to safety by now. There were no storehouses for weapons in Urbiano, and they had made it in time to conceal them in Braida and Micoletto. Through paths that she knew, she accompanied us as far as the entrance to Susa, and then she returned among the rows of vines, singing.

There was no roundup in Susa, but it was full of Germans. When we entered the piazza, it seemed to me that at the other end, right near Teta's store, there was a checkpoint. Then I thought the safest place where we could take refuge was the main cafe, where the Germans came and went in a steady stream. Therefore we went in to get an ice cream. What person with a dirty conscience would have gone into such a place? When I appeared again after a while, the gathering at the other side of the piazza had broken up. Then we went to Teta's store, where we found Ettore somewhat worried. We climbed back up to Meana with him, and warned the partisans from here in case the roundup might extend to this side as well, which I did not think was possible, however.

The cannon on the other side of the Alps had begun to thunder again, and this seemed to be a good omen. Therefore we had optimistic discussions for the entire evening. But in the night the wind picked up, which awakened me, and the optimism of the evening before seemed foolish. For hours I continued to turn over in my mind the anguishes of the past, and to dread the anguishes of the future.

This morning it was sunny, and there was a wind from Provence. Braida and Micoletto were burning. They are poor *grange* and certainly do not contain treasures. The partisans left them in time, but this senseless violence makes my heart sick.

I went down to Susa and saw a lot of people and various women with whom Gruppi di difesa could be created. Then, having returned to Meana when it became dark, we dug up the fuses and the gadgets to make the trains derail and blow out the tires of the trucks. Paolo wanted to bring them back with him in order to begin the activities of the new partisan bands on this modest plane.

26 September, Turin. Paolo and Alberto left again this morning at dawn. It was a splendid night, full of stars. A cannon was thundering far away. On the other hillside they were putting out the fires at Micoletto and Braida.

Around 9:00 a.m., we left for Turin by bicycle. In the vicinity of San Giorio, there was a village that was completely burned, evidently as a consequence of the roundup of the other day. The walls of the houses were standing (the stone from our quarries also resists fire), but the windows seemed like lifeless eyes. Tenacious and patient like ants, the inhabitants were already beginning to rebuild, here a door, there the beam of a roof. Everyone was working, even the children. We felt that, even if it were apparently destroyed, the town was not dead, and did not want to die.

30 September. Having left yesterday morning around 7:00 a.m. from Turin with a huge transport truck, Nada and I arrived in Milan around one in the afternoon. As soon as we arrived, we devoted ourselves to finding our friends again. Toward 2:30 p.m. in the Piazza del Duomo, near the little side portico where we had gone for a brief appointment, I saw a young man come toward me whom I did not recognize at first. It was Giancarlo Pajetta, whom I had last seen when he was a boy, and whom I was meeting again as a grown man.[52] There were also two women whom I did not know and one, whose name was Bruna, said she was responsible for the Gruppi di difesa of Northern Italy. We went to the home of Adriana—who worked with the Gruppi di difesa for the Action Party—and we got to the point immediately, but I realized quite soon that for me the match had been lost from the start.[53]

I had fought up to now to maintain the independence of the Mfgl from the Gruppi di difesa, too obviously communist in origin, attitude, and organization. I thought and upheld that, just as the Garibaldini, the GL, and the Autonomous formations, etc., existed in the military arena, all collaborating and coordinated under the rubric of the Corpo di Volontari della Libertà (Volunteer Corps for Liberty or Cvl) and dependent on the Cln—so the Gruppi di difesa (communist), the Mfgl, the liberal women, socialist women, and perhaps tomorrow the Christian democratic women, should have their independent existence, while collaborating and coordinating with an organization that could be a kind of women's Cln. Instead the Communists maintained that the Gruppi di difesa was exactly the sort of above-party or apolitical body that the various women's groups should join. If that is the case, then which is the communist women's organization? We refuse to have an independent formation, they said. We give the Gruppi di difesa all our strength and activity. This is equivalent to saying that their formation is precisely the Gruppi di difesa, to which they want to attract the other women's movements. But, whatever thing they are creating and however they try to define the thing, I cannot forget

[52] Giancarlo Pajetta was the organizer of the first partisan bands in Barge, an inspector in the Garibalini command, and a representative of the Communist Party in the Clnai.

[53] "Bruna" was Rina Picolato's *nom de guerre*. Picolato was a representative of the Communist Party in the Gruppi di difesa of Northern Italy. Adriana Mendrini was a professor and representative of the Action Party in the Gruppi di difesa of Milan.

that it was the Communists who created the Gruppi di difesa, and that the women upon whom the propaganda work not only nominally but effectively relies are communist women. The link between the Gruppi di difesa and the Communist Party is undeniable, systematic, and unbroken. Their very presence at our meeting with Pajetta (who I believe is from the directorship), while, for example, none of the women from my organization had thought to attend, showed how the Communists might consider the Gruppi di difesa something of their own, and of vital importance.

Now, as far as I'm concerned, I have nothing against the Communists. On the contrary, in addition to an admiration for Gramsci and the movement in the factories that I shared with Piero, my most profound and I will say almost instinctive sympathy goes to them. Many times yesterday, during the meeting, I managed to think with some sense of humor that if I were not a Communist today, it was perhaps simply because of a response that Giancarlo himself, then little more than a boy and just out of prison, but come to think of it, quite dogmatic and sectarian, gave me one day when, tired and irritated by the blissful inconclusiveness of a friend who for me at the time was the crystallization of the Giustizia e Libertà movement, and fascinated by the deliberate seriousness with which Giancarlo was explaining certain organizational methods to me, suddenly I burst out and asked him frankly, "Would you take me to work with you?" "We are not a refuge for souls in pain," he had answered me, somewhat harshly. "If you are not convinced of our ideas and principles, we do not want you." I learned my lesson, and kept quiet. I could not say that I was convinced of their principles, but to tell the truth I did not even really know what they were. On the other hand, of what other political principles was I convinced? What was politics for me then if not fidelity, sentimental nostalgia, and moral aspiration, humanitarian and vague? Basically what else is it for me today, even if from time to time maturity and experience give me a glimpse of truth and perspective? Even if perhaps only now I am beginning to truly understand?

Nevertheless, many years ago the young Giancarlo was right when he defined me as "a soul in pain." Not him; he was not a soul in pain. He knew what he thought, believed in, and wanted, even then. I thought of this yesterday when, while I listened to his measured words, I watched his energetic and marked facial features. He knew what he wanted and he got it. Even this time—aided by the disinterested superiority of my colleagues with respect to "women's affairs"—he had beaten me in advance. While I was in Turin and in Piedmont, trying to give the development of the Mfgl an autonomous and open-ended existence, the representatives of the Clnai had suffocated it under a blanket, recognizing—in a document signed by Leo Valiani—the Gruppi di difesa as "the organization of the feminine masses of the Cln."[54] No sooner had Giancarlo

[54] Leo Valiani, also known as Federico, was a representative of the Clnai.

put this document under my eyes than I understood that I could do no other than accept the situation, trying to obtain the maximum number of guarantees possible. What else could I do? Reject the decision of the Cln? Contest its legitimacy? These are things that a person cannot do in underground life, and that I would probably not do even during normal times. Protest, be obstinate, and create a schism? I would never do such a thing, necessarily unproductive, creator of confusion, and condemned from the first moment to failure. So nothing else remained for me than to endorse it while still continuing to uphold the ideological and organizational independence of the Mfgl outside of the Gruppi di difesa. If our movement is to have breath and vigor, it will be able to get the upper hand even at the heart of the Gruppi di difesa. I agreed to join the secretariat of the Gruppi di difesa for Northern Italy. My presence in the governing body will give our women some satisfaction and security, and I could easily go to Milan every fifteen or twenty days.

It was already late when—after the discussion ended with perfect cordiality—I left the Gruppi di difesa for the Action Party and met with Nada, Momi Banfi, and Rollier again. If Nada and I wanted to return to Turin on the truck that was leaving tomorrow at dawn from a depot that was very far away, beyond the Porta Sempione, we had to get ourselves to the vicinity quickly, before the curfew, and look for a place to sleep there. The prospect did not appeal to us very much, especially because we had had very little time to talk with our friends. Therefore we decided to spend the night in Milan, and face the discomfort and delay of the train the next morning. Nada would sleep at Spinelli's house and I at a cousin of Rollier, where I would also find Vittorio. We spent a moment at the hospital to give our regards to Momi's wife, whose leg had been badly broken during a bombardment (what is more, she is pregnant). Then we went through dark streets and mysterious stairs to a place where we could eat and talk easily, and where we also found Altiero Spinelli.[55] I did not know Spinelli, although I had heard about him for years. Having gotten out of *confino* during Badoglio's forty-five days, when he and Ernesto Rossi had laid down the basis for the Movimento Federalista (Federalist Movement), he immediately found himself in a new battle, without even a moment of rest. But Panta (namely Pantagruel—which is what his friends called him, a bit because of his size, which was more than considerable, and a bit because of the insatiable appetite that many years of prison had left him) quickly grew accustomed to the ways and habits of underground work, where he moves, notwithstanding his mass,

---

[55] Altiero Spinelli (Panta) had been convicted by the Special Tribunal for belonging to the Giustizia e Libertà movement. Spinelli was involved in the creation of the European Federalist Movement in Milan in 1943. The movement later spread to European Resistance fighters. By 1945, a federalist conference in Paris boasted participation by individuals such as George Orwell and Albert Camus.

with remarkable nimbleness. On the other hand, I already knew Leo Valiani, who had come to my house last January, after having crossed the lines, to get in touch with his friends. I confess that, at first, I treated him with notable distrust. It took a while before he convinced me that he was truly the "Federico" whose forthcoming arrival in Northern Italy Nada had announced to me. Now I tried to inform him about the meeting with Pajetta and about the agreement with the Gruppi di difesa, but he did not pay much attention to me. Instead he engaged me in conversation about the possibility of having groups of little houses built for the people in Turin and Milan right after the end of the war, on the model of those created in the previous postwar period by the socialist administration of Vienna.

Then Rollier accompanied me to his cousin's house, where Vittorio arrived a little while later. The pale light of the candle (there was no electricity) did not allow me to see his face well, but from the tone of his voice I had the impression that his anxiety for Lisetta had profoundly shaken him. Luckily Lisetta is no longer in the hands of the Koch Band, but has in turn been arrested by the regular police. She is at San Vittore, from where we hope to make her escape within a few days. Vittorio showed me a little strip of paper that she had sent to him, which said in so many words: "...Do not worry about me because I am doing very well. Do not be making exchanges. Rather, help some man get out. I have my belly, and I will get off lightly at any rate." With emotion and profound relief, I heard in the words of the little note the usual tone of heroic simplicity that I had always so appreciated in her. If they have kept her, it means that nothing serious has happened. Then I unloaded my anxieties about the women's movement onto Vittorio's understanding heart. I do not know if the matter interested him, but he listened to me and advised me patiently, giving me, with his ideas, pretexts with which to back my experience and instincts.

Early this morning I met Nada on the train and we dozed as far as Borgo Vercelli, where they made us get off and travel the six kilometers to Vercelli on foot. But it was not an unpleasant walk. There was beautiful sunshine, and Nada entertained me with little amusing stories about his ancestors. I think I will never forget that Genovese ancestor of his who, for love of classical antiquity, insisted on sleeping, wrapped in a cloak, in the temples at Pesto, until he died of malaria.[56]

We reached Turin after two o'clock. Espedita welcomed me at the front door of the house with an air of festive mystery:

---

[56] Pesto or Paestum is a Greco-Roman city in the Campania region, located south of Naples, which was founded by Greeks from Sybaris around 600 B.C. See www.paestum.de/en/paestum.htm.

"Just guess who has arrived!"

"Who?" I asked.

"Paolo. He came down by bicycle."

I climbed the stairs running, and only when he told me that nothing terrible had happened did I let myself feel the joy of having him nearby. He came to Turin to speak with Valle about certain difficulties that had arisen because of the re-emergence of Autonomous bands in the Upper Valley, after the return of Marcellin from France, which Cesare would like to join with his men, leaving ours.

4 October. When we arrived in Susa the other morning, Monday, we found a strange atmosphere, somewhere between relief and contempt, between hope and disappointment, whose meaning I understood only when Teta told me the latest rumors: "The partisans are about to make an agreement with the Germans. Laghi has been seen in a car with them. The hostilities have been suspended." Upset, I rushed out to Barberis', to Max's, and to Longo's, in search of precise information, and what I received was enough to reassure me, if not exactly to calm me down completely. Laghi had effectively had a meeting with the German command regarding the exchange of certain prisoners, and he had been taken in a car by them they do not know quite where, but he had not spoken about an agreement at all, which they concluded was absolutely unfounded. I let out my breath, but to calm down completely, I had to speak with Laghi directly. Therefore I begged Longo to order a sighting service to identify where he was, and to give me a way to meet him, and I went to Teta's to wait.

It was almost two o'clock when he ran to notify me that Laghi, still accompanied by the Germans, had entered the hospital (the neutral terrain chosen for the meeting). I ran there also and explained what I wanted to a young, intelligent sister, whom I had already met when she had tried to save poor Durbiano. "Come in here," the nun told me, and she had me go into a laboratory, where a few minutes later she also brought in Laghi, whose excited and heroic appearance contrasted comically with the somewhat sterile atmosphere.

"We have not come to terms with the enemy," he said nobly, in response to my hurried questions.

"No, I have not made any agreement. I will explain why I had to accept the truce, but this evening it is over."

"When and where can I see you?" I asked. I had to give him orders and money, and I had to understand his intentions correctly.

"The Germans will bring me by car up to a certain point on the road. The Command is at Mompantero Vecchio. Be there between five and six."

"Fine," I answered.

I let him leave, and then, when I heard that his car had left, I left too. I went to Teta's, and notified Paolo and Ettore also, telling them to go to Meana, where I would join them in the evening. Then I found Longo, whom I begged to accompany me to Mompantero Vecchio. I could not go there by the usual road, through Urbiano and Braida, which were totally occupied by the Germans and the Fascists. I had to take a detour through San Giuseppe, passing through places that I did not know very well. Very familiar with the area, Longo consented willingly and we left immediately. It was around five o'clock when we arrived at Mompantero Vecchio, a small group of *grange* at the bottom of a esplanade of pastures that appeared, like a terrace, on the barren, steep flank of the Rocciamelone. Laghi had not yet arrived. Night was falling and an icy wind was blowing. We retreated to a *grangia*, around a lit fire, with some partisans who told us about the adventures of the group after the last roundup. The bulk of them had already moved toward the Colle della Croce di Ferro, from where, if necessary, it would be possible to go down into the Lanzo Valley. But the situation is not a happy one. It is already cold outside and, at that altitude, it can snow at any moment, which would make any movement extremely dangerous, not to say impossible, while the supply of foodstuffs will become absolutely problematical. Up until now, notwithstanding the roundup, they have gotten off easily by moving at night and hiding in the woods, but what will they do when the last leaves have fallen and their footsteps will leave a mark on the snow?

At 7:00 p.m., Laghi had not yet arrived and Longo decided to climb down. I was unhappy to have him leave me, and even unhappier to lose my guide, but I encouraged him to go. His wife was expecting a child who could be born at any moment, and I would not have wanted to keep him far from his family for anything in the world.

It was around 8:00 p.m. when Laghi arrived, exhausted and worried. "The truce will be over within a few minutes," he announced. We must prepare everything immediately, and leave for the Croce di Ferro. I gave him the money and the necessary communications. Rapidly I informed him about the new situation that had developed in the Upper Valley, and made agreements for future contacts through a system of signals and reports.

While we were still talking, we could hear a violent exchange of shots below, between Urbiano and Braida. The truce had expired and the Germans were attacking. We left the *grangia*. In the valley at the bottom, the tracer bullets left a stream of fleeting lights.

The partisans hurried to make the final preparations to depart and to put the provisions in a safe place. I said goodbye to Laghi, wishing him good luck and, cutting short the protests with which he wanted to send two armed men to accompany me at any cost, I crossed the open space of meadow running, and flung myself into the wooded area. But when I had gone far enough away to be certain that they would no longer try to follow me, exposing themselves to danger uselessly, I confess that I had a moment of very basic fear. It was pitch dark, and I did not know the road. I only remember that, when I climbed up with Longo in the afternoon, we had crossed a stream and walked for a long time in a pine woods. But where were the woods? Where was the stream? I got up my courage and let myself go, like a blind woman. I do not know how to repeat what I did precisely. For a while I continued among the thornbushes, laboriously, with difficulty, and then, at a certain point, I felt the earth give way under my feet, and I rolled for about twenty meters along a kind of little ravine. I absolutely did not know where I was. I only knew that I had to keep to the right, and my only point of orientation was the crackle of Tommy gun shots in the direction of Braida. Suddenly I rolled along what seemed to me to be the bed of a stream until, having been able to stop myself by gripping a protruding rock, I had the sensation of being suspended in a vacuum. No, that would be too much. If I were going to break my neck on the stones, I might as well have stayed with Laghi. I looked at the sky, tinged with a soft glimmer. The moon was about to rise; then at least I could see where I was.

Therefore I waited patiently. I was not cold (evidently I had gotten warm by rolling), but I was terribly hungry. Quite soon it was light enough for me to realize that I was on a layer of rock, which had an overhang of about ten meters in front of it. On the whole, I had done well to stop. I went down carefully from the opposite side, and I recognized the stream that I had crossed in the afternoon, while climbing. I crossed it now from the opposite side, and found the road easily. It seemed like a miracle to me to walk on well-trodden ground. The shots continued to come from the other side, but here everything was quiet.

I crossed two groups of houses, absolutely deserted and apparently immersed in sleep. One had to be the one that, with its compact lawns symmetrically enclosed between parallel rows of poplars, had always appeared to me—when I contemplated it from my window on the other slope—to be an artificial small village, built like a toy. Then I abandoned the road, by now too exposed, and I went down for a stretch among the chestnut trees until I found myself on level ground.

I had arrived, but basically I had not solved very much of anything. Now another problem presented itself: either I cross all of Susa in the dead of night, right in the middle of the curfew, with all the risks that this carried with it, or curl up in a ditch along the road and wait there for the light of morning. I sat on the edge of the road and pondered what to do for a long time. I saw the scattered villages of Meana on the other slope before me, and near the quarry, behind the poplar trees, my white house illuminated by the increasing brightness of the moon. Ettore and Paolo were there, the restful sweetness of their closeness and affection was there, and, I should be less poetic, a bed or a section of bed and a cup of hot tea and a slice of bread were there. I think that essentially it was the

hunger that made me try the "foolish endeavor." I proceeded cautiously, trying to keep myself in the shadow as much as possible. (Now how I cursed that
moon, which I had so invoked and awaited earlier!) But, having arrived at the
height of the bridge that came out into the main piazza, I stopped, hesitating.
Could I cross in the midst of the inhabited area? It was almost impossible that
there would not be surveillance at the entrance and exit. If I were able to reach
and cross the so-called "bridge of the *Alpini*," I would come out directly on the
road for Meana, cutting across outside the inhabited area. But I had made my
calculations without considering the railroad. When, upon leaving the row of
bushes in the shadow of which I had tried to hide, I saw the tracks shine in front
of me, I understood that I had made a mistake. The railroad was certainly the
place that was under the greatest surveillance. Crossing it was the most careless thing I could do, not to mention that this way I was approaching Urbiano,
the nerve center of the roundup.

Therefore I turned back, cautiously. The bridge and the piazza opened
before me, invitingly. The full moon illuminated the façades of the old houses
and the sparkling water of the Dora, making them look like an ordinary
eighteenth-century scene. I could not see or hear anyone. I took off my boots,
which would have too noisily disturbed the prevailing silence, and, holding
them in my hand and bending over as much as possible to take advantage of
any bit of shadow, I rushed forward, very quickly. I felt like a cat. I went beyond
the barracks of the *Alpini,* now occupied by the Germans. I crossed the bridge,
I went beyond the Albergo del Sole where the Command was, and beyond Teta's
store, and I reached the shortcut for Meana. There I stopped, finally letting out
my breath. By now the worst had passed. If they stopped me here, I would have
a thousand plausible justifications: I had come to see a sick relative, I was late,
I had a sick person in Meana, etc., etc.

I proceeded further, cautiously, almost on all fours, for the stretch of the
shortcut visible from the antiaircraft stations in the neighboring field. Then
I straightened up and, with a big sigh, I put my shoes back on and attacked
the climb speedily. By now all that remained for me to go past was one last
dangerous point: the German guard at the railroad crossing keeper's cabin in
Cantalupo, in the vicinity of which I could not help passing. But I knew from
experience that, as soon as night fell, a healthy fear of the partisans induced
the enemy soldiers to barricade themselves inside to sleep. In fact, at the bottom of the climb I saw that they had placed the usual trestles covered with
barbed wire around the crossing keeper's cabin, and I went ahead without further precautions. But, when I was a few meters from the crossing keeper's cabin,
I suddenly saw the shadow of a soldier come out in front of me, unexpected.
I stopped and remained motionless, and he too remained motionless. "Now he
is going to shoot me," I thought. "How stupid to get myself picked up just a few
steps from the house!" But the German still did not move. For some seconds,

which seemed eternal to me, we remained like this, one facing the other. Then slowly, almost insensibly, I turned back, until I reached the protective shadow of a chestnut tree. The other person continued not to move, as if he were petrified. Rapidly, stooping over, I untied my shoes and, creeping, I climbed back up the brief stretch of meadow hidden by the chestnut trees. When I reached the turn of the road above, I stopped for a moment to take out at least a portion of the thorns from the prickly chestnut burs that had planted themselves in my palms. In the meantime, I looked down to see what the German had done. He remained immobile for another moment. Then I heard him emit a long sigh of relief, and I saw him go back in precipitously beyond the barbed wire, to disappear inside the crossing keeper's cabin. I almost started laughing. Evidently he had come outside for a moment to satisfy some natural need, or perhaps, more romantically, to contemplate the moon, and suddenly there he was in front of a mysterious shadow, which he had not guessed was a woman, and which he had certainly taken for a partisan come to attack him. I had been afraid of him, but undoubtedly he had been more afraid of me. Cheered and gladdened by the amusing episode and by its happy ending, I ran the brief stretch that still separated me from my house. Never had I felt such a profound sense of satisfaction in climbing up the stairs.

Inside I found not only Ettore and Paolo but also Alberto, Pillo, and Franco *il Dinamitardo*. The first two had come to Meana to learn about the decisions of the Turin Command in the Upper Valley, and the third to go together with Patria to organize a regular system of *staffette* among the various groups in the Valley with him and with us. But I was too tired and famished to pay attention to them. Only when I had slipped into the "piece of bed" reserved for me, where Paolo and Alberto already were, and I had ingested a considerable quantity of tea and bread, which Ettore had prepared for me, did I have the strength to listen, to narrate when my turn came, and to organize the next day's work. Then I went to sleep immediately, while the others were still talking, exhausted.

The next morning, Alberto and Pillo left at dawn across the mountain to join Patria's group. I, on the other hand, left later with Paolo and Franco, and we crossed the main road to familiarize ourselves with the positions of the German and Fascist troops. We passed Olmo, Gravere, and Chiomonte, full of Germans as usual. We stopped to chat with peasants we met, in the meantime observing the symbols and numbers that we saw on the German cars. But we had such a harmless and easygoing appearance of nice evacuees out for a walk that no one paid us the least attention. At the height of Exilles, we climbed through the woods up to Gran Prà, which, as its name indicates, is a wide expanse of pastures with some *grange*. Patria and his men were waiting for us, and we ate dinner. (We had not eaten such a succulent risotto, made with the fat from the sheep, in a long time!) Then we discussed the situation, and the solution was quick and easy. Patria's group and those of the partisans from Sauze who wanted to be with Cesare will make up a brigade systematically embodied in the other Autonomous forces that Marcellin is reconstructing in the Chisone Valley. The others, and essentially the groups from Beaulard and Savoulx, will form a GL formation, connected with Laghi. Naturally there will have to be constant contact among the various formations, and they will have to be open to carrying out actions together when possible. It will be necessary to organize a regular service of *staffette*, and Franco offered to take care of this directly. There was not a shadow of rancor or distrust on either side, and it seemed to me that in this way we have laid down the basis of a good collaboration, letting each one have the satisfaction of choosing the "color" and designation that he prefers.

The discussion ended and the agreement concluded, Paolo, Alberto, and Pillo left toward Beaulard, and Franco and I returned toward Meana through Gran Combo, Frais, and Losa. The night descended rapidly and a great sadness—the usual desolate sadness I felt every time I was away from Paolo—took over. The autumn beauty of the woods and meadows that we crossed hardly touched me, and I became tired listening to the chatter of good Franco, who told me about his life and its vicissitudes, both material and psychological, through which he had gone from being an officer in the Royal Italian Army to an Allied agent in the service of the War of Liberation.[57]

Today we went down to Susa, and we chatted for a long time with Barberis, Pratis, Max, and Longo. Then we made a run in record time as far as Bussoleno (eight kilometers in fifty minutes), from where the train, after many long stops, put us in Turin around midnight.

In order to leave the station given the curfew, a person needs a special permit. Ettore, in his capacity as an employee of E.I.A.R., had one, and I slipped next to him, saying, "I am his wife." But while we were crossing Corso Vittorio, we heard someone yell "A-da!" We looked around. Who could be calling me at that hour and in that place in that way? We went ahead, but again we heard the same cry, and suddenly we saw a soldier with a pointed Tommy gun in front of us. It was he who had yelled not "A-da!" as we had thought, but *"Alto-là! (Stop!)"* Ettore showed his permit, and we arrived home without other upsets.

5 October. It is raining and cold outside. I saw a number of people. We reviewed the situation in the Valley with Valle, Paolo Menzio, Max, Ferrero, and Trinch. It appears that hope for a rapid Allied advance and an imminent solution have almost completely faded. We will have to face another winter, and the prospect is not a happy one. The partisans cannot remain in the mountains, where the snow makes every movement impossible, and getting provisions becomes more and more difficult. They are thinking of moving into the lowland areas,

[57] The Allied advance in Southern Italy.

where food is abundant, and where it is possible to move and operate. This will be done, it appears, for the groups of the Pellice Valley and for many from the Cuneese, who will go down into the plain at the entrance to the Langhe, but the problem is different for the Susa Valley. Since it is a question of an important communication route, we cannot leave it completely defenseless. Nor has the Lower Valley enough foodstuffs for everybody. We think that Laghi's formations can hold out, at least for the moment, depending on reserves from Susa. As for the group in the Upper Valley, they can subsist only if they organize regular trips into Free France to carry news and bring back weapons, etc., as Paolo has proposed. For such a task they will need individuals who are particularly robust and knowledgeable regarding the mountains, exactly like our boys from Savoulx and Beaulard. We will see, however.

The Allies have landed in Greece.

6 October. Today a Christian democratic woman, Annarosa, appeared, whom I accompanied to Medea's house for the meeting of the Gruppi di difesa.[58] While expressing their reservations about the Gruppi di difesa and about their participation after the end of the war, the Christian democratic women have agreed to work with us. This seems important to me—for today, since there are many of them and they have the organizational experience that we lack and, no matter what happens, they can depend on their parishes for support, and for tomorrow, because if we work together during this difficult period, we will learn to understand and appreciate each other. From the concrete collaboration of today will be born, we hope, a bond destined to endure.

8 October. I came to Milan with Bruna and another friend of the Gruppi di difesa to make contacts with our friends here. We discussed the content and form of *Noi Donne* for a long time. I offered to write the leading article for the next issue. "After all," they said, and they were not mistaken, "It is not our fault that we Communists are essentially doing the newspaper, and that inevitably at times we assume the attitudes of the party. Contribute to it frequently, do it yourselves, and the impression and tone will be different." Therefore I spent the night composing an article that, under the title "Unità," summarizes my thoughts on the subject and on which I hope we will all agree.

In the afternoon, I left for the Vigna with Ettore. We wanted to interest Anita in working among the women. With her intelligence and poise, she will be a valuable addition. At her house I met Paola Levi, mother of the young partisan Geo, a very good friend of Emanuele Artom, who was arrested with him in the Germanasca, but not targeted as a Jew, and only sent to a work camp in

---

[58] Annarosa Gallesio was a journalist and representative of the Christian Democrats in the Gruppi di difesa.

Germany.[59] She agreed to work with us in the field of assistance. I think she is a woman of great courage and significant practical experience.

Thanks to the meeting with her, the balance sheet for today is clearly positive.

12 October. Franco Dusi was killed, in the Canavese.

I am thinking about his mother. But above all I am thinking about him, about him as I saw him as a child when I went to get Paolo at elementary school and smiled at his keen little face and air of considered importance. I remember when he came to take his examination for admission at the "Balbo" and he astounded everyone with his knowledge of the Alpine system, and how I saw him grow, year after year, next to Paolo. I saw them before me, on the same bench, at school, and they gossiped and argued constantly. I saw them together at home when they were preparing for their diploma, and we translated Sophocles and read Dante and Spinoza. We prepared the terms for the *Dizionario Bompiani.*[60] We went together to the mountains. I always felt an intimate maternal satisfaction when I saw him, so handsome and strong and intelligent, and I created the most wonderful dreams for him, as well as for Paolo. When the hour of danger came, I tried to keep him out of it, almost obsessed by a foreboding fear. But Franco joined the same battle. He was not one who could stay out of it. Today he has fallen.

After such blows it seems impossible to be able to keep going ahead.

13 October. Lisetta, having happily escaped from San Vittore, should have arrived in Turin today and settled down at Gigliola's house, but just today Gigliola's house was "burned," and she saved herself by a miracle, escaping from the window. We must stop Lisetta when she arrives to keep her from setting out toward the alleged address, and conduct her elsewhere. They told me that when she arrived, dressed like a Red Cross worker, and they warned her about the complex situation, she said simply, with her usual composure that was half cynical and half amused: "Very good. Indeed, I was a bit tired. This gives me back some of my spirit."

The Allies have occupied Athens and Rimini.

---

[59] Paola Levi Nizza (Ortensia) was an organizer of the Mfgl. Geo Levi was a partisan in the GL formations in the Pellice Valley.

[60] Ada wrote entries for the Bompiani dictionary of literature, which gave her the opportunity to reread a great deal of Italian and American literature. Paolo also wrote some entries for Bompiani on books about the North and South Poles. Between 1947 and 1950, the dictionary was published in nine volumes under the title *Dizionario letterario Bompiani delle opere e dei personaggi di tutti i tempi e di tutte le letterature.*

14 October, Meana. Having left Turin at 6:00 a.m., I arrived in Meana by train directly, without stops or transfers. It has been months since something similar has happened. While recognizing that it is comfortable, I hope with all my heart that this comfort—more useful to the Germans than to us—will not last very long.

Angelo Mussa, Carlo's brother (whose *nom de guerre* is Lino) got off with me in Meana. In his capacity as a member of the Piedmontese Regional Military Command, he had to come to Laghi's to make plans for the winter. We got off together in Susa, and spoke with Max. Then we left for Mompantero Vecchio, where, after the parentheses of the Croce di Ferro, Laghi had returned with the Command. The roundup is finished, and the Germans and Fascists have gone. Therefore it was no longer necessary to make a long detour as far as San Giuseppe, as it was around two weeks ago, and we left instead by the shortest route.

Urbiano, Braida, and Micoletto displayed obvious signs of the passage of the enemy—a number of burned houses, and writings everywhere singing the praises of the Duce, the Führer, and the *milizia*.[61] But the inhabitants, tenacious and industrious, have already begun caring for the wounded, raising walls, protecting roofs, and constructing doors and windows again. The inclement weather will see to it that the writings fade.

We found Laghi in full organizational fervor. Justifiably preoccupied with the problem of provisions —fundamental during this season —he is taking a kind of census of the food resources in the area, with the intention of calling for a kind of contribution from the big landlords, factories, mills, etc., which will be requested graciously and provided willingly, given his excellent rapport with the population. Moreover, he thinks that many of the partisans, natives of this area, will be able to take advantage of their family resources, when it comes to help for them in another form, perhaps for the reconstruction of the houses. He too agrees that the group cannot move to the lowland areas. The street to Moncenisio, the railroad, and the power stations are places that are too important to be abandoned, even momentarily. Therefore, it is better that the group remain on its feet, even if it is reduced to minimal numbers, but immediately be able to count on the greatest number of people possible at every prospective request.

16 October, Turin. Yesterday morning, having taken the train in Meana on which Ettore had arrived from Turin, I reached Oulx around 11:00 without any problem—an almost scandalous convenience! Cesare's father accompanied us as far as Villaretto, where quite soon we saw Paolo arrive running through the fields. He had a lot of things to tell.

---

[61] The Mvsn.

Happily, the group from Beaulard had been formed. The agreement was celebrated with a general drinking bout in which even he and Alberto, in order not to lose face before the mountain boys, had to do their part. When he left, Paulo limited himself to having the impression that the pine trees were running after them very rapidly, jumping high in the sky. Alberto's reactions were more amusing. Having fallen into a deep sleep, he awoke suddenly and, rising to his feet, announced solemnly: "A venta munse la vaca (We have to milk the cow)." Going to the nearby stable, he really milked it. While he had never milked a cow in his life and therefore totally lacked experience, the poor animal, certainly aware of the abnormal conditions, easily let him do it.

After this festive beginning, everything proceeded marvelously. One of the new recruits, a certain Gino Mallen, a forester and aspiring ski instructor, had the idea for the construction of a cabin made of tree trunks in the middle of the woods.[62] Directing the work of the others and working himself with exceptional vigor and ability, he accomplished it in a few days. Now they are organized quite well. Paolo and Pillo made a rapid visit to Sauze, where they were supplied with blankets. Foodstuffs always represent the major difficulty; never abundant in these areas that are not very productive, they are terribly scarce today, but they hope to be able to acquire a sheep from time to time, and have the Municipio of Oulx give them some quantity of foodstuff rations through the Cln.

While Paolo told his story, we continued to climb through the woods in the direction of the cabin. It was all so wonderful, and I was so happy to have him nearby, so animated and satisfied, and to hear him tell the story, that I did not know how to give him the news of Dusi's death. Only when he said to me that they had not yet decided what name to give the new company did I propose that it be named after his friend who had died.

At a certain point, near the glade produced by a taglio raso (clear felling) of pine trees, we met a group of young men. They were partisans from Beaulard, Château, and Savoulx, who had come to inaugurate the cabin. The famous Gino Mallen, who appeared to me to be a young boy who was quite lively, without too many scruples but rich in vitality and initiative, was among them. There was the mild Don Riccardo, parish priest of Château, with his sister, who was studying to be a teacher; Renato, ex-corporal of the carabinieri; Pierre Cote, a very young boy, unusually serious and open; Eligio Pacchiodo, a well-built youngster who was solid and levelheaded like the Carletto of Exilles, and about twenty others.[63] In the cabin, we found Pillo, Alberto, and Bianca, who had arrived yesterday evening. The cabin, constructed of squared pine tree trunks,

[62] Gino Mallen was a farmer and partisan in the "Franco Dusi Column" of the IV Alpine Division of GL.

[63] Renato (no last name given) and Eligio Pacchiodo were partisans in the "Franco Dusi Column" of the IV Alpine Division of GL. Don Riccardo was the parish priest of Château Beaulard.

is truly a little masterpiece. It has foundations, a well-joined floor that is perfectly smooth, the necessary interstices, a well-constructed roof, a very solid door, and a minuscule little window. It seemed to me to be the kind of cabin that 90 percent of the boys and girls of the time dreamed of being able to build, where they could dream of being an explorer. What is more, it is concealed so ably between the trees and against the mountain that a person can pass next to it without noticing it. For now the interior is still in disorder—a rickety stove, some mattresses, and some stools— but quite soon, they say, it will have everything that they need. They are also planning the construction of a minuscule shed nearby that will serve as a depository for the desired provisions and eventually meat from the sheep.

We complimented the builders on their work, and chatted a long time about plans for action in the future. Paolo thinks that he can accomplish the crossing into France as soon as possible. It appears that the most rapid passage is that of the Passo dell'Orso (otherwise known as the Passo della Grande Hoche), but the Germans hold that. Gino, who is very knowledgeable about the area, says that they can go through all the same, and offered himself as a guide. For some time, at least since the liberation of France, Paolo has had it in mind to try the undertaking, and I think that he will end up succeeding. Notwithstanding my natural apprehension, I agree with him that it could open new vistas for all the winter activities of the partisans in the Upper Valley.

When it was dark, the partisans who had family in Beaulard and Château returned home. Only Renato and some others from Savoulx remained with us. We cooked a *polenta* and ate the few provisions that we brought, among which was a cake similar to the one that Valle had called *nutriente* and that the boys affectionately called *la sostanziosa* (something substantial or filling). At the conclusion of the banquet, which nearly ended in the dark, since the carbide of the acetylene lamp had run out, Pillo concluded the festivities by involuntarily overturning the stove with a kick. Then, considering the present insufficiency of bedding and mattresses in the cabin, we decided that Alberto, Bianca, Ettore, Paolo, and I would go to sleep at Villaretto, and we went down through the woods. It was pitch dark, and the ground was wet and slippery. At a certain point Bianca rolled for a good stretch, losing a heel and skinning a magnificent, light-skinned leather bag with a false bottom, furnished by the Party for underground work.

At Villaretto they gave us straw and blankets and we all slept together (the five of us plus the owner's three children) in a small room that was quite soon heated by our warmth. The smallest of our guests (a little boy eleven or twelve years old) must have drunk I do not know what drink because he got up several times during the night and, jumping over those who were sleeping, went to urinate noisily in a receptacle located for such a purpose in the corner of the room. I awoke with a start every time, but instead of cursing him, I was almost grateful to him, for the pleasure that it gave me to hear the calm breathing of Paolo, who was lying next to me.

This morning, having awakened at the filtering of the first light through the steamy panes of the little windows, I saw that Bianca had straightened up to sit and contemplate the face of Alberto, who was still sleeping, while she softly caressed his black hair. We looked at each other and we understood without speaking. The cheerful excitement of the evening party had died down. Now, in the crude light of day, we saw the horrible reality: the winter that was approaching, inexorable, and the hardships, cold, and hunger. The persistent danger still remains—although the cabin is safe and well concealed, the Germans are still too close, and it only takes an accident or a spy for them to be discovered and captured—and if they decide to leave and try the crossing, other much more serious and complex dangers await them. We remained silent for a long time, thinking, until the little boy moved to go to urinate one last time, and even the others woke up.

We went down to the kitchen, but while we were drinking a cup of hot milk, we heard the sound of guttural voices and, looking out the window, we saw two Germans pass. "They are not looking for the partisans," the owner of the house reassured us. "They are going to Château to look for something to eat." But her calmness, all the more admirable because she also has two sons in danger, was not enough to reassure me. What if, just as it essentially happened a little while later, the Germans entered the house, even just to ask for something to eat, and they found all those people? How would we justify our presence?

After a while, Ettore and I set out toward Oulx. Paolo accompanied us for a stretch, and then turned back. There was no sun. A heavy, cold fog concealed the mountains and wet the grass and the trees. When I saw him disappear at a turn, I had to make an effort not to cry.

At Oulx I went to the *Municipio*, where I received from a friend who was employed there a promise of a certain quantity of rationed foodstuffs for the group at "Sapes." (That is what the place near where the cabin stands is called.) Then by bicycle without incident up to Susa, where I made the usual connections with the usual people. At Bussoleno we took the train and again we met Bianca, who told us about her latest adventure. It was a short time after we had left when two Germans had passed by again, and this time, instead of going straight ahead they had gone into the house. The owner's two sons had hidden under the straw, near the cow. Bianca and Alberto had run to the floor above and had thrown themselves down on the straw and embraced each other intimately, thinking that not even the Germans would have had the courage to disturb two people who were innocently making love. Suddenly they heard heavy steps on the stairs. The Germans are here! Instead it was the owner who, having sent away the two Germans, who were only looking for some salami, had come to reassure them, and who did not hide her shocked surprise in seeing them busy making love at a moment of such immediate danger. Paolo, having returned from accompanying us, had seen the Germans enter the house and had taken a stroll in the woods. When he returned, everything was over.

17 October. Another boy has fallen, and another light has been extinguished. Paolo Diena was killed with eight other people in an ambush in the vicinity of Inverso Pinasca. I remember his cordial welcome when we went to the Gianna, the festive joy with which he welcomed the news that his mother would soon go to meet him in the Chisone Valley, and the joyous vitality that his infantile face expressed under his flaming red hair—so strong, so happy, so alive. I absolutely cannot think about his mother.

Lisetta came in the afternoon with her hair dyed blond, eyeglasses, and a very dignified appearance. She is very well in spite of everything and, half amused and half proud, she told me about her adventures. From San Vittore, following her instructions, she was able to get herself transported to a hospital, but in order to do this she had to pretend to faint in a filthy latrine. For her, this was the most disgusting memory of the event. At the hospital, where she was kept under guard, she still pretended to be very seriously ill and unconscious. Meanwhile, under the linens, she devoured the stuffed sandwiches that the nurses, who were accomplices, provided for her, until Gigliola, dressed as a Red Cross worker, arrived with a group of armed partisans and, having locked up doctors and orderlies—who in reality were very happy to let themselves be locked up—picked her up, wrapping her in a cloak. "Ha! Ha!" a doctor laughed, meeting them on the stairs "You are escaping, eh?" Then, dressed and tidied up again, she left for Turin as soon as possible.

Now she is passing for a refugee from Cesena, with proper papers that will allow her to go to the hospital when the time comes. I am thinking with tenderness about her child that is about to be born. I too had excitements and misfortunes when I was expecting Paolo, even if they were less violent, and this has not kept him from being strong and healthy. But I hope that in twenty years Lisetta's son or daughter will not have to face the same events his or her mother has experienced.

18 October. A day that was particularly full.

This morning I went to the Mauriziano, hoping to see Frida who, having fallen asleep with her head on the table while some milk was boiling, had run the risk of being asphyxiated by the gas. But it was not visiting day and, since I do not know anyone at the hospital, they would not let me in. Later, however, I saw her mother, who gave me entirely reassuring news.

Then a meeting with Maria Daviso's young friend, Giorgio Vaccarino, called "the young sparrow" because of the undeniable resemblance of his features and gestures to the feathered little bird. He is working with the Clns of the local businesses.[64] Then, until two o'clock, I worked with Valle typing the plan for the division of the city into zones for the day of the insurrection.

In the afternoon, I had an appointment with Doctor Visentini of the Molinette about the organization of health services.

Then I saw several women, and met one Valle had sent to me, whom everyone called "Aunt Lina." She was so well dressed and tidy that I was really embarrassed about my inveterate indifference to these things. Just as it pleased me to look at her, so gracious and well groomed, it would please others to see me like that, instead of finding me perennially disheveled, wearing something stained or worn out. But this is an illness from which I believe I will have great difficulty recovering.

At the end of the afternoon, three women from R.I.V. and two women from S.E.P.R.A.L. came to my house, for whom Silvia conducted a lesson in political ideology, the first in a series.[65] When they left, excited and satisfied, we planned the second issue of *La Nuova Realtà* with Silvia, Costanza, and Maria Daviso.

21 October. Having left for Milan the day before yesterday at three in the afternoon, I had to do the stretch between Brandizzo and Civasso on foot, given the alarms during the transfer, and then once again, in the middle of the night, the six kilometers from Vercelli to Borgo Vercelli, arriving in Milan at three in the morning. I was able to wait and read in the cafe at the station until five o'clock. Then I had to take refuge in a waiting room filled with the poor of humanity, tired, weary, and bad-smelling, where, if I wanted to sit down, I had to sit on the ground. I left as soon as it was daylight, and, crossing all of Milan on foot, I went to Adriana's house.

Then I saw Vittorio, with whom I walked for a long time, talking about many things and also about the woman question, which troubled me in particular during those days. Then I went to a school to look for a teacher friend, but just as I arrived, the alarm sounded. With anguish I saw the disorganized slowness with which the frightened teachers guided the children into the inadequate shelters. Shuddering, I thought of what would have happened if a bomb had fallen on the school. It was not possible to find the teacher in that confusion; therefore, I left before the alarm ended. I learned quite soon that what I had feared for the school where I went on occasion had actually happened to a school in the suburbs, in Gorla. A bomb had hit the school directly, making carnage out of the defenseless children. While I neared Porta Vittoria, where there is a

---

[64] Giorgio Vaccarino had his doctorate in law. He was an inspector of the GL Piedmontese Regional Command.

[65] R.I.V. (Rubineterrie Italiane Valvole) was a company that made valves for faucets and S.E.P.R.A.L. (Sezione Provinciale dell'Alimentazione) was a provincial department for providing food.

doctor's office, I saw a series of ambulances arrive that were loaded with small children that were horribly lacerated. The people watched, dismayed, with an anguish filled with impotent anger. Many men and women were crying. At a certain point I became aware that I too was sobbing loudly.

In the afternoon, the first full meeting of the Gruppi di difesa was held at Adriana's house. Two Communists whom I already knew, Bruna and Lina; Adriana and I for the Action Party; a Socialist, Lina Merlin; one Liberal; and one Christian Democrat were there.[66] Everyone dressed up for the occasion: one woman had on a fox, another fine embroidered gloves, a third an unusual hat with a red feather. Only the Communists and I (Adriana is always naturally elegant) were dressed simply, as usual. We did not know whether to be ashamed of it or to take satisfaction in it. The discussions were a bit like the dress—many compliments, many abstract statements, and many concerns for each other's feelings. It was certainly not a very conclusive meeting, but there is no question that it resulted in a precise desire on everyone's part to work together fairly. Undoubtedly, this is a good beginning.

This morning, having left at seven, I repeated on foot the stretch between Borgo Vercelli and Vercelli. In a downpour and without Nada's amusing little stories, it was much less pleasant than the other time. At Chivasso, in order not to be compelled to go on foot up to Brandizzo, I took the local tram, which, however, was extremely late. I arrived home after four o'clock, drenched, benumbed with cold, and depressed.

The Yugoslavian partisans have liberated Belgrade, and the Allies have occupied Cesena and Aquisgrana, but all this seems infinitely far away to me.

---

[66] Ada's account of this meeting in Milan points out the errors in information given by historian Jane Slaughter, who wrote of the Gruppi di difesa that "the first group was organized in Milan in November 1943 by Lina Fibbi and Gina Bianchi of the Pci, Pina Palumbo of the Socialists (Psi), Elena Dreher and Ada Gobetti of the Pd'A, and Lucia Corti of the Catholic Left (a group that eventually joined the Pci)." Slaughter acknowledged that accounts differed as to the women who were present at the first meeting of the Gddd, stating that she took her information from Giuliana Beltrami and Mirella Alloisio, *Volontarie della libertà* (Milan: Mazzota, 1981), 30, 131. Jane Slaughter, *Women and the Italian Resistance*, 66, 142 n. 53. On 4 November 1944, Ada wrote that she met a number of women in Milan, including Elena Dreher, whom Ada said "impressed me most of all because of her intelligence and vivacity." She had not met Dreher before this time. Ada mentioned Lucia Corti for the first time on 20 December 1944 in connection with assistance work. She placed Lina Fibbi at the "first full meeting" on 21 October 1944. She never mentioned Gina Bianchi or Pina Palumbo in the *Diario*. Camilla Ravera also placed Ada among the group of women of the Cln who met in Milan in November 1943 to form the basis of an organization open to all women who wanted to fight for liberation, namely the Gruppi di difesa. She erroneously listed the other women as Rina Picolato (Bruna), Lina Merlin, Lina Fibbi, and Giovanna Barcelona. Ada mentioned meeting Rina Picolato, representative of the Communist Party in the Gruppi di difesa of Northern Italy, for the first time on 30 September 1944. She said Lina Merlin attended the "first full meeting" on 21 October 1944. She did not mention Giovanna Barcelona in the *Diario*.

24 October, Meana. As I correctly predicted, the regularity of the trains in the Susa Valley—to our innermost satisfaction, notwithstanding the consequent inconvenience—has been of quite a brief duration. In fact yesterday morning, having left Turin at 6:00 a.m., we had to do the stretch between Rosta and Sant'Antonino on foot, arriving in Meana after noon.

At home we found Paolo, who was just feeling fit again after a kind of poisoning. The work at "Sapes" is proceeding very well. They have happily moved bunks, chairs, and other useful furnishings into the cabin. It is now a shelter, relatively safe and sufficiently equipped. But the fundamental problem always remains that of food.

To resolve it, Paolo went to a hamlet near Desertes to get a sheep. With plenty of good will, the owner gave it to him (almost at the bulk price, which is five hundred lire), but warned him that it would be difficult for him to move a sheep "alone" from one small town to another. "Why is that?" answered Paolo, a victim of the preconception that said that a sheep was the gentlest of animals. "I will drag him behind me, gently or harshly." He took off, self-confident, with the ignorance of a city dweller. But quite soon he had to acknowledge that the mountain man was right. The sheep, used to moving with the herd, absolutely refused to walk alone. He tried to entice it with tender, convincing calls, and offered it handfuls of grass, and some grains of salt that he had in his pocket. It did a few meters, and then it stopped. He tried a strong approach and he yelled terrifying threats at it, but it just looked at him stupidly, "like a sheep," with expressionless eyes. He tried to drag it with the rope it had around his neck, but the animal halted with his four paws on the ground, and there was no way to move it. He had a little more success imitating the bark of a dog, but even this tactic did not last long. Meanwhile night was falling, and he did not have any desire to spend the night in the woods with that stupid sheep. Then he got mad and began to hit it, screaming so much that in the neighboring town those who had seen him on the trip up said to themselves, "The Germans have found a partisan in the woods and are massacring him." One, who was more courageous, went to see what was happening and, when Paolo explained to him the difficulty in which he found himself, he shrugged his shoulders philosophically, repeating the owner's words: "Sheep do not walk alone." Seeing that it was late, he advised him to spend the night in his *grangia*, which was not too far away. "But how will I drag this nasty beast there?" asked Paolo, and I believe that at this point he had truly begun to hate it. "Oh, there is only one system," answered the mountain man, "which is that you carry it on your shoulders." "There," commented Paolo, telling the story, "is the parable of the Good Shepherd. He is carrying the sheep that was found again in his arms, because otherwise he would never have been able to move it."

The morning after, Pillo and Renato arrived and, with a great deal of effort, dragging it a little, convincing it with strange gestures, and carrying it on their shoulders a lot, they were able to get the sheep to the cabin. But after they quartered it, they saw that the unfortunate animal must have been sick with consumption because its lungs were swarming with maggots. They ate it just the same, however. Whether it was the rotten sheep or something else, Paolo had violent symptoms of poisoning, and for several days he was not able to move or do anything. Now, however, he is doing very well, and has decided that this coming week he will go to France with Alberto and Gino.

25 October, Turin. Around 8:00 a.m. Ettore and I went down to Susa, where the truck of Carnino, the driver, was supposed to take us to Turin. But during yesterday evening's trip the truck had capsized in a field, and we did not know when it would arrive. There were no trains until tomorrow, and I was very annoyed because the meeting of the Gruppi di difesa was at three o'clock at Medea's house. Perhaps we would have done well to decide to go down by bicycle at once, but it was pouring rain and this, together with the illusion of obtaining passage on some military vehicle, made us hesitate. In fact, a German truck that was transporting wood brought us as far as Bussoleno, but then it stopped, and we remained in the street, under the rain, waiting to go on. Several motor vehicles passed by, but no one wanted to transport us. Finally we were able to clamber onto a German truck loaded with weapons. I sat down on the barrel of a small cannon, placing my knapsack containing various explosive gadgets at its feet with satisfaction. I hardly had time to be glad about the solution when a German officer, coming out of the hotel opposite us, approached, furious, and (*"raus! raus!"*) forced us to get down. Discouraged, we then got back onto the truck with the timber that was returning to Susa. At least there we could always, in the worst-case scenario, avail ourselves of the bicycles. In the meantime, Carnino's truck had arrived, which took us without incident as far as Piazza Statuto. But in Turin the trams were not running. Therefore, I had to cross the entire city on foot, arriving just in time at Medea's house. The contacts with Milan have been very useful and work is proceeding more cordially and quickly. Today committees for the organization of various sectors were established. The number of members is increasing, and the Central Committee is already inadequate for controlling all of their activities.

26 October. This morning Anna, the woman who comes to do my cleaning, approached me with an air that was half mysterious and half afflicted.[67] In her strange manner of speaking, which was a mixture of Italian and Piedmontese, she began with the usual preamble: "Signora Marchesini, I must tell you something," she said to me. After my departure, she had found a bundle of leaflets in a kitchen drawer. "I did not want to leave them here, and *am rinchersia* (I

---

[67] Anna Latore.

regretted) burning them, and so *l'ai pôrtaie* (I brought them) to my house. Did I do wrong?" Meanwhile she showed me the bundle, which she took out of her shopping bag.

"You did very well," I answered, "but if it happens again, burn them if you wish." But I confess that I was stunned. I had thought that Anna absolutely had not understood anything of what was happening in my house. I had relied on her foolish stupidity, as if a person could rely on a waterproof mattress in the middle of a flooded field. Forced to meet in the kitchen, which is the only room of the house that is light and heated, we spoke in front of her about the most dangerous things that would put us at risk. To my friends, who asked me how in the world I trusted her so much, I responded laughing that, if a bomb had not destroyed the garret where she lived, Anna probably would not have even noticed that there was a war. Nevertheless, I doubted that she knew precisely which states were fighting each other. Once, with a slightly worried air, she had said to me: "Signora Marchesini, they called me to the *fascio* (Fascist headquarters) and I went. Did I do wrong?" "Eh?" I had answered with a kind of start. "What did you go to do? What did they want?" "They wanted me to register with the Republic [of Salò], because before I had joined the *fascio*." (Who had not joined at first?) "What did you say?" *An prinsipi* (At first), I did not want to. Then *a l'an dime* (they said to me), "Don't you want to give five hundred lire for our poor brothers who are fighting?" "*Se a l'è* (if it is) for our poor brothers, *i je dagh pru* (I will certainly give it to them)," I answered, but I work and *i l'ai nen* (I do not have) time to come to the meetings." They answered: "It does not matter. Just give us the five hundred lire." I gave it to them. But now by any chance will *gnente* (nothing) happen to me at all?" "No, no," I answered with a great desire to laugh. "Be calm, and if they come to call for you again, before you go, tell me."[68] Meanwhile I thought: "Magnificent! I certainly had not expected such a cover—a 'Republican' in my house!" That is why her conversation this morning had surprised me. Either I had judged her poorly, or else she had been evolving during these months. Nevertheless, I took good care to make only the slightest remark. Even if she knows, even if she understands, it is better if she has very vague ideas. This is not because I mistrust her, but to put her conscience at ease. If she thinks she is privy to a secret, the sense of responsibility will make her unhappy.

29 October, Meana. The other morning, Friday, having left Turin at 6:00 a.m. under a sky full of stars, I reached Bussoleno at 10:30. Tempted by the hope that the train would continue, I let the local for Susa leave under my nose. I had a heavy bag and if I could avoid making the climb from Susa to Meana on foot, it would be so much better. I was punished for my laziness because the train

---

[68] Anna spoke the *piemontese* dialect.

did not leave and, in addition to the climb from Susa to Meana, I had to do the stretch between Bussoleno and Susa as well. But I was compensated for all my ills when, having arrived at Meana around two in the afternoon, I found Paolo, in good shape and in excellent spirits. He was very satisfied with the document of the Corpo di Volontari della Libertà, which Valle had furnished me, and which would serve as a credential for him when he arrived in France.

The following morning Paolo Menzio arrived, together with Giulio Pardi, head of the Winchester Team (the only one whom I still had not met), who decided to go to France with Paolo and Alberto in order to contact their Command again.[69] We left together, arriving in Beaulard around 1:00 p.m. The Pinna Pintor hospital of Turin has now been evacuated to the old Vittoria Hotel, under the direction of a young doctor, whose name is Bricarello, a friend of Menzio.[70] The news cheered me up a great deal. It is always convenient and often valuable to have a doctor friend within easy reach. Menzio also surmised that he would invite us to dinner. Unfortunately, the doctor was not there, but the good sisters of the hospital, hearing that we were friends, gave us something to eat all the same.

Then we climbed to Château by a road that seemed delightful to me, among red berries and clean young sheep on the somewhat tired and faded vegetation of the autumnal meadows. When we reached the cabin, in the growing darkness, we did not find anyone. Everything was in order, the furnishings had been completed, and the nearby shed had been built. When I had seen it for the first time, it was a big, empty, and disorderly room. Now instead it had the intimate and welcoming appearance of a refuge, with its berths, benches, table, and well-arranged household utensils. Menzio and Giulio, surprised at such "comfort," never stopped expressing their marvel and admiration. Quite soon Alberto arrived with a man who was no longer young, who was in charge of putting together a group in Bardonecchia, and some others. While we exchanged the latest news, the good old man prepared us a stew of sheep meat (this time one that was not sick) and potatoes. Then they brought out the camp beds and spread the mattresses on the floor, arranging everything for sleeping. Cavalierly they assigned a berth to me with a big down quilt and even linens.

This morning when I went to the little window I saw the sky between the branches of the pine trees, dark and menacing, and the boys from here, who had gone out to smell the air, announced that the snow was coming. I was worried about it. It was still early and this year we really did not want a premature snowfall. Paolo immediately declared that, snow or no snow, they would

---

[69] Giulio Debenedetti (Giulio Pardi) was a businessman and head of the English Winchester mission.

[70] Lincoln Bricarello was a doctor and director of the Pinna Pintor hospital, which had been transferred to Beaulard.

attempt the crossing tonight, or at the latest tomorrow night, in order to take advantage of the full moon. They would even try it without Gino, whose father had been "stopped" and who, worried, no longer seemed inclined to leave with them. This news worried me also, since the guidance of Gino, who was very knowledgeable about the area, was for me the only reassuring aspect of the expedition.

Toward noon, Menzio went down to the hospital in search of the doctor, whom he wanted to bring up to date about the situation, asking for his support. After a while I too left for Oulx, where I intended to reach an agreement with the driver for the transport of certain foodstuffs Laghi had promised for the group in Beaulard. Paolo came to accompany me for a stretch. By now it was snowing and, turning around to look at him, I saw at a certain point a line of fine white powder on the edge of his eyelash. It reminded me of so many years ago when I saw him, still a boy, arrive after his first long-distance ski race, with his face red from the effort under his blue wool *mefisto* and his eyelashes edged with snow above his radiant eyes.[71] At the Pierre Menue I embraced him tightly, and he turned back while I, by now alone on the deserted path, took up the descent again.

At Oulx I was able with some difficulty to find the driver and come to an agreement with him. But when I reached the station, I heard them saying that the train was not running. Why? No one knew. Until when? Until tomorrow. Who knows? Or perhaps even the day after tomorrow. Therefore I went to Cesare's house, where I had them lend me his sister's bicycle, but just when I was about to set out, I saw Menzio arrive who, having missed the train, had come to Beaulard on foot. What should I do? Two on a woman's bicycle was not very pleasant, but we could try. "Do you feel like carrying me on the handle-bars?" I asked him. "Certainly, if you feel like being carried," he answered. "Why not?" We arranged ourselves as best we could, under the incredulous and worried eyes of Cesare's father, and we left. I cannot say that it was a comfortable and pleasant trip, but it could have been even worse. An icy wind was blowing, which made the big snowflakes whirl around densely, and the visibility was very bad. The brakes of the bicycle were very bad also, and during the descent, I attached myself tenderly to Menzio's neck, congratulating myself that we had not crashed together against the rocks in the fields down below. Luckily there was not a lot of traffic on the road. At Salbertrand a girl evacuee who was going down to Bussoleno joined us, carrying a big bundle of mistletoe on her handle-bars. With an envious and covetous eye, Menzio observed her handsome new bicycle, of first quality and furnished with excellent brakes. Since she was a girl, evidently wanting to make the trip with company, and she was inclined to continue at our side, I ended up by asking her to make an exchange. She was

[71] A *mefisto* is a woolen ski mask, also called a *balaclava* or a *passamontagna* in Italian.

alone, we were two, and her bicycle was much sturdier. Although evidently she was not very enthusiastic, the girl did not know how to refuse, and we made the exchange. It was lucky, since the worst descent was beginning right then, and the dusk that was rapidly descending increased the difficulty.

We arrived at Susa, which was pitch dark. It was not snowing, but it was pouring rain. The girl complained, whimpering, at having to make the stretch up to Bussoleno alone, and Menzio cavalierly went to accompany her. I climbed up to Meana by the shortcut and began arduously to write reports.

1 November, Turin. It has continued to rain for two days—real All Saints' Day weather.[72]

Yesterday I met quite an extraordinary fellow, a certain Cesco, a man of proven courage and endurance, and a particularly touching sincerity.[73] His Venetian manner of speaking, naturally sweet, did not lack a certain almost feminine tenderness every now and then, and the light that glowed in his eyes, ready to become misty with tears as soon as he got emotional, had no other fanaticism than that of devotion. I accepted enthusiastically the idea of having him come to work for the union organization in Susa. There is an industrial complex in Susa, however modest, and I have the impression that, outside of some old socialist leaders, there are not many organizers among the workers. I think that, with his quality of human empathy, Cesco will be able to do excellent work for the Action Party.

Today two nice girls came to my house who, along with other young people, have created a young people's organization that they call Gioventù d'Azione (Young people of action), linked to the [Action] Party and at the same time organizationally independent, virtually like the Mfgl. They are creating a newspaper, which seems good to me and a very useful endeavor for diffusion among the young people, especially among the students, who, after so many years of miseducation, form a blind and deaf environment that at times is truly worrisome.

2 November. Luisa Monti came to see me. She moved me when she told me about the actions of a roundup in which she found herself, and during which she saved the situation with her composure and knowledge of German.[74]

---

[72] Officially the Solemnity of All Saints in the Roman Catholic Church, this day honors all the saints, known and unknown. On this day, and on the following day, All Souls' Day, the custom in Italy is to visit the graves of dead relatives. See https://www.catholic.org/saints/allsaints/.

[73] Francesco Colato (Cesco) was a worker and union organizer for the Action Party.

[74] Luisa Sturani Monti was Augusto Monti's daughter, a professor and collaborator of the Matteotti formations in the Soana Valley.

In the afternoon, I went to the Red Cross with Alma Vigna, who introduced me to the president, Countess De La Forêt, naturally without saying my name.[75] I wanted to interest her in the Gruppi di difesa, and to ensure that our women could take the first aid courses held by the Red Cross, in view of the insurrection. I found her to be understanding and intelligent. We easily came to an agreement. At the end, she said "Do you know Signora Gobetti?" "I am she," I answered, laughing. Having met her, the precaution of anonymity seemed absolutely unnecessary. We parted on a plane of cordial collaboration.

4 November. Yesterday morning, having left at 7:00 a.m. in a car with Mario Andreis, Valle, and Galimberti, I happily reached Milan at 10:00 a.m. (Three hours instead of the twelve or more that it takes with the train!)

I saw friends and I went to the meeting of the Gruppi di difesa, which was a little less ceremonious but more conclusive, particularly with regard to practical work. I made significant steps toward the constitution of the Mfgl, running all day to the various extremities of Milan and meeting a number of women. One, Elena Dreher, impressed me most of all because of her intelligence and vivacity.

This morning, I waited at around 8:00 a.m. for the car that was supposed to bring us back to Turin, but by nine it still was not there. A telephone call advised me to come to the North Station, where I found Mario and Duccio, worried because they had not yet seen Valle with the car. What if some disaster had befallen him? We waited until 11:00 a.m., a while outside, a while in the atrium of the station, and a while in a cafe. It was almost noon when Valle arrived. In the morning, when he was about to come and get us, he had been stopped by some Fascists who had told him to get out because they needed the car. Valle had protested, showing his (perfect!) papers from the Todt organization, and saying that he was working for the Germans. Perhaps he had protested with too much ardor, so they had taken him to Fascist headquarters and searched him thoroughly. Luckily they did not find anything on him, but they had detained him until the car returned, covered with mud. (What had they done with it? A mystery!) They gave it back to him without further explanation.

Commenting philosophically that all's well that ends well, we finally left for Turin, but the mishaps of the day were not over yet. In the vicinity of Magenta, an air raid surprised us and the Germans of the nearby checkpoint forced us to stop the car. Mario and Valle got out to analyze the situation, while Duccio and I stayed calmly in the car. After a few minutes, we saw them come back running, saying "Get out immediately. The airplanes are coming." We got out skeptically, unwillingly, but we hardly had time to move to the field nearby when a violent exchange

---

[75] Alma Vigna was a music teacher and organizer of the Mfgl. Countess Paola De La Forêt was inspectress of the Volunteer Nurses of the Committee of the Italian Red Cross of Turin.

of shots began. A quick look allowed me to size up the situation. The little square meadow in which we had taken refuge had the provincial road to the left, where we had left the car, the railroad to the right, an antiaircraft station to the north, a few hundred meters away, which was the one that was shooting, and, at a distance of half a kilometer to the south, the bridge over the Ticino, which had already been hit several times, and which was the probable objective today. Valle made us squat down at the edge of a ditch along a row of mulberry bushes, and he put his arm on my shoulders, saying now and again "Courage! Courage!" I was not at all afraid, but I felt his heart pound. (By now, the time when the mere din of antiaircraft artillery made my insides turn upside down, as during the first nearly harmless bombardments of 1940, seemed far away and unreal.) I understood that he was not afraid for himself, but for me, for whom he felt a kind of responsibility. (If he were, he would not have done, and would not be doing, everything he was doing.) His fear began to infect me. Suddenly the antiaircraft artillery was silent. I raised my head to look up. Perhaps it was over? "Down!" ordered Valle, who was paler than usual. "Now they will machine gun. Courage!" He forced me to go down farther into the ditch until my feet touched water. In the meantime, he squashed my face against the nettles of the bank with his hand. "Ta-ta-ta-ta" we heard after an instant, and it seemed like they were machine gunning our car on the nearby road. Then the roar of motors that were going away, growing feeble. Again I raised my head to ask "Is it over?" But this time it was not Valle's hand that drove me back with my face against the nettles, but a strong airflow accompanied by a raining of dirt and pebbles. A bomb had fallen on the bridge not too far away. When, after a few minutes, the airplanes had gone away and the antiaircraft artillery, which had begun to shoot again in the meantime, had become silent, we got up and, shaking, approached the car and found the signs of the machine gun fire. Duccio and I realized that, yes, perhaps we had done well to get out after all.

But now, since the bridge had collapsed, reaching Turin became a problem. We had to make a long detour as far as a small makeshift bridge. "You, little car, go ahead," a German who was directing traffic told us. "Big cars. Do not go ahead." Congratulating ourselves for having a small and not a big "machína," we resumed the trip again.[76] The escape from danger made us cheerful and loquacious, and we chatted pleasantly as far as Turin. In the very clear sky, the Alps uncoiled nearby, immaculate and superb. I looked at the opening of the Susa Valley, at the Rocciamelone, and at the Denti d'Ambin, thinking with anguish of what might be happening up there.

9 November. Complicated, very tiring days. I saw all kinds of people. I went from meeting to committee, and from committee to another meeting.

---

[76] Here Ada is making fun of the German's pronunciation of the Italian word for car (macchina), where the accent is on the first syllable rather than the second.

At my house (God forgive me!) dozens of people began to pass through again every day. Yesterday Visentini accompanied me to the Molinette hospital, and had me speak with a young nun who was intelligent and open. Naturally I kept everything to general topics, in terms of brotherhood and Christian charity, but it seemed that she understood more than I said. I would like to have nuns in the Gruppi di difesa. Besides, are there not sisters in the hospital in Ivrea who, having been trained by one of our women, Cassandra, not only conceal and care for the partisans but also even cooperate to take weapons away from the Germans?[77]

14 November. The other morning we reached Oulx around noon, and around 3:00 p.m. we set out toward Villaretto, and then toward the cabin. Whether it was the high snow that had completely changed the appearance of the scenery or our inadequate sense of direction, the fact remains that we were not able to find it. If on the one hand the matter consoled me ("if we do not find it," I thought "the Germans will not find it either") on the other hand I could not help but worry. Night was falling, and the prospect of spending the night in the open was not very comforting. We wandered for a long time, searching, through the woods. Meanwhile, with painful tenderness, I looked up at the intensely blue sky and the snow-white mountains, which the last lights of the sunset illuminated with rose-colored reflections until, when it was already quite dark, we noticed the tracks and, following them, we arrived at the cabin, almost without seeing it, so well was it camouflaged.

Only Pillo, thin and worn out, was inside. Since it was Sunday, the others could not resist the temptation to pay a visit to their families, and he remained alone and melancholy. Therefore he welcomed us enthusiastically. Even he could not explain the delay of the two boys, except for the bad weather. (They should have been back over a week ago.) The clear sky had only returned two days ago; perhaps they would arrive this very night. We went to bed animated by this optimistic hope, and I fell asleep immediately. But I woke up during the night. The wind that whistled among the pine trees had picked up, and I had the impression that this wind was a portent of snow. Then I lapsed into anguish thinking about the infinite dangers to which the two boys were exposed in the mountains, if they were even on the journey, and if nothing terrible had happened to them yet.

The next morning, as I had predicted, snow was falling, and the cheerful optimism of the night before seemed unfounded and absurd, and not just to me. To rebel, I decided to do a thorough cleaning, which the cabin seemed to need. I had two big pine tree branches cut, and with this improvised broom I swept everywhere, under the beds and in the corners. I picked up articles of

---

[77] Selina Roffino (Cassandra) was an organizer of the Gruppi di difesa in Ivrea.

clothing and tried to tidy them up as best I could. I sent Pillo to get two buckets of water, which I put on the stove to boil, and washed the dirty household utensils.

We had just finished when Gino arrived with some others, a certain Codega among them, organizer of the group from Savoulx.[78] The fellow is an odd Venetian sort who has already been with Marcellin and, it seems, in France as well. He looks much more enterprising than reassuring. He speaks a bizarre mixture of Italian, Piedmontese, and Venetian, into which he introduces strange expressions. He says, for example, "You should *meterghe* (put) a little *muscolo* (and he means "*muschio*" (moss)) on the roof of the *cabana* (cabin)," or even, "The Germans *a l'an pedlame* (*pediname*) (trailed closely behind me) up to here." The two had brought the necessary ingredients to make *tagliatelle*, and we immediately set to work. The others also arrived, and soon the cabin was filled with the festive eagerness that accompanies the preparation of dinner anywhere.

Gino tried to reassure me, saying that if the Germans on guard had taken Paolo and Alberto, they certainly would have known about it in the town, and that if they did not return within a few days, we could go there to look for them. The idea of being able to do something gave me a sense of relief.

When Ettore and I left, Gino came to accompany us as far as Château. It continued to snow. The snow, high by now, had covered the tracks, and his guidance was very useful to us. At Château, we passed in front of the house of Don Riccardo, who invited us inside to *bere una volta* (to have a drink). Remembering that I did not drink red wine (an absurd idiosyncrasy that I absolutely have not able to conquer), he went to look for a little bottle of white wine. "It is what we use for Mass!" he announced.

The train for Turin arrived almost on schedule from Bardonecchia, and we left as usual from Beaulard, but in Oulx it made a long stop, so long that I dozed with my head on Ettore's shoulder.

A violent explosion woke me up suddenly. I opened my eyes and saw that there was no longer anyone in the car. Only a priest's cowl appeared under the seat in front. Everyone had escaped or hidden.

"What happened?" I asked Ettore, who had not even moved, and who answered me placidly: "The Ventoux bridge has been blown up."

"But no!" I protested. "It would have made much more noise!" "Remember that it is quite far away, and that there is the snow," insisted Ettore. As usual, he was right.

Having arrived in Oulx by train many times before, we had observed the numerous boxes of explosives heaped at the two ends of the bridge and under

[78] Armando Codega, a farmer and partisan in the "Franco Dusi Column" of the IV Alpine Division of GL.

the tunnel. Since September the Germans, having anticipated retreat in the face of the Allied advance through the mountains, had mined the bridge to stop them at the right moment. Just this once the problem for us was not to blow up the bridge, but to prevent them from blowing it up. Now what had happened? Having gone down to the station, we started to make heads or tails of the confusing and contradictory rumors. Certainly the Germans had not blown up the bridge. (On the contrary, it appears that the two on guard had been killed in the explosion.) Nor did the partisans. (This we knew for sure.) Therefore the version according to which the explosion had occurred after contact with the excessive moisture produced by the extraordinary snowfall seemed believable.

The stationmaster, who was arguing furiously in the middle of a group of railroad workers, expressed, albeit somewhat coarsely, the state of mind of the surrounding inhabitants of the valley: "These Germans have hidden dynamite everywhere, and obviously they are blowing us up. Let's hope at least that they have also hidden some up their asses!"

But however the explosion had occurred, one thing was certain. The train could not continue. Today we had to be in Turin. Therefore we went to Cesare's house and tried to leave by bicycle, but it was impossible to go ahead in the very high snow. The only thing left was to go down on foot. It was almost five o'clock and, walking quickly, downhill, we could easily be in Susa by eight-thirty, before the curfew. But we made our calculations without considering the snow, which made our progress much slower and more exhausting.

We went ahead quite well up to the bridge, taking advantage of the many tracks that were already laid down. The bridge, an enormous iron structure that was completely destroyed, was a striking spectacle, as if a gigantic force had uprooted the mighty skeleton. The charge must have been very strong. Luckily there were no houses in the surrounding area or else they too would have gone up in the air. The banks of the river and a stretch of road appeared to be ravaged and torn apart.

At the entrance to the tunnel, I saw a new, abandoned, bicycle on the edge of the road, and instinctively I pulled it up and pushed it ahead. "What are you going to do with it?" asked Ettore. "Nothing now, but it can always be useful," I answered stupidly. I carried it carefully as far as the exit of the tunnel, where a German came to meet me and, without a word, took it out of my hands. Had he understood that I wanted to take it away with me? Or rather did he think that I had brought it this far to do him a favor? Of course I will never know. We did not comment, however, and we continued on our way.

Since the road was less trodden, going ahead became more and more exhausting. We greeted with joy the passage of every car that pounded the snow for us, but cars were sparse and the snow was so thick and dense that it covered the tracks again almost immediately. Suddenly in the fog we could see something of a glimmer, perhaps the last quarter of the moon, which was making its way weakly among the clouds.

At 8:00 p.m., we were still not in Chiomonte. It would be impossible to arrive at Susa before the curfew, but just as impossible to stop. Therefore we continued, entrusting our souls to God. When we were at the entrance to Chiomonte, at the place where I knew there was a German guard, I began to talk and laugh out loud, so that they would understand that I was a woman and would not shoot blindly, perhaps out of fear, when they heard the sound of footsteps. The precaution was useful. "Where are you going?" asked a German, coming to meet us with his gun leveled, which he then lowered immediately when he saw our defenseless and harmless appearance. I explained to him in German that the bridge had been blown up and that we had to reach Susa, where we had a child who was sick. "*Ach, gut!* (oh, fine)" commented the German, and he let us go on without question.

We used the same method in Gravere, where they were much more curious, however, and wanted to see our papers. Ettore's were such that they cleared up any of their suspicions, but I realized that they were asking us so many questions because they wanted to chat and likewise to detain us, even going so far as to praise my German pronunciation! I must say to their credit that when they let us pass they sent a noncommissioned officer with us with a flashlight who let us go through the road block at the exit of the town without any more stops.

When we reached Susa it was after nine thirty. We did not see anyone, either at the entry or on the streets. Naturally Teta's store was closed, but as soon as we knocked at the portcullis, we heard her answer immediately and come to open up for us. "My heart told me that you would arrive," she said. She gave us something to eat and somewhere to sleep.

This morning, having left Susa at 6:00 a.m. in a frigid train, we arrived in Turin around ten, benumbed with cold. We found a house full of people, but freezing all the same, without electricity and without coal.

I continued to move about for the entire day, and I did a number of things, but I am terribly unhappy.

15–27 November 1944

And unhappy I continued to be. As the days passed, and hope became weaker, my anguish became stronger.

When I think about it again today, in light of what happened afterward, I must acknowledge that, if even they can seem excessive, my fears were not unfounded. Still I wonder how I came to endure that frightening anxiety. It was not the first time that I was worried about Paolo, but the other times it was a question of a maximum of three or four days and I always knew, more or less precisely, where he was and where I could look for him. Instead, now I was groping in the dark, in a void where sometimes I thought I would go crazy. I continued to see people, and do a bunch of things, a little because I was caught up and went forward by force of habit, and a little because I had the threads of so many things in my hands and I could not let them drop. But in rare moments of rest, I had real crises of desperation, and I howled like a wounded beast.

The notes from those days, fragmentary and incomplete, reveal the confusion of my state of mind. I continued to take part in the usual meetings, introduce people to each other, type, and jot down reports and circulars, but I did so mechanically, as if my internal spring were broken.

On 16 or 17 November I was in Milan again, with Mario and two directors from the Burgo who wanted to get in touch with the Committee of National Liberation of Northern Italy.[1] I saw many women, although a series of misunderstandings and missed appointments caused the projected meeting to fail. I had long conversations with Panta while walking in the darkness along a street, waiting for a fellow who then did not come.

On the 19th, I went to Susa with Ettore and Valle in young Edmondo's *topolino* and from there we went up to Braida, where Laghi was.[2] I remember that

---

[1] Cartiere Burgo was a large paper manufacturing plant.

[2] The popular Fiat 500 or *topolino* (the Italian name for Mickey Mouse) was produced in Italy from 1936 until 1955. It was a favorite of Fiat owner Giovanni Agnelli. Franco Sportoletti (Edmondo) was commander of the citizen squads of the Action Party and representative of the Action Party in the Piazza Command of Turin.

for the entire morning I was almost happy, and it delighted me to see the leaps and buffoonery of two little lambs that had just been born. It was a magnificent day. The mountains toward France stood out, luminous against the clear sky, and it seemed impossible that I would not hear news of Paolo in Susa or Meana. Perhaps I would find him there himself. Instead, I found a group of townspeople in Meana who wanted to found a local Committee of National Liberation, but since there were not representatives of the five parties in the town, they wanted to form it with representatives from each village.[3] I talked with them for a long time, and tried to jot down a rudimentary act of incorporation, and clarify some fundamental ideas. Then I also saw a girl who took charge of forming some Gruppi di difesa locally.

The next evening, we left again for Turin on the train, but the trip was rather eventful. In the car, I was seated next to a German who, when he arrived, with a big sigh of relief, had taken off his belt with its respective revolver and two hand grenades, and had hung it right over my head. Although I was dazed and tired, the possibilities did not escape me. Of course the German might fall asleep. (In fact, he had already fallen asleep immediately.) A little before we arrived in Turin, I had only to stand up and remove the revolver from its case and leave in the dark before he could notice it, and the day would not have been lost. Lulled by the slow rhythm of the train and by the cherished hope for the imminent undertaking, I ended up falling asleep. A violent impact, which threw me against the opposite wall of the car, woke me up. Confusion, screams, uproar. The word "derailment" progressed rapidly along the corridor. But in fact no one did anything. Only at a certain point did the old woman who was seated in front of me begin to cry that she had hurt her nose and that she was losing blood *a brassà* (abundantly). Immediately there were those willing to shine some lights on her, and I could see that she had an insignificant scratch. But the old woman did not give us a moment of peace. "I hit against something hard," she said. "What was it?" Then, raising her eyes, she saw the belt and grenades that were dangling in front of her. "I hit against the grenade!" She began to cry, "I would be dead if the grenade had exploded!" For all that I tried to calm her down and distract her, she dwelled so much on that miserable grenade that at a certain point the German, annoyed, unhooked his belt and went away, spoiling my plan.

I cursed the whimpering old woman in my heart, but even without her, the undertaking would have failed just the same because a little later they made us get off the train and travel some kilometers on foot along the railroad as far as Sant'Antonino. Then, when we got back on, we arrived at Rosta, and there we

---

[3] The five principal antifascist parties that made up a Committee of National Liberation were the Communist, Socialist, Action, Christian Democratic, and Liberal Parties.

made another stop in the dark. We did not know if and when we would depart again. Finally we left, and arrived in Turin after midnight.

The next morning, as soon as it was a decent hour, I called Bianca, who the day before had gone up to "Sapes" and had seen Pillo and the others. But there was no news of Paolo and Alberto. In general Bianca is optimistic and level-headed, but that morning, beneath the conventional phrases with which she gave me the news, I sensed an anguish that was no less than mine. I tried to calm her down. "The little cousins will get much better, you will see," I said. "You know that with this kind of illness there are sometimes unforeseen complications." "Oh, certainly they will get better," answered Bianca, but from her tone I understood that she saw right through my optimism, just like I saw through hers. I remember that when I hung up the receiver, I remained motionless for a moment, staring in front of me, wondering how I would be able to move from there, talk, and go on living. I wanted to close my eyes, to give up without fighting any more, losing myself in that darkness and silence in which I felt myself sink more and more profoundly.

Instead at a certain point I shook myself, went out, saw the usual people, and did the usual things. In the evening, I began to work on several reports for the Susa Valley (military, political, women's), and I spent almost the entire night on them. When I threw myself on the bed, I was so exhausted that I did not have time to think about anything. Suddenly I fell asleep.

I lived the following days in a kind of painful nightmare. I participated in two new committees: the Coordination Committee of the Action Party, in which those responsible for the various branches of work took part; and the Assistance Committee, also of the Action Party, where I tried to divide the tasks among our women who do assistance work in the outlying committees of the Gruppi di difesa. I went to the usual meetings.

Friday morning, when I passed in front of a bookstore, driven by an almost superstitious hope, I went in and bought a pocket edition of the *Ariosto*. Paolo liked poets and nice editions, and now he always carried with him a little Barberà *Diamante* volume of Leopardi's *Canti*, which I had given to his father more than twenty years before.[4] I wanted to welcome him with a little gift upon his return. I leafed through the book at the bottom of my bag with a feeling of profound tenderness that wanted to be hope, but that was essentially desperate nostalgia. The next morning, Saturday the 25th, Ettore and I left. Again, nothing and no one was in Meana. In the afternoon I went up to Braida and

---

[4] Ariosto was the Italian poet who wrote the celebrated narrative poem of the Italian High Renaissance called *Orlando Furioso* (c. 1532). Gaspero Barberà was a publisher in Florence of pocket editions called the *Collezione diamante*. The *Canti* is the major collection of poetry of the poet Giacomo Leopardi (1798–1837).

spoke with Laghi. It was already nighttime when I came back down, and a kind of fine snow was whirling about in the dark air.

The next morning, having left at 9:00 a.m., we reached Beaulard around noon. The weather had cleared up and there was something of a smell of spring in the air. I stopped many times while climbing along the mule track that leads to Château, remembering how I had passed by there around one month ago with Paolo, and how I had admired the fields and red berries and little white sheep. Raising my eyes, I saw before me the snow of the Passo dell'Orso, glimmering in the sun. With this weather that was so beautiful, of course they must be back. Perhaps I would find them in the cabin, they would tell me about everything, and I would laugh about my fears. Perhaps instead I would not find them there. (At this point I felt that my heart had stopped beating.) Then everything would be over, the anxiety and the pain and the torment, because I would stop hoping and give up fighting. But something inside me suddenly said no, that I would not stop hoping, even if they were not there and had not arrived either yesterday or today or tomorrow. I would continue to wait, to live, and to work.

Having reached Château, we stopped for a moment in front of the church to catch our breath. It was a little past one o'clock and the village appeared deserted. Evidently everyone had gone to take a little Sunday siesta in the warmth of their houses. Suddenly we saw a local young partisan approach us, who had certainly taken advantage of the holiday to pay a short visit to his family, and who had seen us from the window of his house.

"How are you?" I asked.

"Very well," responded the boy.

"Are you going up?"

"Yes," I answered, and immediately added, with a tone that I tried to make sound casual: "Have they arrived?"

"Yes."

"No!" I exclaimed, clutching Ettore's arm in order not to fall. "When?"

"Yesterday morning."

"Are they well?"

"Very well."

Then I sat down on the steps of the church and closed my eyes for an instant. It seemed that the universe around me was rotating, as if it had gone crazy. In the meantime I continued to tell myself, "No, it is not possible, I am too happy." When I opened them again, for a moment I had the impression that I did not recognize the place where I was. Yet they were the same mountains, the same sky, the same woods, and the same houses, but it was as if they had a new quality, and the air I was breathing seemed sparkling and exhilarating, like a goblet of *spumante*. I no longer felt any sense of fatigue or heaviness. It seemed that, if I opened my arms, I could go up in the air and fly.

"Let's go, let's go quickly," I said, grabbing Ettore with one arm and the boy with the other, and I began to run up by the path. What I said and what I did during the trip, I do not know. Absolute happiness, like absolute pain, has no beginning and no end. There was the *taglio raso*. There was the cabin, and there was Paolo, on the threshold, alive, healthy, and smiling. "*Ciau, Mi.*" Immediately my exaltation subsided and everything seemed to become normal again. But such a normality is unusual in this world, a normality that appears to us today like a symbol of Paradise, and that perhaps will reign on earth only when the "men of good will" finally are able to reign over their destiny.

We entered the cabin. Alberto was in bed, and Paolo too went back to bed, because, after around twenty-four hours of rest, they still had not recovered from the fatigue and tension of the return trip. Pillo and the others welcomed us festively. How different the atmosphere was from that of my last visit, two weeks before, when everything was dominated by uncertainty, anxiety, and fear.

Paolo took out a little package from his knapsack. "I brought you a gift, *Mi.*" It was a little package of Nescafé. "You just have to dissolve it in a little hot water, and it is ready immediately," explained Alberto. There was hot water on the stove, and they prepared a cup for me right away. Never did a drink seem more comforting, more appreciated, and more extraordinary.

Only then did I ask: "Can you tell me why you were so late? What have you arranged?" Immediately the two boys told the story.

Giulio, Alberto, and Paolo had left according to plan on the night of 31 October. It was snowing lightly, but the moon illuminated the trail (the trail of the Germans). From a mountain climber's perspective, the crossing had not presented much difficulty. At around the middle of the route, at Rocher de la Garde, which, as its name indicates, is at the entry to the last and roughest climb, Paolo had approached the shelter, hoping to be able to go in for a brief stop, but he left in a great hurry when he saw, through the panes of the little windows where he had peered innocently, that the Germans had established themselves there too. With cautious steps he reached the others, and they continued to climb in silence. They passed along the peak of the Passo as light as flies ("real velvet paws" commented Paolo, laughing), at around ten meters from the cabin, where the Germans "on guard" were sleeping peacefully.

No one came outside. Then, beyond the Passo, they threw themselves into "no man's land," and after about three hours of rather exhausting walking in the high snow, which was not marked by tracks, they arrived at a narrow passage in the valley around four o'clock, beyond which presumably the first French checkpoint should have been located. While they continued to advance,

Paolo suddenly bent down, driven by that subconscious instinct that made him notice hidden traps. "There is a wire here. Is there a mine by any chance?" They had lit a flashlight in order to see, but immediately "ta-ta-ta-ta!" and, accompanying the shots, a series of rapid lights ripped through the darkness. (*Las flamelas,* Paolo said in Meanese, telling the story). Evidently the Frenchmen on guard, seeing the light, had begun to fire. The three boys quickly threw themselves on the ground. Then Alberto began to yell with whatever breath he had in his throat: "*Nous sommes du Comité de Libération Italien* (We are from the Italian Committee of Liberation)!" He continued to yell until a voice came out from the darkness: "*Avancez* (Advance)!" Then they went forward, with their hands raised, but instead of the Gallic faces that they were expecting, they found themselves before the black faces of two Moroccans who were waiting for them with guns leveled.[5] "*Vous fifi italien* (Are you Italian Ffi)?" one of them asked.[6] "No, no," Alberto was about to respond, convinced that *fifi* was an insult. "*Nous sommes des partisans* (we are partisans)." Luckily Paolo had a faint idea. Didn't *fifi* mean *Forces Françaises de l'Intérieur* (Ffi, corrupted to *fifi* by the Moroccan voices)? "*Oui, nous fifi italiens* (Yes, we are Italian *fifi*)," he hurried to answer, and took out a document from the Committee of National Liberation. The Moroccans examined it, probably without understanding much of it. They seemed convinced, however. Their black faces brightened into a cordial smile, and guiding them carefully to make them avoid the mines, among great exclamations of "bravo *fifi*," "bravo *italien*," they brought them inside the *blocus* (checkpoint) (called the Clé des Acles) and soothed them with hot coffee, *biscotti* (cookies), and sardines. Then they telephoned up to the Command to receive instructions. But the nocturnal arrival of the three boys had gotten them worried, and for a while they continued to ask if anyone else had come with them. "Is there not someone dead or wounded?" they asked. No, luckily there were no dead or wounded. "If there is someone wounded, please say so," they insisted with an encouraging tone. Then suddenly someone on the lookout thought he saw a shadow (perhaps a hare?), and with mysterious gestures and words, ordered: "*Taisez-vous! Armes aux mains* (Be quiet! Take up your weapons)!" The others stiffened, preparing themselves for the attack that naturally did not come.

Around seven in the morning, evidently following the instructions they had received by telephone, two Moroccans with gun and bayonet hoisted, one in front and one behind, accompanied them up to the Command, in the Alpine village of Plampinet. There lieutenant Roland Grosjean of the Ffi of

---

[5] At the time, Morocco was still a French colony. According to Fofi, Moroccans participated in the war as part of the French troops. *Diario partigiano* (1972), 229 n. 5.

[6] The word *fifi* was a nickname for French Resistance fighters who were part of the Forces Françaises de L'intérieur (French domestic forces).

the Armée Secrète (embodied by now in the regular army as I Compagnie, IV Demi-brigade, I Division, I Armée) welcomed them kindly, and they explained their plan to him.[7]

They had gone to France to offer a *coup de main* (helping hand) that presented relatively light risks and could have interesting developments. It was a question of "conquering" the Passo dell'Orso, taking the eighteen Germans on guard prisoner, and carrying off all of their weapons. At the appointed time, they would go up to the Passo at the same time as our partisans from Beaulard and the French forces from Plampinet. Our men would be in charge of attacking the checkpoint and taking the Germans prisoner—except for one or two, possibly officers or noncommissioned officers, who could be useful for eventual exchanges—who then, however, would be handed over to the French because, given the organization of our group, we would not know what to do with prisoners. On the other hand, the intervention of the French would give the "strike" the character of a war operation, so if they do things properly, they will avoid reprisals on the population on our side of the mountain. But it would remain well understood that we would take the weapons. Having thus cleared out the pass—which the Germans would have significant difficulty getting up the courage to occupy again after the setback—it would open the way for installments of French forces to be organized advantageously in several places in the valley, always in agreement with our partisans, with the goal of disarming the Germans and occupying places of strategic importance. Paolo thought of a certain French general who, in 1754, passing right through the Passo dell'Orso, had pushed forward victoriously as far as Cesana.

Lieutenant Roland listened to the proposal with keen attention. Evidently he liked the idea, but the undertaking was too important for him to take responsibility for it alone. He needed to consult the higher Commands. Therefore he loaded the three boys onto a *bagnole* (cattle cart) and sent them to Nevache (it was there that they saw a jeep for the first time), where a captain, equally understanding and courteous, listened to them with interest and kindness and, fundamentally approving the proposal, sent them up to Briançon.

But at Briançon, at Military Security, they found quite a different ambiance—no longer the fraternal and spontaneous cordiality of the *maquis*, but the bureaucratic distrust and coldness of the regular army.[8] They questioned them in detail, searched them, and examined their documents. Then, after several hours, *"Vite, vite, prenez toutes vos affaires, on va partir tout de suite"* (Quickly, quickly, take all your belongings, you are leaving right away), they loaded them onto a truck with two armed Moroccans, like prisoners (while at

---

[7] Roland Grosjean was a lieutenant in the French army. The Armée secrète (Secret army) became part of the regular army as First Company, 4th Demi-Brigade, First Division, First Army.

[8] *Maquis* (literally "undergrowth") was the name for the French underground.

first they had traveled without an escort), and took them to Embrun. There more endless questions, coldness, and suspicion. While they were waiting, they locked them in a wash house where the Moroccans came to freshen up. It was real enjoyment for them to see how these men undid their turbans to use them as hand towels, and with what skill they reassembled the complicated architecture on their heads, and just as entertaining, even if it was not very appetizing, to observe the aplomb with which they took their chewing gum out of their mouths and stuck it on the wall, later to put it back in their mouths when they had finished washing.

At a certain point the usual order came: "*Vite, vite, prenez toutes vos affaires!*" They brought them to Briançon, to the Devault Barracks, where finally they gave them something to eat, and they put them to sleep in a little room with three folding beds. (It was the first time they had eaten stew and they found it exquisite. They could not imagine that, when it became their only nourishment, they would soon end up becoming sick of it to the point of nausea.) There, who knows why, they remained for three days, without being able to leave, under the strictest surveillance. From the window they saw the courtyard of the barracks and the many practical jokes of the Moroccans from the window. These men had been among the troops at the landing in Southern Italy, and they spoke some words in corrupted Neapolitan. "*Aruà, aruà!*" they muttered frequently. "What does *aruà* mean?" they asked the little Moroccan constantly on guard at their door. "It means *vieni accà* (come here)," he answered laughing. One morning they awoke hearing *O sole mio!* sung at the top of their voices.

Finally when, having made the best of things, they had begun to get settled and organize themselves a bit, suddenly they were made to leave ("*Vite, vite*"), around the evening of the second day, and were brought to Embrun, where they had to sleep on the ground with some blankets, in the guardroom. Naturally every hour someone came to change places and sound the trumpet, which disturbed Alberto and Giulio (but not Paolo, whose sleep is really bombproof). At four in the morning ("*Vite, vite*"), they were loaded onto a truck with the usual escort of Moroccans, brought up to Grenoble, and there directly to the Hotel Lesdiguières, where the High Command of the entire Alpine area was located, and left to wait while those who accompanied them went to confer with the "important people." They felt as though they had arrived in a palace from *Mille e una notte* (A thousand and one nights)—shiny floors, ornate mirrors, dim lights, and Moroccans dressed in white, with turbans, who moved silently with gestures that were almost solemn and who, expressionless, bowed down with folded arms.[9] But their enchantment did not last long. At Military Security on

[9] The *Thousand and One Nights*, also known as the *Arabian Nights*, is a series of anonymous stories originally written in Arabic and including the stories of Ali Baba, Sinbad the Sailor, and Aladdin.

Rue Condorcet, where they were taken immediately, they found the same banal atmosphere, half office and half barracks. Again they were questioned for a long time until a certain Moretti, well esteemed by the French authorities with whom he had already worked for a long time, and who had met Alberto and Paolo during their crossing with the group from Patria, came out of nowhere to resolve the situation.[10] But he did not know Giulio, and therefore he could not vouch for him. Paolo and Alberto got all worked up in vain, declaring that they knew him very well and that he was one of them. What is more, Giulio, who evidently had his reasons for doing it, withdrew into a kind of obstinate silence, saying that he would not give any more explanations until they put him in contact with someone from the Allied Command. Then one of those absurd events that happen often in the bureaucratic world took place. Giulio, who was regularly regimented in the Allied army, was detained at Military Security as a suspect, while Alberto and Paolo, armed only with their good will and with a little piece of paper from the Corpo di Volontari della Libertà (which in their case was authentic, but which could have very well been false) were from that moment onward, thanks to the recognition of someone whom they met by chance, considered to be colleagues and treated with trust and respect.

Then they left, in the company of three officers, and passing through the *route du Lautaret* (Lautaret road), they reached Briançon, where a lieutenant who specialized in *coups de mains* (sudden attacks) accompanied them to Plampinet. The High Command approved the attack on the Germans at the Passo dell'Orso, but instead of waiting to do it with the collaboration of the partisans, they wanted to do it immediately, with only the French forces, making use of the guidance of the two *maquisards italiens*. It was not exactly what our boys wanted; however, what was important was that the action took place. Therefore they accepted, asking and obtaining, however, that all the weapons taken from the Germans be left to us.

It was Sunday, and the soldiers had organized a type of spectacle at Plampinet, in which a certain Indochinese Tin-Tin had a big part, and during which Alberto and Paolo learned a song that was quite in vogue in France at the time, *C'est aujourd'hui dimanche* (Today is Sunday), and they participated in an *enchère américquaine* (American gambling).[11] They stayed in Plampinet for two days while they made the preparations for the "strike."

They finally left on the evening of the 7th. The French had done things on a big scale. For an undertaking for which seven or eight people were sufficient, they had set a bunch of people in motion. About twenty *éclaireurs-skieurs* (skier-scouts) went ahead. Then came the group that was supposed to carry out the strike, comprising about thirty people. (Alberto and Paolo went with

---

[10] Moretti was a liaison officer with the Allies.

[11] Tin-Tin was a popular French cartoon character.

these men, but they were not armed. They had given Paolo a bazooka rocket to carry.) Finally a group of reinforcements would come, made up of another thirty men. At Châlet des Acles, where a stretch of flat land begins, two companies of Moroccans would be placed, armed with mortars. Then at Plampinet another three reserve companies would move in. A brigadier general would even come up for the occasion. It was the first action of such importance after the September advance that they would carry out on this front, and the "big shots" evidently hoped to derive honor and glory and perhaps a citation in the bulletin from it, hence the importance given to the matter.

But their ambitions were frustrated because the strike did not succeed. When, having gotten through the long stretch of flat land without incident, they had attacked the climb toward the Passo, a terrible blizzard arose and a widespread *glissade* began.[12] The snow conditions had completely changed from when Paolo and Alberto had gone through around one week before, and advancing became very difficult. At a certain point the *éclaireurs-skieurs* had stopped, no longer able to go ahead. Paolo and Alberto had continued to climb with their group, which, however, was becoming more and more lean. The blizzard on the Passo was very violent, and they could not see one meter ahead. Suddenly they found that only three of them were left, the two of them and an officer. Then even the officer disappeared. Suddenly, yelling in the snow squall to make themselves heard, Alberto and Paolo realized that the two of them were alone and that they were speaking French. By now they were on the Italian side, at perhaps about a hundred meters from the cabin occupied by the Germans, but what could they do alone and without weapons? Certainly they could not try the strike, thus sounding a warning; nor could they push ahead and return to Italy, as perhaps they felt tempted to do at the bottom of their hearts, which would have been neither appropriate nor right. Therefore they decided to turn back, and the expression of joy and relief that emerged on the officer's face when he saw them reappear in the middle of the storm revealed how little faith he had in them, at least up to that moment. This is why they had not armed them. Now, seeing them disappear, they had thought it was an ambush for sure. "*Reculez, reculez* (Move back, move back)!" the officer, very excited, had yelled to the men who were moving about in the blizzard. Seeing them reappear, he understood that he was mistaken. "*Reculez!*" he continued to order, but more serenely, as if it were a matter of routine.

Even though the undertaking did not succeed, the return trip had a triumphal character. If the matter had not gone well it had been because of an act of God, the fault of the elements, but they had done what they could, and the two Italians had conducted themselves magnificently. At Plampinet they were

---

[12] *Glissade* literally means skid or slide.

welcomed at the officers' mess, and a kind of banquet was given in their honor. There was a festive cordiality in the air, as if they thought: "This time it went this way, but now we have found trustworthy friends, and we will be able to do great things together."

Nevertheless, without their knowing it, the outcome had been achieved. The next day the Germans abandoned the Pass, and they did not return there again. Were they surprised when they saw the tracks around the cabin? Were they afraid of a new attack, which they thought would be difficult to resist? Or maybe they had already decided to go away beforehand, because winter made provisions and travel more and more difficult, and the failed attack had persuaded them to hurry their departure? Or had they simply obeyed an order of a general nature, without any reference to the particular circumstances? We will never know. Nevertheless, we had obtained what we wanted: the Passo was free.

The next day Paolo and Alberto returned to Briançon, to the Devault Barracks. Now they were no longer considered prisoners, but soldiers like the others. They went down to sit in the courtyard in the sun, and all the Moroccans came to shake their hands. (The Moroccans' passion for shaking hands is strange. When two Moroccan drivers meet while driving a car on the road, whether in the mountains or in the middle of the snow, they stop their automobiles and get out to shake each other's hands and to shake the hands of all of the passengers in the two motor vehicles!) Taking advantage of the off-duty time, they went to take a short walk around Briançon. The next day, with a jeep, they returned to Grenoble, to Military Security, where a Belgian whose name was Maurice made them a proposal. Would they agree to organize a regular wartime information service in Italy for the French Command? If so, they would have to stay in Grenoble for about ten days to take a course of instruction, and then return to Italy to collect the *renseignements* (information) that they would then bring back or have brought back to France.

Alberto and Paolo took a few hours before responding. They understood very well that the notorious Deuxième Bureau, that is, a secret espionage service, was probably hidden behind this "information bureau." But now they were at war and, however different their objectives and moral and political persuasion, on a practical plane they were pursuing the same goals. It was a question of clarifying their own position precisely, and not jeopardizing their own freedom of action in any way. Once these points were established, they could very well provide the information, which would naturally all end up at the Allied Command. The support of the French would be very useful in all present and future developments in the partisan struggle.

After having thought about if for a while, they ended up accepting, provided that everything was quite clear. They were Italian partisans, and the only authority they answered to was the Corpo di Volontari della Libertà.

They agreed to work with the French army, providing information of a warlike nature, as long as this collaboration was compatible with their orders from the Cvl, and helpful to the battle of the Italian partisans. Naturally they remained free to collaborate with the English and American Commands in all actions where their aid could be useful. In exchange for the information, the French Command would give them weapons for the partisans.

The French did not have any objections to such declarations. Having clarified the situation in this manner, Paolo and Alberto were lodged in the Hotel Rochambeau, *réquisitionné* (requisitioned) by the Military Command. They began the course, consisting of a series of lessons about the various German ranks, the uniforms of the various divisions, the marks on the tanks, *Sold Buch*, and things of this nature.[13] After several days, they saw Giulio and Franco (who had reached France from another side in the meantime) also arrive in Rochambeau. Giulio had finally been able to clarify his own position and get in touch with his command. Therefore he also put Alberto and Paolo in touch with a Major Hamilton, head of the Allied mission in Grenoble.[14] They had promised a significant quantity of weapons and the group from Beaulard would be mobilized for their transport, linking the transport and information services. The days passed quickly, not at all unpleasant as a whole.

On 22 November, furnished with all the weapons they could carry, they returned to Plampinet and immediately set out on the return trip. Tired because of the heavy load, they reached the plain in broad daylight, in view of the German positions. Therefore they waited, hiding as best they could in a forest, which was a bit darker. Then, instead of continuing toward the Passo dell'Orso, they decided to pass through the Col des Aiguilles, which was closer. In the evening they reached the Colle della Santà, joined by a trail to the Passo della Mulatera, which was occupied by the Germans. The trail was inviting, but of course, armed and weighted down like they were, they could not run the risk of encountering some enemy patrol. Therefore they moved to the opposite side, and pushed ahead in the darkness. After a while, they began to slide. The terrain was becoming steeper and steeper, and in order not to fall, they were forced to dig out steps in the snow until they found themselves before a drop whose bottom they could not see in the darkness. The moon that had lit their way before had disappeared, and a kind of fine snow was falling. Trampling

---

[13] According to one source, "the *Soldbuch* was issued to all members of the German military once conscripted. Literally meaning 'paybook', the *Soldbuch* was the main form of identification for all members of the Wehrmacht. In the *Soldbuch* were the soldier's name, rank, military registration number, physical description (later a photograph), current unit, training unit, issued equipment, medical information, awards issued and pay group information." See http://www.angelfire.com/tn3/luftwaffefeld/research.html.

[14] The Belgian Léonard Blanchaert (Hamilton) was a major in the English army and head of a mission in Piedmont.

carefully with their feet, they enlarged the step until they made a kind of landing or terrace out of it, on which they stopped to study the situation. Finally they decided that one of them would be let down to explore. They drew lots and it fell to Paolo. They tied together the four strips of canvas from the skis, and even the jump rope that Alberto always carried in his knapsack.[15] Then Paolo lowered himself down in the void, while Alberto held the rope, but no matter how much he stretched out, he was not able to either touch or see the bottom. There was nothing he could do from that side, and he climbed back up to the small landing. Now it was necessary to try from the other side. Again they drew lots and this time it fell to Alberto. First they threw down an empty canteen and after a while they heard it stop. Therefore the drop must not be huge. They fixed a ski pole solidly on the ground, to which they tied a rope to increase the range, and Alberto lowered himself down. When he reached the end of the rope, he had the feeling that he was almost at the bottom and let himself go. In fact he touched ground, but the bottom was so steep and slippery that he rolled down for quite a stretch. Then he climbed back up laboriously, until he found the rope again and shook it to attract Paolo's attention. But in the meantime Paolo had fallen asleep. (More than sleep, I think that it was a kind of delirium owing to fatigue, because he recounted having seen the mountains before him change into a gigantic fireplace, decorated with vases, figurines, and flowers.) He called him for a while, yet without daring to raise his voice too much, until Paolo awakened and came to his senses. He put down the knapsacks, guns, and skis, and then he jumped down, but he did not notice the last section of rope, and detached himself from it before the end. The very long drop made him skid even faster. Alberto tried in vain to stop him, and for a while they rolled together. Then, when they stopped, they patiently climbed back up to look for their things again: the knapsacks were open, Alberto's Sten had lost its barrel, and the *biscotti* and other objects were scattered here and there on the snow. They collected what they found as best they could, and then continued to climb down.

Meanwhile a good part of the night had passed, and when they reached the woods at the bottom it was almost 7:00 a.m. and had begun to get light. Around 9:00 a.m. they reached Pleynet, a group of *grange* not too far from Château, which were not inhabited during the winter. There they let themselves fall on the ground, exhausted, without even the strength to find shelter for themselves, and fell asleep immediately. The sound of steps and voices woke them up after several hours. Paolo, with his eyes half shut, saw two armed figures who were approaching. One wore the hat of the *Alpini* and the other a German cap. "We are finished!" he thought with a sense of fatality. He looked at the Sten that he had next to him, but before he had time to make any decision, a

---

[15] They put these strips of seal skin under the skis in order to climb up the hill.

familiar voice stunned him: "To', here they are!" It was Pillo with another partisan. In those days they had made several successful strikes, disarming *Alpini* from Monte Rosa and Germans, and they hoisted their spoils in a sign of victory. Having exchanged reciprocal congratulations, they went together to the cabin, where Alberto and Paolo finally went to sleep. The adventure was over.

Certainly the story the boys told me that day was not so explicit and well organized, but somewhat muddled, and interrupted by frequent recollections, flashbacks, and presentations of supporting evidence: newspapers, maps, books, *biscotti*, pans of food, etc. The K rations, containing all that was necessary for a meal, struck me most of all: *biscotti*, ham, eggs, jam, cheese, chocolate, along with what is needed to make soup, coffee, and lemonade, and finally cigarettes, matches, and even toilet paper—all condensed to the maximum in the least amount of space.

I absolutely do not remember what we ate that evening, and at what time we went to bed. I continued to navigate in an unreal euphoria, as if the semidark cabin in the thick of the pine trees was a magic island, miraculously detached from all the sadness of the universe and miraculously illuminated by the sun of happiness.

The next morning the euphoria vanished, and new problems and responsibilities got the upper hand.

If Paolo and Alberto's undertaking was to bear fruit, we needed to organize the double information service and weapons transport as soon as possible. But the matter was too important for us to carry it out without the authorization and agreement of the Central Command. Therefore we decided that Paolo himself would go down to Turin with us that very day, and would give a detailed report of the trip to Galimberti and Valle. On the return trip he would pass by Laghi's to bring him up to date and to gain his approval and support.

But even the local situation presented problems that were somewhat worrisome. During the last ten days, Pillo and the others, animated by the spirit of initiative, had taken the offensive, so to speak, disarming several *Alpini* and Germans, eliminating a spy, and taking another prisoner, a girl that they brought to the cabin, but who then was able to escape. The presence of this girl in the village, who by now knew the location of the cabin, represented ongoing danger. Therefore we needed to either eliminate the girl, of whose guilt they did not have absolute proof—a solution that everyone was against unanimously— or change headquarters. We opted for the second solution. Gino decided that the construction of a new cabin would be begun immediately, right above Beaulard, almost on the edge of the stream where, if they climbed along it, they could avoid leaving visible tracks.

Having made the final arrangements, Ettore, Paolo, and I went down toward Beaulard. It was a splendid day and the Passo dell'Orso stood out, luminous against the sky. I looked at it without any more fear, almost with a feeling of gratitude, while I squeezed Paolo's arm hard. "Do you think that I too will be able to make the crossing?" I asked suddenly. "I think so," answered Paolo. His response was the beginning of many other things.

At Beaulard we took the train and arrived in Turin before the curfew, without incident. We went into the concierge's place for a moment to notify her of our return. Good Espedita, who evidently thought Paolo was lost, gave free reign to such manifestations of joy and tenderness when she saw him that I, who had been able to maintain some composure at the time when I saw him face to face, even though I was overcome and enraptured, began to cry too.

Then we went to sleep, and I had the joy of tucking Paolo in his bed, as if he were not a partisan and someone who had crossed mountains, but the boy of long ago. I remember that, more than once during the night, I woke up and said to myself, "He has returned, he is here in the next room." I got up to go and look at him; it seemed so impossible to me, as if, having just come out of a long dark tunnel, I could not believe the marvelous reality of the sunlight.

28 November–25 December 1944

28 November, Turin. Today, which began with the best of omens, ended instead with very grave news: Valle and Duccio, surprised in a bakery that they were using as an address, have been arrested. It appears that they had damaging documents in their pockets. In addition to worrying about their personal position, I cannot help but think of the disarray that their arrest will cause the entire organization, just at a time when the situation is becoming more and more delicate and difficult, with winter approaching.

29 November. More bad news. They have also arrested Marelli, which means that the police action, which began with the arrest of Duccio and Valle, is not over yet.[1]

In the afternoon I went with young Edmondo into the furnished room that Duccio last occupied, under a false name of course; the police have not yet discovered it, but they could do so at any moment. It was a matter of convincing the concierge and the landlord to let us go in and remove the damaging things. Basically the task was not very difficult. The concierge was easily convinced by Edmondo's generous tip that he bestowed munificently, while my respectable appearance served to satisfy the scruples of the owner of the house. "You wouldn't happen to be police, would you?" he asked at first, suspicious. I could not help but think of the strange inversion of values that has occurred today, even in the simplest of souls. Once, in similar circumstances, a landlord would certainly have asked, "You wouldn't happen to be crooks, would you?" Today the enemy is no longer the common delinquent, but the police.

As quickly as possible, we went on to carry out a careful search, which brought us to the discovery of a well-hidden suitcase, filled with letters, reports, and circulars from the Piedmontese Regional Military Command. Hurriedly,

---

[1] Luigi Masciadri (Marelli), an industry executive, was an inspector of the Piedmontese Regional GL Command and later political commissar of the VIII zone.

crammed into Edmondo's *topolino*, we brought it to two old seamstresses who were completely unsuspecting.

1 December. Yesterday morning I went to Casalegno's house for the meeting of the Committee of Coordination, but the meeting did not take place because Casalegno's son was born that very night.[2] Today, at the meeting of the Gruppi di difesa, the Communist Gennarino was absent because she had had a baby girl as well.[3] This flowering of births should have been a good omen and should have brought us luck. (By now even Lisetta's son or daughter should not wait too long to come into the world.) Instead, these days everything is going badly.

Valle and Duccio are still in prison, and it appears that their release will present many difficulties. Today Mumo, who after his release from prison in Milan has been living more or less in hiding with his sister, on hearing a banging at the door, insistent and with an unconventional rhythm, while he was alone in the house, convinced that it was the police, tried to flee by jumping down from the window. But he broke both of his legs and had to be transported to the hospital. Later Giorgio Diena, having gone to his house to look for news, ran the risk of being captured and, fleeing, had to get rid of a packet of documents it would be better not to have in circulation.

This morning General Alexander sent a message by radio to the Italian partisans, telling them unemotionally that from now until the good weather, the Allied forces would not continue their advance. Therefore, he advised them to retreat and stop and wait for the entire winter.[4] As if, surrounded, harassed, and pursued as we are, we can wait without doing anything. I very well understand how, in the general and immense picture of the war, the battle of the Italian partisans might be but an episode, but for those like us who are involved, the message has been quite a hard blow. Moreover, we are now without that sense of support—perhaps more imagined than real—that the proximity of the Allies gave us. We know that they are still nearby, but as long as the winter lasts, they have completely lost interest in us, and we should not expect anything from them. Never mind! We will fend for ourselves. I am more and more convinced that we must not rely on foreign help, but on our own forces. Yet we feel a certain bitterness.

2 December. Cesare arrived early in the morning with not very cheerful news from the Susa Valley. In the area of Oulx, there was an unexpected and rather sweeping roundup. All the bases of the Autonomous forces were surrounded and ravaged. Taschier's cabin (where their command was) was burned.

---

[2] Carlo Casalegno was a professor and inspector of the GL Piedmontese Regional Command.

[3] Giuseppina Vittone (Gennarino) was an organizer of the Gruppi di difesa in Turin.

[4] Harold Alexander, an English marshal, was commander in chief of the Allied forces in Italy.

Partisans were arrested. The Fascists also went to Beaulard, but they did not find the cabin.

Later Bianca, who arrived last night from Beaulard, confirmed the news for me. She had another strange adventure. When she arrived the other morning, she found herself in the middle of the roundup without knowing it. Since she was not able to find the cabin in the woods, at a certain point she began to shout: "Pillo! Alberto!" so that they would come to meet her. Meanwhile at the same time the Germans and Fascists, who miraculously passed near the cabin without seeing her, were coming up from the other side. Our boys in the cabin were not aware of the movement of those who were carrying out the roundup either. They only realized it later, when they were warned in the town and saw the visible tracks in the snow.

Such unbelievable good fortune seems due to several factors: in the first place, to good luck and a benign Providence; then to the safe, camouflaged location of the cabin; in the third place, to the wisdom of our boys in wanting to remain independent from the local Autonomous forces; and finally to the aid of the townspeople, including the notorious girl who was taken away as a spy and then fled. She had only to go to the head of the squad to have them all caught red-handed.

Nevertheless, we must not exaggerate. It went well today, but it could also go badly tomorrow. Therefore it would be good if the relocation of the cabin happened as soon as possible. As for the Autonomous forces who were arrested, their situation does not seem serious. It appears that they offered to have them work for the Germans on a civilian basis.

Tomorrow I will go and see.

3 December. Having arrived at Beaulard around 10:00 a.m., I set out through the woods, toward the mountain stream. But at a certain point I stopped, my heart pounding. I had seen the cap of an *Alpino* through the trees. Could it be the Monte Rosa? Instead it was only Pillo who, having anticipated my coming, had come down to meet me, dressed and armed from head to toe. After a while Alberto joined us, with the Sten over his shoulder and a long and shapeless sheepskin jacket. Together we climbed back up the river to the new cabin, which is much larger and brighter that the previous one, and to which they are transporting the furniture and household goods a little at a time.

On the whole the situation is quite peculiar. Evidently well-informed regarding Alexander's announcement, the Germans have launched a proclamation in the valley, promising impunity and work of a civilian nature to all partisans who present themselves by 8 December. They think that this way they will protect themselves from the nuisance and danger that guerrilla warfare represents for them, at least during the winter, taking advantage of the difficulty and discouraged state of mind the formations inevitably must be experiencing, after being deserted by the Allies. The maneuver might even partially succeed, especially where organizational ties are not solid and political training is lacking. In our group from Beaulard, not even one thought of presenting himself. In the group from Savoulx, on the other hand—more detached and dominated by the suspicious Codega—almost all of them wanted to present themselves, except of course for the very steadfast and irreproachable Corallo brothers.[5] As for the Autonomous forces, in addition to those who have already been captured, a strong movement well disposed toward the order appears to exist among them. Someone, more or less in good faith, must have passed the rumor among them that even the Turin Command approved of the order—as a contingent and temporary expedient. It is obvious that we have to do something quickly with very specific rallying cries. The boys will do their part locally, while I will try to trigger the most influential persons of rank of the Autonomous forces in Turin.

In the meantime, while we were talking, we cooked the rice. We sent it up with many good wishes, although it was really not very appetizing, since it lacked salt entirely. We agreed that tomorrow I would make the final arrangements in Turin. Then I would pass by Laghi's house in Susa with Paolo, and I would go back up with him to decide about the next trip to France. Meanwhile, during these two or three days, the situation could stabilize and we would be able to evaluate the consequences of the proclamation.

When I returned to Turin, I had unpleasant news. Salvatorelli's house, where Lisetta had settled a few days before, had been "burned."[6] Luckily she was not home, but she lost the entire layette for the baby that her companions from San Vittore had prepared for her, and the few provisions she was counting on for the next few months.

4 December. This morning, I went with Paolo to the home of Tonino, who, as we predicted, proved to be absolutely against the idea of the order. In his capacity as commander of the Autonomous forces, he gave us a precise message for the partisans in the Susa Valley, who belonged to Marcellin's ex-formations.

We will have to go to look for Patria, who seems to me to be the most intelligent and active among those who are left, and consult him as to how he might explain the excessively accommodating propaganda of the enemy to his men.

Later, at Giorgio's, I had news. They had managed to get Valle out, whether with an exchange or by paying a certain amount, I do not know. For Duccio, on the other hand, the situation was more complicated. Giorgio fears the Fascists from Cuneo might be able to make the Germans hand him over, and this would be terribly dangerous.

---

[5] Eraldo and Virgilio Corallo were partisans in the "Franco Dusi Column" of the IV Alpine Division of GL.

[6] The home of antifascist historian and journalist Luigi Salvatorelli.

5 December, Meana. At 6:00 a.m. we left Turin, whose atmosphere was cold, icy, and foggy, and we reached Susa at 10:00 a.m. under a sky that was flooded with golden sunlight, swept violently by the wind from Provence. At Micoletto, Laghi was overjoyed when he saw Paolo, he too having thought that Paolo was lost for sure. Seated outside in the sun, we chatted for a long time about the trips into France, as well as about the local situation. He too knew about the proclamation, but did not even consider it. "What kind of partisans are we," he said with a nobility that was not just symbolic, "if we make pacts with the enemy, even if only temporarily?" We could reduce our activities somewhat, and in given cases let the local partisans spend the winter at their own homes in order to simplify the problem of provisions, but the formations absolutely must not be dissolved, and the partisans must be ready to act at any moment, as soon as the occasion arises. An agreement of such a nature with the occupying forces would be to betray the most cherished meaning of the partisan battle.

When we returned to Susa, we met a new individual, namely a commissioner of police, a certain Cozzolino, who expressed sympathy and respect for us and warned us of a denunciation that had been made concerning us, which in fact later proved to be the by-now-very-outdated denunciation at the police office at Vercelli.[7]

Having climbed back up to Meana under a sky full of stars, we reached an understanding with the heads of two Meanese squads. Here no one is thinking of presenting himself, although basically they are not making a big deal of it, but during this waiting period we cannot demand too much.

6 December. This morning, it was snowing heavily, and we left here with the not-very-cheerful prospect of returning on foot from Salbertrand to Exilles (where there is no station), and then climbing toward the *grange* of Gran Prà in the problematic search for Patria. Instead circumstances were favorable to us. The train stopped for a minute at the crossing keeper's cabin before Exilles (which was enough so that we could scurry to get off). We had begun the climb amidst the snow for only a short time when we saw a hooded, cloaked figure, who turned out to be Patria in person. We went down to his house together where, in front of a comfortable, lit fire, I conveyed to him the message from Tonino. He hastened to say I was right, and seemed to me to be convinced of the need to keep the formations on their feet at any cost, albeit at a reduced level, even if he could not give me very precise news about the stability of the Autonomous groups in the area of Exilles. Nevertheless he would get me an accurate report on the local situation as soon as possible.

---

[7] Dr. Pasquale Cozzolino, commissioner of public safety, was a collaborator of the partisans.

8 December. Having gone down to Susa to go to Laghi's, I saw the news of Duccio's murder in the newspaper. The newspaper said that they shot him while he was trying to flee, near Cuneo. As Giorgio had feared, the Fascists were able to make the Germans hand him over.

The news struck me like a blow. I knew he was in danger, but I was almost certain that they would be able to get him out, as they did for Valle and Marelli. My despair is still tinged with disbelief.

I confess that at that moment I did not worry very much about the damage that his death would bring to the organization of the GL formations. If only Duccio were still alive, even if he were far away, even if he were in prison, it seems that everything would go well all the same. But I am thinking about him, a living creature, and about how it seems impossible to me that such strength and ardor can be extinguished forever. Of all of the qualities that make up Duccio's power and appeal, I have always fundamentally admired his marvelous vitality, which manifested itself not only in political and organizational preparedness and ability but also in his rich and cordial humanity, in the tender and joyous love with which he knew how to make a woman in love happy, in his liking for all things (a beautiful poem as well as a beautiful mountain, a cheerful little story as well as a good meal), and in the free and easy humor with which he knew how to regard even the most serious things.

I remember when we went together to the Chisone Valley. If I am not mistaken, the attempt against Hitler had been the day before, and Duccio had composed a little song about the event to the tune of *Vecchio organino*.[8] "Yes," I had commented afterward, "and to think that if the attempt had been successful, now everything would be over, or almost over. How magnificent, no?" Suddenly under his strength, resistance, and almost legendary gaiety, I had felt a sense of fatigue and nostalgia for a life that was safe and serene, that nostalgia we all feel sometimes, but to which he almost always was able to appear immune. At that instant, through that moment of weakness, I had truly felt his heroic dimension.

I remembered the last time I saw him, about one month ago, at Giorgio's house. Suddenly he had appeared on the threshold, bowing ridiculously: "Oh, here is Signor Ulysses! How are you, Signor Ulysses?" ("Ulysses" is the undercover name that Laghi had tried to saddle me with out of prudence and that, applied to me, naturally sounds a bit comical.) He laughed, and took off his hat, and I very nearly became irritated.

My God, but is it possible that Duccio is no more? And that we must continue the battle without him?

---

[8] The assassination attempt of 20 July 1944 led by Colonel Claus Count von Stauffenberg. See http://www.youtube.com/watch?v=ZbWxaDnrJ5Y for a rendition of Luigi Orlando's *Vecchio organino*.

11 December, Turin. Here we are again, after three somewhat intense and complicated days.

On Saturday the 9th, we went to Beaulard and then, with Alberto and Pillo, who were waiting for us at the station, we continued as far as Bardonecchia.

Bardonecchia was very crowded with Fascists, Germans, and soldiers of every kind. I wondered how much longer it would be wise to travel in their midst with three boys of draft age, sunburned, and with hair that was quite long and arranged bizarrely. (Pillo even had on a pair of gray-green soldier's pants that were very visible underneath his greatcoat.) Notwithstanding this—or perhaps really out of respect for our recklessness—no one said anything to us. Calmly we set out on the road to Melezet, where Alberto and Pillo told us how things were.

The boys from Beaulard, who were very enthusiastic and excited about the expedition into France, had talked a bit too much about it—only with their family members, of course, with their fiancées, and with their friends, but practically the entire town was aware of the project and discussed it and commented on it. How could we be sure that the news had not also reached where it should not reach, by the most indirect ways? Even if the Germans in residence at Beaulard are surprisingly stolid and indifferent (at times I could say downright blind, deaf, and dumb), the Fascists, much more curious and alert, continue to circulate. Just the other day they had cut off the hair of a girl named Benedettina, the daughter of the owner of a hotel in Sauze, with whom Pillo had danced one night, accusing her of being in love with "the bandit Pirlo (!)," in whose direction they had later uttered the most terrible threats. Evidently they are very well acquainted with the existence of our group, even if up until now they have not been able to single out the members and discover the headquarters. But they can succeed at any moment, and at the worst moment.

If we organized the expedition under such conditions, we would run the risk of having everyone captured, with documents and belongings of every kind, at the moment of departure. I think that at some point even I must place a limit on optimism and irresponsibility. I proposed that the expedition be postponed for several days, telling the boys that it was suspended *sine die*, following orders received from France, so that the present excitement could fade.[9] Ten days will suffice so that no one is talking about the matter any more. Then, without notifying anyone first, we will be able to embark on the trip, taking the most trustworthy and least loquacious individuals for now. Meanwhile we will do the preparatory work for the collection of news, and Paolo, Alberto, and Pillo will go to Turin for a few days to let the waters subside and suspicions rest. Then they will return to collect the information. Having studied the new situation, we will see how to organize the passage.

---

[9] *sine die* is Latin for "without day," meaning without assigning a specific day for an event.

Having made this decision, we returned to Bardonecchia, where Alberto went to a certain dealer in wholesale timber, whom they call *il Piccolo* (the little one), although he is really very large, and who gave us precise news about the movement of troops, and about German means of transport of every kind. During the last few days they have planted a howitzer 380 in Bardonecchia, with which evidently they are thinking about shooting into France.[10] Then we returned to Beaulard on foot. On the road we encountered several German patrols, who did not even look at us. But, farther ahead, we found Dr. Bricarello, who was very irritated because the Germans—probably the same ones who had passed by near us—had stopped him, notwithstanding the red cross that he wore in a manner that was as visible as can be on his white windbreaker. Before letting him go ahead, they had examined his documents carefully and meticulously, which luckily were perfect.

When we climbed back up to the cabin, we found a group of boys there. The cabin is now perfectly equipped and comfortable; there is a good stove, a good acetylene lamp, and even a phonograph. They prepared a bed for me with blankets, linens, and a down quilt right next to the stove. "We will even give you a pillow," Pillo said candidly, putting the object in question on the bed in a case of an indefinable color. Although I rightly knew how to appreciate even the greasy and the dirty, I still preferred to wrap my head in a scarf. "Why are you wrapping your head?" protested Pillo. "It is not at all cold." He did not understand— and was very careful to tell me so—that I preferred not to come directly into contact with his precious pillow. Nevertheless, I fell asleep immediately and slept magnificently, while the boys played *morra* and bounced and jumped on the bed until late, emitting the strangest cries.[11]

The next morning, the entire group arrived and we had a general briefing. I announced that we had to postpone the trip to France. I explained the expediency of giving the impression that we did not exist for a while, and of intensifying the collection of information. We resolved various questions that had remained undecided, among which was the one regarding the girl who had been arrested as a spy and then escaped. I read the memoranda of the interrogators accurately, and was convinced that she was not responsible for anything critical. On the other hand, if she had really wanted to, she could have had everyone captured after her escape. Therefore we decided to file away the experience. I restricted myself to recommending that we tell them, or have them told—perhaps by Don Riccardo—that it would be good if they continued to keep their mouths shut. Then I distributed the money sent by the Command, which will help them make ends meet during these days. They all belonged to

---

[10] A howitzer 380 mm artillery gun.

[11] *Morra* is a game for two players where each shouts a number at the same time as showing a number of fingers. The one who shouts the correct total number of fingers wins.

poor families. (Here the land is barren and no one is rich.) Before the war, the boys helped by working in Bardonecchia or in Susa or directly in Turin. Now, being essentially outside the law and not able to move, they rely heavily on their already meager family resources.

After the briefing, Alberto, Pillo, Paolo, and I went down and calmly took the train. I breathed a sigh of relief for the moment. I thought that in a few hours we would be in Turin, where we would split up, and where the presence of three boys in a close group would no longer have such a specific connotation. I did not know, (naïve!), what other complications awaited us.

At Salbertrand, the train stopped and remained stopped for a period of time. First I did not think anything of it. Then, after more than an hour had passed, someone began to get irritated and got off to inquire. There was no electricity. Would it return? "I do not know!" Again we waited for a long time. It was terribly cold in the train and I was completely frozen, and I thought with ever-increasing worry about the possibility of arriving in Turin after the curfew.

Finally—it was around 7:00 p.m.—we learned that the train would not leave that evening. Perhaps it would depart the next morning, around 9:00 a.m. We could not stay in the train, starving and fraught with cold. Therefore we set out toward the town in search of food and shelter. But finding it was not easy. We did not know anyone in Salbertrand. It was pitch dark, and we absolutely did not know where to go. Finally Paolo remembered a partisan who must have family in Salbertrand. With some difficulty, we were able to find his house. Naturally the boy was not there, and neither was his father or his mother. Fortunately one of his sisters, who recognized Paolo and agreed to put us up, was there. She brought us into a stable where a *veillà* was unfolding.[12] There was an old woman who was spinning, a little man who was getting some stakes of wood ready, little boys and girls who were playing cards, and some girls who were knitting. The young men were absent, of course, and the arrival of my three musketeers made some impression. The girl introduced us generically and vaguely as "friends" and, making us sit around the stove, gave us potatoes with butter, which we devoured voraciously. The little man—probably an uncle—regarded us with some diffidence and made several strange remarks to us, from which we guessed that he had taken us for Fascists. We did not worry about enlightening him. We savored the good warmth of the stable delightfully, happy to have found shelter. When it was time to go to sleep, we stretched out on the straw, and the calm breathing of the animals provided a lullaby.

The next morning—which was this morning—we were at the station before 8:00 a.m. But the train had already left, how and why we truly did not

---

[12] The *veillà* was a long evening spent in a barn doing activities such as spinning wool, playing cards, or just chatting.

understand, because the same railway official and the other railroad men arrived after us, cool and ignorant. We could not hope for other means of transport for the entire day. If we wanted to arrive in Susa, where perhaps we could take the evening train, we would have to set out on foot. The railroad men and some others were walking and we joined them, hoping in this way to be less conspicuous. Everything went smoothly.

In Susa, Teta comforted us in various ways and even had a trustworthy barber come to cut Alberto's and Pillo's conspicuous long, thick hair. At 4:00 p.m. we left, but the train for Turin was not in Bussoleno. What to do? Return to Susa on foot? Look for hospitality in Bussoleno? The prospect was not very encouraging.

But then, there was the sound of a train. They said it was a cargo train that was going to Turin. Of course we got on. I was so accustomed to bad luck that I waited for the train to stop at any moment, at the worst place, naturally. Instead it did not stop, not even once, until Quadrivio Zappata, where Alberto and Pillo chose to get off and leave on a tram. Paolo and I disembarked happily at Porta Nuova. It was 8:00 p.m. and therefore exactly twenty-six hours from when we left Beaulard. It would very nearly have been faster to come on foot.

Ettore was not at home, but he arrived a little later. He had been with Lisetta at the "burned" house to see if they could recover something. There must have been Fascists inside and around because Ettore, who had gone ahead, had hardly appeared at the window when the concierge, without letting him speak, made expressive gestures to him with a terrified air to bid him to leave, which naturally he did, picking up Lisetta, who had stayed at the front gate to wait. It had gone well, but they (especially Lisetta) had run a big risk. Certainly it had been rash, but I understand so well Lisetta's desire to recover at least something of her belongings. I think that, in her position, I would have done exactly the same thing.

13 December. Today, a little by coincidence and a little because they had appointments, a large group of partisan leaders and members of the Cln of the Susa Valley were at my house. At a certain point—when there was not an empty room in the entire house, and there were even people who were chatting not only in the kitchen, under the inattentive eyes of Anna, who was cleaning spinach in the meantime, but also in the bathroom—Espedita arrived to warn us that two individuals with a suspicious appearance were walking in front of the main gate. Therefore I begged my guests to disperse discreetly, one at a time. Either it was a false alarm, or one of the persons present had been shadowed. Nevertheless nothing has happened so far. Certainly it would not be that bad to close the house for two or three days. I am leaving for Milan tonight, where I will stay for a week, and Ettore and Paolo will go into the valley to gather news.

20 December. I was in Milan for a week, and I hope not in vain. I saw a bunch of people and I walked an infinite number of steps.

I had several interesting conversations with Lucia Corti regarding assistance work. She said—and quite truthfully, I think—that to get women involved, and not merely to excite them uselessly, it is necessary to interest them in social work, toward which they are instinctively inclined. She showed me the program for certain social service training courses held by the Cardinal Ferrari Institution. Evidently the Catholic Church, which has had a long and vast experience in this arena, has understood what tomorrow's work among women must be. Why can't we do something similar, in this way breaking up the by-now-century-old Catholic and Vatican monopoly on assistance? Certainly we lack training and experience, yet we must begin sometime! "Our women's organizations should gain experience with this kind of work!" she repeated several times. I agree with her completely, but I fear that, as long as the battle is not over, we will not be able to lay the kind of foundation we would like to have for this type of work.

I also attended a meeting of the Executive Committee of the Action Party, where I had to report about the women's movement, and I did it as best I could. Everyone agreed with me, even if I am not quite sure whether they had really listened to everything I said.

These are the serious things about my stay in Milan. As for the picturesque side, nothing in particular happened. I slept alternately at the houses of Adriana, Nanni Vasari, and Panta.[13] I ate in the most mysterious places and with the strangest people. (One evening, since it had become late, I even went without supper, and at night I could not get to sleep because I was so hungry.) I traveled kilometers, from one end of Milan to the other, sometimes arriving on time, and sometimes missing appointments. I passed by Garzanti, Bompiani, and Bianchi-Giovini just to create alibis for my presence in Milan.[14] I talked so much that I was worn out. At times I was calm and optimistic, at other times sad, worried, and anxious for the future.

Finally, last night I left again. At Vercelli, it half scared me to death when the soldiers began to search my neighbors' luggage, and I was carrying documents and several newspapers. In reality they were simply looking for tobacco, whose trade, as I was able to learn, had its center in the Veneto and flourished on this line. At three in the morning, they made us get off and do the stretch between Chivasso and Brandizzo on foot. There was mud and slime. I was sleepy and I slipped, and every once in a while I lost something that I had a hard time finding in the dark. When I got back on the train, I slept up until Porta Susa.

---

[13] Nanni Vasari was a collaborator with the Action Party and an organizer of the Mfgl.

[14] Garzanti, Bompiani, and Bianchi-Giovini were publishing houses. Ada frequently went to such publishing houses to conduct business regarding translations she was doing for them.

While I went to the house by Via Cernaia, for the first time I saw the enormous searchlights that illuminated the vicinity of the soldiers' barracks, which were decorated with a gigantic black banner.

At home I found Paolo and Ettore, who had returned from the Susa Valley. In Bardonecchia, in addition to collecting information from Piccolo, they met individuals suitable for the formation of the Cln, among whom was a fellow who might be the future mayor. Then they had been to Cesana and Fénils to learn about the location of two 420 cannons, located between Cesana and Clavières, and about points where the road toward France is mined.

Then today we held a type of war council with Pillo, Alberto, and Bianca, to decide about the next trip. By now, with what they already collected, what they would still collect in the valley, and what I had received in Milan, there is a good bit of news to bring to our French friends. They decided to go there right after Christmas, bringing only the two Corallo brothers with them, after whom—if everything goes well—Pacchiodo and the others would follow, in stages. I think that I will be able to go with them too. By now, the work among women is well established and can move ahead very well without me for about eight or ten days. Besides, when we arrive in Grenoble, I will be able to contact the French women. (Paolo told me that he had seen the headquarters of l'Union des femmes françaises or Uff, nearly equivalent to our Gruppi di difesa.)[15] Undoubtedly I will learn many things that will be useful to our work here, availing myself of their experiences during the period of the underground and liberation. Furthermore, our connections can be the basis of an effective collaboration in the future.

Then I saw a great many people, Valle among them, who, having gotten out of prison, was getting ready to go to live in Milan, since it would be difficult for him to work here. A certain man came from Genoa with disastrous news. Many have been arrested; Lanfranco has been deported to Germany; Zino and Marchisio were saved by a miracle.[16]

24 December. Lisetta's child was born: a baby girl. Everything went very well, and it truly seemed to be a miracle. Thanks to her splendid false papers, she was able to be admitted to the Molinette hospital, where she is safe and well cared for. Vittorio, relieved and happy, came to give me the announcement.[17]

We chatted for a long time about many matters. Among other things, he told me that our friends from the Action Party leadership have arranged to have me

---

[15] L'Union des femmes françaises (Union of French women) was created in the autumn of 1944 and was linked to the Communist Party.

[16] Eros Lanfranco, a lawyer and representative of the Action Party in Genoa, was deported and died in Germany.

[17] Molinette was the largest hospital in Turin.

nominated vice mayor after the liberation. I confess that I burst out laughing and thought Vittorio was joking. Instead he was most serious. My desire to laugh began to change into alarm.

"But I do not have a shadow of administrative experience!" I protested. "I am not made for this kind of work."

"You will gain the experience," he answered me steadily. "I assure you it is precisely the work that you need. Think about how many problems there are to solve, simple problems, almost domestic, in order to reorganize the lives of half a million people. I cannot think of anyone more qualified."

I looked at him with my mouth open. He was really serious. What if he were right? Yes, certainly, once all of this is over, there will be a great deal to do, and it is true that I like to get busy, *metter la pelle sul bastone* (put my hide to the stick), as my father used to say expressively, to help people, and to make things go well, even one small thing. I had so dreamed of returning to the peaceful quiet of my studies! But I am more and more convinced that it will not be possible.

25 December. Christmas. Yesterday it snowed. Today it is sunny and the outdoor scenery is peacefully traditional. It is the second Christmas of occupation. Will it be the last? I do not dare make predictions any more. Certainly even this period will come to an end, as everything in this world has an end. At times I have the impression that, even when the liberation comes, we will no longer be able to be happy. We have lost too many friends along the way. The strain inflicted on our nerves and on our hearts, in order to dominate the pain and resist, has perhaps dried up our capacity for joy forever. Or perhaps it will not be like this, because life continues, inexorably, and it is stronger than everything. New babies will be born to replace those who have been lost, and they will affirm life's immortality.

This afternoon Paolo and I went to meet Lisetta's daughter. She is a beautiful, healthy baby girl to whom they have given the name Annalisa. Lisetta entertained me by telling me that her baby girl will be duly registered in the Registry of Births and Deaths under the name of Annalisa Rizzini by showing us her marriage certificate, on which her supposed husband was represented by the photograph of a nineteenth-century gentleman. (He is English, it appears, and a relative of Lucia Corti.)

When we left the hospital, a splendid moon illuminated the river and the hill that was covered with snow. Paolo said that the moonlight would help us in the crossing. I still have things to do for a few days to settle various affairs, and must spend time in Susa and Meana to see how things are going. Then we will leave. If everything goes well, we will be in France before the New Year.

30 December 1944–26 February 1945

To be honest, I left for the mission, which though not really dangerous still presented risks of every kind, in a state of mind of absurd, reckless delight, as if I were going on vacation, as if I were leaving on one of those adventures of which my solitary childhood had been deprived, and for which I had tried to find compensation by living a new childhood, free and adventurous, through my son.

Today I wondered. Was this widespread foolhardiness really absurd (of which mine was only a particularly vivid example), or rather a heaven-sent remedy for the unremitting, excessive tension that we would not be able to withstand otherwise?

No matter what it was, having left routinely from Meana on the morning of 30 December, we reached Beaulard around 10:00 a.m. Alberto, who had gone ahead of us with Pillo, jumped on the train, and went to Bardonecchia with Paolo. Ettore and I got off and set out toward the hospital in the company of Pillo, who gave us the latest news in the meantime. Everything was in order. We could have dinner at the hospital and remain there until the time of departure. The Corallo brothers would come with us, but they would leave several hours before us, and wait for us at the top at the Colle dell'Orso. No one else knew about our departure. Alberto and Pillo's stay had been too brief to put the wheels of suspicion in motion. There was still important news about the location of pieces of ordnance to collect that Piccolo had gathered. This is why Alberto and Paolo had gone to Bardonecchia.

Bianca and Alberto's brother Bruno, with his wife, Juanita, had also arrived on the same train as ours and joined us quite early at the hospital, but they had left from Turin. Bruno, a surgeon by profession, had been captured as a Jew and held in prison for some time. Having gotten out by a miracle, now he intended to join us on the crossing. Once he reached France, he would ask to be taken to Southern Italy, where he has another brother, and there enlist in the Liberation Army as a doctor.[1]

---

[1] Bruno Salmoni wanted to join the Southern Italian Army that fought alongside the Allies and took part in the Allied advance.

Immediately we began to prepare our belongings, knapsacks, and articles of clothing. Virgilio, the youngest Corallo, arrived, a handsome boy of sixteen with a splendid physique, and with the blond hair and blue eyes that characterize the ancient Celtic race here. He and his brother were about to leave. They came to see if we wanted to give them something to carry, seeing that they were going up unladen. My eyes fell on a big coil of ropes that seemed absolutely useless to me, and that instead Paolo had wanted to bring at any cost. Wasn't the Passo dell'Orso an easy little walk? I thought that, by entrusting them to Virgilio, I would be doing something clever, because later we would have them anyway, without the effort of carrying them. Indeed, but if the ropes were to be useful, they would be so during the climb, as occurred in reality. For once, Paolo rightly observed that my decision revealed my lack of any "rudimentary knowledge." (No one knows of what, perhaps of everything.) In any event, in his absence, no one dared oppose my intelligent decision, and the boy left with the coil of ropes in his knapsack.

We dined, and then I left to rest a little in a room that dear Bricarello had put at our disposal. I was tired and, considering the upcoming trip, I thought it advisable to get a bit of rest when I could. I threw myself on the bed and fell asleep immediately. I woke up after about an hour after hearing someone enter the room. It was Alberto and Paolo, with an unknown and mysterious man who took off his boots as soon as he entered, and out fell papers and documents. It was the information that Piccolo had gathered, which he had preferred not to entrust to Paolo and Alberto, fearing that they would stop them on the train. Instead he sent them by means of one of his reliable men, who had his documents in order.

By now everything was ready and we could leave. I stuffed myself with documents, and we set out toward the mountain and through the town. By now it was dusk, and the Germans were traveling from one house to the other with pots of rations. Today I still wonder how the passing of that group of people, thoroughly rigged out, who, at that hour and during that season, were moving toward the mountains, did not arouse their suspicions. What is more, at a certain point Bianca and Juanita stopped and, before turning back, for a long time stayed to say good bye to the group that was leaving, with expressive hand gestures, if not exactly waving their handkerchiefs. Evidently the Germans in residence in Beaulard—as was already tested and as was also demonstrated later—did not have a particular hostility for either the population or the partisans, and took good care not to take any initiative against them. No one had given the order to stop us; therefore they observed us leaving without the least interest. Only two or three days later, when an anonymous denouncement regarding our departure reached them—we never knew from whom—did they go to look for Gino, tagged by them as a guide and ski instructor, and force him to accompany them through the mountains in search of us. But the storm had completely erased our tracks, and Gino, who knows the area thoroughly, brought them to places that were so difficult and dangerous and impossible that they, in all honesty, could state that under similar snow conditions no one could have carried out the crossing.

While the others were going up to the cabin, where we would make a stop and wait for the moon to rise, Alberto and I went to Pacchiodo's house, where some of our partisans had gathered. We handed the money for the month of January over to them, gave them final instructions and a few newspapers (I had brought up *Il Partigiano Alpino* with the news of Duccio's death and his photograph), and agreed that, if everything went smoothly, we would have them notified, or someone would come to get them. They would be ready to leave immediately as soon as they were notified, in small successive squads, without the news spreading.

Then we too went up to the cabin. I was so tired that I was thinking with terror about the exertion that awaited me. At that moment the Passo dell'Orso seemed to me to be infinitely far away, almost unreachable, and I almost did not *consumai l'impresa* (bring the enterprise to an end).[2] I could say goodbye to those who were leaving and turn back. I thought with hopeless nostalgia about the little room in the hospital where I had rested for a moment in the afternoon: the pretty clean little bed, the radiator on, and the hot running water, instead of the cold, the darkness, and the fatigue, above all the fatigue. Basically I was just a woman and they could do without me very well. What was more, in the very end I only represented an obstacle. For a moment the temptation was very strong, but I reacted quite quickly to the physical laziness that had inspired me, taking a tablet of *simpamina*, and when I reached the end of the climb, I was again more determined than ever.[3]

We found the others in the cabin, in the dark, not as a measure of prudence but because there was no coal for the acetylene lamp. In the uncertain light of the stove that was lit, we ate something, and then we remained seated in the darkness, tranquil, and sang old mountain songs, waiting for the moon to rise.

It was almost 10:00 p.m. when we left. The snow glistened in the moonlight, and the big dark fir trees seemed to be so many Christmas trees decorated with shining stars. It was so magnificent that a feeling of happy exaltation followed my depression of a little while before. "How lucky I am!" I said to myself,

---

[2] The phrase "consumai l'impresa" comes from Dante's *Inferno*: "Perché pensando consumai la impresa, che fu nel cominciar cotanto tosta (For when I thought thereon I brought to an end the enterprise which had been so hasty in its inception)." Translation by William Warren Vernon.

[3] *Simpamina* or amphetamine sulfate is a drug that stimulates the central nervous system and was probably used in this instance to treat fatigue.

proceeding in what seemed to me a fairy tale land. "To think that I would never have been able to see something like this!"

Suddenly, I heard suffocated sounds and curses behind me. It was Pillo, who had gotten his foot caught in a hare trap. It was not difficult to free it, and he immediately continued on his way. This was his first mishap.

At 2:00 a.m. we reached Rocher de La Garde. The cabin was empty and the door was open, just as the Germans had left it when they went away about a month before. There were bunk beds, a bit of straw, empty cans, and an old blanket. We went in and decided to make a brief stop. Paolo announced that we were about half way from the summit, but that now the hardest part was beginning. It was terribly cold and we tried to light a bit of fire with the straw, but it was wet and we were not able to set it aflame. Suddenly we felt the wind rise whistling in the valley. We listened, with our hearts in suspense. If a blizzard were breaking out, it would be difficult for us to be able to continue. But the wind did not reach us. The air continued to be still, the sky clear, and the moon bright. The blizzard remained below, raging, and providentially erased our tracks. Bianca and Juanita, down at the hospital, and the boys who knew about our departure, awakened by the hissing roar, wondered anxiously what had happened to us, and if we had turned back.

But near us the night continued to be clear and still, and after about ten minutes, we continued on our way. At the moment when we left, I realized that my gloves were soaked. Naturally I had another pair, but they were at the bottom of Ettore's knapsack, and I did not want to make him lose more time looking for them. Therefore I got the blanket that was abandoned by the Germans and threw it on my shoulders, wrapping my hands in its two ends. I left, very proud of my solution. I felt picturesque, like a figure in a Goya print, and my hands wrapped up like this were freer and warmer than they were with the gloves.

That last stretch proved to be really difficult, however. The Germans' tracks, which had made Paolo and Alberto's crossing so much easier the last time, were no longer there. The wind had swept away the soft snow, and we had to proceed by making steps in the ice along the naked ridge, at a considerable slope, above an overhanging rock of two or three hundred meters. But that night I was not aware of the difficulty. I realized the danger that we confronted only when, on the trip back, I saw, from the other side, the frightening incline of our route over the abyss. Alberto and Paolo, the only ones who were really aware of the situation, remembered it. But Alberto's shoes (Valle's ill-fated shoes) did not grip and tended to slide. Therefore Paolo went ahead, made steps in the ice with his ice ax, and then tried them with his feet, scrupulously, slowly, before trusting his weight on them and making more of them. Alberto, who adjusted and hardened the steps with his feet, came after him. Then I came, panting and protesting. Paolo's precautions seemed truly excessive. (Why was he not going faster? I was beginning to feel cold.) Behind me, Bruno, then Pillo, and last, Ettore. I had told him, "Stay behind. That way you can close ranks and we will not lose anyone." He faithfully performed the task entrusted to him. But the tracks that Paolo marked so accurately and that Alberto and I maintained and hardened, then became badly crushed, broken, and practically destroyed by the feet of Bruno and Pillo, who were not mountain dwellers. Therefore poor Ettore, who is not a mountain dweller in the least, had to laboriously remake the track for himself. When I think of my foolhardiness that night with regard to him, I feel really guilty. I admire the calm equilibrium that enables him, under similar conditions of inferiority, to quietly go through the ordeal. If only we had the rope! But I had sent it ahead! When I confessed it to Paolo, in response to his question, he shook his head, more amused than infuriated: "It's OK!" he said "We will manage without it."

As a matter of fact, thanks to I do not know what saint, we did manage very well without it, and after about four hours we were at the Passo. A rag was fluttering, hung on a rope between two poles, and for a second my heart shuddered at the thought that the Germans might have preceded us, closing in on us. Paolo went down to call the Corallo brothers, who came outside immediately. A little because of their joy at our arrival, and a little to stretch their legs, they began to run like chamois halfway up the slope that led to the other side. While I watched them go away, smiling, I saw a figure break loose from the group that had waited for us at about fifty meters from the cabin and begin to hop behind them. But suddenly my smile changed into a cry of anguish, because the figure in motion—Pillo? Bruno? Ettore?—had unexpectedly fallen and was sliding rapidly along the frozen slope toward the precipice. Distraught, I hurried ahead with Paolo, even though we knew perfectly well that there was nothing to be done. But, by I do not know what miracle, when he arrived at the edge of the abyss, the poor wretch stopped suddenly. Perhaps he had found a rise in the land, or perhaps he had been able to stop himself. Counting the others who also had approached, I realized that it was Pillo, who now was trying laboriously to climb back up the slope. The Corallo brothers ran to help him and, after a few minutes, he was at our side. Even in the moonlight, I could see that he was very pale and was trembling violently, and with reason, because he had had a narrow escape. This was his second mishap. I gave him a bit of brandy, which he swallowed in one gulp, and then courageously got back on his way, flanked by the two Corallo brothers. But by now the dangerous part was over because, having gotten over the Passo, the descent began into a tranquil ravine, without a hint of precipices or overhanging rocks.

I had barely finished rejoicing over the dangerous escape when I noticed a strange sensation in my hands. In the excitement of the last few minutes, I had forgotten to keep them wrapped in the hems of the blanket. Now, looking at them, I saw them becoming a strange color, between yellow and brown, absolutely unnatural. I understood immediately—it did not take much—that they were freezing. I would never have believed that it could happen so quickly! I began to hit them, rub them, and beat them under my armpits. After a few minutes, a thousand little stabs and the resumption of a normal color revealed that the circulation was back and the danger of frostbite was over.

Then I thrust myself ahead for the descent with a kind of drunkenness. "We are in France!" I continued to repeat while I went down with long leaps, sinking in the soft snow. "We did it! Now we are safe!" Instead, even if we had crossed the prewar border, we were not now in France, but in "no man's land," when at any moment we could run into some German patrol on reconnaissance, and where we were within sight of the German emplacements at the Col des Acles, visible to the naked eye.

It was 6:00 a.m. when, having completed the descent, we began our march on level land. The moon had set, but the sky was already illuminated by the light of dawn. Nature was slowly awakening, and we could even hear the song of a bird at the top of a pine tree, tender and touching in that icy silence.

We had to move quickly to get out of the stretch within sight before broad daylight. But we were all a little tired, and advancing in the soft snow was extraordinarily difficult. Therefore the sun was already illuminating the tops of the mountains when we reached Châlet des Acles, a group of *grange* used in the summer season, in peacetime, by herdsmen who brought their animals to pasture, and of course deserted now.

Still we made a short stop. Ettore took two photographs of the group. (Why not immortalize such an event?) I combed my hair and made myself up as best I could. I had it in mind that I should embrace the first French person that I met, and I wanted to be presentable. In 1940, when Italy had entered the war against France, I had sworn that when the war was over and I crossed the border, I would throw my arms around the neck of the first Frenchman I saw. Certainly the event was happening in circumstances different from the ones I had foreseen, but the promise was valid just the same, and the time to keep it was approaching.

We had resumed the march for a short time when the roar of a shot from a firearm gave me a brutal start. "How stupid!" I said to myself. "Here there is really no reason to be afraid. The Germans must be practicing." It was the Germans all right, and yes, they were practicing, but practicing firing at our line, which, winding dark against the whiteness of the snow at the bottom of the valley, constituted a moving but perfectly visible target. Yet I continued to navigate in my state of almost unreal bliss. I did not even comprehend the situation when we heard a second roar, this time notably closer. "Perhaps they are blowing up mines," I thought.

"Quick, quick!" Paolo took care to say. "Quicken your step if you can!" Again I scarcely listened to him. Why hurry? We were doing so well! Nevertheless we all walked a little more hurriedly while the shots recurred, at intervals that were shorter and shorter, louder and louder, and closer and closer, until we reached the narrow gorge that, between two high walls of rock, led to the Clé des Acles, the French checkpoint. There, finally safe, Alberto and Paolo made us stop. Then Alberto, followed by Paolo, advanced carefully toward the guard post, with a white handkerchief hoisted on the tip of a stick and yelling at full voice: "*Vendettà! Vendettà!*" the code word that had been given to them the time before.

But the garrison of the checkpoint had been changed. The Moroccans were no longer there; no one from before was there any more. Still, even though they did not recognize the code word, someone came outside to talk with them, and what they said must have convinced them because they turned to us immediately, making a sign to come ahead. When we had approached, and after they looked us up and down and were certain that we were not Fascists in disguise, they removed the mines to let us in. One cavalierly offered me his hand to help me to pass over the barbed wire. "*On vous a tiré dessus avec le mortier!* (They fired on you with the mortar)," they said in the meantime, excited. "*On entendait les coups et on n'y comprenait rien. C'était pour vous, alors* (We heard the shots and we did not understand anything. They were for you, then)!" "*Vraiment* (Really)?" I answered, with the most radiant of my smiles. "*Cela se peut bien* (That could very well be)." But at the bottom of my heart, I still did not believe it.

When we were in the *baraccamento*—a cabin only a little bigger than ours in Sapes—they subjected us to a formal but superficial search, after which, having removed any suspicion, they indulged in manifestations of cordial hospitality.[4] They were *maquisards* of the Ffi and almost all of them had a *bouc*, which was an unkempt little goatee. They were down-to-earth, solid, dear, and sincere, like our mountain folk from the other side of the Passo. They gave us cookies and chocolate, bread, sardines, salmon, and above all coffee, real coffee, two *quarts* (quarter liters) of which I gulped down immediately, and which truly restored my soul. Meanwhile one continued to transmit with a telephone from the camp. "*Allô, Mouton* (Hello, Sheep), he yelled, all cheerful, evidently using conventional names. "*C'est ici Lapin, Lapin qui parle. Appelle-moi Cochon! Eh, dis donc: nous avons ici huit partisans italiens, sept homes e une femme. Qu'est-ce qu'il faut faire? Oui, c'est moi, c'est Lapin qui parle* (This is Rabbit, it is Rabbit speaking. Call me, Pig! Hey, by the way: We have eight Italian partisans here, seven men, and one woman. What should we do? Yes, it's me, it is Rabbit speaking)."

Suddenly I remembered that, in the anxiety of our arrival, I had forgotten my promise. I looked at the *maquis*, choosing the one who seemed to promise the least rough skin and the least pungent beard. My choice fell on the young man next to me who had just now filled my *quart* of boiling coffee for the third

---

[4] A *baraccamento* is a small building of gray stone typical of military buildings.

time. "*Est-ce que je peux vous embrasser* (May I embrace you)?" I asked him laughing. "*Mais oui, sans doute* (yes, of course)," he answered, reddening under his *bouc* and sun tan. I kissed him loudly on both cheeks, eliciting the warm-hearted laughter of the others who, when I explained to them the origin and reason for my gestures, explained to me in turn that I had chosen to kiss the very one who, before becoming a partisan, had been a seminarian. "*C'est qu'on l'appelle 'le curé' vous savez* (We call him 'the priest', you know)," they said laughing. Then I was afraid I had embarrassed him, and tried to make amends by saying that there was really nothing wrong in it, because I could very well have been his mother. The *curé*, rather than being sorry, seemed rather flattered and satisfied because a moment later he pulled me aside and, pouring me more coffee, told me seriously: "*N'oubliez pas. On m'appelle le 'curé'. Si jamais vous avez besoin de quelque chose, appellez-moi e je serai toujours à vot'service* (Don't forget. They call me the 'priest'. If you ever need anything, call me and I will be at your service)."

Pillo complained, saying that one of his feet hurt, and I advised him to take off his shoe. It was not an easy undertaking. It took four of us to pull, two on one side and two on the other. When the shoe finally came off, bringing with it the sock that was stuck on it, the foot seemed black and blue and swollen to our eyes. I bet it hurt, poor boy. The shoe, evidently too tight, had stopped his circulation, and his foot was on the road to frostbite. Immediately we hastened to guard against it, beating it, rubbing it with the snow, and warming it. Some feeling returned, but it still remained in bad condition. This was Pillo's third and final mishap.

Meanwhile, with the new changing of the guard, which was supposed to replace the group from Clé, two French policemen charged with accompanying us up to Plampinet arrived. They became very excited when they heard that there was a *blessé* (a wounded man) among us. "*Est-ce qu'il faut faire venir un brancard* (Should we have a stretcher brought)?" they asked. No, Pillo did not want the stretcher, and he said that he felt like going down on foot, provided that they give him some footwear for his foot, which he could not pour back into the fatal shoe. They quickly found a rubber boot, with which he declared that he could walk. "*Bon* (good)," the head policeman then concluded. "*La dame va nous précéder avec le blessé. Ainsi on n'ira pas trop vite* (The woman will go ahead of us with the wounded man. That way we will not go too quickly)." Then we set out, in a procession, along the mule track: Pillo and I in front, arm in arm, then the policeman, then, at random, our men and the French men who came down after having finished their turn, and finally the other policeman.

I do not think I will ever forget our descent in the sun and our glorious arrival in the village. It was Sunday, and the entire population of the town, having been notified of our arrival, had gathered to wait for us. "*Ce sont des italiens, des maquis italiens* (They are Italians, Italian *maquis*)," they said. "*Voyez, il y a aussi une femme* (Look, there is also a woman)." They greeted us festively, with their hands and with their smiles.

They had us go into the Command Post (P.C.), and while Alberto, assuming his part as *chef de l'équipe* (team leader), withdrew with an officer, explaining to him who we were and showing him our credentials, the others surrounded us affectionately, made Pillo stretch out on a mattress, and gave us something to eat. Evidently, before the liberation, the house had been the headquarters of a German command, because everywhere we could see drawings and writings that the French had spiritedly modified. For example, *Ein Reich* (one Reich) was written on a wall, and the French had commented: *en ruines* (in ruins); *ein Volk* (one people)...*décimé* (decimated); *ein Führer* (one leader)...*aux abois* (in dire straits).

When we finished eating, the boys threw themselves on the mattress next to Pillo, whose foot was covered with water blisters and still hurt him, and fell asleep. The policeman came to propose that Ettore, Bruno, and I, the older ones, go to sleep in his room for a while. I accepted with gratitude. With the excitement over, I was beginning to feel quite tired. There were two beds in the room and the stove was lit. I threw myself down and dozed lightly. Half asleep, I heard Bruno, who instead of going to sleep had sat down near the stove and was talking with the policeman. He was speaking a strange French. For example, he said "*lon qu'on dit, lon qu'on fait* (when one says, when one does)." At a certain point he spoke about one of his "*ami qui avait une ville dans la rivière* (friend who had a city in the river)," evidently meaning that he had a villa on the Riviera. Lulled by his conversation, I fell sound asleep. I awakened upon hearing the wind whistling menacingly. Was I dreaming or was it real? It was, because Ettore, who was stretched out next to me, had also heard it. Another policeman, who had entered the room a little while later, announced that it had begun to snow. I wrapped myself in the blanket that they had thrown over me with a sense of well-being and profound gratitude. I did not have much time to make myself comfortable, however. Alberto came to call us. A car sent from Briançon had arrived to bring us up there, but it could only carry three people, and naturally they wanted the "leaders." Alberto thought that he, Paolo, and I should go.

Regretfully, I tore myself away from the pleasant warmth of the room and returned to the Command. Pillo had a slight fever. "*On va l'emmener à l'hôpital et le soigner comme il faut* (We are going to take him to the hospital and care for him properly)," an officer assured me. But my heart wept at leaving him when he was not perfectly well. Even Paolo had a slightly dazed appearance, although he did not acknowledge any pain. The others, aside from fatigue, were in excellent condition, and the French assured us that they would come to join us quite soon, with another car, the next morning, or perhaps this very evening.

An officer came in, running: "*Vite, vite, on va partir tout de suite* (Hurry, hurry, we are leaving right away)!" I snatched my things quickly and embraced Ettore very tightly. It made me very sad to begin the New Year away from him. Whether it was the pain that sounded in my voice in saying goodbye to him or the tenderness of my embrace, the fact remains that the French officer, the one who had previously refused my request ("*pas possible... la voiture est surchargée* (impossible, the car is overcrowded)"), proposed with some hesitation: "*Mais, enfin... si vous voulez... prenez vos affaires... on peut se reserrer encore un peu...* (Well, OK, if you wish, get your things; we can squeeze together a little more)." He did not have to tell us twice. Ettore ran to get his knapsack, and for once he was very fast. We squeezed together incredibly to make space for him. Finally we left. The car, a little bigger than an "1100," was effectively *surchargée* because, in addition to the four of us, crowded in the back, there were three in front—the driver, the officer, and a girl who belonged to an auxiliary corps who, even though it was not very comfortable, continued for the entire trip to sing a little song that had for a refrain: *Chez Beber!*[5]

A brief stop in Briançon, and then we left again for Embrun. After a few kilometers we could see the lights lit, like in peacetime. "*Oh, la lumière* (Oh, light)!" I exclaimed, happily surprised. "*Oui*," said the officer. *Ici finit le blécou* (Here there is no more *blécou*)." "What is a *blécou*?" I wanted to ask, but at that moment a sign answered my question. It said "*Fin du Black out* (the end of the blackout)," and I understood that *blécou* was none other than the dreadful French distortion of the English word used for blackout.

At Embrun, where we arrived after nine, our *chef* (leader) was not able to find the individual who was supposed to look after us. He went around from one office to the other, but it was New Year's Eve and no one was there. He finally brought us to the hospital and from there, having telephoned right and left, was able to make blankets and food arrive. Then he left us in the care of the nurse on duty, a soldier boy with puffy eyes who spoke a strange French, and who wanted to offer everyone one of his bottles of very bad cognac at any cost. Then he brought us to sleep in a room with four beds and a stove. I was too tired to make observations or comments. Ettore tucked me in really well. (I think he also gave me his blanket). So, sleeping, we entered 1945.

The arrival of a soldier with four loaves of bread and four cups of a black broth, defined by him as a *jus* (juice), woke us up in the morning. We wished him a Happy New Year, to which he responded with little enthusiasm. "*Avec cette sacrée guerre* (with this blasted war)!" he sighed. I understood that he must have been weary of the *naia* (cobra), and I learned later that during those very

---

[5] The Fiat 1100 was first introduced in 1937.

days the Germans had launched a new offensive against the Allied front in the Ardennes, and there was some apprehension in the air.[6]

I wanted more than anything to take a bath, or at least to wash myself with some comfort, but on the floor where we were, I was not able to find a washbasin. There was only a toilet whose pipes were broken because of the cold and that, consequently, was overflowing. What is more, since the door handle was missing ("*les allemands les ont emportées toutes* (the Germans took them all away)"), I might remain shut in there until someone came to free me. I was about to go down into the nurse's little room, where we had eaten the night before, and where it seemed that the only available faucet was located, when I saw the officer who had accompanied us as far as here arrived. "*Vite, vite*," he said, and he brought us immediately to the Command.

While we were waiting to be introduced, we met two pretty, nice girls in uniform who drove the ambulances (*ambulancières*, they described themselves). I confided in them freely that, together with my love for France and my wish for the war to end soon, I also wanted to wash up. "*Mais venez chez nous* (then come with us)!" they cried, understanding right away. "*On vous donnera de l'eau chaud et tout ce qu'il faut* (we will give you hot water and everything you need)." I could not take advantage of their offer because right at that very moment they brought us into the office where they subjected us to a long, idiotic, and very intense interrogation. As a result, they issued a report, which they gave me to read later. It was a real masterpiece of idiotic bureaucracy where, for example, they said that "*sept partisans italiens avec leur mère* (seven partisans with their mother)" had arrived, whose *mère*, by the peculiar phenomenon of prematurity, was born in 1922 (rather than in 1902). (Good gracious! I did not know that I had so many sons, and so grown up!)

Among the others there was a fat officer, whose porcine face clashed peculiarly under the elegant cap of the *chasseurs des Alpes* (Alpine hunters), and who brightened up greatly when he heard that we had specific information about the German artillery in the Susa Valley. He begged us to give him a summary of the information that we brought and translate it, which we innocently agreed to do. To us it was important to support and help the war operations. We were not aware of the touchiness and spite of the various commanders, who only wanted to get ahead and put themselves in good light with their superiors. Certainly we could not know that by giving a report to the officials at Embrun, we were upsetting those at Grenoble.

Therefore, with Alberto and Paolo's help, we worked hard all morning long, summarizing, translating, and typing the most important details of our

---

[6] Operation Cobra, which took place between 25 July 1944 and 31 July 1944, was part of the Normandy Invasion. The German offensive in the Ardennes, known as the Battle of the Bulge, occurred between 16 December 1944 and 30 January 1945.

information. At a certain point we saw Bruno and the two Corallo brothers arrive. They had been worse off than we had been because in Briançon they had essentially slept on the ground in a guard post. What is more, right at midnight, as if to greet the New Year, the German cannons (those located near us) had begun to fire, stirring up a certain panic, fortunately without consequence. Pillo had been taken to the hospital the night before, and they did not know anything more about it. I begged the officer with the face of a piglet to call for news about him by telephone. He was so happy about the trick that he was playing on his colleagues from Grenoble—thanks to our naiveté—that he obliged me immediately. *Lieutenant* Spriano was better. His foot had second-degree frostbite, but they had already begun to treat it with certain marvelous special injections, and in about two weeks he would be healed. Not to worry because he has received all the necessary care.

It was past noon when we finished our work. Then they brought us into a large, empty room, which must have been used to hold lessons because it contained a blackboard, and where there had evidently been a Christmas party, because you could still see holly branches, tinfoil stars, and cotton snowflakes hanging. There was a table, chairs, and a stove that had been extinguished. They told us to wait, because soon they would bring us something to eat. It was very cold and I was beginning to become terribly hungry, because the morning *jus* had not been very nourishing. Immediately Ettore got busy and lit the stove. He made an inspection tour of the various neighboring offices, gathering all the wood that he could find, and was able to create a pleasing and comfortable blaze. But the meal did not arrive. Suddenly we heard footsteps approaching. "Here it is!" we shouted enthusiastically. Instead it was a young soldier who was coming to ask us if we had mess tins and cutlery. No, we answered, how could we have them? We were not regular soldiers. At which the young soldier scratched his head, saying that it was a big problem. They did not have extra plates or cutlery. They could buy them, but it was a holiday and the stores were closed. At first I thought that he was pulling our leg, but then I realized that he was very serious. He went away with a worried look, and we did not see anyone else for quite a while. Virgilio killed time writing his own name with big flourishes on the blackboard. Paolo began to complain, saying that the big toe of his right foot hurt, and maintaining he must have gotten frostbite, but I was too exhausted to pay attention to him.

Finally, around two thirty, a succession of soldiers arrived, bringing everything we needed: plates and cutlery (Had they bought them, or had they gone to get them in the neighboring town?), and not the usual stew but some excellent broth, and a magnificent casserole with potatoes, and even peaches in syrup.

We had barely finished the meal when there came our guide. "*Vite, vite!*" We were leaving for Grenoble. We said goodbye to Bruno and the Corallo brothers, who, they assured us, would join us the next morning, and we left. The car was not so crowded because the girl was no longer there, and the officer himself drove.

I was stunned to see that he took a Thompson.[7] "*On ne sait jamais* (we never know),"
he explained. "*On pourrait rencontrer des collabos* (we could run into collaborators)."

Instead we did not encounter anyone, and it was an enchanting trip along
the Route Napoléon, surrounded by a regular succession of marvelous Alpine
scenery. We crossed small rivers with expressive Provençal names (like the
Rabioux). We went through villages where children tobogganed like the children in Meana. We went down and climbed back up pure white valleys, and
we drove alongside a large frozen lake for a while, on which the fisherman had
constructed straw huts, and over which an equestrian statue of Napoleon had a
commanding position from on high.

It was already dark when we got to Grenoble, and we stopped in front of the
Hotel Lesdiguières, headquarters of the Commands. But we barely had time
to get out when Alberto and Paolo cried simultaneously: "Palisse!"[8] They had
seen Lieutenant Palisse, navy officer in charge of the information service, with
whom they had negotiated and made agreements the time before. He must have
thought that they would not return again because, on seeing them, he lapsed into
manifestations of cordiality and joy that seemed to me to be somewhat excessive. He even became downright frenetic when, in response to his questions,
they told him that they had the location of pieces of German artillery. "*Vous avez
les 420!* (You have identified the 420s)," he cried, ecstatic, jumping up and down.[9]
"*Vite, vite*," he said then to the officer who had accompanied us. "*Emmenez-les au
Rochambeau. Je vais venir tout de suite* (Take them to the Rochambeau. I will come
right away)." He had not even noticed my presence, nor that of Ettore.

At the Rochambeau, the *réquisitionné* (requisitioned) hotel at the other end
of Grenoble, a gracious *mademoiselle* showed us into a room that was very modest, but that, after a night spent in the barracks, seemed downright luxurious
to me. There was a washbasin with hot running water, on which I flung myself
and washed up without delay. Then I went into the lavatory, which was clean
and not frozen. But I had only just gone in when I heard the sound of footsteps
and the voice of Palisse, who was talking with the boys, which then intensi-
fied suddenly, disturbed and excited: "*Non, mais non, la dame ne peut pas rester
ici* (No, but no, the lady cannot stay here)!" I felt my heart skip a beat. The *lady*
could only be me. "The next thing you know," I thought with some apprehension, "they will keep the others here and will send me to a concentration camp,
and I cannot do anything about it!" I no longer had the courage to come out. But
I could not stay in the lavatory forever, even if it were clean and comfortable.
Therefore I got up my courage and, having come out, went to introduce myself

---

[7] The Thompson, a submachine gun, was also known as the "Tommy gun."

[8] Bernard Palisse, a lieutenant in the French Army, was in charge of the information service
on the border with Savoy.

[9] The 420 mm howitzer.

with the most beautiful of my smiles. The storm had been placated by then, and the situation had been explained. Palisse and the other officer who was with him, Lieutenant Campin, welcomed me cordially.[10] They calmed down immediately when they learned that I was Paolo's mother. But they could not make a decision. We had to speak to the general.

Again they loaded us into a car, and they brought us to the Hotel Lesdiguières, where this time we went in. Yes, there were the polished sidewalks and hazy lights Paolo had described, but there were no longer Moroccans in turbans, and even the atmosphere of the *Thousand and One Nights* was missing. They conducted us to the first floor, and made us wait several minutes in a long hallway. Poor Ettore, who did not have time to avail himself of the lavatory, where I had remained much longer than I should have and wanted to, desperately began to look for one. Suddenly we saw him turn, contented and determined, toward a door where *Chef de Cabinet* (supervisor) was written. "No, no!" we shouted with energetic signs of opposition. Then he ran to the end of the hallway where he threw open a door and went in, first turning to us with a radiant smile and stretching out his arm in the Roman salute!

He had just returned when they showed us into the general's office. He was most polite, greeted us cordially, and gave a nice speech, praising the work of Alberto and Paolo and thanking them for the valuable news they had brought. "But," he concluded, "we were expecting two of you and eight arrived. Naturally I must ask you who the others are." And after all, he was not wrong.

It was easy to explain the position of the Corallos. They were two mountaineers, guides and carriers, useful for the transport of weapons that they hoped to obtain. Pillo was a young partisan officer who had cooperated in the search for information, and who had to be put into contact with the French authorities in case Alberto and Paolo could not come personally to bring the news—a kind of deputy, in effect. Even Bruno—a persecuted Jew and surgeon who wanted to join the Liberation Army and who offered to work as an aid in some French hospital in the meantime—was quickly justified. It was my presence that they could not manage to accept. What had I come to do? The traditional masculine idea of the woman, which arose from natural distrust, made them unable to understand, and although I did not resemble Mata Hari in the least, I still aroused some suspicion in them.[11]

I tried to explain that I wanted to establish connections with the French women in order to profit from the experience they had gained after the liberation, and to lay down the basis for collaboration in the future. "*Mais c'est justement ce que vous ne pouvez pas faire!* (But that is exactly what you must

---

[10] Campin was a lieutenant in the French Army.

[11] According to Bonnie G. Smith, who provided a photograph of Mata-Hari, the female spy "became a symbol of women's power to seduce men away from their duty to the fatherland." Bonnie

not do)," exclaimed the general. He went on to say that diplomatic relations between Italy and France did not yet exist, and that therefore they could not permit contacts of a political nature between the French women's organizations and me. "Oh no," I answered, having finally become aware of his typically military phobia for politics, "Nothing political, for heaven's sake." I gave him a magnificent idiotic speech in which the words *humanité, philanthropie, soins pour les blessés et les malades, crèches pour les enfants, e retraite pour les vieux* (humanity, philanthropy, care for the wounded and the sick, day-nurseries for babies, and old age homes for the elderly) entered continuously, and I concluded emotionally by saying that it would be cruel for me (*une cruelle deception* (a cruel deception)) if, after having faced so many and such grave dangers for such a purpose (here I exaggerated a bit), I would be forbidden from performing my job.

Certainly the general was not convinced by my words, but he did not know what to say to me. Perhaps he thought I was a little crazy and that it was better to agree with me, if for no other reason than out of respect for those capable young men who had accompanied me, and from whom they had received such important information. "*Eh, bien* (Oh well)," he said "*on va y penser, et dans quelques jours on vous dira avec qui vous pouzez vous contacter* (we will think about it, and in a few days we will tell you whom you can contact)." Therefore I might remain at the Rochambeau. The next day I would have a *carte de circulation* (travel pass) like the others, with which I would be able to go around freely, but for the moment I should not try to approach any women's organization. "*Je vous remercie* (thank you)," I answered with a smile, which could be interpreted as an assent or as a promise, but which really meant, "Leave it to me, and I will be very careful only to *me contacter* (contact) the people who interest me."

So I too was set. As for Ettore, who was the very one who had the least to do with it (the mission), they asked him absolutely nothing. "How nice to be a minor detail!" he commented, congratulating himself while they went down the stairs.

Again we climbed up by car, and again we went down to the Rochambeau. But this time no one came to threaten to take us away. The rooms were not heated, but the kitchen range pipe passed underneath the one Ettore and I occupied, so there was some heat. We ate alone in a big dining room on the ground floor, served by an old cook with the classic (red) nose of a drunkard. At the end of the meal, Paolo took out a bottle of Port, duly padded, which he had carried through the mountains. With that, thinking of those close by and far away, we toasted 1945.

The next morning, we were all upset and suffering from a cold, a natural reaction to the fatigue and excitement. Paolo was limping. I examined his foot. The big toe was puffy and swollen and covered with little blisters; it appeared frostbitten indeed. Nevertheless, he could walk and he went with Alberto to the home of Palisse, who had sent a car to get them.

After a while, Ettore and I also went out. There was a newspaper store at the corner of Rue Rochambeau, where the hotel was located, and Corso Jean Jaurès. I hurried to buy everything that seemed interesting. It was like a miracle to be able to buy newspapers freely where we could read news that could only be printed clandestinely at home. I found the local dailies: *Les Allobroges*, organ of the Resistance; *Le Travailleur Alpin* (The Alpine worker), organ of the Communist Party; *Le Réveil* (The Awakening), organ of the *Mouvement Républicain Populaire* (popular republican movement) (corresponding to our Christian Democrats); and a women's newspaper, *Femmes Dauphinoises*, which would help me to find out about the existing organizations.[12]

Then we found a pharmacy not too far away on the main street, where I went in to look for remedies for our various illnesses. But they had neither syrups nor cough lozenges, and we had to be satisfied with some *cachets* (tablets).

When we went back into the hotel, we found the two boys with Palisse and Campin who had come to accompany them and bring us our *cartes de circulation*, which in realty were typed pieces of paper that were furnished with a stamp. Palisse reprimanded us amiably for having gone out before having them in our possession. "*Vous voyez, il y a souvent des rafles, et on aurait des ennuis* (You see, there are often raids, and we could have problems)." (In reality, for the entire time we remained in Grenoble, we never came across a *rafle*, either by day or by night, but evidently soldiers cannot be too careful.) Then he asked me to translate into French the information bulletin of the Committee of Liberation of Northern Italy that I had brought, which I gladly agreed to do, as long as they gave me a typewriter. They brought it to me right away, and I set to work immediately.

At four in the afternoon, Palisse came to collect what I had done and accompanied Paolo and me to the hospital, where the doctor (a strange chap, visibly Jewish, who had bare feet in his shoes "in order not to get cold," he said), examined the big toe of his foot, and diagnosed third degree frostbite, but fortunately on quite a small area. With two or three injections he would be cured. He quickly got ready to give the first one. Paolo, who loathes doctors and medicine and gets sick if he just passes by a hospital, did not look very pleased. "*Est-ce qu'il est un peu douillet?* (Is he a little bit of a softie?)" the doctor asked me. No, of course not, I protested energetically, he was a partisan, the deuce! But the partisan reacted to the injection with a whining frown, to which the doctor

G. Smith, *Changing Lives: Women in European History Since 1700* (Lexington, Massachusetts: D. C. Heath, 1989), 372–373.

[12] The Allobroges were an ancient Celtic tribe in Gaul.

commented, shaking his head: "*Oh, il est bien un petit peu douillet quand même* (Oh, he is really a little bit of a softie all the same)!"

When we went out it was sunset. The fog, which weighed down on the city in the morning, lifted for a moment. For the first time I saw the circle of mountains that surrounded the capital of the Dauphiné, shaded with clouds. I thought with a pang of nostalgia about the circle of Alps around Turin. I had left it only three days ago, but it seemed far away, unreachable, as if in another world.

We went by the pharmacy to get the prescribed medicines, and then we returned home. Paolo had a high fever and went to bed immediately. Ettore and Alberto were very cold and sleepy. Bruno and the Corallos had not arrived yet. There was no news about Pillo.

Slowly a feeling of deep depression began to take possession of me, against which I tried to react by working on translating the report.

This was the first of a long series of days that followed each other, now happy, now sad, now calm, now anxious, but all dominated by a strange sense of unreality, as if we were not really the ones who lived in the Rochambeau, went out on the streets of Grenoble, and talked with so many people, but others, whom we watched live with a feeling of detachment, only dimly interested, as if the very essence of our lives had remained far away, beyond the Alps.

We thought we would remain for a maximum of about ten days, and instead we stayed for more than a month. The French Command wanted to give us the address of a certain man from Cuneo, with whom we should keep in touch regularly. In order to get this address, Palisse had to go to the Nice Command in person. Hindered by that year's exceptional snowfall that blocked all the access roads to the Dauphiné for several days, he was more than a week late in returning. Then, realizing that Ettore was a radio engineer, he wanted to give us a broadcasting apparatus, which would have enabled us to keep in contact with them directly. But it took a lot of time to get the transmitter out and explain a very complicated code to us (the Marchetti code).[13] In short we were hung up in the military system, bureaucratic and slow to the point of exasperation, and which it was not in our power to accelerate, as much as we tried.

Therefore we remained in Grenoble for the entire month of January and the first week of February. The mountains that surrounded the city (the Bastille, at the bottom, and behind her, the massif of the Chartreuse; the glorious Vercors on one side, and on the other the multifaceted and snow-ridden background of the Savoyard Alps) became familiar to us, but—at least as far

---

[13] Most likely Ada means the Morse Code. Nello Marchetti, tutor of the inventor of wireless telegraphy, Guglielmo Marconi, and a retired telegrapher himself, taught Marconi the Morse Code.

as I was concerned—without becoming part of our innermost being.[14] We learned to know and travel Avenue Jean Juarès, which led to the center of town from our suburban Rochambeau; the Cours Berryat, which crossed it at a certain point arriving on one side as far as the Drac river; the long Rue Thiers (on which opened the streets that led to the hospital and to Military Security, and where we found a newsstand that had Swiss newspapers); Place Victor Hugo, with its garden and grand hotels; and Place Grenette, where the headquarters of l'Union des femmes françaises was located. We discovered the ancient charm of the little piazza, where the Palais de Justice (*Municipio*) and the cathedral grace the monument to Baiardo *"chevalier sans peur et sans reproche* (the fearless, irreproachable knight)."[15] Distracted and pensive, we contemplated the flowing waters of the Isère, at the foot of the hill that vaguely reminded us of that of Turin. We ended up finding it natural to go out in the evening without a curfew and without a blackout, and spending every day at the editor's office of the *Allo* (*Les Allobroges*), where the war bulletins were published, and where we could follow the progress of the Allied armies on an enormous map.

The weather was almost always harsh, gloomy, and unpleasant. It snowed continuously and, since no one removed the snow from the streets, walking was quite difficult at times. Enormous icicles hung from the balconies and gutters. Even the ground was often icy, and more than once we managed to find ourselves seated on the ground, as usually happened even to the local people, moreover. Sometimes, returning home at night, when we crossed the overpass situated at the intersection of two roads we were violently knocked down by icy, violent, tumultuous gusts of wind from a snowstorm in the high mountains. But, despite this and even though at home it was not very well heated, I never really suffered from the cold. Perhaps this was because I was sufficiently covered. I had a good five pairs of socks in my shoes, and several sweaters and, over everything, the old faithful fur coat. Besides, almost all the women that I saw around me were bundled up and wore trousers. Therefore I could mill around in a state like this without attracting attention. Only during the first days of February, when it stopped snowing and the temperature improved, did we have days that were almost like spring. But walking became even more difficult, because we waded through a kind of quagmire of mud on the streets and roads that were not cleaned.

---

[14] For a history of the battle between French Resistance fighters and the Germans that took place in the Vercors plateau in July 1944, see http://www.vercors-net.com/dossiers/histoire/resistance.html. According to Fofi, 750 *maquisards* were killed in the battle, which he called "one of the most glorious and dramatic of the French Resistance." *Diario partigiano* (1972), 276 n. 2.

[15] Pierre Terrail, the Chevalier de Bayard (1473–1524), was known as the "the good knight without fear and without reproach."

Along with the presence of a number of people in the most diverse uniforms, and groups of German prisoners that we encountered from time to time with *P.G.* (prisoner of war) on their backs, the streets' lack of cleanliness was one of the most visible signs of the state of war in the city, which, not having endured serious bombardments, exhibited neither defacements nor ruins. Another sign, less visible but even more noticeable, was the shortage in the stores. There was destitution during those times at home as well, but we still found many things, even without ration cards. It was always possible to buy fruits and vegetables in stores and markets that were more or less nice-looking and more or less expensive. Instead here we found absolutely nothing. Four years of German occupation had exhausted all the reserves, and the difficulty of transport, especially during the winter season, seriously cut into supplies. In recompense, however, rationing, even if not lavish, proceeded regularly, not with exceptions and by chance as it did at home. But for the foreigner, not equipped with *tickets d'alimentation* (ration cards), the stores offered very few resources. The only thing there was an abundance of was salt. Instead at home, especially among the mountain folk, who were eaters of *polenta* and soup at all hours, it was really missed. (In fact, the two Corallos, drunk from such abundance, bought several kilos of it, and we had a hard time convincing them not to bring it back with them on the return passage.) Another thing that was available and convenient was Cologne water and perfumes—at Galeries Nouvelles, the biggest department store in Grenoble. But this did not constitute a great resource. When we went into a cafe to talk with a friend or to flee the icy winds of the streets for a moment, we absolutely did not know what to order. Our "substitutes" of that period in Italy were a veritable nectar compared to the horrendous *tisanes saccarinate* or *praliné* (saccharine or praline herbal teas) that they prepared for us in Grenoble. There was good beer, but it cooled us down rather than warmed us up, and the classic Pernod, a favorite of the French of any social class, was a bit alcoholic for our tastes. Only toward the end of our stay did we discover the existence of some excellent fruit juices, which, mixed with a bit of water, made a reasonable drink.

We were neither well off nor poorly off at the Hotel Rochambeau. It was a small hotel, which at that time lodged only us and from time to time some mysterious character (certainly some other "spy"), who stayed at most only one day, however. The owner was a short little man with a Jewish nose and a beret that he always wore on his head. While he boasted about I no longer know what athletic ability, he was almost always sick, and they cured him with methods that were horrifying to us: *ventouses* (leeches) in abundance, and poultices of pigeon dung! His daughter was a beautiful girl with the typically French *minois* (fresh young face) and extremely polite, with whom we exchanged a real battle of verbal courtesies every evening.

"*Bon soir* (good evening)," she said with a smile, coming out of the dining room.

"*Bon soir*," we answered in chorus.

"*Et bonne nuit* (and good night)," she hurried to add.

"*A vous aussi* (to you too)," we retorted.

"*Reposez-vous bien* (sleep well),"she insisted, unrelenting.

"*A demain* (until tomorrow)," we continued.

And so forth. But it was quite difficult for us to have the last word.

The maid, Madame Rose, was the widow of an Italian political exile, a native of Bordighera, who was killed by the Germans, by accident, during the days of the liberation. She was an ordinary little woman, insignificant and colorless, who had a single refrain: "*Ah, oui, c'est pénible* (oh yes, it is tough)!"

The cook, Madame Roche, was much more picturesque, with her big drunkard's nose and a "goduriosa" tendency that was typically *gauloise*.[16] She spoke quite an expressive French, and she always told strange, terrible stories, such as, for example, that she fell while she was crossing Place Championnet on her bicycle and had completely *partagée la langue* (split her tongue)! We loved how much she loathed the owners (whom she defined as misers and thieves), and when at times, in the evening, we played and sang (there was an old, forgotten piano, which Bruno and I took advantage of from time to time), she appeared from the kitchen and delighted in singing various French songs with gestures and expressions that reminded us of cafe concerts of the *can-can* era.[17] One evening Alberto offered her a cigarette, which she accepted with eyes that were bright (more than usual) and moved. "*Je la fumerai pensant à vous* (I will smoke it thinking of you)," she said. She added, with an inviting smile that was all languor: "*A moins que vous ne vouliez venir la fumer avec moi dans ma chambre* (Unless you want to come and smoke it with me in my bedroom)!" a proposition which literally terrorized Alberto.

As for the food, we passed through several changes. At first they gave us French military *ravitaillement* (provisions), comprising, at least as far as we were concerned, essentially vegetables and *pain mouillé* (moistened bread). After a few days, however, they replaced it with American *ravitaillement*, consisting exclusively of food in cans. So we went from vegetarian meals (*pain mouillé*, potatoes, carrots, and cauliflower) to meals that contained meat and were very spicy (stew, salmon, corned beef, and pork paté). We asked timidly if we could alternate

---

[16] A "goduriosa" is a woman who likes her pleasures.

[17] As a young girl, Ada studied piano under Ermenegildo Gilardini at the piano school of Boerio-Ferraria-Gilardini and voice with Stella Calcina. Her teachers judged her to be sufficiently talented to pursue a professional career in music.

between the two regimens, but we were asking for something impossible for sure, because the bureaucratic machine could not conceive of such a sensible solution. Only toward the end did the meals begin to improve. When, after the big snow-falls ended, the transports began to function, there were a few fresh vegetables. One day—oh what a miracle!—they even gave us a salad of greens.

Jokes aside, there was really nothing to complain about. The American meals, even if they were nauseating, were nutritious. And—something especially important to me—we had tea and coffee (albeit an amalgamation) in abun-dance. Moreover, Major Hamilton, head of the English mission in Grenoble, supplied us with biscuits, butter, and jam. I still remember the sensation that I felt on opening a jar of Cirio apricot jam, made in San Giovanni a Teduccio in the spring of 1944, even if it had inscriptions and explanations in English, as if I had found the familiar face of a person held dear, though in a strange uni-form.[18] But when the French learned about these gifts from the English, with Latin sensitivity they felt degraded, and did not want to be outdone.

One evening when we came home, we were greeted by the *mademoiselle*, who shouted to us festively: "*Venez voir! Il y a le Père Noël pour vous* (Come and see. Father Christmas came for you)!" In fact on the table, in front of each person's plate, there was a little multicolored pile of chocolates, cigarettes, and chew-ing gum. The latter represented a new experience for the younger of the two Corallo brothers, Virgilio, who had never seen it, and who did not know what it was. The next day he reported to us, half angry and half annoyed, that he really did not like those American candies. He had chewed and chewed them and then, seeing that they did not melt, he "swallowed" them! Fortunately not even the ingestion of various packets of chewing gum could hurt his cast-iron stomach.

Certainly, if we had known from the beginning that we had to stay for so long, we would have been able to organize ourselves and make the most of our days. Instead we were up in the air and in suspense, waiting to leave from one minute to the next. Despite my passion for plans, we absolutely were not able to make any beyond the day.

What is more, we were almost all more or less sick, as if, the tension and the danger being relaxed for the moment, the body, abused, overworked, and neglected, had reaffirmed its inconvenient rights.

First it was Paolo's turn. After the injection, the big toe of his foot resumed an almost normal appearance, and the doctor with the bare feet, who came to see him after several days, declared, to the great satisfaction of the patient, that the circulation had returned and that more injections would not be necessary. But the high fever that had taken hold of him on his return from the hospital

---

[18] Cirio was an Italian company located in San Giovanni a Teduccio, a town near Naples.

lasted for more than ten days, annoying and obstinate. We all believed—doctors included—that it was a question of a typical, ordinary flu. Instead it was probably the first sign of those rheumatic problems which then resulted in so violent an attack on our return to Italy, and which caused the heart murmur that Bruno noticed when he visited him before he began the return trip.

Paolo was barely well and had begun to go out when Ettore got sick: a high fever, a cold, and a cough. He too had to remain in bed for several days. He suffered a slight pleuritic rub of which the roughness of the voyage, which should have harmed him, instead cured him completely.

Then, with Ettore barely cured, Paolo began to have a fever again, not so high and not continuous, but vexing and worrisome nonetheless.

Then Alberto was sick for a few days, then Bruno (who had arrived in Grenoble with the Corallos three days after us), and then I too, although only mildly. Only the two Corallos stayed well, even though they also caught cold and often had crises of depression.

Since the warmest room was mine, the person whose turn it was to be sick moved to my bed and we gathered around him, "forming a circle." Our Italian and English friends who came to visit us, seeing a different person in the bed each time, could not make heads or tails of it, and the juiciest rumors began about our relationships. It was clear at once that the two mountaineers were the guides. I was a woman, and Bruno was the "surgeon," but the others? At a certain point when, having gotten to know us better, they had finally clarified the situation, they confessed to me that at first they thought Alberto was my husband (something that for me was quite flattering since he is around twenty years younger) and that the one they had the most difficulty in identifying was Ettore: "The one with the eyeglasses, we did not really understand who he was then!"

On the first of February Pillo too arrived, practically cured. The miraculous injections—they had given him five or six—had saved his foot, which hurt him only sometimes. He could walk very well, albeit with a wooden shoe that, together with a cane—absolutely unnecessary, in my opinion—and a gray wool face mask that he pulled down over his ears, gave his face and stride quite a sinister appearance, half pirate and half moneylender. At Briançon, he was quite well taken care of and surrounded by attention, on the part of both the French and the Italian community of the place. His companions in the hospital ward had naturally all been French soldiers with whom he had struck up a friendship, thus enhancing his education with respect to the French language by a rich patrimony of jargon from the barracks, which he used, in the euphoria of convalescence, both at the right moment and at the wrong moment. One evening, having gone out with Alberto and Paolo, he risked becoming entangled in a dose of punches from a soldier who, passing near them, had believed directed at him the name *sale con* (dirty idiot), which Pillo had yelled without the least personal intention, but rather out of mere expressive exuberance, thumping the ground hard with the notorious, useless, cane.

It was not that we refrained from doing anything. Our days, even if not organized, were full and at times even productive.

We had a visit from the French almost daily: Palisse or his assistant, Campin. They always wanted some explanation, or had some news to give us. We discussed and perfected our plans for activity in the future. We studied the radio code. They kept us up to date on changes that took place in the insignia and acronyms of the Germans, so that our observations could then be accurate and precise, and they consulted us about the equipment and weapons that we needed for the return trip.

Our contacts with the English mission were also frequent. Major Hamilton, settled in a villa on the outskirts of Grenoble, sent for us with his jeep, and did not just offer us biscuits and jam but promised us weapons (which he later gave us) and discussed with us the possibility of organizing strikes in the Susa Valley (which afterward he did not have time to do). Through him we met Vernon, an officer of the P.W.B. (Psychological Warfare Bureau), a young Englishman who resembled a little blond angel with his blue eyes, and whose white cloth jacket and strange cap adorned with ribbons gave him the appearance either of a schoolboy or a sailor, I cannot say which. He was an intelligent and kind boy, with many interests and open to all ideas. We could speak frankly and talk with him—much more than with Hamilton, bound by his professional discretion as an agent of the Intelligence Service, and more than with Palisse, who was restrained by the bureaucratic shackles of the Deuxième Bureau. He came from Naples and had intelligent ideas about the Italian situation, even if they were not very specific. To use a term that came into fashion some time afterward, I could say that his political orientation was quite "progressive." I saw him again in Turin, two or three days after the liberation, before the Allied troops arrived. He was full of admiration and moved, and he gave me what for an Englishman must have been the greatest compliment: "You carried out the revolution," he said, "and everything is so quiet and orderly. I feel like I am in England!"

Our friendship and the frequency of our contacts with the English evidently got on the nerves of our French friends. Lots of distrust, quarrels, and spite existed between the two commands, ever more gangrenous since, unable to be vented, they became more and more ruthlessly acerbic under the obligatory veneer of proper respect. The hostility of the officers of the Deuxième Bureau for the Intelligence Service, in whose organization they unwillingly had to recognize a model much superior to theirs, and one that would be difficult to attain, became more intense than ever. It was natural, therefore, that they resented our intimacy with the English and judged it, on their part, to be a kind of illicit rivalry.

But our position was clear, and had always been clear. We were working with them because circumstances put us in touch with each other. All the same, we remained free to establish relationships with anyone who could help us in our war of liberation, which was our only goal. Solely to its leaders did we owe obedience and discipline.

They could not object to anything regarding such a position, which was perfectly legal and correct, even from a strictly military point of view. But the heads of the service, if they accepted and even appreciated it theoretically, in daily practice were annoyed about it. They got even with poor Palisse, who therefore found himself between the devil and the deep blue sea. On the one hand, he had to please his superiors, who certainly held him responsible for each of our actions. (I think I heard them say: "*Qu'est-ce que ces italiens ont à se f…avec les anglais* (what business do these Italians have with the English)?"). On the other hand, he did not want to irritate us, whom he genuinely respected. So at times his discomfort materialized in observations or questions whose impertinence he tried to veil with irony. (For example, he asked Alberto, "*Combien de fois par jour voyez-vous M. Hamilton* (How many times a day do you see Major Hamilton)?" At other times it appeared in precautions that seemed like childish annoyances, as when, having found the English with us two days in row, he had a big cow bell applied to the entrance door of the hotel, which had opened silently before. We did not know if it was supposed to give us the impression of being restrained, to intimidate visitors, or to warn us, when he was with us, about the arrival of the…enemy!

Even before we left Italy, we knew that there must be Italian partisans in Grenoble, who had crossed the border from the Lanzo Valley and the Aosta Valley during the last German roundups, and we immediately tried to get in touch with them. The French, in deference to their useless and irritating discretion, were purposely rather vague and evasive. Despite this, it was not very difficult to find responsible individuals quite soon, among whom was Professor Corti, who explained the situation to us.[19]

In Grenoble there were around seven hundred partisans, who had come from the Aosta Valley toward the end of November, with him, with Chabod, and with the chaplain Don Solero and some other officers.[20] At first they had been locked in a concentration camp; then they had then been quartered in Fort Robot, on the hillside of Grenoble, half way down the road from the Bastille. In the beginning, they were rather poorly off as far as *ravitaillement*. (From this standpoint, the month of December must have been bad for the army and the French population as well.) But for some time the situation had become better,

---

[19] Alfredo Corti was a university professor and a partisan in the formations of the Aosta Valley.

[20] Federico Chabod was a professor of history and collaborator of the partisans in the Aosta Valley. Don Solero was a chaplain of the partisans in the Aosta Valley.

and now they did not have any serious complaints. The French did not want anything to do with arming them or organizing them militarily, but now the Anglo-Americans were paying attention to them, and it seemed that things were taking a turn for the better. There was also a group of partisans from the Lanzo Valley who had arrived a month before the *valdostani*, but having arrived a few at a time, disbanded, without leaders, and often with their wives and small children, they were in part scattered here and there, finding work in Grenoble itself or in the neighboring countryside.[21]

The morning after the meeting with Professor Corti, we left for Fort Robot, where he had us visit the local inhabitants and speak with the partisans. They were accommodated in a barracks-style settlement, but certainly better than the one that they would have had a short time ago in Italy. The rations, which they distributed while we were present, were excellent, and they could come and go as they pleased. (In fact, when we went outside in the evening we always ran into someone.) Then they were still dressed in their clothes, but after some time we saw them go about in American uniforms, furnished by the Allies, on which was sewn a piece of ribbon with the Italian colors as a badge. Those with whom we spoke confirmed for us the things that Corti had said. They were capable and nice boys, even if it did not seem to me—at least through the few words that we exchanged—that they had a definite and certain political orientation. Neither, however, did their leaders: a certain De Francesco, an excellent and efficient organizer; a Captain Plik, whose real name we never knew; and the dear and very compassionate Don Solero. Corti was an old and experienced antifascist, but like many of us, he was one essentially for moral reasons. His almost austere unselfishness, absolute lack of opportunism and ambition, and candid optimism made it difficult for him to find his bearings in the complicated and treacherous game of self-interests that affected the relationship among the French, the Anglo-Americans, and us at that time. But precisely because of this, he was a charming man, and I cannot without tenderness think about our meetings and chats of that period, on the gelid streets or in the not-very-hospitable corner of some cafe, when, under his courageous and cool demeanor, I felt the nostalgia of a man, who was no longer young, for his native country, his family, and his home.

The only one among all of them who had a political vision of the situation was Federico Chabod, who had crossed over the mountains with his wife and faithful dog, Bobby, and who, he himself being a *valdostano*, was naturally more sensitive to the danger that was developing. As he explained to us, the French did not want to arm the partisans of the Aosta Valley and organize them militarily because they wanted to avoid having them be the ones to go down into the Valley at the time of the liberation, where the French had—as was shown

---

[21] *Valdostani* were individuals from the Aosta Valley.

by some articles that appeared a little while ago in French journals of a nationalistic tone—very specific objectives, based on the separatist leanings of some movements. The Anglo-Americans, on the other hand, who were naturally opposed to the French ambitions in this arena, were in favor of the formation of an Italian expedition corps, destined to stop them and fight them.[22] In the end, as was predictable, the Anglo-Americans prevailed. I confess, however, that at the time—while I valued the factual information disclosed to me by Chabod, and had complete faith in his judgment and intuition —the entire question seemed to me to be a simple quarrel among the Allied Commands. It seemed impossible to me that, after a war of an ideological nature, as I believed the one that we were fighting was, they still had to have a dispute over the nationality of a piece of land. But I was deceiving myself, and even if Chabod's fears were not realized, they were, however, as was demonstrated later, perfectly well founded.

It was also Chabod who brought us a bundle of newspapers that came from liberated Italy. Many issues of *L'Italia Libera* were among them, with almost all of the articles signed by people I knew. It made a strange impression on me, as the French newspapers had earlier, to see publicly in print names that had to be spoken lowering our voices at home.

Then, a few days later, we met another Italian representative, Dugoni, who was there from Switzerland as an emissary of the Committee of National Liberation of Northern Italy.[23] Unlike Corti and Chabod, essentially intellectual and moralistic, he impressed me with his tone of practical efficiency and diplomatic ability. He wore the uniform of an American officer, and told us to constrain our activity in order to avoid the trouble that the French might give him. He was very courteous and cordial to us, interested in our work, and gave us useful information and advice. It was from him that we received—on January 17, I remember the day perfectly—news of Parri's arrest. From that moment I no longer had any peace. Who else had been arrested? How were things going at home, in Turin? What had happened to all of our friends? What

---

[22] Historian Gianni Oliva has provided several reasons the French government did not want to fully support the Italian partisans. De Gaulle's program of self-preservation could not envision a neighbor beyond the Alps where Communists, Actionists, and Socialists were too strong. The program of annexation of the Alpine valleys (which the Gaullist troops tried to carry out in May 1945) could be accomplished only with an Italy that was weak and deprived of new forces capable of governing it. Finally, the position of France with respect to the postwar European order would benefit from an Italy liberated by Allied forces rather than one that rebelled autonomously. On the other hand, as Oliva observed, military objectives would be well served by helping the Italian partisans, who through their acts of sabotage and attack on German positions, were useful in keeping roads and other communication links between France and Italy open. Gianni Oliva, "I rapporti fra i partigiani piemontesi e la Francia libera: estate 1944–primavera 1945," *Mezzosecolo* 9 (1993): 358–359.

[23] Eugenio Dugoni was an industrial manager and representative of the Socialist Party.

were they thinking, not seeing us return? These were questions and thoughts that, continuous and insistent like those in a nightmare, kept me in a state of long-drawn-out anguish, without allowing me the relaxation of tension that external circumstances would have been able to do.

It goes without saying that I did not wait for permission from the authorities to get in touch with the French women, which in reality was given to me two or three days after my arrival, but in a very limited form. "*Puisque vous avez si bien travaillé pour nous* (since you have done such good work for us)," Palisse told me with an air of granting me a big favor, "*on a décidé que vous pouvez vous contacter avec la Croix Rouge* (we have decided that you can contact the Red Cross)." He also gave me a letter of introduction to the president. I went there, although I was not very enthusiastic. They welcomed me courteously, but they did not have anything extraordinary to tell me, nor I to ask them. The Red Cross is an international organization founded on fundamentals that I already understood perfectly, and they could not teach me anything about its operations that I could not learn directly from De La Forêt. But they spoke to me about certain *équipes d'urgences* (emergency teams) that had been very useful during the liberation and even afterward, whose leader and organizer was a certain gentleman whose name I do not remember. So I went to his house and he gave me plenty of explanations and suggestions. He had formed *équipes* (teams) during the occupation to give aid to air raid victims. But there had been very few air raids in Grenoble, and the *équipes* (made up of citizens of every political orientation, but all anti-German and anti-Pétain) had been able, under the auspices of the Red Cross, to develop genuine and appropriate assistance for the partisans, with whom the surrounding mountains were filled.

But before, even without being authorized, I had already contacted the women of the French Resistance. There was an office of the local seat of the Uff on Place Grenette that was open to the public. It was with a sense of nostalgia and at the same time of high hopes (who knows when the Gruppi di difesa will be able to have a headquarters open to the public, in broad daylight?) that, the day immediately after my arrival, I pushed open the door to the small office. There were, in some glass cases and hung on the walls, photographs and inscriptions that would become familiar to me afterward, but that appeared new and marvelous then. There were portraits of Danielle Casanova and Bertie Albrecht and other women murdered by the Nazis.[24] There were photographs of smiling babies and women at work and documents of women's participation in the reconstruction of the country. There were some inscriptions with slogans

---

[24] Danielle Casanova and Bertie Albrecht were heroines of the French Resistance. Casanova, a militant Communist, founded l'Union des Jeunes Filles de France. She was deported to Auschwitz in 1943 and died in May of that year. Albrecht was a French partisan who died in the Fresnes Prison in the Val-de-Marne in 1943.

that seemed singularly happy and impressive: "*Si toutes les femmes du monde voulaient se donner la main,*" one said, "*on pourrait faire une ronde, une ronde autour du monde* (If all the women of the world wanted to hold hands, we could make a circle, a circle around the world)!" And another: "*Nous voulons créer pour nos enfants les lendemains qui chantent* (We want to create for our children tomorrows that sing)."

The woman in charge, Jeanne, who had very sweet eyes and entirely French good manners, after giving me the explanations I asked for, directed me to Claude Dunoyer, editor of *Femmes Dauphinoises*, who certainly would be happy to meet me. I could even find her right away at the headquarters of *Les Allobroges*, where she was a reporter.[25]

In fact I found her immediately, and when she learned who I was and what it was about, she welcomed me with enthusiastic cordiality. She was a small woman, around my height and age, whose features vaguely resembled Claudette Colbert. "*Mais c'est épatant* (but that's marvelous)!" she kept on repeating, "*On va enfin pouvoir parler des femmes italiennes* (we can finally speak about Italian women)!" She called a stenographer and began to interview me. I realized quickly from her questions how little they knew about us in general in France, and how many vague or downright wrong ideas they had as far as we were concerned. Therefore I spoke for more than an hour, trying to clarify how our *Resistenza* had not been born simply from an uprising of revolt against the invader, but had its roots in the twenty-year period of antifascism of many Italians. I spoke about what the women were doing, explained who the Gruppi di difesa were and what they intended to do, and gave figures, information, and precise statements. Claude Dunoyer listened approvingly, at times asking me something, and launching into explanations and clarifications in turn. It was from her that I heard mention of the sadly notorious camp of Auschwitz for the first time, and of the tens of thousands of women who had lost their lives there.

When I left her we embraced cordially, with the understanding that I would return two days later to read the interview before it was published. I arrived home late for dinner, but in a state of personal euphoria.

I returned two days later to read the interview, which had to be modified a bit. In my enthusiasm, I had responded so profusely and with such precision to the questions asked of me that my person could not be confused with anyone else. It was certainly unlikely that *Femmes Dauphinoises* would arrive in Italy and fall into the hands of the Fascists, but the possibilities are infinite, and it was better to be prudent. Therefore by common agreement we modified the article, taking out all of the references of a personal nature, and not hinting at the crossing through the mountains at all. On the contrary, we decided to date the interview from Geneva in order to divert any possible suspicion. But even

---

[25] Journalist Claude Dunoyer was also an editor at *Les Allobroges*.

as far as women's activities in Italy were concerned, there were several inac-
curacies that we corrected. It was the first interview that I had given in my life,
and I had not yet learned that, if I did not want to be misunderstood, I should
talk as little as possible, say few precise things, and continue to emphasize
them using the same words. Instead, at that time, in the effervescence of this
first experiment, I had blurted out a flood of words among which it was natural
that the French journalist, new to the topic and to the milieu, did not always
know how to find her bearings. She fell to work with good will and rewrote the
article completely. When I returned the next day, I no longer had any important
objections to make.

The issue of *Femmes Dauphinoises* of the following week came out with the
interview on the first page, with a title in big letters that contained the entire
heading: *Les femmes italiennes contre les nazi-fascistes* (Italian women against
the Nazi-Fascists), and underneath, the view of a city—that truly I did not
recognize and that could have been any city of the North —with the inscription: *Turin, la capitale de la Résistance* (Turin, capital of the Resistance). I confess
that when, going about on the streets of Grenoble, I saw the newspaper with its
remarkable title exposed in the shop windows and in the news stands, I could
not hold back a sense of pleasure and genuine pride. It was a small thing, a very
small thing, without a doubt, but after so many years of silence—worse, of
shame—it was really great to see the name of Italian women gain world recognition in the land of France.

Quite soon Claude introduced me to another interesting woman, Denise
Varelle, an artist and a pupil of Le Corbusier.[26] Her Spanish heritage revealed
itself in the warm pallor of her beautiful, expressive face, as well as in the passion that she put into every word. She was young, learned, and intelligent, with
at times the contradictions and candor of genial temperaments. We established
a close friendship right away. The respites in her delightful, warm kitchen are
for me one of the most soothing and pleasant memories of that period.

Denise introduced me to almost all of her friends, and invited me straight
away to participate in the meetings of the Directing Committee of the Uff,
where I was welcomed without a shadow of mistrust. They even allowed me to
speak, and more than once my suggestions were accepted. For the first time
during those meetings, I heard mention of subjects fundamentally similar
to those that we wanted to encourage in Italy after the liberation: assistance
to families of partisans and victims of war, milk for children, *ravitaillement*
(the transport by truck of potatoes and cheese from certain isolated mountain regions of Savoy seemed to me to be an excellent initiative), defense of
the values of the *Resistenza*, rapport with other women's groups, penetration
into the masses of women who were still politically uninformed, and above all

[26] Denise Varelle was an artist and organizer of the Uff in Grenoble.

the battle to make understood, through initiatives that were even simpler and more banal, that politics are not intrigue or conspiracy, but an essential form of life.

During these meetings, I learned to appreciate Jeanne's abilities and spirit of self-denial, one of those modest "workers" on whose activities and incessant sacrifice the existence and functioning of an organization were often based. At that moment, they were trying to create outlying sections of the Uff in the various neighborhoods of Grenoble. Several times she drove me with her to preliminary meetings. I always admired her tact in dealing with new people, intuition for finding convincing arguments time after time, and clarity in imposing questions. I learned many things that could be useful to me later.

I had learned from Dugoni that there was a Socialist in Lyon, a certain Gina Lombardi, an old organizer, trustworthy and intelligent, whose address he gave me. I wanted very much to meet her. But to get a train ticket in France at that time it was necessary to complete certain formalities that I, a foreigner and an illegal one at that, could not execute. Therefore I spoke with the French about it, saying of course that I wanted to go to Lyon to meet a childhood friend there. "On va voir d'arranger cela (we will see about arranging it)!" Palisse said with a promising air. I already anticipated the pleasure not only of meeting a smart woman, but also of seeing Lyon, which I did not know, of having a look at the bookstores, certainly better equipped than those appalling ones in Grenoble, and perhaps of making a brief visit to the editor's office of *Lione Libre* (Free Lyon) and meeting Ferrat there.[27] The next day, with a satisfied and triumphant air, Palisse announced to me that I could go to Lyon on Monday (it was then Saturday) with a military car that would take me back to Grenoble the same evening, a solution that limited my plans somewhat, but that I still accepted with due gratitude.

On Monday morning, punctually at 7:00 a.m., the car came to get me at the small hotel. There were two French officers with me and a noncommissioned officer who drove. It was a frigid day, perhaps the coldest of that very cold winter, and we had hardly left Grenoble when the motor, frozen, stopped functioning. After quite a while it began working again, but it continued to become clogged from time to time. Every time the driver had to get out, and every time—I could not make out whether because of propriety, discipline, or prudence—he took off his jacket and put on a work smock, even when he simply had to raise the cover of the hood to see what had happened, which undeniably provided some variety to the scene, but certainly did not serve to speed things up. At a certain point the fog became so dense the unfortunate fellow was forced to drive holding his head outside the small window for more than two kilometers.

---

[27] André Ferrat was the editor of *Lyon Libre*.

It was almost noon when we arrived in Lyon. They accompanied me to Villeurbanne, a huge, crowded suburb where my friend lived, and we agreed that the car would come to get me around three o'clock in the afternoon.

I climbed the stairs—the classic wooden stairs of so many French houses—wondering if I would find Signora Lombardi at home, and how she would receive me. She was there, purely by accident, as she explained to me. There was no electricity in the factory where she worked, and therefore she had stayed home. I thanked my good fortune, and told her the reason for my visit. She knew my name, and said she was happy to speak with me.

She was an ordinary woman, but deeply earnest, with clear ideas and valuable experience. She told me at great length the story of her life in France, where she had emigrated a little after the advent of fascism in order to flee persecution, described people and surroundings to me, and spoke to me about organizations and movements of which I had never heard mention. From her attitude I could sense what the mentality of exile must have been for most people, its struggles and discouragement, accumulating hurtfully, month after month, year after year, small ambitions, resentments, and quarrels that were doomed, since they could not be vented openly, to poison relationships and obscure the very visions they had in common. I believe that one needs an ideal sense of security and a better-than-normal strength of spirit to be able to preserve one's lucidity and equilibrium during exile. Listening to Gina, I thought about the words that Piero had said to me on that day, so many years before, at the time when he left for France: "In Paris, we must try not to be exiles, *fuorusciti*, but to force ourselves to remain Italian and become European."

At a certain point, Gina's husband came home from work, and he too was approachable and nice. With the cordiality of humble people, they invited me to dinner, even though I was basically a stranger, and we continued to chat. When I spoke with Gina about women, about what I thought should be done, I asked her how she thought we could lay the foundations of work for today and for tomorrow. She told me her ideas, supported by extensive experience, almost all in agreement with mine. She confessed to me that after the liberation she had not concerned herself with anything extraordinary, a bit due to fatigue, and a bit because she was annoyed about so many things. "But now I will begin to get involved again," she promised in the end. When, the car having come to get me, we parted with an affectionate embrace, I had the impression of having found in her a friend and collaborator.

The return trip was much more rapid and comfortable. The sun had dissipated the fog, it was no longer so cold, and the car ran like a dream. The only black mark was the strange phenomenon of incomprehension that was expressed between the driver and me. I sat next to him (the two officers had remained in Lyon) thinking that I would entertain him with my chatter. But it did not work. He did not understand what I was saying, and I did not understand what he was saying. At a certain point, seeing a burned and semi-destroyed house, I observed: "*On voit que les boches sont passés par là* (We can see that the Germans have passed by there)." "*Mais pas du tout* (Oh not at all)," he answered me. "*On ne passe pas par là. La route est par ici* (We do not go that way. The route is this way)." I was quiet for a while, until he asked me to take something out (I did not understand what) from the glove compartment I had in front of me. I opened it and saw a bar of American chocolate that I took out and handed to him. "*Non*," he said, smiling "*prenez, prenez* (take it, take it)..." I thought that he was offering it to me and therefore I broke off a little piece, but evidently I had not understood well: "...*le chiffon* (the rag)." He wanted the rag to clean the window, and I had eaten his chocolate! After this experience, I did not try to converse with him any more, limiting myself, when he left me at the door of the small hotel, to telling him, "*Merci et bon soir* (thank you and good evening)." This time evidently he understood because he responded smiling: "*Au revoir.*"

Meanwhile Alberto, Paolo, and Pillo devoted themselves to organizing and directing the liaison service between the Susa Valley and France.

The first to arrive, three or four days after us and without waiting for our direction, were Eligio Pacchiodo with another two. Circumstances justified the initiative. The day after our departure, some French prisoners, having fled the Germans in Bardonecchia, had gone to Beaulard, where they knew that there were partisans, to beg them to accompany them to France, across the border. The French were in danger, and it was urgent to get them to a safe place. Eligio, who would have been an excellent noncommissioned officer in a regular army, had taken the responsibility for organizing the crossing. Everything had gone very well. Having crossed the border, they came into contact with the American mission stationed at Guillestre, half way between Briançon and Embrun, which, on their request, had sent them to join us in Grenoble. Then we too came into contact with the American mission, in particular with Major Richard, who was the leader and who promised to give the three men, when they returned to Italy, all the weapons and materiel that they could carry. He would continue to do the same with all of the subsequent patrols that crossed the border with the same purpose. Thus the supplying of weapons was effectively organized and begun. Two days later, Eligio and the others departed again with their load of weapons, carrying newspapers and other messages in addition. After around ten days, Eligio returned with five more men. The American mission, convinced by now of the regularity of the patrols, decided to create a *Centre d'acceuil* (reception camp) at Plampinet, with an officer placed at the head of the service. In this way (in the end it was a problem), the Passo dell'Orso became an almost official thoroughfare, just like the Colle della Galisia, whose reception camp was in the Isère Valley, where the *staffette* and partisan patrols from the Lanzo and Canavese Valleys flocked. Movement became more and more speedy and continuous, and the Americans—with their usual lack of any prudence regarding clandestine activities—went as far as to print on one of their propaganda leaflets, destined for diffusion in Italy, the photograph of a partisan who, armed and loaded, was crossing the Colle della Galisia.

In truth this happened somewhat later. Then, notwithstanding the intensity and frequency of the crossings, the publicity had not yet reached these extremes. Our boys from Beaulard went back and forth several times, without the least difficulty.

On 8 February, we also saw Carletto, one of Laghi's trustworthy men, arrive with another two from Beaulard to look for us and get our news. Since, by pure accident, Carletto had not met the Americans, we thought instead of putting him, together with his two companions, in touch with the mission of Hamilton, who was very happy to welcome them and agreed to arm and equip them for the return trip.

In this way we had set up three liaison services: one with the French, essentially consisting of the transmission of news and which, because of its particular sensitivity, would have to be centralized in our hands and occur essentially via the Corallo brothers; another with the Americans for the transport of weapons, in which squads of five or six of our sturdiest mountaineers would have to follow each other almost uninterruptedly; and a third with the English, centralized around the very dependable Carletto, for the communication of news and the transport of various materials, newspapers, and propaganda.

As can be seen from all this, our days were full of movement, inquiries, and meetings. Yet we still had a certain margin of free time left, more than we had been used to having during recent times in Italy.

We took advantage of it to go to the cinema sometimes, although Grenoble's screens did not offer much of interest at that time. I saw some films that I had missed up to that time, even though I had wanted to see them, such as *Pépé le Moko* and *Les gens du voyage*. I saw some others again, among them Charlot's *La febbre d'oro*, which struck me for its inexorable vitality. The only new ones were three Soviet films: *l'Assedio di Leningrado, Una giornata di guerra nell'U.R.S.S.,* and *Arcobaleno*.[28] I was enthusiastic about the first two, not only because of their present-day interest and their brisk pace but more than anything because the faces of the actors, soldiers, bourgeois, and workers, struck me. On all of them, and on those of the women as well, and even on those of the children, you could read an absolute and precise commitment, assumed with enthusiasm. I could

---

[28] *Pepe le Moko* (1937) was a crime drama directed by Julien Duvivier. The drama *Les gens du voyage* (1938) was a German film directed by Jacques Feyder. *La febbre d'oro* (The Gold Rush) (1925), was one of Charlie Chaplin's best films. Chaplin was known as Charlot in France. *Arcobaleno* (The Rainbow), 1944, directed by Mark Donskoi, was an anti-Nazi film about partisan resistance. *L'Assedio di Leningrado* (The Siege of Leningrad) and *Una giornata di guerra nell'U.R.S.S.* (A Day of war in the USSR) were probably documentaries.

not, looking at those faces, doubt the victory. Instead *Arcobaleno* left me perplexed. It was quite alluring and had convincing episodes, but in the woman's final invective against the Germans, she brandished such a fury of hatred that it left me dismayed. Yes, she was in a war, it was true, but it seemed to me that the tragic reality of the facts—which the film crudely narrated—was enough to inspire in the spectators the implacable wish to resist and conquer. One day we went to see a Franco-Soviet exhibition, by means of which the reality of the new Russia seemed, beneath its propagandist veneer, profoundly alive and vital. Another evening we went to a commemoration of Lenin, on the anniversary of his death, and I was profoundly moved, remembering how, twenty years before, I had seen the news of his death during a lecture Piero had given in an underground passage of the Sforzesco Castle for the Proletariat University of Milan before a public that was essentially made up of workers. "Our Ivan Illic is dead," the announcer had said simply. In the silence that had suddenly fallen over the crowd, I saw the face of more than one of these ordinary men streak with tears. The atmosphere of the commemoration held in Grenoble was much less tragic and intense, but the words and phrases of Lenin, read or cited by the lecturers, sounded alive, contemporary, and heavy with meaning and promise, like twenty years before, and perhaps even more so.

Another day we went to hear a rally of Jacques Duclos, assistant secretary of the French Communist Party, who, notwithstanding the unfavorable weather conditions, attracted an immense and enthusiastic crowd to the Palais de la houille blanche, an enormous, frigid room with big windows on the outskirts of the city.[29] But I did not like his speech: too little Communism and too much nationalism, too many words and too little substance. His verbose rhetoric, and even his stout figure, seemed to me to be typical of a political man of old, all of one mentality, all of one style, that at the time I deluded myself into believing had disappeared forever, and that instead I saw resurge, affirm itself, and have its way almost everywhere afterward.

We also went to some concerts and to a performance of Molière's *L'Avare* (The Miser), which was followed by the recitation of verses of various poets of the *Resistenza*. At that time I heard the names of Aragon and Éluard for the first time.[30] The short poem by Aragon, "La balade de celui qui chanta les supplices" (The ballad of one who sang supplications) made a huge impression on me. How many times later on, at moments of particular anguish or fatigue, did I repeat two of its verses to myself, to give myself courage, like a magic formula:

---

[29] After the signing of the Nazi-Soviet Pact in 1939, the Communist Party was banned in France. Jacques Duclos went into hiding and later joined the communist underground, helping to edit the underground newspaper *L'Humanité* and helping to establish the *Front National*, a communist-based resistance group.

[30] French poets Louis Aragon and Paul Éluard were both active in the French Resistance.

Et si c'était à refaire,
je refairais ce chemin!
(If I had to do it over,
I would take this road again).

In the evening we were almost always free, and I would have liked to take advantage of this to read, but as I think I already said, the bookstores of Grenoble were at that time quite inadequate. Besides the newspapers and some rare magazines, we did not find anything extraordinary. I launched into reading the classics (Racine, Corneille, Voltaire) and some modest English novels. There was absolutely nothing new.

And I wrote a variety of reports, for the French, for the English, for the Americans, for the French women about the activities of the Italian women, and for the Italian women of liberated Italy about the activities of the women of occupied Italy and about the French.

At times we spent the evening conversing and discussing animatedly, or we played and sang popular old French songs whose music we had found, or we had races and jump rope tournaments to keep ourselves agile and in shape.

I remember with pleasure that we always got along perfectly, without even a shadow of those small acts of meanness that could have arisen so easily in the atmosphere of irritation produced by a stay that was forcibly prolonged. Alberto, Paolo, Pillo, and I, to whom in effect the initiative belonged, agreed on fundamental matters. Not one of us ever did anything without first consulting the others, and the slightest disagreement never arose. Ettore, with whom it was impossible not to get along, was his usual calm self, always ready to help everyone. Don Medoro Benefà (Don Medoro do good), we called him lovingly. Bruno was a very pleasant companion, interested in everything, amusing in conversation, spirited, and keen in his commentary. The Corallo brothers were literally golden boys, disciplined and patient. They endured cheerfully the long stay in a country where inevitably they felt isolated. I saw them become agitated only one time, and with reason, namely when the last patrol that had come from the valley gave them the news that their father had been arrested by the Fascists and taken to Turin. The elder, Eraldo, a former *carabiniere*, possessed all of the most fundamental and traditional virtues. The younger, Virgilio, was spontaneous, fresh, and naïve, like a force of nature. I already mentioned the sincerity with which he recounted having "gulped down" the chewing gum. I will never forget the wonder his big blue eyes expressed when staring at some innocent magic tricks Ettore performed. "Ettore is an evil spirit," he said shaking his head. Even when he disclosed the trick to him, he did not seem completely convinced.

Today, when I think again of our stay in Grenoble, I wonder if its most positive aspect—other than the organization of liaison services and contacts made with so many people—was not the very perfect understanding achieved among people that were so different in temperament, education, mentality, and profession, and if it were not this very understanding, this profound fraternity—on a level that naturally was much more widespread—that was the essential goal to which everyone would have to strive and will have to strive once again.

Finally, after an unnerving succession of orders and counter orders, postponements and delays, our departure was set for 13 February.

Only five of us would go back. Pillo's foot, though almost healed, did not permit him to face a journey in the snow that was so long and tiring; and Bruno, while waiting to be transferred to liberated Italy, would serve in a hospital in Grenoble. In compensation Carletto and the two from Beaulard who had come with him would join us for the return trip, and, passing through Guillestre, we would also join the last so-called American patrol.

Everything was ready. The last instructions were given and the last agreements made. Ettore had given and received the explanations necessary for the broadcasts, the radio apparatus was in order, and the Marchetti code was well clarified. The French had provided the equipment for the trip: skis, fur jackets, white jackets and trousers, and an entire case of K rations. The English had given each of us a Sten gun with many cartridges. One morning an official arrived with a mysterious knapsack out of which came weapons that I concealed carefully in my room. Then at the last minute Vernon arrived with two enormous bundles of newspapers containing some caricatures put together by the Psychological Warfare Bureau for propaganda in Italy. But it was propaganda that was so generic that it would not be very useful to us. If they threw it out of airplanes, fine, but for us to carry it across the Alps seemed excessive to me. All the same, we decided to bring it as far as Briançon. Then, having assessed our load, we would decide whether to take it or leave it.

It was not easy to pack our bags. In more than one month's stay, we had acquired or received as a gift many things—especially books and newspapers—and we hated to part with them. We decided to be relentless, however. It was absurd to have to stop at a some point because we had brought things that were not absolutely necessary, and it was stupid to leave them by the road. I was merciless with myself and abandoned almost everything, among which were some particularly interesting books.

When, the night before we left, I looked around the room dominated by the disorder that precedes all departures, the feeling of unreality that had possessed me for all that time struck me, more acute than ever. We had not really been in this room where it appeared that we had slept, talked, and moved. Therefore I—usually so romantically nostalgic at the slightest separation—could not feel the least sense of regret in leaving it.

Later I went out with Ettore and Paolo and we climbed for a while toward Fort Robot. We contemplated the illuminated city from the top of the hill, beyond the Isère, and we wondered when, from the top of the Monte dei Cappucini, we would see the lights of Turin shine again beyond the twinkling reflections of the Po. "To think that in three days we will be in Turin!" I said suddenly. "If all goes well," I added almost superstitiously. "Let's hope so!" Paolo and Ettore said together, as if they had responded: "Amen!"

We waited around 8:00 a.m. for the car that was to bring us to Plampinet, where we would begin the crossing, but we were already in motion two hours before because, as usually happens at the time of departure, there were still many things to organize and decide.

Our hosts were very excited. Madame Rose, with her voice more tearful than usual, repeated "*Saluez pour moi l'Italie* (Say hello to Italy for me)!" Madame Roche kept embracing me, evidently not daring to embrace Alberto. (In the end she got up the courage and also embraced him.) Mademoiselle ran to and fro, visibly moved. Even the owner came out of his sick room, leaving the poultices of pigeon excrement for a moment to come to say goodbye to us personally and wish us a good trip. Just think that good Palisse had recommended the maximum secrecy to us. In the small hotel they were definitely not to know where we were going. ("*On ne sais jamais* (You never know)!" he had concluded with a mysterious air.) But where in the devil could six Italian partisans go, who were leaving with skis, equipped for the mountains, and laden with weapons and munitions and propaganda newspapers in Italian? To Nice to go swimming in the ocean? Or to the mountains for winter sports or to hunt chamois? No one respects secrecy more than I do, when something is really secret. But when it is Pulcinella's secret, it seems like a piece of buffoonery to me, more than useless, damaging. I think it is better, when absolute secrecy is not possible, to engage the loyal complicity of others with frank honesty.[31]

A little before 8:00 a.m. Palisse arrived to say goodbye to us and give us his final recommendations. He said that a young lieutenant would come to accompany us, un *type dégourdi* (resourceful chap) who would see to whatever we wanted during the trip. He would leave us in Plampinet. But Palisse hoped and wished that the crossing would not be too tiring, especially for me (he said, with a chivalrous smile), the weather splendid, and the trip *heureusement* (happily) not too long. Instead, just the night before, he received news of Moretti and his wife, who, having entered Italy again by way of the Modane-Ambin-Exilles road, had been *tués* (killed). I gave a start. What? They killed them? Who? The Germans? "*Mais non,*" he then explained. "*Ils sont arrivés tués de fatigue* (No, they arrived worn out with fatigue.)" I breathed a sigh of relief.

Instead of at 8:00 a.m., the car came to get us at nine. The *dégourdi*, a young officer equipped with a very elegant *bouc* (goatee), with phony, effervescent

---

[31] Pulcinella was a stock character in the *Commedia dell'Arte* who could never keep a secret.

energy, much more *dégourdi* for himself than for others—as he demonstrated later on—dwelled on long, complicated excuses. The car was a covered truck. I settled down in front, between the *dégourdi* and the driver, while the five men got in the back, with the bags and the weapons.

The trip took place without incident. We made a detour at Guillestre to collect the six men from Beaulard who would come with us. The officers from the American mission—settled in a gracious *chalet* adorned with hunting trophies and chamois horns—furnished the Corallo brothers with socks and sweaters, as they had already done for the others. When we were about to leave, Major Richard offered me in particular some sweets and a toothbrush that bore on its handle the emblem of a great Park Avenue store, an unusual provision for a journey for a woman who was about to cross the German lines at a height of three thousand meters, but I was duly grateful for it nevertheless, and when, after having used it for more than a year, I had to throw away the historical toothbrush, I felt some regret.

It was still daylight when we reached Briançon. The light of the sunset illuminated the mountains that separated us from Clavières. An old road sign signaled "Oulx, 30 kilometers." "To think that," I reflected aloud "if the Germans were not here, we would be at the border in half an hour without even going down by car. "Ah!" commented the *dégourdi* in the tone of a *farceur* (clown or practical joker). "*Ces allemands. Ils gâtent tout* (These Germans. They spoil everything)!"

At the entrance to the town, the car stopped. The *dégourdi* made us get out with our weapons and our luggage, said that he would come to get us the next morning, and left to take care of his own affairs. Alberto and Paolo went up to the Command to notify them of our arrival and get instructions, but they returned quite soon. The Command said we should manage for ourselves. A willing young soldier, who passed by here by chance, gave us useful information. He sent us to the Albergo della Stazione where, according to him, we would find a place to eat and sleep. It was the first stretch that we traveled on foot with our baggage. I realized right away that the load was excessive. In addition to a heavy bag containing foodstuffs, munitions, radio parts, and other things, each person carried one or two Sten guns and a bundle of newspapers. We decided for sure that we would eliminate the newspapers at the first opportunity. Personally I thought that I should have lightened my bag even more, although it really was not very heavy, and perhaps abandon my Sten gun as well—but I would resign myself to this only *in extremis* (at the last moment).

It was a gay evening. The feeling of being so close to Italy made us all euphoric and optimistic. Paolo seemed to be in excellent physical condition and amused himself by playing skittles with the boys from Beaulard on a billiard table in the hotel. The Corallo brothers were enchanted with the Bren machine gun that had been consigned to us by the English. They came to assemble it in my bed-room, and Ettore and I slept with the Bren at the foot of the bed.[32]

The next morning, after some difficulties of a bureaucratic order were resolved, we left. But we found an atmosphere of alarm at Plampinet. At sun-rise one of our patrols (which included the two Pacchiodo brothers), which had arrived a few days before, had left to return home to Italy with their load of weapons. But at the Clé des Acles, the French on guard at the border would not let them pass. In the last few hours they had noticed suspicious movements in the valley. It appears that there were patrols circulating. Perhaps the Germans were aware of the trafficking and were watching the narrow mountain pass? Perhaps someone was spying? With a keen sense of responsibility, the French had detained our men, preferring to send one of their groups ahead in recon-naissance, made up of an officer, a noncommissioned officer, and two soldiers. They had been gone a little more than an hour when gunshots were heard. Evidently the alarm had not been unfounded. After having waited for a while, since no one wanted to go back, our six men had left in reconnaissance in turn (without baggage), together with a good escort of very well-armed French men. We did not know yet if they had been able to continue or not and, until there was precise news, it was not expedient for us to start off.

The news did not bother me excessively. I was convinced that it was a ques-tion of excessive prudence and almost of spite on the part of the French. Nevertheless, we could do nothing but wait. With Ettore and Paolo we set out for a short walk along a narrow lane that skirted the mountain. We could see the Colle della Scala below. On the other side were Bardonecchia, Melezet, and Sette Fontane, there, within easy reach. It seemed impossible that any obsta-cles could arise.

When we went back toward the village, however, the French officers ran to meet us, very excited. "*Les allemands ont fait monter des petits ballons* (The Germans have sent up little balloons)," they said. "*Regardez* (Look)!" They handed me some binoculars. *Pour quoi faire* (to do what)?—I asked, taking them. "*On ne sait pas. On n'a jamais vu rien pareil* (We do not know. We have never seen anything like it)." We looked through the binoculars, but no matter how hard we tried, we could only see minuscule little clouds that did not seem to be able to be called balloons.

But when I was just about to convince myself that they were useless fears and that there was no reason to worry, there arrived the Pacchiodo brothers with the other four Italians and a French squad. When they arrived in the vicinity of Châlet des Acles, they had found traces of blood and some cartridges scattered on the ground. The marks made by the skis entwined in all directions.

---

[32] The English army was introduced to the lightweight, machine-fed Bren machine gun in 1937.

Evidently the French had been surprised and taken prisoner. Presumably the Germans had then hidden to wait for our patrol farther ahead, at the narrow pass in the valley, at the point where the French guide should have abandoned it. Having analyzed how the situation stood, the group had turned back and gone down to Plampinet to get orders.

My reaction to the news was one of anguish for the French. "*Vous avez perdu quatre hommes pour nous. Je le regrette de tout mon coeur* (You have lost four men because of us. I regret it with all my heart)," I told the officers. "*Nous ne le regrettons pas* (We have no regrets)," one of them responded with a tone that I would never forget. "*Ils seront traités comme des prisonniers de guerre. Si les allemands vous avaient pris, vous, ils vous auraient tués sur le champ* (They will be treated like prisoners of war. If the Germans had captured you, they would have killed you on the spot)." I had to admit that they were right, but my pain was not lessened. (When I returned to Italy, I learned afterward that the four Frenchmen were in prison in Bussoleno where they were not bad off, and that after the Liberation, they returned to their country, safe and sound.)

Now the problem was: What to do? The French declared that we had to postpone the crossing. The area was *alertée* (on the alert) and we had to wait for a few days until the surveillance slackened and ceased completely. For a moment, I saw Paolo's face stiffen into an expression of obstinate will. "We will leave tonight," he said. "By day there will be patrols but by night we could go across quite well." Certainly if it had been he and Alberto alone, like the first time, they would have done it, and probably it would have gone well. But there was the load of weapons, there was the radio, there was I, who could not follow the pace of their step in an escape, and above all there was the responsibility toward the valley dwellers who would have come with us. We could not run the risk of having all of us caught in an ambush. These reasons were so valid that he finally gave in.

Now we had a choice: remain in Plampinet (or in Briançon) until the alarm was over, or try to return home by way of another route. We rejected the first hypothesis quickly: the wait could be prolonged for several days, or possibly for several weeks. By now we had been away from Italy for too long and the prospect of another delay (what is more, it would have been a period of inaction and endless suspense) seemed unbearable to us. The two squads could be left, having arrived only a few days before. A period of rest certainly would do them good. But we had to return home. We would try another road. Immediately we had them give us a map for studying the various itineraries, but alas, excluding the Passo del Orso, the shortest route was precisely the Modane-Ambin-Exilles route that the Moretti brothers had taken, arriving *tués* (dead tired) in the end. Nevertheless there was little choice, and with this route, having crossed the last mountain pass (we had to cross three valleys instead of one), we could descend directly on Savoulx, making a stop at some *grange* where we would find the mother of the Corallo brothers.

Having made this decision, we had to go back to Briançon to confer with the Command. But the truck that had brought us up had left, because the *dégourdi* had thought it appropriate to turn back immediately after having unloaded us. The officers telephoned for them to send a car to get us, and we went to the Centro italiano (Italian center) to wait.

There was an American officer in charge of the service, and several other Italians besides us. There was one among them who, having been taken prisoner in 1940, had remained in France and, after the liberation, joined the partisans. He did not know how to speak Italian anymore, and he did not know French yet. He said "*ho visto una lumiera* (I saw a light)" and "*ho la migrana* (I have a migraine)" and "*il fusile mitragliore* (the machine gun)."[33] We spoke about several things, and decided that one group would remain in Plampinet, waiting, and another would return to Guillestre. In the meantime the faithful Carletto, who did not want to leave us, decided to come with us.

Soon the truck arrived to get us. We retraced our steps on the road we had traveled a few hours before, but the flowery names of the villages (Val-des-Près, Rosier) that had seemed to be filled with good omen and promise in the morning had lost their enchantment.

At Briançon we climbed up all together to the big hotel requisitioned by the army, where the Command resided. Alberto and Paolo went to make contact, and I stopped with the others to wait for them in the big veranda that must have been very elegant once, but that was empty now, with broken glass and filled with dust and litter. There was not even a chair, and we sat on the ground. We were tired, not so much out of physical fatigue as out of nervous tension. Ettore and the three mountaineers went to sleep immediately. I watched the forbidding, white mountains in the radiance of the sun at sunset. At a certain point, I began to feel like they were enemies. A dark sense of uneasiness, of anguish that was almost panicky—to which I still did not dare to give the name of fear—began to take possession of me. The silence and solitude of the veranda, with these four men abandoned on earth like dead men, irritated my nerves, which were strained to the point of trembling. For a moment I had the feeling that I would go crazy. Then I realized that I would have to deal with it at any cost. I saw a book with its leaves turned over amidst the litter and I picked it up, as if it were an anchor of safety. It was a German translation of *Delitto e castigo* (Crime and Punishment), evidently left there by the occupants when they escaped. I tried to read, and the effort I made to understand the unfamiliar language made me regain my equilibrium.

---

[33] These phrases involve a curious mixture of French and Italian spelling.

When Alberto and Paolo came back in, chattering noisily, it seemed to me that life, which had been frightfully suspended, had taken up its normal rhythm again. Even the others woke up. Everything was set. The next morning we would return to Grenoble, and then leave again in the opposite direction for the new mission. Meanwhile we would eat at the *popote* for the *sous-off* (mess hall for the noncommissioned officers). Then they would give us a place to sleep somewhere.

At table, perhaps in response to the fatigue and disappointment of before, we suddenly became extraordinarily cheerful. Having finished dinner, we began to sing and whistle in chorus the French songs we had learned in Grenoble: "Les Allobroges," "La Madelon," and "Le Régiment de Sambre et Meuse."[34] From the neighboring tables the *sous-off* stopped talking in order to listen to us. When we made a move to leave, they clapped their hands begging: *"Encore! Encore!"* We satisfied them. Then some of them came outside with us. *"Attendez* (wait)," one of them said suddenly. He conducted us to the house of an officer who had taken a drive into Italy that morning. We went enthusiastically, hoping for who-knows-what news, but in reality that person had only driven by car some hundred meters into "no man's land," and could not tell us anything important. But he was a nice young man with whom we soon passed from military and topographical topics to speaking about political problems. He wanted to offer us a coffee and invited a group of friends to join us, and the conversation was lively and interesting.

There were the good and the bad among them, rather the intelligent and the stupid, better yet the politically oriented and the inveterate chauvinists, more or less acknowledged or aware. Suddenly, one began a diatribe against the Italians, speaking of the usual *"poignard dans le dos* (stab in the back)."[35] *"Votre Mussolini* (Your Mussolini)..." he began. Immediately another scolded him: *"Tais-toi! Est-ce que nous n'avons pas eu notre Pétain* (Be quiet. Did we not have our Pétain)?" I realized that in that atmosphere, which was not fundamentally military (they were all officers and noncommissioned officers), De Gaulle was not an undisputed and idolized myth, like he appeared to be among the military men and good bourgeois of Grenoble. I felt a sense of relief and pleasure in it, since the abundance of images of the tall general in all postures and at all ages (*Charles à sept ans, Charles à quinze ans* (Charles at seven, Charles at ten) never failed to be a particular nuisance to me.

When it was time to go to sleep, our new friends brought us to a very luxurious hotel, where they gave me a magnificent room with very thick carpets, dim

---

[34] "Les Allobroges" was a patriotic Savoy hymn written in 1856. "La Madelon" was a popular song created by the singer Bach (C. J. Pasquier) in 1914. "Le Régiment de Sambre et Meuse" was a song and military march written by Robert Planquette, with words by Paul Cezano, around 1870.

[35] Italy declared war on France on 10 June 1940.

lights, and the softest bed I had ever slept in. Naturally there was a washbasin and a bathroom, but there was not even a drop of water: the ice had broken the pipes, they explained.

All of a sudden I fell asleep, but I woke up quite soon with a big thumping in my heart and a strange sense of anguish and dryness in my throat. Finally I understood. I was afraid, a fear I had tried to dominate and ward off for the entire day. With terror's ruthless lucidity, I saw what would have happened if the French had not sent the patrol ahead on reconnaissance: while we were moving ahead, unaware and confident, the Germans, lying in wait at the critical moment, surrounded us and captured us. We did not even have time to disappear, to defend ourselves. Perhaps I would have been able to throw in the snow the most important documents, which I always had within easy reach, and hide them by trampling on them, but what we had in the bags was much too conspicuous. We were Italians in the service of the enemy, spies, caught in the act, and there was not the least doubt about our activities. It was useless to take the trouble to bring us to Italy, to subject us to any trial: the evidence was more than adequate. They would shoot us immediately. Perhaps it was better like this. In a kind of lucid delirium, I saw Paolo and Alberto fall, and I saw Ettore, Carletto, and the Corallo brothers stretched out on the ground, lifeless, like I had seen them on the veranda. The thought of the narrow escape almost made me go crazy. For the entire night I tossed and turned in a kind of feverish nightmare, my teeth chattering in retrospective fear. Only at dawn did I fall asleep, exhausted.

When I woke up, it was bright daylight. The nightmare had vanished and everything took on normal proportions again. What vexed me most when I woke up was the lack of water for washing my face even crudely. Ettore, having left in reconnaissance, returned to announce to me triumphantly that down on the main floor, in the corner of a dismantled kitchen, there was a faucet with water, but the washbasin was a little dirty. . . . He did not have to tell me twice. There was water and I took advantage of it as best I could. The washbasin was the dirtiest washbasin I had ever seen, and given my deep, invincible loathing for dirty washbasins, I certainly would have rolled up my sleeves and tried to clean it, perhaps going outside to get a little gravel and some snow, had they not come to advise me to hurry up because it was time to leave.

Naturally I did not tell anyone—except for Ettore—about my nighttime agonies. Instead, amused, I stopped to listen to the much more pleasant adventures of Paolo and Alberto, who had only just fallen asleep the previous evening in their very soft bed when the door to the room was thrown wide open. Two French officers, completely drunk, had entered the room and, seeing them, had approached threateningly: "*Qu'est-ce que vous faites ici? La chambre est à nous* (What are you doing here? This is our room)," they had said. Paolo, who when he sleeps does not move, had mumbled something, pulling the covers over his head. Alberto had sat up and, half asleep as well, had tried to explain: "*Nous sommes des partisans italiens...on nous a mis à coucher ici...mais si c'est votre chambre...*(We are Italian partisans...they put us here to sleep...but if it is your room)." "*Mais non* (Oh no)," they had responded, immediately pacified and very polite. "*Ça ne fait rien. Si vous êtes des fifi italiens, c'est tout a fait normal* (It's nothing. If you are Italian *fifi*, it is quite all right)!" Emerging into the hallway, they had shouted: "*Venez ici. Il y a des italiens...des fifi italiens...*(Come here. There are some Italians...some Italian *fifi*)." In a moment the room was filled with all sorts of chaps, all rather drunk and in diverse stages of undress. All of them had emitted exclamations of surprise and made declarations of friendship, and all of them wanted to shake Alberto's hand, and even Paolo's, who let his be shaken while continuing to sleep. They had collected their things and, noisily wishing them *bonne nuit* (good night), had gone to sleep *ailleurs* (elsewhere).

We left on a public service motorbus, amidst women loaded with packages and baskets who gave the distinct impression of being part of the black market. At Embrun we took a diesel train reserved for the military, and we were in Grenoble by five.

When we got out, we were delighted to see the face of Pillo who, having been notified of our arrival, had come to get us at the station. While we were leaving, a French officer whom I had met several times, seeing me loaded down, offered to take me to the hotel in a small car that was waiting for him. I accepted with gratitude and, to make the most of the unexpected good fortune, had the others give me as many weapons and bags as possible. But evil befell me because, at a certain point, the officer who was driving, noticing the time, began to curse. He had wasted time and would arrive late at his appointment with the general! When we were at the height of Avenue Rochambeau, he said "*Je regrette, Madame* (I am sorry, Madame)," and he dumped me, bag and baggage (never was the expression more appropriate), in the middle of Cours Jean Jaurès. And there I was, on the ground, with four bags, four guns, three pairs of skis, and several bundles of newspapers. From there to the small hotel was not more than a few hundred meters, but I could not take a single step with all that load; nor could I place it in the middle of the street in order to go and ask for help. Therefore I made the move in installments, a few meters at a time, until I was near enough to the small hotel to be heard. Then everyone came out—Madame Rose and Madame Roche and Mademoiselle—and with great exclamations they brought everything inside for me. They welcomed me so much and seemed so glad to see me that for an instant I had the feeling of truly having returned home.

In the meantime the others arrived too. Then Bruno returned from the hospital and told us the episode of the day. While he was operating on the appendix of a certain man, the head physician turned to him and said, through his mask, "*unpocodacquà.*" He repeated it several times, with smiling eyes, while Bruno tormented himself thinking what on the earth did the strange word mean and could it possibly be the name of a new French disinfectant. Finally he understood. Out of kindness for his colleague, the head physician had wanted to express himself in Italian. The mysterious word simply meant, "*Un poco d'acqua* (a little water)."

After supper, in the absence of Palisse, who had gone to Nice, Campin came. We told him how things had gone and how we had decided to try the crossing from another side. He promised us that he would get the necessary permissions and that, save for some unforeseen difficulty, we would be able to depart the day after tomorrow.

The next day, 16 February, is still vivid in my memory as the most unreal of those unreal days, as if closed and isolated in an uneasy haze of tenderness and nostalgia between two black abysses of anguish.

Outside it was a perfectly normal, ordinary day, a day of vacation. I got up late, hung around in the room for a long time, and then went to look out the window and stayed to enjoy the sun while I listened to Paolo and Pillo's chatter. After dinner, we brought a little table and chairs outside, in the little courtyard of the small hotel. Mademoiselle had coffee brought to us and we took pictures, like at the end of a summer in the country.

The temperature was that of early spring, and looking at the roses climbing, which naturally were still bare and which covered the walls of the little garden, I tried to imagine how beautiful it would be when they were all in bloom in the summer. (I passed by later in June, on the way back from Paris, but the flowering period had passed and the roses hung from the vines withered, dejected, and covered with dust.)

Then the others went to the movies. Paolo and I took the *funivia* and went up to the Bastille.[36] The sky was very clear, and there were mountains on all sides as far as the eye could see. We sat in the sun and remained in contemplation for a long time. At a certain point, I stopped looking at the mountains, and turned to look at Paolo. With a kind of lucid intuition, I seemed to see him become transparent and to notice the signs that the events of the last months had engraved on his adolescent body, and above all on his heart. I thought of Piero who, eighteen years before (that day was his very anniversary), had died because his heart could not endure the strain that had been inflicted on it.[37] I thought of the exertion of the long trip back, of all that still awaited us in Italy, and a sense of hopeless fatigue overcame me. I remained there for a long time, as if I were petrified, until the sun began to cast longer and softer shadows, and Paolo too recovered from his meditations.

[36] A *funivia* is a suspended cable car.
[37] On 16 February 1926, Piero Gobetti died in exile in Paris at the age of twenty-four.

We went down, running, and the exercise served to cheer me up a bit. We crossed gardens where a number of mothers and their babies were enjoying the sun. (Oh, how happy I had been, perhaps without knowing it, when I too brought mine outside in a little carriage, or to play with the small shovel or little pail.) I went to buy a pipe that I wanted to give Pillo as a gift, and then returned home. I realized that I had lost a pin, a small brooch with a bunch of flowers with the French colors that I liked because it did not have any special significance, and I could even wear it in Italy. Seeing my displeasure, Ettore ran to buy me another. His simple kindness moved me, and gave me a feeling of security. If he were there, I thought, everything would go well.

Again the next morning, 17 February, the car that came to get us was very late. Again the six men (this time Carletto was there too) got in back. Again I sat in front, between the driver and the guide, who this time was no longer the *dégourdi*, but a young lieutenant with a serious air and of few words, who proved to be much more experienced and efficient than the other. Again the trip progressed without incident. As we advanced toward the border, the valley narrowed considerably, and the signs of occupation and war became more and more evident: houses demolished, power stations destroyed, trees and poles smashed, and above all bridges in fragments. For kilometers and kilometers we did not see a single bridge that was whole or had been rebuilt. But Modane made the most desolate impression on us. The single long street that passed in front of the station ran between two continuous rows of rubble. (I remembered it very well for having strolled on it during the obligatory stops, between one train and the other, while entering or leaving France.) Not a single house had remained standing. The station was a pile of ruins. Even the neighboring hamlets, on the sides of the mountain and in the valley below, appeared terribly damaged.

It was nearly sundown when we reached the little town of Bramans. The serious young officer accompanied Alberto and Paolo to the commander, and we entered a kind of inn where there was a stove lit and where we put together a little dinner with the help of the K rations. "*Vous êtes des italiens* (Are you Italians)?" the host, a typical mountaineer who could have easily been born in Bardonecchia or Oulx, asked. "*Oui,*" we answered. He shook his head, without commenting, but something in the expression on his face disclosed to me that his experience with Italians during the brief occupation had not been pleasant. Without being even the least bit responsible, I felt a burning shame.[38]

Quite soon Alberto and Paulo returned. Everything was set. We would leave tomorrow at sundown. The French would accompany us for a while with mules. Then they would carry the bags and weapons for us as far as they could in order

[38] Italy's ten-month occupation of southeastern France began in November 1942.

to lessen our physical exertion a bit. In the meantime, we tried to go out and be seen in the village as little as possible.

I did not know whether to be mad or laugh when they told me that a girl employed by the Command had been very surprised to hear that there was a woman in the group who would also make the crossing. She would come to meet us tomorrow, because she wanted to see the *espionne* (female spy).

After we finished our rapid dinner, the officer conducted us to an isolated little house, evidently used by vacationers during the summer season. We slept peacefully and stayed for almost the entire next day, which was Sunday, resting and conserving our strength to the utmost.

In the afternoon, the female employee who wanted to see the *espionne* arrived. She was a pretty girl who had the look of an imbecile, with enormous galalite earrings and an elaborate *cocoricò* hairdo, which came into style in Italy several years later.[39] Her conversation was so idiotic that my initial resentment gave way to amused indulgence. Instead of bluntly correcting her definition, as I had intended to do, I ended up by going along with her attitude of amazement by assuming tones of cryptic mystery.

Around five o'clock, the young officer came to get us, and we went with him to the Command, where a company of *chasseurs* was waiting for us with mules. We loaded our bags, skis, and guns on them, and we set out in a long column by a passageway quite similar to our Stretta Valley. The colors of the sunset filled the sky with delicate shades. An incurable romantic, I thanked fate one more time for granting me such exalting experiences.

After about two hours of climbing, we reached a demolished *grangia*. At that point the valley narrowed until it became a simple passageway. We had to pass at the foot of the Piccolo Moncenisio, where there were German emplacements within hearing and seeing distance. The mules turned back. Our friends loaded our belongings on their backs. By now it was almost dark. While the last gleams from the sunset were dying out in the west, suddenly, raising my eyes, I saw before me a faint star glimmering deep in the sky.

"*Passez votre cagoule* (Put on your hoods)," the officer whispered to us. Then we pulled the hoods of our white jackets over our heads. We were so perfectly camouflaged that in that uncertain light it was impossible to distinguish us from the surrounding snowy whiteness. We continued in silence. At a certain point, the person at the head of the line stopped and, making a sign, lifted a curtain that hid an opening in the rock and went in. We followed him. It was the last French checkpoint, a kind of communication trench dug out of the earth and stone. There was a lit stove, and they offered us beer, wine, and coffee. We were all very thirsty, and we gulped down several glasses of icy water.

---

[39] A hairdo where hair was piled on the head like the comb of a rooster.

Then we left again. We were soon out of the narrow passage and the valley became wider. We were no longer close to the enemy, and we could proceed without so much caution. At a certain point, the binding of one of my skis broke. The Frenchman next to me took it and told me to go ahead. He would fix it and catch up to me. But it was not pleasant continuing in the soft snow with only one ski. Fortunately he caught up to me quickly, and I took up my normal stride again.

The climb became steeper and more tiring. We had to go around a small frozen lake. The snow around the edges was icy, and it was not an easy task for anyone. One of our valley dwellers slipped and almost fell to the bottom. I was afraid I would do the same, but the two men who were next to me were able to help me, and I came through the difficult passage without incident.

The French left us one by one. They had to hurry to turn back so as not to find themselves in view of the German positions at dawn. We said goodbye cordially with warm, mutual good wishes, and then we took up the climb again, alone. But we were already tired. Evidently the long stay in Grenoble, with the absolute lack of physical exercise, had weakened us, and our loads were perhaps excessive (except for mine, since the weight of my bag was insignificant and I had given up carrying the Sten, although with great regret). Nevertheless, we walked another two hours. We wanted to reach the Baraque d'Ambin, which must not have been far away, and to make a stop there, but although the moon was still high, we were not able to find it. At a certain point, exhausted, we stopped to catch our breath in the shelter of a rock. Everyone was panting heavily. We remained motionless so that we could catch our breath. We watched the moon set in silence until we got cold and started again. After another half hour of difficult climbing, we found the Baraque, which we had not seen before because its roof, which was almost at ground level, was completely covered in snow.

The door was open and we went in, going down the short ladder. Inside there was a table, stools, and wooden floors filled with straw. We unloaded and collapsed, exhausted. I had barely begun to become drowsy when Virgilio sat up, terrified. "There is some one here! They knocked at the door!" he said. I listened, my heart in my throat, but I did not hear anything but the rustling of the wind on the snow. "No," protested the others, who did not want to move. "No one is here!" But the boy did not give us any peace. "I really heard it. I heard it myself!" he kept on insisting. "Well, go and see then!" another told him, irritated. But Virgilio, who was afraid of confronting any danger whatsoever in the open air, now, enclosed in a kind of trap, was afraid and did not dare go out. He continued to mutter and move about until he even transmitted a little of his worry to me.

Then I decided to get up. I would no longer be able to sleep in any case. I put my shoes back on, climbed the short ladder, and went outside. No one was there, as I well knew. In the blue light of the early dawn our tracks could be distinguished clearly, but no others could be seen on any side. Leaning against a wall of the hut, I saw one of our Stens, which someone must have propped there before going down, and then forgotten. I went back down with the weapon and showed it to Virgilio, who still did not seem convinced. "Doesn't it seem that the Germans at least would have taken the Sten?" I said. "Furthermore, if there are not any tracks, perhaps they flew?" "Nevertheless, I really heard it," the boy insisted, stubborn and evidently overexcited. I advised him to calm down, and to put himself down to bed. I was not sleepy and would stay up and be on guard. I told him not to worry, that I would not let him be caught in a trap.

I went back up the short ladder and sat at the top, looking outside. I saw the last stars go out, the light advance slowly in the sky, and the mountain wake up in the immense silence. I was perfectly calm. I no longer felt exaltation or anguish or regret or anxiety or longing. I was in a state of mind of perfect, almost sensual, connection with reality. A subconscious defense instinct kept me from thinking and worrying. This always happens to me: while I worry about anxieties that are absurd when plainly there is nothing to fear, instead, in moments of danger, I feel an inhuman, lucid serenity.

When it was bright daylight, I pulled the *cagoule* over my head. We were in view of the Piccolo Moncenisio, but even with very strong binoculars it would not have been possible to distinguish my hood from the pile of surrounding snow. But we could not set out by day, under the eyes of the enemy, who would have been able to inform the other stations that were closer, and have some patrol catch us unawares. Therefore I went down into the hut to discuss the situation. We would sleep and rest, since we could not depart before sundown.

I got a book, one of the very few that I had brought with me: *Les yeux ouverts dans Paris insurgé* by Claude Roy, and I went up to read at the top of the small ladder, serving as a guard at the same time.[40] The insurrection of Paris seemed like a dream, a passionate dream, but unreal. I did not want to think about what the insurrection of Turin would be like.

After a while, Paolo came outside, too, and he crouched down in the shelter of the cabin, getting some sunlight. We talked and discussed and joked as if we were in the most normal of circumstances. The others preferred to remain below and sleep. Around noon, someone said that he was hungry, and everyone seconded him. We could have lit the fire very easily, but the smoke might betray us. Therefore we limited ourselves to burning some paraffin wrappers from the K rations, which enabled us to heat up a little water to make a broth. We ate the usual biscuits, and the usual hot chocolate with vitamins.

---

[40] *Les yeux ouverts dans Paris insurgé*, written in 1944 by the communist journalist Claude Roy, recounted the liberation of Paris from 19 to 27 August 1944.

Around three o'clock, a cloud arose, the first of the day, and deposited itself right on the Piccolo Moncenisio. We decided to take advantage of it. We made up our loads again in a hurry, left, and rushed down for the descent. By the time the cloud disappeared, we would already be out of sight.

We traveled for a long while almost on level ground, leaving the Denti d'Ambin to our left. Then we began to climb again toward the Sommeiller glacier through the Colle del Gran Cordonnier. The last stretch was terrible. It was a very steep climb, but one that in the summer, without snow, could have been done in half an hour. Instead we spent more than three hours surmounting it. Our skis did not grab onto the frozen snow. There were no stumps or stones to lean on. We did two steps forward and three back. I had had enough. Paolo, who was in front of me, suddenly let himself fall to the ground as if he were dead. "What is the matter?" I asked stupidly. "Nothing, nothing!" he responded angrily. From the enraged fury of his answer, I understood that his endurance must have reached its limit. Nor were the others much better off: Carletto was vomiting and Eraldo was moaning from a stomach ache. Virgilio, motionless, looked around as if he were stupefied. Ettore did what he could. Yes, everyone had taken a good dose of *simpamina*. But the drug, so valuable during certain moments of mental tension, proved to be useless and injurious in this case.

It was Alberto who saved the situation. Without saying a word, he took the lead, and advancing slowly, with difficulty, in a zigzag, and with the aid of his ski poles, he was able to trace, with infinite patience, a kind of stairway on which everyone followed him, one after the other.

When we reached the top, notwithstanding my fatigue and breathlessness, I could not help but let out a cry of marvel and admiration. The moon had risen and the upper part of the Sommeiller glacier sparkled blue like a miraculous, immobile waterfall, while the flat part opened underneath us, velvety and soft, like a magic trail.

The boys dashed forward, almost running. I remained behind with Ettore. I did my best, but I could not hurry like the others, and soon lost them from view. I knew that they would wait for us at the end of the glacier, but not seeing them there made me feel absurdly anxious. When I noticed them on the edge, near some stones, seated in waiting, I let myself fall to the ground, exhausted. I think I fainted because for some time—I will never know whether it was brief or long—I was not conscious of anything. No one approached me, and no one came to talk to me. By now we had reached the point at which human relationships were reduced to their essential importance. If it had happened in any normal situation, everyone would have flocked around me, tried to help me, and spoken a number of words. Everything, words and gestures, was absolutely useless, because if I were dead, they would not have been able to revive me, and if I had simply fainted, I would have also come to by myself, which in fact is what happened. At some point, I regained consciousness, perhaps also because the cold had begun to stimulate me. I remembered the anxious run along the white trail of the glacier. I saw the six men, motionless as statues, with their heads bowed, just as I had seen them upon arriving. I realized we had to move. I got up with difficulty. "Let's go," I said in a low voice. Everyone silently obeyed. Paolo came near me and unstrung my modest knapsack from my shoulders, attaching it to his, and my despondency was so great that, even though I recognized his fatigue, I did not have the strength to stop him, nor to react.

Now it was a matter of crossing the deep Rochemolles ravine, halfway up the hill, and of reaching a narrow mountain pass from which we would proceed into the Fredda Valley. For a while we went along quite easily. Then the moon set, and going forward in the dark became much more difficult. We had to go carefully because the Germans were not very far away, the trail was not marked, and if we lost sight of each other, we could not call to each other. Every once in a while someone slid. Several times my ski pole slipped from my hand and Ettore went to get it for me, with incredible patience, without even swearing. Suddenly, Virgilio stopped, whispering in fear. "Shh! I heard voices." We remained motionless, with our hearts suspended. But, like the night before, we could only hear the rustling of the wind. Suddenly I wondered what would have happened if, that night which was so incredibly calm and serene, a blizzard had broken out. I thought about this to console myself. To give myself courage, I kept on singing to myself the songs I had learned in Grenoble, one *couplet* after the other. Madelon, with her *caporal en képi de fantaisie* (corporal with his fancy soldier's cap), always returned to my mind, and I though of Madame Roche. Every once in a while, at the worst moments, I repeated the verses of Aragon:

> *Et si c'était à refaire*
> *je refairais ce chemin!*

After several hours of walking, we felt the need to make a stop. We were also hungry, since we had not eaten since morning, but had simply chewed a bit of sugar and chocolate while walking. But there was no shelter nearby. We squatted down for a moment under an enormous protruding rock, but it was not very comfortable. What is more, I was afraid that the rock, which seemed to be wavering, would tumble down at a certain point, crushing us. Therefore, I insisted that we start again, and, while I was waiting for the others to get up again and get going, I leaned my head against my ski poles and dozed. When I woke up again, I lifted my eyes and saw the sky amazingly studded with stars, but these stars no longer had the witty, human wink of the little star that I had seen flourish on our departure from Bramans. These were cold, hostile, almost scoffing, and the geometric designs that they traced in the sky seemed faulty and absurd, like they had come out of an unhinged mind.

But even that night—the longest I could remember—came to an end. Sunrise found us in a kind of hollow full of rocks, in front of another climb that we had to make. "But haven't we finished climbing?" I protested. "Courage! This is the last climb. Then we will only have to descend." Paolo comforted me. The Corallos confirmed his words. Instead, as we would see, it was not true.

But when, huffing and complaining, I reached the summit, I suddenly forgot any fatigue, the view that it offered my eyes was so spectacular. It was a vast scene, in which the mountains succeeded one another, one chain after the next, endlessly: peaks, spires, and massifs, fused into a single enchantment by the rose-colored light of the sunrise. Olympus? Valhalla? Every comparison seemed inadequate, just as any attempt at description seems inadequate today.[41] Human words are insufficient. At that moment, I had the impression of an eternal and superhuman reality that all the effort of man's brainpower would never completely be able to understand and dominate. "He who goes to the mountains, it is as if he went to his mother," I thought. In the impassible solidity of the mountain, I felt something primeval, essentially and fundamentally maternal.

When I had contemplated enough, we went down a small stretch in order to reach the others who, having crouched down in the shelter of some rocks, were trying to melt a bit of snow to make coffee by using some awful solid alcohol.[42] They succeeded in the end. Since it was the first hot drink that we had swallowed down since our departure from the Baraque, it was a great comfort, even if each of us only tasted one sip of it. Then we chewed biscuits and chocolate again, and stretched out in the sun, on the rocks, and rested a bit until we decided to leave again and attack the descent. I protested violently when I saw that, at the bottom of the ravine, we had to climb back up the other side, contrary to what everyone had told me. But everyone assured me in unison that this climb was really the last.

There was not one cloud in the sky. There was not a puff of wind blowing in the sheltered ravine, and its isolated and uninteresting location made an encounter with any German patrol extremely unlikely. The cohesiveness of the group eased, and individual preferences regained the upper hand. Carletto attacked the climb in a straight run. I do not know how he kept from tumbling backwards, but the very strong sun had made the snow soft, and sliding was more difficult. Alberto, applying his usual technique, began to climb in a zigzag. Virgilio went up erratically, a bit straight and a bit in a zigzag himself. Eraldo had fallen asleep before finishing the descent, and we had a hard time

---

[41] Mount Olympus was the dwelling place of the ancient Greek gods. In Norse mythology, Valhalla was the great hall of the dead warriors, a kind of heaven for the Vikings. From his throne in Valhalla, the god Odin could look out over all the heavens and the earth.

[42] They used cans of denatured and jellied alcohol similar to Sterno for fuel.

waking him up. Ettore thought about taking off his jacket right away in order to get some sun. Paolo began to make marvelous ice cream, mixing the snow with a little sugar and a packet of Nescafé. I was terribly thirsty and thought of all the fresh drinks that I would have been able to drink in a bar.[43] I seemed to feel the cool sparkling of seltzer water, to hear the tinkling of crystal, and to see the polished reflections of the espresso machine, and I felt a desperate nostalgia for these familiar things that spoke of normal life.

Finally, we too decided to climb. Eraldo and Paolo were soon at the top, but Ettore and I found it incredibly difficult. I was absolutely exhausted. Ettore was sliding and could not turn around. There was the track made by the others, a track of stairs, and every time that I had to turn, I pointed my ski poles against Ettore's skis to keep him from sliding backwards. And every time I trembled at the thought of seeing him fall, not because of the danger—since he would stop on the soft snow at the bottom—but because then he would have to climb back up. Meanwhile the sun had set, the snow had begun to freeze, and moving became harder and harder. It took us more than three hours to do a stretch that under favorable conditions we would have covered in one hour maximum.

Paolo was waiting for us at the top. The others had already gone down to reach the barracks of the Séguret, which the valley dwellers called *Vin vert* (sour wine), where we hoped to find shelter for the night. "Where were these huts?" I asked with some anxiety. Paolo showed them to me: small buildings of gray stone, typical of the military, like all the other similar huts of the Assietta, Gran Serin, and Cà d'Asti, visible in the last light of the sunset. They did not even seem so far away. Above all, there was nothing more to climb.

Therefore we attacked the descent, but night fell unexpectedly, as often happens in the mountains. In the dark we lost the trail made by the others. Then I felt a sense of profound discouragement. I did not feel like going ahead any more, and even less like spending the night in a temporary encampment. I sat with Ettore on a pile of snow while Paolo looked for the trail with a torch. Then a strange thing happened to both of us. It seemed to us that we saw two figures dressed and hooded in white, with guns on their shoulders, pass speedily in front of us on skis. Instinctively I opened my mouth to call to them, thinking they were our men, but Ettore held me back. "Shh!" he whispered to me. "They could be Germans." I held my tongue, in suspense. Suddenly I heard the sound of voices. I closed my eyes. I could not and did not want to understand anything anymore. Paolo's return shook me. "Two men passed by," I told him. "Who could have passed by?" he answered. "We saw them. Ettore saw them too, and we heard them talking." Paolo shook his head: "Absolutely no one passed by. It was I who was talking to myself because I could not find the trail. You saw a bush

---

[43] "Bars" in Turin serve coffee, pastries, sandwiches, and cold drinks, as well as alcoholic beverages.

move. Get up, come!" We got up again with great difficulty, but we were not at all convinced. Today I still wonder about the origin of that strange hallucination that appeared not only to my overexcited imagination, but also to Ettore's calm, practical, very steady eyes.

We followed Paolo tiredly. I had really reached the limit of my physical strength. I went ahead like a sleepwalker, with the feeling that I would never be able to stop. In vain I resorted to my usual therapeutic methods, recited poetry, sang songs to myself, and repeated several times:

> *Et si c'était à refaire*
> *je refairais ce chemin!*

I was bewildered. The strangest things and most absurd memories came into my mind: scenes of my childhood, my old house, objects I had forgotten about. At some point (Ettore told me because I do not remember) I began to talk to my grandmother—who had died twenty-five years before—about some curtains and linens placed in I do not know what mysterious armoire.

Alberto's voice awakened me from this sort of delirium. "The cabin is here on the right. I came to meet you. We prepared coffee for you." I remember that I held onto his neck and let my head fall on his chest with a sense of profound tranquility, as if I had found something precious that I thought was lost for good. Suddenly I felt incredibly light, with a sense of not being myself any longer, of being able, at any moment, to step out of my heavy shell and vanish, light and happy, into the air.

In the cabin, there was a lit fire and a flask of hot coffee that I gulped down all in one mouthful. Only then did I regain a sense of reality, which in the end was not so consoling. What had seemed to be a welcoming cabin when I went in, in contrast to the darkness outside, was in reality a hut in ruins whose roof the snow and foul weather had almost completely burst open, leaving only some beams. Therefore it was filled with snow, except for the most sheltered corners, where the boys had placed as benches pieces of the doors from the neighboring huts, which were in even worse condition. The fire was lit on the wooden floor, which broke every once in a while, burning. No, the dwelling was not comfortable, but there was no choice. If I were more dead than alive, the others were not fooling either. They were all lying on the benches and on the ground, in postures that betrayed a state of extreme fatigue and the loss of the most elementary control.

We arranged ourselves for sleeping as best we could. Every once in a while someone stirred the fire, went to look for more wood, and added a bit of snow to the container that they had put near the fire to have a bit of water. After a while it began to rain: the snow which had accumulated on the surviving beams of the roof melted with the heat from the flame underneath. For the entire night the constant dripping continued, heavy and insistent, onto our jackets, which fortunately were waterproof.

I slept in stretches, a heavy sleep of senseless nightmares. At times I felt my feet burn through the climbing boots that I had put too close to the flame, and I hurried to pull them back. From time to time I reached out to take a handful of snow from the nearby pile to placate the burning thirst that I continued to feel in my throat.

No, it was not a pleasant night. Nevertheless, I felt a sense of acute regret when the flame waned at the first light of dawn, and I had to shake myself from that sort of stupor.

But as soon as I went outside, my fatigue suddenly seemed to disappear. The spectacle that it offered my eyes was much less grandiose than the one I had seen the previous morning. But they were our mountains: there was the massive shape of the Chaberton, there was Punta Clotès, and there was the bend of the Passo dell'Orso. I felt my eyes fill with tears. We had arrived. We were in Italy, finally. An absurd sense of euphoria overtook me as if the danger were over at last, not that now instead the most hazardous part had just begun.

For the time being, one thing was certain: there would be no more climbing. A long slope opened before us, at the bottom of which we would find the so-much-desired and dreamed-about *grangia* of the Corallos. "Mama is down there, there's a cow, and there's a fire," Eraldo continued to repeat, to encourage himself and me. That simple phrase "Mama is there" sounded to my ears like music from Paradise. To see the face of a woman seemed to me to be a marvelous thing. I felt dirty, unkempt, and in tatters. I had on trousers in rags. It seemed to me that only a woman could understand all these things and help me, if only with her silent affection, a woman who would prepare something for us to eat, who would fix up a couch for us, to whom I would be able to cede the responsibility (that I felt, even without completely executing it) for organizing the basic necessities of life for the others.

We brought our things outside the barracks, where only a few embers and a black hole in the floor betrayed the nighttime fire. We tied our skis and poles together, since we would descend through the woods and stony land, and skis on our feet would have only been an encumbrance. We said goodbye to Carletto, who preferred, by skirting the Séguret, to go directly down to Exilles. We saw him leave, almost running under the heavy load, invigorated by the night's rest and by the hope of being home soon. Then, with a final wave of goodbye, we disappeared at the first turn.

Then we too left, going straight down, without paying attention to roads or paths. When we found a stretch on a gradient covered with snow, we began to sit and let ourselves slide down. When we were in front of a drop of rock, we let our skis and packs fall. In the end we went downhill too. After some hours of these gymnastics, we were rather tired. While we were passing through a forest of spruce trees, Paolo let himself go onto a stretch of dry ground and closed his eyes. "Go ahead, I will join you right away," he said. I went ahead for a little bit unwillingly; then, not seeing him arrive, I turned back. He was there, motionless, with his eyes closed, as I had left him. I had a hard time waking him up. While I was touching him, I thought that his forehead felt quite hot, but I wanted to attribute it to the sun and to fatigue.

It was noon when we arrived in view of the *grange*, exactly sixty-seven hours after our departure from Bramans: three nights and three days when we had barely eaten or slept.

But a terrible disappointment awaited us. From a certain distance, Virgilio had already observed with some anxiety: "I cannot see any smoke. How can it be?" The closer we got, the more the *grangia* gave the impression of being abandoned: no utensils or containers scattered around, no clothes hung in the sun, no odor of fresh manure. The two brothers rushed to the door, but it was locked and no one responded to their knocks and calls. What had happened? Without too much difficulty, we opened the door. Inside, a big mess (stools overturned, sacks spilled, bundles of sticks and straw scattered here and there) gave the impression that the *grangia* had not been left normally, given the orderly care the mountain folk had for their houses. Something unusual must have happened. Eraldo, who upon entering had immediately rushed behind a pile of wood bundles, let out a muffled cry.

"The weapons are no longer here. The Germans must have been here!"

"Your relatives could have had them taken away to hide them in a safer place," I said to calm him down, but without conviction.

"It is impossible. They would not have left everything in disarray, and the hole open."

He showed me the empty hiding place, which must have been covered by some big stones that were next to it.

Perhaps Eraldo was right. Truly we should have expected it. Having arrested their father, the Germans must have raided the house, down at Savoulx, then climbed up to the *grangia*, found the weapons, and then.... Tragic questions were posed, to which no one knew how to respond.

One thing was certain: we could not stay there. The Germans, having come once, and not without success, could return at any moment. We, with our weapons, the radio, and all that stuff (from our skis to our trousers, from our sweaters to the cigarettes and the matches) that betrayed where we had come from! We had to go. But where? Since we did not know what had really happened and how things were, we could not decide to which side to direct our steps in order to find another less-dangerous shelter. We had to go down to the village to ask for news, and it was obvious that only I could go.

Goodbye, longed-for dream of a female presence and of abandonment to the warmth of maternal comfort! I told the boys to light the fire, make a little broth, and pull some small cans out of the packs. I washed my hands and face, combed my hair as best I could, took off my trousers, which were in rags by now, and put on the dress that, fortunately, I still carried in my pack. I went down, hoping that there would not be some surprise in the meantime.

I did not meet anyone on the street. During that season, there was not yet any traffic on the mountain. But on entering the village down below (Signol), I had a terrible impression: it was full of Germans who were drawing water from the fountain, sawing wood, and sitting smoking on the doorstep of various houses. I seemed to be entering the Russian village that I had seen in *Arcobaleno*, even if here, fortunately, I did not see silhouettes of men hanging. The same atmosphere of hatred and fear predominated around here. Perhaps I felt it with particular acuteness because I had come from a country where the nightmare had disappeared by now, and the only Germans we met any more had *P.G.* on their backs.

Trying not to attract attention, I found the house of a married sister of the Corallos. I met her in the little courtyard, and quickly informed her of the situation. She became as pale as a dead person. Then, with a nod, she had me go into a kind of hall filled with wood where, in a low voice, she told me what had happened. They had arrested the father and brought him to Turin (this we already knew). They also had wanted to arrest the mother. The Fascists had taken one of their young cousins, a partisan, and had torn away his fingernails to try to make him say where the two Corallo brothers had gone. They had gone up to the *grangia*, had found the weapons, and certainly would return. She concluded with anguish: "But why did my brothers return home? I was so happy to know they were safe! They cannot remain here. They must go away, immediately!"

I tried to calm her down. We would leave the next morning, or perhaps that very night, and we would find a place to stay, but in the meantime could she provide a little bread and something to eat for us? We had lived on chocolate and biscuits for three days.

She excused herself then, regretting that anxiety and fear had made her forget the duties of hospitality. She would go up to the *grangia* with me, bringing what she could. In the meantime, she had me go into the stable.

It was the first really welcoming place I had seen since my departure from Grenoble, and immediately I felt a sense of relaxation. The cows, which were chewing their cud calmly, were on the ground floor, there was a baby a few years old in the high chair, and there was a man seated in front of me at the table on which three bowls of soup were steaming. Perhaps I smelled the fragrance with too much pleasure because the woman said to me: "Do you want a dish of soup?

"Thank you," I answered gratefully, and immediately began to eat. While the spoonfuls of hot food went down into my stomach, I realized how starved I had been before. Never had food seemed so tasty or so exquisite to me. Perhaps this kind of ecstatic rapture revealed itself in my manner of eating, because after a while I realized that the woman and the man (who was her husband) were staring at me instead of eating too. Suddenly, with a tone not of someone who was asking a question, but of someone who was stating a fact, the man said: "She is Paolo's mother." "How did you know?" I asked, impressed. "You have the same eyes," he answered simply. But the strange thing was that, as I learned later, Ernesto (as that was the man's name) had only seen Paolo once, in passing, and what is more, it was in the wan light of an oil lamp.

My hunger satisfied, I set out with the woman toward the mountain, veering off a little so as not to cross the village. It was not a big climb—around an hour of walking under normal conditions—but I was so exhausted that it was difficult for me to keep pace with the village woman, and more than once I had to stop to catch my breath. "No," I thought to myself in the meantime, "tonight we will not move, no matter what happens. Tonight I want to sleep."

But we could not have left, even if we had decided to. At the *grangia*, I found Paolo flopped on the straw-filled mattress, burning with fever. He was complaining of severe pains in his knees, wrists, and ankles, which, as soon as they were uncovered, proved to be surprisingly swollen. The Corallos' sister advised us to rub him with a bit of fat that by chance she had brought with the other provisions, and Ettore, willing and energetic, did it right away, but I had the impression that he did not enjoy it very much. We had aspirin tablets. I gave him one, followed by a hot drink. What else could I do?

After dinner, which, to my great relief, the woman provided, the three Corallos chatted for a long time, deep in conversation, in patois, narrating their reciprocal experiences. Alberto threw himself down on the other rollaway bed. He had a bad cough and it seemed to me that he also had a fever. Ettore and the three Corallos made up an improvised bed with straw and some blankets near the fire.

I understood that it was imprudent to the point of madness not to post a guard for the night, but how could I ask the others to do what I did not feel like doing myself? By now I was at that point of depression where a person becomes indifferent and fatalistic.

Soon my body reaffirmed its rights and, notwithstanding my worry and anxiety, I fell asleep. I woke up a number of times in the night. Paolo tossed and turned, moaning in his sleep, and I caressed his painful ankles and burning forehead with futile tenderness.

When I awakened in the morning, the Corallos' sister was combing her hair in front of the fragment of a mirror. Sunlight was coming in the narrow window, the stove was lit, and the household utensils from the night before were washed. Paolo was sleeping calmly, and feeling his forehead, I noticed that the fever had gone down. When he too woke up after a few minutes, he said that he felt good and that he hardly felt any more pain. Then I had a moment of optimistic euphoria, and began to think about what to do.

It was urgent that we leave the *grangia*. The Corallos would move to another *grangia* that belonged to some of their relatives and was not far away, and from there they would get in touch with the group from Beaulard again. We could do two things: either go on foot as far as Beaulard, skirting the mountain, and ask for hospitality at the hospital for a few days, or even run the risk of taking the train to Oulx and arriving as far as Meana, with the hope that nothing new had happened there in the meantime.

The plans proved to be premature, however, since when Paolo got up he realized that he could not stand: his knees hurt him a little less, but his ankles were still swollen and he absolutely could not tie his shoes. He could not go down in stocking feet without shoes; nor could we carry him in our arms, when the essential thing was not to attract attention in any way.

I had a moment of true despair. Then I decided that the only thing to do was to go as far as the hospital and ask the doctor for advice. I sent the Corallos and Ettore to dig a hole not too far away to bury the weapons and the radio and, with a spirit that was anything but relaxed, I set out toward Beaulard.

Fortunately Bricarello was there and made his diagnosis immediately: an acute attack of rheumatism. He gave me what was necessary to make an enema of salicylate and an injection of I do not know what substance.[44] With this remedy, the swelling in his ankles should go down the next day. We should avail ourselves of it immediately if we wanted to move, because there was no telling if they would swell up again.

I thanked him and started on the road back again. But in the middle of the road I ran into Ernesto, who came up with me. In the meantime we spoke about the local situation, the impossibility of keeping some partisan bands in place in such immediate vicinity of the Germans, at least as long as there was snow, and the opportunity for intensifying exchanges with France and collecting information at the same time. He, for example, worked repairing roads: no one could give us more precise news about the traffic along the road. I told him how he should do it. He was a very capable young man, rich in intuition, and he understood me immediately.

Luckily, nothing had happened up above. The radio and weapons had been buried, and the most damaging articles of clothing carefully hidden. Paolo was swollen like before. Alberto had a terrible cough and was burning with fever. I gave him an aspirin, and wondered who would become sick next. Even the

---

[44] Salicylate is a salt of salicylic acid used to treat rheumatism.

Corallo brothers were coughing and looked pale. The only ones who did not have anything were Ettore and I, the oldest; perhaps it was for this very reason.

It was not easy to give the enema and the injection, without alcohol, with little light, and without any conveniences. While I professed a somewhat deplorable indifference to hygienic scruples, there are limits beneath which I cannot go. Moreover, I believe that Paolo had not had an enema since he was two years old. As for injections, I had no other experience than that very recent one in Grenoble. His profound aversion to any kind of medical care certainly did not facilitate the task, for which we, Ettore and I, prepared ourselves with much good will. We tried to boil the syringe as best we could. When I brandished it to complete the operation, however, Paolo protested for I do not know what reasons. I made a gesture that was a bit brisk, and the needle fell in the middle of the straw. It took us quite a while to find it again with the light of a flashlight, and certainly we should have boiled it again. But I confess that instead I just cleaned it with my handkerchief and used it nonetheless.

Even so, in the end both operations were happily completed. Ettore was sweating as if he had been carrying boulders, and I was literally exhausted.

Our efforts were not in vain, however. The next morning, the swelling in his ankles had gone down, and Paolo could put on his shoes and try to walk. He did it. Alberto still had a cough and a fever but, although he was tottering, he too was on his feet. Therefore we decided to leave immediately, according to the doctor's advice, before any other complication arose. In order to be extra careful, we decided to divide up. Ettore would accompany Alberto to Beaulard and leave him at the hospital (where Bricarello had told me the other day that he could put him up), and Paolo and I would go down to Oulx. From there we would take the train to Meana.

Everything went well. While Eraldo accompanied Ettore and Alberto, Virgilio, by paths known to him alone, conducted Paolo and me speedily until we were above Oulx. Then he turned back, and we went down on the main road at a place and time when no one was there. We went ahead without a problem, arm in arm. We had in our knapsacks, and I had in my bosom, enough stuff to have us shot *sur le champ* (immediately), as the French would say. But I in my threadbare fur coat and Paolo in his very ordinary raincoat could very easily pass for two displaced persons on a trip from one hamlet to the next in search of eggs and butter. We crossed the bridge, watched by four Germans armed to the hilt who did not even deign to glance at us. We passed in front of the Command, where a group of bare-chested German officers were sunning themselves, and in front of the barracks, still chatting animatedly, stopping from time to time to look at something, with the untroubled appearance of lazy people who were not at all in a hurry.

After a stop at Cesare's hospitable home, we took the train, where we found Ettore. It had gone well for them too. Eraldo had accompanied them through the mountains up to Beaulard. Alberto was staggering because of the fever, but he remained standing until the end. Then, having left Eraldo, they went down on the main road and, with the most indifferent air in the world, they crossed the train tracks. The Germans on guard did not say anything, but after they had already passed one called them back, suspicious. "Where are you going?" he asked. "To the hospital," Ettore said, prepared, "where the doctor is waiting for us." The other did not say anything more.

As soon as he arrived at the hospital, Alberto collapsed. Bricarello had him put to bed, took his temperature (it was higher than forty), and diagnosed him with common bronchitis.[45] Ettore, seeing that Alberto was safe, took the train, counting on meeting us again in Oulx, as in fact happened.

Then I had an idea. Why stop in Meana? There was neither a doctor nor a pharmacist in Meana and, if Paolo were sick again it would be a disaster. Not to mention that, after so long an absence, I would have a number of things to do in Turin, and he would remain alone. Why not go directly to Turin, where we would have doctors and medicine and where, if nothing else, we would all be together? The proposal was accepted immediately, and we let the station in Meana pass by without getting off. But at the bottom of my heart, I was anything but relaxed. Provided there is not another disaster and the train does not stop, and everyone is not searched, I said to myself, as had happened at other times. Provided that we arrive before the curfew. Provided that our house has not been "burned," and we have to go look for shelter for the night.

Instead everything went well. The train arrived on schedule. We took the tram, and we went home without incident. Espedita was touched when she saw us again, and told us the latest news. Nothing had happened, and she had not seen anyone suspicious. At times some friends had come over whom she knew well. As far as she knew, there had not been any serious arrests. We could very well go up and stay in the house. And we did, almost incredulous. Then I begged her for a favor. Could she try to fire up the hot water heater? There must still be a little coal and wood. Then we would have hot water. I wanted very badly to take a bath. Espedita did not have to be told twice and, with the aid of her exceptional [husband] Giuseppe, she lit a nice fire right away. But suddenly we saw water spilling onto the floor. The ice had frozen the pipes, which threatened to flood the house.

It was this absurdity that was the straw that broke the camel's back.[46] In a short time I began to cry from exasperation. But I had not accounted for Ettore's infinite resources. While Espedita and Giuseppe hurried to dry and remedy the disaster, with some of his mysterious electrical wires he was able

---

[45] Forty degrees centigrade or 104 degrees Fahrenheit.

[46] While I translated *la goccia che fece traboccare il vaso* as "the straw that broke the camel's back," literally the phrase means "the drop that made the vase overflow."

to heat water in the bathtub for me, where I immersed myself with incredible delight after all.

Paolo was in his bed, calm and satisfied, and said he felt just fine. When Ettore and I entered ours as well, we confessed to each other that we had not thought we would ever return to sleep there again.

The next day, normal life began again. I went out to go shopping, and it seemed strange to see the vegetable stalls and familiar faces at the market on Corso Palestro. I saw children coming out of school, and wondered if and when I would teach again.

I saw Mario Andreis, whom I had notified of our arrival, and I heard the news from him. Parri had been released in Switzerland through an exchange, and this relieved me greatly.[47] Naturally the activity of our partisan bands in the mountains had slowed a bit, for reasons of weather. But in the Cuneese, Livio Bianco—who had duly succeeded Duccio as commander of the Piedmont Giustizia e Libertà formations—had made important agreements with Juvenal, head of the French *maquis* in the area.[48] The Gruppo mobile operativo (Mobile Operations Group or Gmo), which had gone into the Langhe, was prospering and was amazingly active. In the city, everything was going on as usual. The press came out regularly and in abundance. The young people were organizing themselves into the Gioventù d'Azione. The doctors had almost completed preparations in the health arena, and the women's movement was moving forward.

Then, briefly, I told him about our venture and, when he left, I began to jot down the various reports.

The parenthesis was closed. Life took up that rhythm of orderly anxiety to which I was accustomed by now, and in whose absence I had experienced somewhat of a feeling of longing during the days I spent in Grenoble. Intuitively, I felt that the end was near, and that we had to reach it.

---

[47] For more information on Parri's release, see Michael Salter, *Nazi War Crimes, U.S. Intelligence and Selective Prosecution at Nuremburg: Controversies Regarding the Role of the Office of Strategic Services* (New York: Routledge-Cavendish, 2007), 99–103, 142.

[48] Max Juvenal was a lawyer and leader of the 2e Région des Mouvements Unis de Résistance.

27 February–25 April 1945

27 February 1945, Turin. We have taken up life as before, as if the interruption was one of only a few days. I am seeing friends again, one after the other, resuming contacts, and bringing myself up to date regarding the work that has developed in the various sectors.

I have the impression that the orientation has changed, and that now it is no longer so much a question of fighting and harassing the enemy (whose defeat appears certain by now), as one of preparing for the insurrection, which should be imminent, and arranging things in such a way that the victory will not be in vain. In the meantime, the Gap and citizen action squads are being prepared specifically for the first purpose, and Committees of Liberation are springing up everywhere for the second: in the factories, offices, stores, and wards of the city.[1] It will be these Clns—live nuclei of what the democracy of tomorrow, founded on popular initiative and participation, must be—that will prevent the victory from being thwarted, in order to achieve the democratic revolution.

Naturally, a state of mind of panic in the enemy, which manifests itself in frequent acts of terrorism, mass killings, and indiscriminate hangings, coincides with our state of mind of certainty. Maximum caution must be imposed. By now we already have too many martyrs, and we need to conserve our strength to the maximum.

1 March. This morning, a meeting at the Garibaldi Monument of various people responsible for the work in the Susa Valley. There was fog on the river and I could not even see the hillside again, which I had thought about so much while I was staring at the blue waters of the Isère in France.

The situation in the Susa Valley worries everyone a great deal, especially because it appears that, as a result of pressure from the Allies, they are forming a single Command for all of the zones. Who will be the commander of the Susa

[1] The Gruppi di azione patriottica or Gap were responsible for carrying on the partisan battle in the cities.

Valley? Practically speaking, it is divided into three parts: the Lower Valley is Garibaldini, the Middle Valley is Giustizia e Libertà, and the Upper Valley is Autonomi (with the exception of the little group from Beaulard). Between the two clearly opposing factions, the Garibaldini and the Autonomi, the work of balance of power and mediation will be up to Giustizia e Libertà explicitly. How can they place Laghi, with his anti-communism, his militaristic-bureaucratic crazes, and his lack of a political sense, in command of the entire valley, right now when, with the possible arrival of the Allies, the political component will become more and more important? The Garibaldini will not accept him, and neither will the Autonomi, who oppose him with the good Ferrua as a candidate for commander. It will be necessary to replace him with another capable member of GL who is sensible and whom everyone accepts. But apart from the fact that we would not know where to find this other person—who on the other hand would have the disadvantage of not knowing the men or the area—it does not seem to me that Laghi has any intention of letting himself be replaced. The situation is therefore quite complex, and there does not seem to be a way out.

How much better, clearer, and more comforting it was in the autumn of 1943, when we fought with spontaneous enthusiasm, and truly had the feeling of carrying out a revolution with every action, albeit modestly, instead of arguing over matters of prestige, balance, and parity (not to mention the back-biting) as they do today, with a spirit that I thought had been buried forever! Perhaps even this is a crisis of growth, a necessary passage, but I still feel a sense of depression and anguish.

In the afternoon, I went to the Concerio Fiorio (Fiorio Tannery), where the general headquarters of the Committee of National Liberation was located. There I found Giorgio, Greco, and Antonicelli, whom I had not seen in years.[2] I was very pleased to see him again. In my opinion it was as if his keen intellectual capacity had grown stronger when faced with the reality of these past few months, and given him a considerable new lease on life.

Then I went to find a health inspector willing to work with us. For all intents and purposes, I think it will be useful to get people who are technically trained.

At home, I found Paolo in very bad shape. The extremely high doses of the salicylate treatment—prescribed for him by the doctors for the pain that had come back so violently—had debilitated him to such an extent that he could not even sit up in bed. I stayed near him for a long time, and we talked about a great many things, nearby and far away, about people, books, and music. Eventually he felt a little better, and I too was able to regain my serenity.

---

[2] Franco Antonicelli was a writer and president of the Piedmontese Regional Cln. He spent time in prison, in particular the Regina Coeli prison in Rome, for his antifascist activities.

3 March. Following a morning phone call, I ran to Livio Bianco's house, where I found a kind of war council assembled: Giorgio, Nada, Penati, and Jacopo.[3] We spoke about the general situation and about that of the Susa Valley in particular. In his capacity as commander, Livio—whom I did not know well up to now—made an excellent impression on me, I felt that he was not only sure of himself regarding the general questions, but also perfectly well informed about the various local circumstances, and without that high-minded contempt for particular small events that recurs so frequently among our friends and is so uncomfortable for the people who must base their work on these very particular events.

In the afternoon I went to Sylvia's house and we planned the second issue of *La Nuova Realtà*, which would be printed in Milan. One of these days I will bring the manuscript and will make arrangements with our male and female friends there.

4 March. Today Ettore and I went to the Lingotto, where we were supposed to meet with Mino and help him transport some suitcases filled with newspapers into the center of town.[4] But the typographer—set up in a strange semi-ruined house on the banks of the Po—was late and, in order to wait for him without attracting attention, we went to sit down for a while in a thicket that forms a kind of islet in the middle of the river. Instinctively, I sat down looking at the hillside and turning my shoulders to the mountains. It is a truly strange phenomenon. Just looking at the mountains covered with snow made me physically nauseous, perhaps because I had eaten too much. The other evening, at Natalia's house, I had to move so as not to see a photograph of glaciers that was hung on the wall. To think that once just looking at the figure of a mountain comforted my heart. Now when I do, a feeling of anguish weighs heavily on me.

It was already evening when, having collected the newspapers, we went to take them to safety at the Borello, at the other end of the city. This "Borello"— which I had heard so much about but had never seen before today—is a lovely old house with a vast garden that, with remarkable generosity and courage, Maria Daviso had placed at the disposal of the Action Party as a meeting place and depository for newspapers, while in the meantime she was reduced to living with her mother in small lodgings nearby.

When we arrived, Lisa Ricci, who was rearranging the newspapers into two big armoires, was also there. What a lot of material had been printed in a little

---

[3] Giorgio Agosti, Franco Venturi (Nada), Fausto Penati, and Cesare Moscone (Jacopo). Moscone was the chief of general staff of the Piedmontese Regional Military GL Command.

[4] The Lingotto was a Fiat automobile factory that was completed in 1923 and that was closed in 1982. It featured a spiral assembly line and was the second largest automobile factory in the world. The Lingotto was transformed into a massive public space that includes a convention center. Emilio Castellani (Mino) was a publicist and inspector of the Piedmontese Regional GL Command.

more than a year! How interesting it would be to keep it in a well-organized archive! I have tried to do it several times, but always, at the unforeseen appearance of some alarm, I had to send everything away, and many things ended up being lost. I hope that what I have not been able to do, someone else will do.

5 March. Sylvia introduced me to a new friend, Giulia Lucca (who called herself Valeria), who has agreed to work to organize the housewives.[5] The problem of the housewives—the most stubborn, I believe, in their opposition to any political training, and the most difficult to reach—will be one of the most difficult to solve if we want to create a new society. I confess that I do not have many ideas about it, but Silvia seems to have some, and even seems to feel them with some passion. Let's hope that, with the help of Valeria, something concrete can be achieved.

6 March. I went down with Ettore to inspect the materials that we had in the cellar. We had hidden a very small amount of newspapers—ones we just could not do without—under the floor of the underground passage, where, by removing a board and some bricks, Ettore had constructed a spacious hiding place. But a policeman who was on the ball, and who really wanted to, would find it immediately. Therefore it did not seem to me to be advisable to put the machinery for making false papers there as well, since it is after all the riskiest thing because it reveals the existence of an organization. After much thinking and investigation, we found what seemed to me an almost perfect solution. In the communal hallway of the cellar there is a small niche. In this niche there is a nook in the wall. By digging into this wall, we made a hole wide enough to hold ration cards and stamps that we could easily enclose with two bricks and a little gravel. Beyond the fact that it is very difficult to find, there is the advantage that it is not in our personal cellar but in the hallway, where anyone can enter during air raids, which makes it possible for us to deny without putting anyone at risk.

7 March. I went to look for Alberto, who was at Bianca's house, sick. The bronchitis, which he caught during the crossing and from which he thought he was cured after a few days, came back instead. Now he has a fever again and an ugly, worrisome cough. What is more, he is depressed and worried because, on the one hand, he understands the danger that his presence represents for Bianca, and on the other hand, he is annoyed because he cannot return to the mountains. On this point I tried to console him. For now, it is useless for him to return to the Susa Valley. Our partisans from Beaulard are practically all in France. The Command, anything but formal, can be entrusted to some officer

---

[5] Giulia Lucca (Valeria) was an organizer of the Mfgl.

who is already a resident of the valley, who makes a stop at Beaulard from time to time to order the movements of the groups and to take care of the weapons and materiel brought there, without dwelling there permanently, which would be useless and dangerous.

When I returned home, I received the news that this morning they had searched the Canelli Hotel, headquarters for the Socialists, where several people who were being hunted resided, and where they regularly have the riskiest meetings. But the owners, who were warned in time, had gotten everyone to escape, and the police did not find anything or anyone.

In the afternoon, there was a special meeting of the Gruppi di difesa. Tomorrow is 8 March, which, beginning in 1910, a group of women pioneers had chosen as "international women's day," and which must be equivalent to the workers' holiday of the first of May.[6] I confess that I had never heard of it, but the idea of affirming women's wish for peace with a date seemed like an excellent idea. They prepared little leaflets that we will have circulated in the factories and delivered in mailboxes, and that we will try to pass out in the markets tomorrow. We will see if we can have little meetings here and there as well. It is dangerous, but undoubtedly useful at this time, to give our women the feeling that they are not isolated, but ideologically linked to women of all of the other countries in the world, who are fighting with the same spirit and for the same goals.

10 March. I still tremble at the fear I felt following a stupid alarm. Tonight—it was around 3:00 a.m.—I woke up after hearing a car pass by. Today there are not many cars that travel at night on our street, and every time one passes by, I wake up and remain in suspense until I hear that it has gone away. This time, hearing that it was stopping instead, I jumped up from the bed and ran to the little window that overlooks the stairway. I heard knocking at the front gate. "This time we are done," I thought. Even Ettore had gotten up and come near me. "We must wake up Paolo," he said. While Ettore tried to wake him up so he could get dressed as best he could, and escape through the balcony into the flat next door, I heard the concierge ask, "Who is it?" and someone with an unmistakable accent respond sharply, "Police!"

Paolo had sat up on the bed, but he was not yet completely awake, and did not understand what had happened. I thought I should hurry up, move, but I remained near the little window as if I were nailed down. Suddenly, right while two strangers were getting ready to climb the stairs, I heard the voice of Doctor Banaudi, who lived two floors above us. "I am coming!" said the voice. "Wait for me, I am coming right away." Then I understood. Doctor Banaudi is

---

[6] International Women's Day was proposed in 1910 by the German socialist leader and women's rights activist Clara Zetkin (1857–1933) and is celebrated on 8 March.

the doctor for the police and some chief who felt sick had sent for him. (He told me this himself later.) Then I collapsed into a chair, without any more strength. "It is nothing," I said to Ettore. "Tell Paolo not to worry either." But Paolo was not at all worried. On the contrary, he had lain back down and was sleeping again like an angel. I remained near the window until I saw the doctor go down, heard the front gate close, and saw the car drive away. Then I went back to bed, feeling my legs go weak, as if I were convalescing after a serious illness.

11 March. During these two days, nothing of much importance. Adriana brought me another health inspector. On the occasion of the 8th of March, I spoke with and spread propaganda to the owners of my bakery and my poultry shop, who seemed trustworthy but with whom I had never spoken openly. I gave them newspapers and leaflets. The storeowners were among the women who were the most difficult to convince. Today it is possible, and we must take advantage of it.

Bianca gave me a book on the vote for women that told the entire story of the suffragist movement. It is an old book, and does not discuss present day arguments. At times I am embarrassed, given that, willingly or unwillingly, I am working on women's problems and know so little about the whole movement. I feel the need to bridge the gap in my ignorance, even if only partially.

12 March. A long wait with Vera in various parts of the city to move several suitcases of newspapers to the hillside, at one of her friend's who is boarding with the nuns. (Should we find a safer place?) Vera is very serious and lively. To think that, one year ago, she was a child without many ideas and with little initiative. Today she travels back and forth with dangerous responsibilities, makes contacts, and spreads propaganda intelligently.[7] It is extraordinary how today's atmosphere matures minds. From one day to the next, we see young boys and girls transformed overnight into men and women.

Following a mysterious telephone appointment, I went to the hillside, where at some point I saw jump out Franco *il Dinamitardo*, whom I had not heard anything about for a long time. He was still lame because of a wound he received to his leg while he was fleeing from the barracks of the Cuneo *militia*, which had arrested him on his return from France. He told me about his far-from-pleasant adventures, but from which he was able to escape, without leaving important documents he was carrying in the hands of the enemy. Now he has been released from his team, and he would like to work with us. I will speak with Livio, and I will put him in touch with someone.

---

[7] Vera Marchesini was Ettore's niece, the daughter of his brother Mario. She was a student and a *staffetta* in the city squads.

13 March. A diabolical day. No electricity. No gas. Paolo had a high fever again and was terribly depressed, and I could not stay with him for one minute during the entire day. I made a bunch of useless, futile trips. I went to look for Tonino (who was not there), Mario Andreis (who was not there either), and Vittorio (and I did not find him). At Natalia's house, our women were restless and unhappy, and we were not able to get them to agree. To complete the day, there was the news that Cesare was arrested and was at the Sitea [hotel], the headquarters of the SS. I am tired and mad at everyone. I want to go to sleep and not wake up again.

15 March. Two days that were much calmer and more decisive followed the exasperating day before yesterday. Paola Levi reappeared on the horizon— with the name of Ortensia—and, along with Alma, agreed to take the reins of our Assistance Committee. She is an active and intelligent woman with some experience in accounting, and will be a great help.

I was at the interparty committee for help for political prisoners, which meets in the house of the Montalenti sisters on the other side of the Po.[8] The blond Albertino, who had been working on the matter for a while, came with me. He is a boy full of initiative and with extraordinary gusto, and is enthusiastic to the point of becoming emotional about everything he is doing. The sending of packages to prisoners—initiated about a year ago on a quite modest scale—has now assumed considerable proportions. The matter has been simplified by the fact that, with the number of political prisoners increasing, an organization was formed among them (tolerated by the jailers, who by now sense that the end is near, and want to take advantage of it). They have their Cln, corresponding to those on the outside, and they attend to the distribution of foodstuffs according to need. To such an internal organization should correspond an external organization that does not divide into groups and factions but provides for everyone in a unified manner. It seems to me that they are on the right path. They have pooled their funds. Every party assumes a task for which it has the greatest chance for success. One procures provisions, another makes the packages, and another takes care of delivering them. Various connections and terms have been worked out so that they ensure that the goods arrive quickly and well. A large number of capable girls (among whom, for us, are Paola Jarre and Nicoletta Neri) are getting down to it and obtaining notable results.[9] If we continue in this direction, this will be one of the most

---

[8] Bianca Montalenti was a professor and collaborator of the Assistance Committee of the Cln of Turin and an organizer of the Gruppi di difesa. Mila Montalenti was an accountant and organizer of the Gruppi di difesa.

[9] Nicoletta Neri was a professor and collaborator of the Assistance Committee of the Cln of Turin.

complete and efficient services. I found Nino Malvezzi among the members of the committee.[10]

The news arrived that Cesare has been released and has left immediately for the mountains. It appears that Sibille, who was arrested with him, is conducting himself very well and shouldering all the responsibilities himself, so Cesare, about whom nothing has been found, was able to get off easily. They are now talking about an exchange for Sibille.[11]

17 March. The other night a terrible thing happened.

Pretending to be partisans, with false papers, two Fascists had themselves put up for the night by a family of workers, the Arduino family. Then at some point they made them come out of the house and they killed them all: the father, the son, and the two sisters, Vera and Libera, active organizers of the Gruppi di difesa. The son's wife, who was pregnant, threw herself into the Dora river and was able to save herself while they continued to fire at her. Miraculously, she reached the house of a friend, where she took shelter and was taken care of. It appears that she is quite well, and that even the baby is safe.

The ferocious crime has excited a wave of indignation throughout the city. It is these very monstrosities, together with the conversion of broader and broader layers of the population, that make me feel the end is imminent.

This morning was to be the funeral of the two sisters. The Gruppi di difesa wanted to be present, in a manner that would give the ceremony the tone of a demonstration, albeit a clandestine one. I wanted to go, but they forbade me. Many other friends went instead, some of whom were arrested by the police who—something unheard of!—were present at the entrance to the cemetery and filled several trucks with girls who had taken part in the funeral procession. Miraculously, Frida—who, if she were captured again, could find herself in a dangerous position—was able to avoid being caught by attaching herself to the arm of a widow who was following the coffin of her husband, and hiding her showy blond hair with a handkerchief that she borrowed from a willing stranger. Nevertheless, various bunches of flowers with tricolor ribbons and the initials G.D.D. have been placed on the tombs. Almost all of the girls who were stopped were released after several hours and a summary interrogation. One has the impression that the enemy is displaying its fury in isolated acts, with almost individual initiatives, which therefore are all the more heinous, but that the organization necessary to implement repression systematically at this level of ferociousness is intimately and profoundly disintegrating. In the

---

[10] Nino Malvezzi (Andrea) was a member of the Assistance Committee of the Cln of Turin.

[11] Luciano Sibille was a student and vice commander of the Monte Assietta Brigade in the Chisone Valley.

meantime, our organization is becoming more solid, more extensive, and more secure, encouraged and thrust ahead by a breath of hope.

Tomorrow I will go to Meana, and then continue on to Beaulard in search of the Corallo brothers in order to send them to France with the latest news.

19 March. Having awakened yesterday morning at 4:00 a.m., after an almost sleepless night, peopled with nightmares and anxieties, I left on the first train, crossing the city still immersed in the curfew, silent, empty, and dark, like a dead city.

At 7:30 a.m., we were already in Meana. I found Esterina sick with pleurisy and Guido, Aunt Lina's son, settled down in the house while waiting for Moretti, with whom he had to put together a dispatch of news and information for the Allies.

Then I went down to Susa, among the first flowering shrubs, while I thought about the March of the year before, about the Germanasca Valley, and about so many things that had followed, wondering in the meantime if this spring that was coming would truly be the last of war, and what the future would hold for us.

At Susa I found a group of women willing to work with the Gruppi di difesa. They are all bourgeoises, observant Catholics, and Dames of St. Vincent. They exchanged many formalities, and they are really afraid of the Communists and have a particular aversion to them, even if they do not say so. The important thing, however, is that they have agreed to work together. We hope that, from practical collaboration, later even understanding might emerge.

I saw several other people and then I returned to Meana, where in the meantime Aunt Lina had arrived to bring her son a package of documents to pass on. I confess that the thought of putting her up for the night made me somewhat embarrassed. She is always so neat, so well groomed, and so elegant! My house in Meana, notwithstanding my periodical radical cleanings, is so poorly kept up, so ruined, and the household utensils so insufficient! There is cooked rice for the morning that is reheated for the evening. "You will see," I said to Ettore, "that she will not eat this reheated rice. And I have nothing better to give her." Instead I was mistaken. Despite her refined appearance, Aunt Lina in fact did not turn up her nose in contempt at my table without a tablecloth and my messy plates. She ate the reheated rice with an excellent appetite, and she adapted with the greatest ease to sleeping between sheets where at least a dozen people had already slept. Like the pea of the famous princess, this proved to me that she has the stuff of an authentic partisan.[12]

---

[12] Here Ada is referring to the story of the Princess and the Pea, which tells the tale of a true princess who could feel a pea under a layer of mattresses.

Then, when I had sent everyone to bed, I worked almost until morning writing a long letter to Palisse, explaining the situation to him, and describing the documents that I was sending him.

This morning, having arrived in Oulx around 9:30 a.m. as expected, I set out on foot toward Signol, hoping in some way to track down the two Corallos. But I did not need to go as far as the village because at some point I ran into Ernesto [Pont] in his dual function as road worker and informer. He gave me the latest news, and told me that the Corallos were waiting for me in the vicinity of the usual *grangia*, where they had returned a few days ago, thinking that I would go to look for them.

I left, but the *grangia* was locked and no one was there. I sat in the sun, near the fountain, waiting. In the meantime I looked at the mountains that were nearby and far away, the Alps of Savoy, blue in the distance, and the Colle dell'Orso, still white with snow and harsh and inhospitable. I thought about the morning of anguish spent in that very place around a month ago, when Paolo could not walk and Alberto had a fever and the Germans could have arrived at any moment. Then everything had gone well. But will it go well up until the end?

A rustling of branches nearby shook me from these thoughts, and there peeped out Virgilio, next to me, with his green jacket of the French *maquis* and his Alpine hat decorated with the crest of Grenoble. We were very happy to see each other; quite soon Eraldo, who had seen me from a distance, joined us too. After a brief sojourn with their relatives, they had returned to their *grangia*, convinced that I would need them. ("I felt it, I really felt it," said Eraldo.) They accepted enthusiastically my proposal that they go to France and bring the sealed envelope containing important documents to Palisse. "When do you think you will leave?" I asked. "Right away," responded Virgilio. In spirit, the two were already on the move. "We will leave this evening and, if everything goes well, we will be in France the day after tomorrow," added Eraldo. I gave them the packet, with the usual recommendations, entrusted them with our greetings to Pillo, Bruno, and Palisse, and then left them, wishing them *in bocca al lupo*.[13]

When I went back down on the main road it was almost one o'clock. Instead of returning to Oulx, I decided to go as far as Beaulard to collect some letters and stamps that we had left at the hospital.

Bricarello informed me about the local situation, gave me the things that I was looking for and, since there were still two hours before the train's departure, offered me his room to rest. I accepted with gratitude, but although I was very tired, I was not able to sleep. While I was walking, I had begun to think about an article for the new issue of *La Nuova Realtà*: a call to all women to

---

[13] *In bocca al lupo*, literally "into the mouth of the wolf," means "good luck."

devote themselves completely to the battle, reminding them that at times like these nothing is more ineffective than egotistical prudence, since we were living during times when what usually happened to *others* could happen to *us*. I had thought about it with some fervor, and I felt it inside. Such moments of inspiration are so rare in me that it seemed a shame not to take advantage of them. Therefore I put the result of my musings on a piece of paper. By the time I finished, it was time to leave.

The trip was very, very uneventful. I did not find anything new in Turin. I thought about the Corallos, who perhaps at that moment were crossing the Sommeiller glacier.

21 March. I had not seen Monti for so long![14] What joy I felt in finding him still alive, still keen, with his witty manner of speaking, and with his tone that was didactic, but absolutely devoid of pedantry. The Committee of National Liberation had appointed him regional superintendent for instruction. Sometimes he came down from Chieri's house, where he was staying hidden as an evacuee, to make agreements with future colleagues. I would like very much to work with him in the school sector, instead of facing that terrible responsibility of vice mayor, to which I believed I was surely condemned.

Then I went to Valeria's house, where I found Francesca, the health inspector, and I met Odette, the sister of a partisan leader from the Biellese, who is taking responsibility for working with the women.[15] She made an excellent impression on me. She has a decisive and energetic manner, and the light of intelligent devotion in her eyes. If we had enough women like this one, intimately "dedicated" to the cause, I think that our work would have undreamed-of possibilities.

In the evening, Lamberti arrived. He is tired and not very well. The work that he is doing at Fiat, even if not burdensome, evidently is too much for him. Besides, he would like to write that economic program for the Action Party that he began and was not able to finish. We had fun creating a nice plan. It seems that, not too far from Turin, there is a house with a garden, belonging to a friend of Natalia's, which they will hand over to her willingly. Lamberti could go there for around a month, and finish his work in this peaceful place. Paolo could go with him. It would be better and safer than here at home. They could keep each other company, talk, and read good books. The custodian of the villa would provide meals. And I could go to see them often.

24 March. A meeting of the Provincial Committee of the Gruppi di difesa. Representatives from the Susa Valley, from the Pinerolo, from the Canavese,

---

[14] Augusto Monti was a professor who had been convicted by the Special Tribunal for belonging to the GL movement and who was a member of the Cln for the schools in Piedmont.

[15] Susanna Piazzo (Odette) was a partisan *staffetta* and an organizer of the Mfgl.

and from the hillside were there. They reported on their work, often still uncertain, but beginning to bear fruit. There must be a single center, however small, where there is a nucleus of active women. If the women can work on doing this, soon they will multiply, and the initiatives will multiply as well.

Then a meeting of the Action Party group for the schools. Monti, Gliozzi, and Widmar were there.[16] Again I was sorry that I was not chosen to work on the schools. It is the only field where I have ideas and plans, however vague they still are. It seems to me that it is absolutely not enough to—on the contrary, that we must not—return to the schools before fascism, not even to the humanistic *ginnasio* that I had loved so much, and whose ruination I had disfavored so strongly.[17] If, as I hope, a new society will be born out of our agony, we must also have new schools. From now on we must think about creating these new schools—which will be both a reflection of and a creative component of our democratic revolution. But not one of the friends whom I saw today seemed to be on this course. Monti upholds that, in a regime of liberty, the schools must not pretend to be "character-building." It is enough that they teach reading and writing and arithmetic, namely, that they be only "technical." The family, clubs, newspapers, and cinema will provide the real education. But this presupposes a society already perfectly liberated and democratized, which I did not delude myself into thinking that tomorrow's society would be immediately. It will fall to the schools to create this society, but how can the schools create it if they are simply designed according to the requirements of the labor market, and not to build the character and the integrity of the students?[18] For me, the professors and teachers are the main problem. In any kind of school or school system, a man like Monti, for example, will carry out the work of education. (He even did it in the fascist schools.) But how many men like Monti are there in the Italian schools? It is a question of training them, of creating colleges and seminars for this purpose. We must do away with the old universities completely, since they no longer meet the needs of the present even minimally. In my opinion—after the opportunistic and lackluster performance of the majority of university professors and students during the *Resistenza*—I would close the universities for twenty years. (Perhaps I am exaggerating; ten might be enough.) In this way we will have time to prepare better institutions, and we will avoid throwing on the market thousands of ignorant and presumptuous degreed individuals, condemned to misery and

[16] Bruno Widmar was a member of the Cln for the schools.

[17] *Ginnasio* refers to the first two years of the *liceo classico*, or senior high school specializing in classical studies. Ada attended such a school, the Ginnasio Cavour. Fascist reforms attempted to limit enrollments in the *ginnasio*, the only path to a university education, thus thwarting upward mobility of the population.

[18] *Diario partigiano* (1972), 334 n. 3.

because of this very misery, paradoxically, to a violent hatred for the working classes.[19]

28 March. Great commotion. At various times they came to tell me that none other than the undersecretary of occupied territories (if I understood well) had arrived in Turin, probably by air, namely a certain Medici, a member of the Italian government of Rome.[20] He met with members of the Committee of National Liberation and I do not think—at least from the comments that reached me—that the meeting was entirely peaceful. Some lack of understanding is natural between the representatives of a legal government and the representatives of an underground and revolutionary movement. I do not think this initial contact with "the other Italy" drew much enthusiasm.

In the afternoon the undersecretary was to receive the representatives of the various organizations, among them the Gruppi di difesa. Therefore I was invited to attend along with Franca, the Communist.[21] My friends implored me to say this, address that, during the meeting. . . .

At the appointed time, I found Franca near Via Cibrario, and we walked together back and forth until, at an agreed signal, we entered a front gate and went up to an apartment where there were several people already, almost all well known. The undersecretary made us wait a good while, and then arrived all out of breath to say that the Germans had been informed of his presence, and that therefore he had to leave immediately. He was sorry that he was not able to stay and speak with us for very long. But, after this preamble, he began a long speech in which he told us none other than the story of our *Resistenza*. When he was finished, one of the attendees followed suit, in the name of the Camera del Lavoro, and he too recounted the whole story, going back to the beginning of fascism. Then a third spoke and said the same thing. I listened, a bit discouraged. It seemed to me that I had returned to that meeting in my house in Meana, in November of '43, when that man with the tumor on his eye began to speak of the "tombstone of fascism." But those were down-to-earth, candid people, old antifascists without training or experience. Today instead it is a question of an important meeting, with a quasi minister and representatives of the best among us, and all these empty, useless speeches upset me. I vowed to myself that, when it was my turn, at the cost of passing for stupid, I would say only "goodbye and thank you." But I was even spared this trouble because, while the third person was still speaking, someone arrived to say that the

---

[19] Ada's dreams for the universities were not realized. See her article on the student protests of the 1960s, Ada Marchesini Gobetti, "Gli studenti hanno ragione," *Il Giornale dei Genitori*, Year X, n. 1, (January 1968): 12–14.

[20] Aldobrando Medici-Tornaquinci, undersecretary of state in the Ministry of Occupied Italy.

[21] Franca was Maria Negarville.

airplane was about to leave early, and the undersecretary had to leave quickly. So the meeting concluded sooner than I had expected. Medici shook everyone's hand. When it was my turn and Franca's, he said what he had already said to our friends from the Cln, namely that he had brought a flag embroidered by the women from Rome, which restricted us to responding "thank you" and leaving the "arrivederci" for the next time.

1 April. Today is Sunday. The sun is bright, and it is beginning to feel like spring. These past few days have been terribly full and frenzied, but today instead it seems like I am on vacation. I was even on the balcony for a while, in the sun, watching people who, undaunted, were playing *bocce* or watching. (They never stopped, not even during the worst period of the bombardments.)

Lamberti came over, whom I convinced to move into the hospital at Beaulard for about a month, given that the plan for the house in the country had failed for many reasons, among which was that the house was full of bedbugs. He will be cared for there, and he will find in Bricarello a congenial companion. In the meantime, he will be able to work on the formation of Clns in the Upper Valley, which I find to be rather behind, and yet will have a particular significance, especially if there is a French occupation.[22]

Then we chatted for a long time, easily, about a number of things: the economy, politics, and morale. A problem today, which is more acute than ever and which is absolutely not resolved for me, is that of justice. Is it just, for example, to bring the traitors to trial and condemn them to death? Lamberti says no, and Paolo agrees with him. So do I, theoretically, because I think that no man has the right to kill another man, for any reason. In practice the matter is a bit different. In practice it can be necessary to kill, if only for legitimate defense, and legitimate defense can be not only defense against someone who makes an attempt on a person's life, but against someone who threatens and puts in danger an idea that a person believes to be right. In such cases, however, it seems to me to be extremely dangerous to talk about justice in the usual sense, and to give it the blessing of legality, however vague. Killing must never be legal, but always an appalling emergency measure.

3 April. I met Gina, the concierge from Via Cibrario, a woman who is extraordinarily vibrant and intelligent. We understood each other right away. The work that concierges can do today, and even more what they can do tomorrow, is immeasurable. When I think that there are women like Gina and Espedita among them, it seems that it is really worthwhile to cultivate them.[23]

---

[22] Here Ada is referring to De Gaulle's program of annexation of the Alpine valleys, which the Gaullist troops tried to carry out in May 1945.

[23] The widowed Maria Giaccone Tommasini (Gina) was the concierge for the building on Via Cibrario.

Then, for the entire morning, I worked with Momi to write the statute of the Movimento femminile Giustizia e Libertà. I confess that I absolutely do not see its usefulness, but this is based on my genuine incapacity to take formal rules seriously. I think that what counts in an association is an agreement and a willingness to cooperate among its members. Otherwise, no matter how perfect the statutes and regulations are, they will not be able to decide anything successfully. I think that things will go really well when there is no longer a need for statutes (have we not done without them, at least during this period?), and when what Elena Croce calls my "foolish trust in human nature" finally will seem justified.

8 April. A day filled with encounters, meetings, and "committees." Today is Sunday, and again it has been a bit calmer than usual.

This morning Manfredini brought me several texts on administrative law. If I really do become vice mayor, I should at least have an idea, however rudimentary, of what are the tasks and functions of the *Comune* (town council). I have already studied the structure of the various "departments," and I feel lost up against problems and services that are so diverse and complex. I hope that there will be a distribution of tasks, and that I will have to work only on things (such as assistance and education) where, even without having specific competence, I feel that I can more easily find my bearings. What will I do if I have to be responsible for markets or fire brigades or city cleaning?

10 April. I was awakened by Tonino and Patria, who wanted to come to an agreement with us about the complicated Single Command of the Susa Valley that had been discussed. Then a disagreement between Momi and Silvia about a controversial point of the statute for the Movimento femminile 'Giustizia e Libertà'. Then a girl from the Pellice Valley, then another from the hillside, then Vera and Laura for the female Gioventù d'Azione.[24] Then Pinella, who had an urgent need for a *staffetta* in the Langhe. I tracked down Franca Formica who, although she was not feeling very well, left immediately on her bicycle with true self-sacrifice.[25] Then I ran to look for Livio to inform him about Tonino's proposals, and to know how to respond. Then a meeting with two new girls, Rosy and Liliana, whom I brought into the circuit of assistance. Then after a very short break between 1:00 p.m. and 2:00 p.m., the music began again: Sylvia and Valeria for the organization of housewives, then Paola Bologna for the women in the Canavese, then Adriana, and then Alma. To conclude, a meeting in Angelini's house with Tonino and Giorgio about the Command of the Susa Valley. Then Giorgio accompanied me back to my house. I am in a good

---

[24] Laura Sisto was a student and organizer of the Gioventù d'Azione.
[25] Franca Formica was a partisan *staffetta*.

mood because it appears that the Allies have resumed their offensive toward the north, and that the end should be imminent. But this evening I am so tired that I really cannot believe it after all. Sometimes I think that this frenzied life is destined to be prolonged indefinitely, for eternity.

13 April. I was in Milan for two days, and the trip was quite busy from beginning to end. The meeting place was yesterday morning at 5:30 a.m., in front of the Rivoli Station. Therefore I left the house when it was still curfew, and took advantage of it to write various kinds of notices on walls of the porticos of the Piazza Statuto with a small piece of chalk that I always carry in my pocket in case I need it. At Rivoli Station I found Nada, who was very punctual, but instead the car made us wait for quite a while. It was almost 7:00 a.m. when it arrived. What is more, we had hardly reached the highway when, because of I do not know what mysterious mechanical failure, we had to turn back to the garage, which was in the vicinity of Corso Cirié. Fortunately the malfunction was remedied quickly (it was a matter of changing I do not know what part), and we could leave again. But by now it was late, broad daylight, and the danger of machine gun fire along the road persistent.

In fact, near Magenta, airplanes began to fly above the highway. The driver turned to us: "Should we stop? "No, no," Nada and I answered simultaneously, "If you are not afraid, let's continue somehow." "Then let's go," the driver said simply. We continued to travel at the highest speed possible, notwithstanding the more or less distant din produced from time to time by the bombs that were falling. Near the end of the highway we saw a big black cloud darken the sky. A bomb had fallen on a fuel warehouse; the fire brigades acted quickly.

But by now we had arrived. We left the car with the driver, congratulating each other, and we took the tram to get to the center. I found Lucia Corti in the vicinity of Piazza Cavour where, without excessive prudence, we exchanged yellow envelopes containing bulletins and news. On the other hand, what place was safer than the vicinity around *Il Popolo d'Italia*?[26] It seems that the other day one of our friends, passing by those parts with a big purse full of documents coming from Switzerland, had been stopped by an agent who asked him what the purse contained. "Information bulletins," the friend answered coolly, opening the purse voluntarily, and making a gesture of taking out the sheets of paper. "I am an employee of the Information Service." "Very well," responded the agent without insisting. The friend went away without a problem. The strange thing is that he had told the truth.

Elena Dreher, Nanni Vasari, and I reviewed the new issue of *La Nuova Realtà* that we had put together with Silvia in Turin and delivered into the hands of

---

[26] Mussolini founded the right-wing newspaper *Il Popolo d'Italia* in 1914.

young Procopio, who had organized the copy perfectly.[27] Then we discussed the statute of the movement with other GL women. Finally, I went to the meeting of the Gruppi di difesa with Elena.

At 5:00 p.m. I was at Porta Sempione, where I was supposed to find Nada and the car to return to Turin. The car was there. Nada arrived shortly with Leo.[28] She would not be leaving with me, since she had to stay for a meeting she had that evening. In her place, two friends she introduced me to would come to Turin with me. At the last minute Leo hurriedly gave me a big yellow envelope to give to Livio, entrusting it to me privately.

We left immediately. The big envelope worried me. Usually, when I had to transport important documents, I hid them in various parts of my body. Up until now, I had never been searched, and this gave me somewhat of a sense of immunity. I would have done the same today, had I been alone in the car, but there were three of us, shoulder to shoulder. I could not open the envelope without the others seeing what it contained. Even though they were friends, I did not know to what extent they had been informed about matters. Therefore I decided not to open the package. I simply hid it at the bottom of my briefcase, putting a sweater over it. "After all," I thought, "they had never searched the car before."

But when, having just left the highway, we arrived at the checkpoint at the entrance to Turin, the driver began to curse. "Damn it!" He pointed to a German officer who was approaching, accompanied by two Fascists. "The other evening they even made us empty the sack of coal!" (The car ran on gazogene.) The officer approached and made us get out, and then began to search the car in detail. Luckily it had not occurred to me to hide the famous envelope. I held it like a precious object in the briefcase under my arm. In the meantime, I thought desperately of what to do. I did not care at all what happened to me, but the envelope contained important documents, perhaps orders, and plans for the imminent insurrection. I thought with anguish of the consequences there would be if they fell into the hands of the Germans. For a moment, I thought of escaping by hurling myself down on the escarpment and throwing the envelope away in the meantime. But they would have caught me immediately (they had cars, motorcycles, and machine guns), and they certainly would have found the envelope. Therefore I remained motionless and very composed, in that kind of oblivious stupidity in which I often took refuge during the most difficult moments.

"Your papers," demanded the officer. We handed over our papers, which he returned to us after having examined them thoroughly. They were all in order. Then

---

[27] Mario Dal Pra (Procopio) was a *libero docente* (university teacher not on the regular staff), editor of *L'Italia Libera*, and a representative of the Action Party.

[28] Leo Valiani.

he went on to examine the purses and briefcases of the others, until he was in front of me, who had remained at the end of the line. "What do you have in that brief-case?" he asked. "A sweater," I answered with a voice that did not seem to be mine. The officer stretched out his hand and took the briefcase. He opened it, took out the sweater, and then the famous envelope. "What is in here?" "Letters," I answered indifferently. "Ah!" the German said, and he replaced the envelope and the sweater in the briefcase, closed it again, and handed it to me. "Thank you," I said.

We got back into the car. When it left again I dropped backwards for a moment. I felt like I no longer had a drop of blood in my veins. The others were not aware of anything. I thought that a second of hesitation would have been enough, and I blessed my providential foolishness.

The car brought us back to the garage. While I was waiting for the tram to return home, I noticed a group of excited people nearby who were handing each other leaflets and commenting with vivacious enthusiasm. A car had gone by a few minutes before, throwing them out abundantly. "What courage!" everyone commented; in the meantime they read avidly. They were Gap leaflets. I deemed it better that I distance myself without taking the tram. I could not have any peace until l had brought the famous envelope to its destination, and only when I had delivered it into Livio's hands did I breathe a long sigh of relief.

14 April. Today several members of the future administration of the *Comune* were supposed to be at the Canelli Hotel for an initial meeting: the mayor, Roveda, a Communist, and the three vice mayors, one a Socialist (the good Chiaramello), one a Christian Democrat (Quarello), and the third from the Action Party (me).[29]

But Roveda was not there today. After his adventurous flight from Verona, they are keeping him carefully hidden, and they are acting very appropriately, since it is really not worth the trouble making him run the risk of being recog-nized by someone for the pleasure of having him participate in meetings of a purely formal nature. Therefore the get-together was reduced to a conversation among Chiaramello, Quarello, and me. I cannot say that I was enthusiastic about it. When I think about the responsibilities that I am about to assume before a population that is disoriented and in need of everything, materially and morally, and about the difficulties of every kind that will arise over the resolution of even the smallest of problems in order to bring people to an even modestly civil level, who by now had been used to living under the laws of the jungle for years—I

---

[29] Giovanni Roveda was a union organizer convicted by the Special Tribunal for belonging to the Communist Party. He was the political representative for all of the Garibaldini forces in Piedmont. Domenico Chiaramello was a businessman and representative of the Socialist Party in the municipal Cln. Gioacchino Quarello was an industrialist and representative of the Christian Democratic Party.

confess that it makes me breathless. I thought that my future colleagues—even if they are older and more experienced than I am—must have also been feeling the same concern. Instead the two that I saw today were composed and satisfied like heirs who were finally coming into possession of an inheritance to which they were entitled, and regarding whose ownership there was no longer any doubt. In vain did I try to speak with them about concrete problems: the internees, the ex-prisoners who were returning, the houses without roofs, the schools, and the families of the political victims. I quickly understood that my problems did not interest them very much. Quarello says it will be necessary to put benches back on the avenues immediately. (Yes, of course, but it does not seem to me that this is the most urgent thing.) Chiaramello is thinking of a delightful season of lyric opera. (This is also good, but my God!) Since I insisted, perhaps a bit too much, on the greater urgency of the other problems, Quarello suddenly said to me with the air of a "weasel": "Pay attention to me, Signora, do not get flustered; remember that we are in this position today not for what we will do, but for what we have not done," alluding to our twenty years of self-restraint and to our lack of devotion to fascism. I was seething; antifascism was certainly a sacrosanct thing, but only if the passive resistance of yesterday, transformed, at least for us, into active resistance during these last twenty months, will continue to be a wish for renewal, revolutionary activity, and reconstruction. It does not seem to me that this is the right time to retire into the dignity of our past, and boast that we deserve and claim offices and honors as a reward. Today we must work more than ever. For me an office means only a duty to serve the country. I told the two men these things, perhaps with too much candid fervor. Quarello shook his head with an air of indulgent superiority. Chiaramello, confident of our old friendship, took the liberty to give me amiable pats on the head, saying, "But look now at what revolutionary ideas our Ada has put in her head! Ah, ah, pretty, bizarre, little head! I did not think you so peculiar!"

On this tone of Sunday-like oratory, where, curious thing, the reverend was a Socialist, the meeting ended.

I left the Canelli, discouraged and humiliated. When I ran into Vittorio later and told him about my anxiety, he consoled me by reassuring me that Roveda was a completely different sort, and that I could work with and get on well with him. Let's hope so!

But the disappointments were not over yet. At the Office of the Superintendent of Fine Arts, where Aldo Bertini and Signora Brizio are creating a splendid and very safe meeting place, there was a meeting of the committee for the purge of the schools, where they wanted me to participate also, I do not know why.[30] It is

[30] Aldo Bertini was a teacher and collaborator of the Action Party involved the printing and falsification of documents. Anna Maria Brizio was a university professor. I believe the committe was meeting to discuss how to reduce or eliminate the fascist influence on the schools.

true that I had voiced my desire to work with the schools more than once, but of all the activities that concern them, the purge, however necessary, seems to me to be the least constructive. Nevertheless, I went. Solari should have presided over the commission, but given his deafness, which would have forced the others to scream names and things—violating all conspiratorial rules—he decided to postpone his participation until times that were less dangerous. Therefore the commission comprised Bertini, Signora Pajetta, a young Socialist, Lemmi, and me. Lemmi had been my teacher at the *liceo*.[31] I even remember the demonstration of affection that we students showed him when, during the other war, in order to respond to the challenge from Cian, that wicked erudite, he enlisted voluntarily.[32] He is an honest man, and I have the greatest esteem and even affection for him. But today was a disaster. Recently he has evidently remained isolated (something very justified, given his age and the condition of his health), and our conversation, all in acronyms (Cln, FdG, PdA), sounded incomprehensible to him. It took us another half an hour to explain to him the composition of the Cln and its relationship to the schools. He gave a summary, diligently, but he did not seem convinced to me. Again I felt a sense of dismay. Are these the men with whom we will have to work tomorrow? Good, honest, dear, but "of yesterday," embalmed in a correct and noble, but by now sterile, dignity. Certainly it is not their fault if during the past twenty years they had to remain outside of active life, but it is as if they were dried up. Today we need new people, or people who are old but still approach new problems, not with a didactic tone but with candid humility.

I took a little comfort in the meeting about assistance. Here, if nothing else, they are talking about real things, however modest.

Toward evening, in Piazza Sabotino, I met a certain Nuccia, a worker from the Mirafiori plant who is working with the Gruppi di difesa in the Susa Valley, and with whom I arranged a meeting in Susa for tomorrow.[33] She is a down-to-earth and courageous woman, and today we speak the same language. When I left her I felt more serene. The Lemmis, the Chiaramellos, and the Querellos do not matter. It is with these "new" women that tomorrow will be built. I began to hope again.

16 April. Yesterday morning we went to Meana, where the Germans had requisitioned our house. Fortunately Mario Cordola had thought to carry away the damaging things in time.

---

[31] Francesco Lemmi was a teacher.

[32] Vittorio Cian, a renowned professor at the University of Turin, was a founder of the Nationalist Party in 1910 and later a supporter of fascism.

[33] Annetta Donini (Nuccia) was a worker at the Mirafiori plant, a partisan *staffetta*, and an organizer of the Gruppi di difesa in the Susa Valley.

We found Moretti intent on sketching designs of fortifications to send to France. I gave him the envelope of information I had brought from Milan. Tomorrow a squad will leave with the Corallos, who will bring everything to Palisse. This way, only one trip will be made.

Then we went down to Susa, where, for the entire morning, in Teta's back shop, I continued to see people of every sort, a little like at home—men and women, old and young, military and civilian. In the afternoon, I went to Silvia Mazzola's house, where, after much waiting, inquiries, arguments, and post-ponements, we were able to arrange a meeting of the Gruppi di difesa.[34]

When the meeting was over, Ettore and I went back up to Meana. It was a sweet evening with a last ray of sun at the summit of the Rocciamelone. The flowers of the bushes, which had blossomed two weeks before, had already changed into leaves. We climbed slowly, in silence. I had talked all day long. I was tired, and I thought about how it would have been nice to go away and sleep peacefully in our house.

Instead we went to sleep at the Jarres' flat which, having been occupied by the Germans this autumn, now instead was free. This morning, when we left to go down to the station, it was pitch dark. Evidently there was still a curfew because at various places in the road *chevaux-de-frise* had been dragged, which we surmounted by moving them slightly.[35]

But at the station an unexpected complication awaited us. In order to leave, a person needed special permission from the German Command, which a non-commissioned officer was requesting and controlling. Ettore's travel document satisfied them, but my railroad pass did not. In vain did I declare that I was an employee of the state, who taught school in Turin, etc., etc. "*Nicht* (no)," the German continued to repeat, "*nicht, Signora.* Come to Susa with me." Wisely, Ettore did not intervene, as if he did not know me. It was useless for both of us to get into a fix. But I was furious. It was not that there was the least danger, since it was a question of a purely bureaucratic arrest. Strangely enough, hav-ing unloaded all the damaging materials into Moretti's hands, for once I did not have even one dangerous document on me. At Susa they would certainly have let me go. But I would have lost the entire morning, missing a number of appointments.

At some point, having been called by a colleague, the German moved a few steps away. Taking advantage of the semi-darkness of the dawn, I left rapidly and slipped into the "men's" lavatory, where I hid behind the door, which I left open. After a few minutes, I heard the German yell: "*Signora, Signora,* do not leave, *Signora!*" I heard him run up and down. He also came in front of the bath-room and looked inside. It appeared empty to him, and he left. In the meantime

[34] Silvia Mazzola was a professor and collaborator of the Gruppi di difesa.

[35] A *cheval-de-frise* (plural *chevaux-de-frise*) was a portable frame covered with barbed wire.

the train arrived. I ran outside like a thunderbolt, got on, and found Ettore, who had set out ahead silently. We still heard him yell one or two times: "*Signora*, where are you, do not leave!" Then, after a moment that seemed like an eternity to me, the train moved. Ettore and I looked each other in the face and burst out laughing.

The trick I had played on the *cruco* filled me with cheerfulness, but when I arrived in Turin, I did not have time to think about it any longer, since there began the usual jumble of people, from which I have now just emerged, absolutely exhausted.

18 April. Today, dress rehearsal. For several days, they have been talking about this strike, which was supposed to be both a demonstration and a census of our forces. Some saw the need for it, while others hesitated dubiously, fearing serious reprisals as a consequence. Instead it all went very well, much better than we had hoped, and on a larger scale than we had imagined.

We were all perfectly confident regarding the strike in the factories. Had the workers not had strikes several times in 1944, and previously in 1943? But I thought that the strike would stop there, like all the other times, with only a timid demonstration of sympathy in other areas. Instead it was complete and total, even on the part of those classes and categories traditionally devoid of any courage, such as employees and storeowners. I can see that the fruit is truly ripe.

After I went to Bianco's house, I went down to Via Po, where I had made an appointment with Paola Jarre and the blond-haired Caterina, the Liberal who was working on assistance to those who were in jail.[36] I was marveling that I did not see either one arrive (in those days everyone was extraordinarily punctual) when I realized that something exceptional had happened. In the meantime, the trams had stopped running, which explained the missed appointment. People popped out from everywhere, lively and happy, as if they were on an impromptu vacation: young schoolchildren and students with books under their arms, employees with the classic briefcase. At a certain point, with somewhat of a clamor, the rolling shop shutters of the stores were lowered.

Then I understood. This strike had not only been successful in the factories. It was the whole population that was saying "Enough!" and was saying it without truculence or ostentation, with the placid Turinese grace that does not get upset, or even look menacingly at anyone when it knows that it has victory within its grasp. The very extent of the strike had averted the danger of reprisals. The Germans certainly cannot arrest half a million people. In reality, the few that we see about have the appearance of beaten dogs.

[36] Kitty Bruno (Caterina) was a representative of the Liberal Party in the Assistance Committee of the Cln of Turin.

I ran home, comforted again and exultant. "We made it," I thought in my heart. The fact that even the unperturbed *bocce* players had abandoned the garden confirmed for me that the matter was serious. Paolo, still nearly immobilized by a recurrence of his aches and pains, was also satisfied. "When I saw that the cafe on the corner (visible from his window) had removed the little tables and lowered the shop shutters, I understood that it had gone well," he told me. After a while Ettore arrived, also happy about how things had gone at E.I.A.R. The Fascists did not even dare to be seen. Evidently they feel the end is near. Everyone I saw during the day brought the same comforting news from the most diverse parts.

This evening, while I was coming home from the Red Cross, where I had gone to speak with Signora De la Forêt, I saw a German, laden with weapons, knapsack, and suitcase, accompanied by a woman who looked like a prostitute who did not cost very much. The terrified glances that the highly armed soldier threw around him, and his attachment to the woman as a defense, made me realize, more than any other thing perhaps, that they felt truly finished. Despite my inveterate sympathy for the conquered, I could not feel sorry for them. I remembered only too well their arrogance and their cold, inhuman impassibility from the time when they felt like they were masters. Today they are conquered, and they are afraid. I would not act cruelly toward them, but I feel that the condemnation is just. Everyone feels like I do: the hostility, the silent persecution that accompanied the passage of the German—almost a symbol—was so common that it could be almost physically felt, even if no one said or did anything. Today all of our people are united, not only in purpose but also in sentiment.

21 April. After the other day's rehearsal for the insurrection, it is as if there is a sense of certain promise in the air. Nature itself seems to want to encourage us, smiling in its immutable rhythm. For several days the trees of the valleys have been covered with tender green, the sun is warm and pleasant, and the distant mountains, no longer white with snow, are silhouetted against the blue.

The change in temperature has been good for Paolo, who no longer has a fever and is in less pain. After long discussions with his friends, he has ended up by agreeing to represent the Gioventù d'Azione in the Fronte della Gioventù. He too runs to committees and meetings, sometimes returning irritated, often dubious, and rarely satisfied.

The rhythm of preparations—appointments, meetings, printed material— is still rapid. But even in the feverish rhythm, it is as though there is a feeling of relaxation, like someone who, after a long tiring race, sees the finish line near, and, holding out with all of his strength, lets out his breath, deeply relieved.

Today I went to the Canelli Hotel again, with Chiaramello and Querello. Pier Luigi Passoni, chosen by the Cln as prefect of Turin, was also there.[37] Things, although not very exciting, went a little better than the other time. We are, roughly speaking, distributing the tasks. Chiaramello would like to work on markets, real estate, and taxes, things for which he has practical experience, thanks to his profession as a businessman. Querello is interested in public utilities (the tram, the electric company). I have been assigned assistance, education, and fine arts, all areas that, to tell the truth, are new to me, but where I will try to do my best, taking advantage of everyone's counsel and help. I asked if it would be possible from now on to have some contact with the local authorities—on whose antifascism we can rely—not only for insurrectional and purging purposes (there have already been such contacts for some time) but also to become informed about the functioning of the various services, and know where and whom to call for the carrying out of the most urgent measures so that they can be set up immediately.

This evening the news circulated that Bologna is insurgent and is, for all practical purposes, free. Is it true that things are coming to a head? That we are truly at the end?

22 April. To shake me from the excessive optimism of the last few days, this morning Sandro Galante came with the news that Aldo Guerraz had been seriously wounded in the leg while he tried to flee the Fascists who had gone to arrest him.[38] It seems they have to amputate it. The matter is all the more cruel because, up until now, despite his incessant, very dangerous activities, he has always managed to escape. The fact reminded me that our anxieties and struggles are not over yet. However depressed, however certain of defeat by now, the Nazi-Fascists will not give up without a fight. Perhaps the most terrible things are yet to come.

24 April. Around six this evening, after a day filled to excess with the usual matters, I was at the home of De Angeli the surveyor, who, in a flat on Corso Vinzaglio that I do not know how he found, has established a splendid office—underground, naturally—for the creation of false papers with stamps and signatures, everything that is necessary.[39] How different from the plain identification cards Ettore manufactured (which were still a godsend for so many

---

[37] Passoni represented the Socialist Party in the Piedmontese Regional Cln.

[38] Aldo Guerraz was a judicial officer and inspector of the Piedmontese Regional GL Command.

[39] Giuseppe De Angeli, a surveyor, was head of the U.F.O. (Ufficio falsi e organizzazione or Office of False Papers and Organization) of the Action Party, and was an inspector of the Piedmontese Regional GL Command.

people), and my signatures imitating that of the engineer Giuglini! The surveyor put things on a downright scientific plane right away, and his documents
are absolutely perfect. Moreover, he is responsible for a number of other things
necessary for the insurrection: badges, ration cards, and templates for flags.
I made him give me one. I did not want to wait even a minute to have my red
flag with GL's flaming sword.

After leaving the surveyor's place, I thought about stopping at Bianco's
house for a moment to get the latest news, since it was not far. My instincts
were correct because I turned up just in time, in the middle of a war council.

Everyone was there: Mario Andreis, Nada, Penati, and those in charge of
various city services. An order arrived (Aldo says 26 + I), by which it appears
that the insurrection must begin the day after tomorrow. The workers will
occupy the factories, and the action squads will drive out the Germans and the
Fascists with the help of partisan formations, who will descend on the city at
the same time from all directions. We must act quickly so that the liberation
will happen before the arrival of the Allies, who are approaching, so that they
will find everything in order, and the new government firmly in place.

It was decided that from the day after tomorrow onward I must stay at the
Borello, headquarters for Pinella's *staffette*, who will see to it to that liaisons
among the various commands are maintained. The work of the *staffette* will be
essential because, during an insurrectional period, women can go about much
more easily than men.

When I arrived home, I gave the news to Ettore and Paolo, and also to the
faithful Espedita, who immediately began to dye clothes and curtains red in
order to make flags out of them. When I saw the red GL flag, just out of Ettore's
hands and hung to dry in the kitchen, I cried with emotion.

25 April. I ran all day like someone possessed, but I have the feeling—or the
illusion—of having done everything I had to do.

Every one of my women know where they must go, whom to contact, and
what to do. In turn, today those who have organizational or group responsibilities have gathered together their followers. During the final meeting, held
this evening in Natalia's house, they reported the results to me. It seems like
everything is going well. There is not a neighborhood or organization where we
do not have a representative. A swarm of girls supplied with bicycles will act as
liaisons. In the dreadful event that the enemies blow up the bridges on the Po,
Mila Montalenti will provide a boat for crossing the river. So not even the other
side of the Po will remain isolated.

In the meantime, with Espedita's considerable help with the dyeing,
Ettore has prepared a number of GL flags of all sizes. Moreover, a sales
clerk from the Bianchi warehouses, one of our supporters, has delivered to
me in care of Maria Daviso an enormous package with French, English, and

American flags and pennants. Naturally the Russian ones are missing, but by this time does the red flag not have a universal meaning?

Tomorrow morning, Ettore will go to the Cln of E.I.A.R. and will see what there is to do there. Paolo has been designated—given that he has difficulty moving—to remain at the headquarters of the Gioventù d'Azione, in the home of Federico Dumontel.[40] I will go to the Borello. So, at the decisive moment, we will be divided.

It is strange, but I do not feel excited in the least: neither anxiety nor worry nor exaltation. I am extraordinarily lucid and serene. But it is this very serenity, which is almost reckless, that is the symptom that signals for me the advent of the gravest of times.

---

[40] Federico Dumontel was a student and an organizer of the Gioventù d'Azione.

26–28 April 1945

Today, as I reread and rearrange my diary from the days preceding the insurrection at a distance of several years, I realize that, despite my unassuming attitude of serenity and almost of indifference, I had the expectation of something big, heroic, and final. Incorrigibly imbued with the patriotism of 1848, on which my exultant adolescence thrived, I was dreaming, perhaps without admitting it to myself, of fiery, glorious feats where I would have been able to worthily conclude the heroic aspirations, always vivid and always thwarted, of my entire life.[1] But, even while recognizing the limits and flaws of its origin, I can say in good conscience that this longing of mine was not superficial rhetoric; it was an honest desire for sacrifice.

Evidently, however, I was not worthy of martyrdom. Fate—which had for accomplices and instruments my friends who relegated me to the Borello—perhaps intended me for the more bitter and melancholy experience of monotonous work on tasks that were apparently without consequence, rather than for immediate and total sacrifice. It is a fact that those days—which my fantasy had imagined to be so warlike and glorious—unfolded almost with an ordinary administrative rhythm. If there were also brief moments that were touching or exciting, on the whole they lacked any risk or heroism for me.

The morning of 26 April dawned gray and cloudy. When I left the house a little after 6:00 a.m. on my very old bicycle, the city was almost deserted, and the absence of trams revealed the unusual situation. I found the Riccis at the Borello, and a little later all the others arrived, but there were no orders, and we did not know what to do. We sat in the empty house, waiting. In the meantime, it had begun to rain, and a sense of cold and uselessness began to overcome us.

Mario arrived around 9:00 a.m., irritated and in a bad mood. He unleashed the youngest girls on the various Commands, and he wanted the older women with a respectable appearance, who had convened thinking that they would

---

[1] The revolutions of 1848, beginning on 8 January in Palermo, resulted in constitutions in all of the Italian states except for Lombardy-Venetia, including the famous *Statuto* of Piedmont.

be useful precisely because they did not attract any suspicion, to stay home. "If we need you, we will call you," he said. "There is nothing to do here now." Then, with childish impatience, I begged him to send me to some other place to do something, seeing that there was nothing to do there. "You stay here," he responded briskly, and he left without further explanation.

Meanwhile, however, people began to arrive from various parts with the most disparate news: they had occupied the factories and the partisans were approaching. The blond Carmelina, the first partisan *staffetta* who entered the city, arrived by bicycle, with the tricolor ribbon on her chest.[2] Then someone else arrived to say that there had been a counterorder, and that for that day the partisans would not enter. Then they came to contradict the news. The insurrectional movement was slowly going forward. They knew that the regional Cln, the city Cln, the Cmrp, and the Piazza Command were sitting in permanent session, and from time to time news and messages arrived from one or the other.[3] With bureaucratic pedantry, intended to placate the nervous tension that I was feeling, I began to organize the papers that were arriving into various folders. At a certain point Nada arrived, who told me he had seen Paolo, who was suffering but in good spirits, at the headquarters for the Gioventù d'Azione. Toward noon we began to hear some shots being fired. Mino arrived with some bread and a piece of cheese, and we began to eat.

In the meantime several messages had arrived. The trade unionists were asking for women to act as liaisons. Having sent my "madame" (older women) home (who, to tell the truth, really had not done anything up until that time), there was no one to send out. I tried to telephone, but as was expected the telephone did not work. Then, taking advantage of Mino's presence, I decided to make a quick trip home, stopping to notify the women who were in my part of town in the meantime.

At home, I found neither Paolo nor Ettore. Anna, imperturbable as always, was tranquilly working in the kitchen and had not seen either one of them. Espedita did not know anything either. She went to call one of her nieces, who took charge of carrying the various messages. While I was writing some brief notes, I begged Espedita to sew a GL badge inside my jacket (the one Duccio had given me so many months before, with joking words of homage). I might run into road blocks or partisan squads, and a sign of recognition would be useful.

I left again for the Borello right away. I was almost at the end of Via Cibrario when I heard an agitated sound of footsteps on the semideserted street. Then several shots of Tommy gun fire sounded, dense and furious, while the characteristic odor of gunpowder spread. At the height of the Maria Vittoria hospital,

[2] Carmelina Piccolis was a painter and a partisan *staffetta*.

[3] The Cmrp was the Commando militare regionale piemontese or Piedmontese Regional Military Command.

I saw that they were transporting the wounded. Fascists? Partisans? I just kept pedaling faster. I did not want to be stopped.

Nothing had happened at the Borello during my brief absence, but there was no longer the sleepy and disorderly atmosphere of the morning. *Staffette*, orders, and news came and went with a rhythm that was progressively more rapid.

When it was evening, the men left, and about a dozen women remained: there were the Riccis, Carmelina, Pinella, Alda, and Ester. It was unthinkable that all of them would leave. Crossing the city was extremely dangerous, and it would be even more dangerous to cross it again the next morning. It was pointless to do so unnecessarily. Therefore we decided to remain together. Naturally I gave up making the dash home that I had hoped to make. At a certain point, Jacopo arrived and said that he would spend the night with us. I was happy to share with him—a member of the Cmrp—the responsibility that I felt was weighing on me.

Pinella prepared a little dinner and lit the fire in the fireplace. A great peace reigned around us, broken only from time to time by some distant shot. The warmth of the fire, the security that being together gave us, the feeling of caring for each other, of being all for one another, and the feeling that we were not alone, gave us a sense of relaxation, almost of joy, to which, more or less unconsciously, we abandoned ourselves, and the same feeling that united us was that which was enlivening, in our city, in our country, and even beyond the borders, all men and women of good will. We began to sing: mountain songs of Italy and France, partisan songs, those I already knew and—from the formations of the Cuneese—those that I had never heard.

Suddenly I noticed that in a corner, in the shadows, Ester was crying. For her the imminent liberation could not be joyous, because Sandro would not return. Even Carmelina's eyes were full of tears. The wait was hopeless for her as well. Alive in Nenne's good, melancholy eyes, was the memory of another young fellow who had vanished forever. Who could say if each one of us, before the end, would not still have to surrender to a new tragedy, a new struggle? We were quiet for a long time, each to her own anxiety and her own pain, which was not closed and selfish but united and communal. When we looked into each other's eyes again, we all felt that we could smile. Without useless words, we had understood each other profoundly. Our dead, those of today, those of tomorrow, those of yesterday, were with us. They would be with us forever, for us and *for everyone*.

Finally we roused ourselves, and I insisted that we go to bed. The next day would certainly be very tiring, and it would be better to confront it rested and strong. Pinella and the girls went to sleep on the floor above where, in case of an alarm, they could pass through the attic into the barn of the neighboring farmhouse, and from there escape into the fields, if ever the Borello were surrounded. Jacopo and I would remain below. At the first sign of danger, we would give them a signal.

Pinella wanted at any cost to prepare a rollaway bed for me near the fire, which was going out. But I did not sleep much. Now and again Pluto, the Borello dog, began to bark. Then Jacopo and I went out prudently, with weapons in our hands. But there was no attack. It had begun to rain and at times the moon made a fleeting appearance between the clouds. The good dog, faithful to his ancestral instincts and unaware of the anxiety that he was causing us, greeted it every time by barking.

As soon as it was light and I thought the danger of a nighttime attack was over, I decided, leaving Jacopo still on guard, to make a rapid jaunt home, before the day's work began again.

I found Ettore and Paolo still in bed. Paolo was very excited because he had heard the Clns of Genoa and Milan speak on the radio. Lucia Corti had spoken in Milan in the name of the women. So Milan and Genoa were free. Now it was Turin's turn.

I returned immediately to the Borello, cheered up by the good news. A timid, pale sun ripped open the gray mantle of the sky, and the saplings and little leaves of the garden seemed to smile at me with a sense of unfailing promise.

The girls left quite early for their various tasks. Then began an unremitting coming and going of people, a succession of orders, messages, and news, and a whirlwind of needs, all urgent and all different, in comparison to which the rhythm that I was used to at home during the last few months became a downright *adagio*.[4] Naturally I do not recall everything that was done and everything that was said; nor would I know how to distinguish precisely the various phases of the day. But I recall that the most worrisome and insistent theme was the request for aid on the part of the factories. As soon as the order was received, the workers had occupied them, relying on the arrival of the partisans. Instead, the partisans had not yet arrived. (There had been a counterorder, a disagreement with the Allies who wanted to arrive first themselves.) The workers had resisted, and were continuing to resist, but now the Germans had surrounded the factories with tanks. We had to help them.

At a certain point I saw good, serene Alma arrive; I would have never imagined she would be so dismissive of the danger. She came from the Lancia factory; our men were asking for a GL flag. I told her to go and get one at my house. A little while later I learned from someone else that the red flag with the flaming sword was waving at the top of the factory, defying the enemy's tanks.

Then Giosuè, a partisan from the Chisone Valley, the one who played the organ with the tricolor ribbon in his long hair, arrived. Now he no longer had

---

[4] *Adagio* is a tempo marking for music that is to be played slowly.

either the little ribbon or the long hair, but instead he brought me a Tommy gun that he immediately began to lubricate and assemble.

Then Ettore came too, bringing a radio that he thought could be useful to us. In fact we were longing for news, but how to find the time to stay and listen to it? The radio put in place, he left in search of a truck with which to go and recover the parts of a transmitter—which were hidden in various places—to make the radio function immediately in case the Germans had destroyed the equipment as they were leaving. (In fact they did destroy it, but thanks to the foresight of the engineers from E.I.A.R., the very evening of the liberation we could begin to broadcast again.)

Around 11:00 a.m., a rumor circulated that the Germans had left. A festive cry arose in the village. Flags appeared on the balconies and at the windows. Sergio Pettinati arrived, commander of a squad of the Gruppo mobile operativo, gallant and happy in his big camouflage jacket, his eyes sparkling in his handsome face, tanned by the sun.[5] Then the partisans arrived, and someone came saying that the city squads had occupied the *Municipio*.

But quite quickly an ebb tide followed this flood of good news and consequent euphoria. No, the Germans had not left. On the contrary, they were stopping, arresting, and shooting. The *Municipio* had been recaptured by the Fascists. The entrance of the partisans into the city had suffered a setback. The flags disappeared from the windows, one after the other. A silence made of apprehension dominated the roads that had been jubilant before.

And there came Mino, defeated, with the news that Albertino, stopped at the checkpoint of Reaglie while he was carrying the order to descend to the formations in the hillside, had been shot immediately: Albertino, Giorgio Latis, who had escaped unharmed from the most dangerous and audacious undertakings, who repeatedly ridiculed the police, going about with his bleach blond hair and that violently blue jacket which, in my opinion, should have attracted the notice of even the most half-witted policeman. Albertino, so generous, so ready to do and to give. Albertino, who the last time I had been with him, returning from a meeting by tram, had spoken to me, telling me everything about his passion for painting and especially for Botticelli. . . .

But there was no time to stir up memories and cry. We had to continue *his* battle. There was one more to make come to life again with our passion, one more who was forcing us to keep our promises, *all* our promises.

Maria Daviso returned from a factory, which she had been able to penetrate notwithstanding the encirclement of the enemy. She was exultant and moved by the spirit of solidarity and confidence that she had felt among the workers. Carmelina, who had crossed the city a good three times to carry orders and

---

[5] Sergio Pettinati was a doctor and a partisan in the V Alpine GL Division. The Gruppo Mobile Operativo was a GL formation.

news to the formations that were stopped at Moncalieri, announced that the disagreement had been resolved, and the partisan formations were arriving regularly by now, with an orderly and repetitive rhythm.

In the early afternoon, Vera arrived, elated and exhausted. She let go of her bicycle on the lawn and came in shouting: "Auntie, the war is over! Hitler has fallen!" I understood immediately that it had to be one of those rumors that spread at peak times from who knows where. (Didn't they spread roughly the same rumor on 26 July 1943? And then even I had believed them.) Mario, who was writing, raised his head, irritated. "Who is this crazy girl? Send her away!" "She is my niece, and she is not crazy," I answered, and I led the girl into the next room. "But it's true, Auntie," Vera continued to insist. "Everyone is saying it.... "Where did you hear it?" I asked. "I heard it everywhere. I heard it from...." She interrupted herself. Suddenly, she realized the falsity and absurdity of the unfounded news. With a moan, she collapsed into a chair, disheartened. "Oh, Auntie!" The chair where she was seated broke, perhaps because it was old and worm-eaten. The banal accident should have made her laugh; instead, it made her cry. She threw her arms around my neck, sobbing loudly. I gauged from this outpouring of feelings how very tired and stressed she was. I let her cry a little, content to close the door so that they could not hear her in the next room. Then, thinking that the best way to calm her down was to have her do something practical, I sent her to bring the printed materials to various places.

People continued to arrive, and the most absurd, strange, and terrible pieces of news continued to follow one another.

Someone said that they had seen a wagon loaded with lifeless bodies pass by in the vicinity of Porta Nuova: dead or wounded? A woman with a big white flag on which a cross was outlined in blood was walking in front. The news, linked with other rumors according to which the Germans, before leaving, had massacred all the *politici* (political prisoners) locked up in jail, filled us with indescribable anguish. We thought about all our men who were still inside and, given some terrible precedents, the cruel barbarity of such a gesture was totally likely. Luckily a little while later one of the Ricci sisters arrived, accompanying two partisans who had just gotten out of prison, who did not know where to go, and whom she had run into seated on the steps of a house not too far away. (Her brother-in-law, Massimo Visalberghi, was at that very moment at the Carceri Nuove.)[6] Then the news of the massacre was not true, even if the two men, who still appeared bewildered and disoriented, could not tell us anything important. They had let them go, and they were out. We gave them something to eat, and we made them comfortable, feeling ourselves comforted in turn.

---

[6] Aldo Visalberghi (Massimo) was a professor and chief of staff of the Regional Piedmontese Command.

Around evening Silvia arrived, with the armband of the Red Cross and the news that they were fighting in the vicinity of the Cittadella garden. It was the last zone of defense of the Fascists and the Germans who had their Commands there, the *Guardia Nera* (Black guard) in the Caserma della Cernaia (Cernaia barracks) and the *Questura* (Police headquarters). Similar news, the thought of the danger that Paolo and Ettore were in, and the impossibility of running to learn what happened would have filled me with unbearable anxiety at another time. But I was truly on that plane of acceptance where *our* affairs were not worth more than *other people's* affairs. I understood that we did not have to think about what was happening at the Cittadella. There were too many things to prepare for the next day. If truly the next day we would be free, we needed to print a new issue of *La Nuova Realtà* immediately, we needed to prepare a flyer, a proclamation to women, for the Gruppi di difesa and for the women of GL, and we needed to think about a brief speech to deliver on the radio. Luckily Silvia, who was much more clever than I, was there.

Again, Pinella lit the fire around which we gathered. Everyone from the night before was there, plus some others. But no one wanted to go to sleep, and it did not occur to anyone to sing. For a long time we could hear insistent shooting, from various parts, far away. Then everything was silent. A good sign? A bad sign?

Carmelina and the Ricci girls, who had traveled kilometers and kilometers by bicycle, fell asleep with their heads on the back of their chairs. Pinella, small, attentive vestal that she was, kept the fire lit, and kept her ears on the alert, full of anxiety. Sometimes she smiled with hope, and sometimes she shook her head. Silvia began to write; in a few hours she had dashed off four pages of the newspaper. I was not so inspired. I drew up a leaflet as best I could, and then I attacked what might be a speech or manifesto. "Piedmontese women," I began, and then I was not able to continue. I managed not to think about the present, but the past, invincible, pressed on my memory and on my heart. All the past, our entire battle, from 10 September, with those first Germans, impassive, at the corners of our streets, and then the first weapons, and the sabotage of the bridges, and the first fallen soldiers. Then the Germanasca with the roundup, and the tragic light in the sky at Massello. Then the Chisone Valley, and the narrow mountain pass of the Colle delle Finestre, all in bloom with rhododendrons. The fire in Meana, and the poor boy who was hanged. Then Beaulard and the cabin, and France, and the return trip, and the endless night on the glacier. "Piedmontese women," I began, and again my mind went astray. I was counting the dead, and I was remembering their faces and their voices: Braccini, Sandro Delmastro, Paolo Diena, Franco Dusi, Duccio, Albertino. . . . The crackle of wood on the fire roused me, and the incessant grating of Silvia's indefatigable pen. "Piedmontese women. . . ." Only toward morning did I make up my mind to conclude. "Today, all women who have grief in their hearts," I said. "May this grief not have been in vain." Something like that. At the moment I was not able to say anything else. I was as tired as if I had written an entire volume.

The dawn arose gray, dominated by a silence that could have been as much a breath of relief as a threatening and deadly lull.

As soon as it was light, I felt like I could make a trip to the house, in search of news. I did not meet a living soul until Corso Tassoni where, at the corner with Via Amedeo Peyron, two or three men who looked like workers had stopped. "Well?" I shouted to them, slowing down my bicycle. Such was the nature of sentiments and thoughts in those days that they understood the meaning of my question quite well, and although they did not know me and I did not know them, they answered with a cheerful gesture of their hands: "They went away!"

I began pedaling again at a good pace. Again I did not run into anyone until Piazza San Martino, where, almost unconsciously, by my old habit of always avoiding Via Cernaia with its military barracks whenever possible, I slipped into Via Juvara directly. As I was nearing the house, signs of the recent battle became evident: broken mirrors, scraped walls. With my heart in my throat, more from anxiety than from the ride, I finally flew onto Via Fabro. There was Ettore with his tricolor armband of the Cln. I threw my arms around his neck. "Paolo?" "Here he is," he responded with a gesture. Indeed I saw him arrive, at the steering wheel of a *topolino*. There was Espedita, who embraced me, tearful and moved. There were our fellow lodgers, who came out on the street and shook my hand, rejoicing and congratulating each other. There was a sense of festive relief in everyone, even in those who were the least politically conscious, as after the disappearance of a long nightmare.

I went into the house with Ettore and Paolo, where I found an indescribable disorder. They had just returned home the day before—Paolo from the Gioventù d'Azione and Ettore from collecting parts for the transmitter—when, around 2:00 p.m., a company of partisans arrived, the 49th Garibaldi Brigade, who occupied our house and the neighboring houses, preparing to launch the attack against the Cernaia Barracks from there. Paolo joined them immediately, going to take the old Model '91 gun we found on 10 September out of the cellar. In the meantime, expecting that it would "get hot," Ettore had advised the neighbors to go down into the cellar, into the shelter, where no one had gone down for some time, and where he replaced the light. The afternoon was spent in preparations and anticipation. The Garibaldini were well armed, with rifles, machine guns, *panzerfaust*, and even a bazooka, and they settled down in the house, taking steps to assemble and prepare the weapons, waiting for night to descend in order to attack.[7] Ettore devoted himself to helping them, from fixing or finding a missing screw to bandaging the feet of a boy who was

---

[7] The *panzerfaust* was a handheld, single-shot German antitank weapon. The *bazooka* was an American antitank weapon, which the Germans had copied.

wounded there. Espedita and the other tenants of the house (naturally the most unpretentious) brought food and relief.

As soon as night fell, they heard the sound of motor vehicles and saw an armed column wind onto the main street, beyond the garden: the Germans were trying to go to the High Command on Corso Oporto.[8] Immediately our men began to fire from the windows overlooking the garden, and hit several motor vehicles. The others responded. A violent exchange of shots followed, the traces of which could be seen on the façade of the house and on the pedestal of the monument to Ettore De Sonnaz, which had resisted nonetheless, undaunted, like during the bombardments.[9] The battle dragged on, at intervals, for the entire night. At a certain point, hearing the shooting from Corso Palestra (it probably had to do with Fascists from the Cernaia Barracks), they thought that the enemy was about to surround the block, but luckily the alarm was unfounded.

Continuing to shoot, they struck a truck with a trailer full of munitions that caught fire, continuing to explode for a long time. At the first light of dawn, Paolo and another individual crossed the garden to learn of the losses inflicted on the enemy. They set an armored vehicle and the truck with the trailer on fire, immobilized another four trucks and four or five cars, and hit a *topolino*, which certainly, judging from what it contained, belonged to the Feld-Gendarmerie, and was still serviceable, despite a flat tire.[10] Paolo changed the tire and, having loaded into the little car as many Garibaldini as were there, they went to the Cernaia barracks, which appeared empty and abandoned. Having left the group of partisans on guard, he returned to load up some others to take them to the Stipel.[11]

While Ettore and Paolo were telling the story, I felt a burning regret, almost of rancor: they were fighting, but I had remained immobilized and nearly inactive for the entire night at the Borello. Even so, looking at Paolo and Ettore safe and sound, I immediately reproached myself for this absurd gesture of rebellion. New tasks had imposed themselves, less romantic but just as important.

Meanwhile, I had to return to the Borello, get precise news, and learn what I had to do. I wanted to wash up and change (after two days and two nights without sleeping, I felt somewhat *fanée* (withered), but I was too tired to take the necessary initiative. I remained seated in the kitchen, in the midst of the

---

[8] Corso Oporto is now Corso Matteotti.

[9] Ettore De Sonnaz was one of Cavour's generals during the 1849 War for Italian Independence. He was also minister of war under Gioberti.

[10] Members of the Feld-Gendarmerie were drawn from the German civil police and had a distinctive uniform.

[11] The Società Telefonica Italiana per il Piemonte e la Liguria (Stipel) was the telephone company for Turin.

empty weapons and the dirty pans and plates, without making up my mind to move. Seeing my state of collapse, Ettore remembered the existence of a handful of real coffee that he had providentially put aside, and he got ready to prepare it for me.

In the meantime, the imperturbable Anna arrived—at 9:00 a.m., not one minute before and not one minute after. "Let's see," I said, laughing to myself. "This time even she will have to say something!" In fact she did say something: "Good morning." After which, tranquilly, like every day, she proceeded to change her shoes into comfortable slippers, slip into an apron, and tie a handkerchief in a knot on her head. Then, looking around without amazement, she said simply "*A smia* (It seems) that in this house *sta neuit a sia staje* (last night there was) a bit of movement." It was her only comment. Calm and impassible, she began to dust the guns and gather and organize the household utensils.

Having had my coffee, I began to feel a little better. Then the doorbell began to ring and people began to arrive, not friends, companions in battle whom I would have welcomed with enthusiastic joy, but people whom I did not know very well, or whom I once knew. Having seen the winds change and perhaps having heard news of the responsibility that awaited me, they were hurrying to come to be remembered, to congratulate each other, and to commend themselves.

Therefore I decided to cut things short, abandoning them, and giving up tidying myself and changing. Ettore returned to E.I.A.R. to see what there was to do. Paolo, decked out in the iron collar of the Deutsche Polizei (German police) that he had found in the *topolino*, got on his bicycle and came to accompany me.

I will never forget that ride. The sky, gray and unpredictable during the past few days, had definitely cleared up. The April sun illuminated the surviving trees adorned with new buds on the avenues, the more or less ragged houses, and the streets and piazzas on which the people timidly began to move again. As I advanced toward the outskirts, the flags became denser. Men, women, and children called to each other festively while they exhibited them from house to house. Some had cut away the coat of arms of the House of Savoy, some had covered it with a piece of cloth or paper, and some had limited themselves to putting it upside down.[12] The bells of the churches sounded in festivity. The passersby, even without knowing each other, exchanged news, greetings, cries of "long live Italy," and joy. Sometimes they embraced each other.

At the Borello, an atmosphere of demobilization emanated instead. The insurrection finished, its function was finished as well. Almost all the girls had gone away. Mino was there with some others. Pinella, who advised me not to leave and to remain there because they would come to get me to take me to

---

[12] The monarchy, the House of Savoy, had collaborated with the Fascists.

the *Municipio*, was there. Here I was again, nailed down there while I thought there were so many things to do. Above all, I was obsessed with worry about the *politici* who had been released from prison and who, not being from Turin, did not know where to go. It was necessary to requisition a hotel, prepare it for them, think of their comfort, and welcome them. I would have liked to track down the women of the Gruppi di difesa and organize the matter with them. In the meantime, I spoke with Pinella about it. I saw that she was tired, and I observed in her that subtle sense of nostalgic regret that I too was feeling, and that often follows the achievement of a goal and the realization of a dream: the melancholy that comes after a *cueilleson du rêve* (the realization of a dream). "How wonderful it was last night!" she told me suddenly, with a sigh. Yes it was wonderful: that harmony, that understanding, that being and working together, that forgetting oneself in all the others, that feeling part of a unified whole. Now instead, everyone has become single, isolated individuals again, each one with different leanings, responsibilities, and ambitions. It was sad, but it was reality, and we had to confront it with courage.

Soon someone arrived running to tell me that I had to go to the *Municipio* at once. I immediately got on my old bicycle. Pinella protested: "Do you think it is right that the vice mayor should arrive at the *Municipio* on such a bicycle? Is there no car to come to get you?" Notwithstanding her protests, I left just the same. While I was going through the gate, which was thrown wide open by now, our men and some passersby gave me a kind of ovation. I do not know whether it was directed at the authority that I was about to assume, or at the splendor of my *toilette* (dress).

At the height of Via Cibrario, I stopped, hearing myself summoned. It was the car that had gone to the Borello to get me and that Pinella had sent after me. I do not remember who was driving. Instead I remember very well the dark-haired Stefania, seated at the side of the driver, with a Tommy gun pointed outside the little window.[13] I let my bicycle go without bothering about it anymore, and I got into the car. (The bike was so damaged and I had used it so much that I could afford very well to lose it. Instead—how ironical!—someone picked it up and brought it to me at home.)

At the entrance to Via Saccarelli—where at the time the city Cln had its headquarters in the Istituto per l'Infanzia (Children's Institute)—we saw a row of cars in motion. It was the new city authority that was going to take its place. A car came and stopped near mine. They told me to get out and switch. A big hand held itself out to help me get in, while a voice was saying, "Are you Signora Gobetti? I am Roveda." "Oh, finally!" I exclaimed with a feeling of joy, and

---

[13] Bianca Aloisio (Stefania) was a city *staffetta* for the Action Party.

looking him in the face, I understood that I had found a friend. "Let's address each other with *tu*," said Roveda, after having acknowledged me in turn.

We crossed Piazza Statuto and entered Via Garibaldi. A truck loaded with armed partisans opened the procession. Then came our cars, then other cars with armed men. They were still shooting from the windows and from the corners of the streets, but the people, heedless of the danger, flowed onto the street in the way of our passage. "Long live Italy! Long live the partisans! Long live the Cln!" They cried, and they threw flowers, and mothers raised their babies and held them toward us, so that they could see, so that they could remember. While we were stopped for an instant at the intersection with Corso Valdocco, a certain man, with the appearance of an old worker, went up to the car and recognized my companion. "Roveda!" he said, with a voice that I will never forget. It was evidently an old worker, who had fought and hoped with him, who had believed in him, and who, after 8 September, had cried for him, thinking he was lost. Now he saw him there in front of him, ready to take the destiny of his city into his hands. I saw tears stream down his face while, with a deferential gesture, he took off his hat and bowed. At that moment I understood what real authority was.

We were supposed to stop at the *Municipio*, but in Piazza di Città the shooting was so violent that we decided to go first to the *Prefettura* (prefecture). As soon as we got out of the car in Piazza Castello, someone fired from the roofs of the neighboring houses, and the partisans responded with a fury of fire that seemed excessive to me: guns, Tommy guns, and bazooka fired for more than a quarter of an hour, making an infernal din. "Throw yourselves on the ground! Take shelter behind the cars!" someone yelled. But we did not even think of it. On foot, smiling, we filled our lungs with the air of freedom. To us, the shots seemed like fireworks of joy. "They want to show that they have a lot of weapons, and to consume a little ammunition!" I said at a certain point, laughing. "Who believed in *cecchini*?" Indeed I did not believe in them, but I was wrong.[14]

In a moment of respite we got out at the Palazzo del governo (Government office building), where Passoni, the prefect, welcomed us, and where we joyously found Penati, Lucca, Signora Verretto, and Signora Savio, representatives of the Gruppi di difesa in the new *Giunta* (council), with whom I immediately made arrangements to organize the hotel where the ex-prisoners could be welcomed.[15] We decided to choose the "Patria" in Via Cernaia, which had been

---

[14] *Cecchini* was a name for Fascist snipers. According to Fofi, these last Republicans did not want to surrender because they would have much for which to atone in order to settle the score for their crimes. *Diario partigiano* (1972), 370 n. 1.

[15] Alfredo Lucca was a pediatrician and representative of the Action Party on the Cln of Turin. Piera Verretto and Maria Savio (Renza) were representatives of the Gruppi di difesa on the Cln of Turin.

occupied by the Germans until the day before, and we took the necessary measures so that the women of the Gruppi di difesa could work on it immediately.

In the piazza they continued to shoot. In a little room set apart, which opened onto the Giardino Reale (Royal gardens), the first meeting of the Giunta Popolare (People's council) was held; we said but a few words of reciprocal greeting, postponing until the next day the discussion of more concrete problems.

It was already well into the afternoon when, across the Giardino Reale, we reached the *Municipio*, a few at a time. We climbed the stairs of the Palazzo del Comune (Municipal office building) amidst the applause of the clerks who were taking part in the municipal Cln, and the bailiffs. "Finally!" the imposing head bailiff, Bertone, said to us with tears in his eyes, while he led us into the room. "We have dreamed of this moment so much, when people worthy of the position they were occupying had their turn to serve."

We chose the respective rooms where we would work. Then, having found a *topolino* in the courtyard with an available driver (the excellent Manzoli, who later was my faithful and affectionate working companion for almost two years), Signora Verretto and I left to see how the welcome to the ex-prisoners was going.[16] At the "Patria" everything was in order. The women of the Gruppi di difesa, and above all Adda Corti, had performed miracles.[17] The rooms were ready, the food provided, and there were even flowers. But where were the guests? How would they know to come, if they did not know about it? We would need the collaboration of the director of prisons, who would be able to give us the necessary information.

Therefore we left at the turn for the Nuove. But it was not easy to enter. The partisans who had occupied it did not want to hear about letting me in. In vain did I explain the reasons for my request and invoke my authority as vice mayor. "I do not believe it," the big boy who was acting as sentinel said to me. "Even *le fûmele* (a woman) is now the vice mayor?" Suddenly I had a flash of genius. I still had my GL badge sewed on the inside of my jacket. I showed it to him, saying "I am a partisan commander. Go call your leader, and hurry!" This was an authority that he had learned to recognize and respect. He left after he stood at attention, and returned a short while later accompanied by... Pratis who, since the day before, together with Gallo, the attorney, a member of the Cln for prisons, was working to resolve the practical matters for the liberation of the *politici*, in this way avoiding releasing the common delinquents indiscriminately at the same time.[18] It was easy to reach an agreement with him. He would affix a sign

---

[16] Luigi Manzoli, the driver for the *Comune* of Turin.

[17] Adda Corti was an organizer of the Gruppi di difesa.

[18] Vittorio Gallo, the lawyer and English vice consul in Turin who had been arrested and accused of being a spy, was the organizer of the Cln in the Carceri Nuove prison, and was the director of this prison after the Liberation.

to the exit, and he would personally notify the ex-prisoners who did not reside in Turin. The initiative seemed first-rate to him.

Then we spent a moment at the Borello to deliver some newspapers. There were people whom I did not know, and the enchantment was definitely broken.

We returned to the *Municipio*. There I finally had a long meeting with Roveda. I told him about my concerns regarding the ex-prisoners and the need to take steps to receive them decently. We spoke about a number of things, and we decided on several points, finding each other fundamentally in agreement and putting down the basis for a cordial, productive collaboration that was to last, unclouded and without obstacles, for the entire time of our working together. "Well *brava!*" He told me suddenly. (He then repeated the same phrase later, several times.) "They did not even tell me you were a teacher!" Although I am not at all embarrassed to be a teacher, understanding what he meant by that judgment I was deeply flattered.

Suddenly the door opened, letting a woman in who, laughing and crying, threw her arms around Roveda's neck. "*Gioânin,*" she cried. "Oh, *Gioânin!*" It was his wife, the faithful, courageous companion who had fought and suffered with him, who had been able to save him by having him escape from the prison in Verona, and who, after the beginning of the insurrection, had not seen him any more. Now she had found him again, safe and sound, and the "mayor." Relief, joy, and pride transfigured her.

I left the spouses in the joy of finding each other, and decided to finally return home. But the front gate of the *Municipio* was barred, and the bailiffs ardently advised me not to leave. "They are shooting! There are *cecchini!*" they told me. I left just the same, shrugging my shoulders. Who believed in *cecchini?*

At the entrance to Via Garibaldi, which was completely deserted, a squad of partisans blocked my passage. "You cannot go through. They are shooting," they said. I showed them my badge, the card of the Cln, and they let me go. I continued rapidly along the empty street, thinking that the *cecchini* were pure fantasy, when I heard a bullet whirr that proceeded to drive itself into wall a few centimeters over my head. So the *cecchini* did exist, even if their aim was not perfect. I continued along my way, internally blaming myself. Mine was not courage, but stupidity. Given the responsibilities that awaited me, I did not have the right to risk my life out of reckless bravado. I swore to myself that I would never do it again.

At home, after a short time, Paolo and Ettore also arrived. We ate something in a hurry. Then I decided to go find Mario Andreis. I wanted to tell him what I had done and what I planned to do, and to feel that I was somehow supported and guided in the not-easy task that awaited me. Ettore and Paolo decided to accompany me. I did not have my bicycle (they brought it to me later), so Ettore took me on the handlebar of his.

We crossed the city, which was utterly quiet and deserted. Livio, who was shaving, was also at Mario's house. I realized right away that neither of them wanted to listen to me. They were tired and bewildered, each burdened with a thousand problems and a thousand worries. "Fine, fine," Mario responded to everything I said. "You have done a very good job. Whatever you have to do is fine." He was in a great hurry to send us away. "It is better that you do not go about late in the evening," he said.

We returned home in silence. We went to sleep in the beds that the incomparable Anna had laundered and made up again. Regardless of how very tired I was, however, I was not able to sleep.

I thought about everything that had happened during that very long day, but above all I thought about tomorrow. The shots that I could still hear in the distance from time to time reminded me that, notwithstanding the festive exaltation of that day, the war was not over yet. I knew that large German forces were still not far from Turin, in Grugliasco in the Canavese.[19] But it was not this that worried me profoundly. The bloody struggle—even if there could still be terrible incidents—was virtually over. The Reich, according to the prophetic inscription I read at the French Command in Plampinet, was truly *en ruines*. Soon the Allies would arrive. There would no longer be bombs, fires, roundups, arrests, killings, hangings, and massacres. This was a great thing.

Nor did the practical and material difficulties that I had to confront in order to reconstruct a disorganized and devastated country frighten me, because the most unexpected and unheard of solutions for each matter would be found in the boundless resources of our people.

Yet, confusedly, I sensed that another battle was beginning: longer, more difficult, and more extensive, albeit less bloody. Now it was no longer a question of fighting against arrogance, cruelty, and violence—easy to detect and to hate—but against interests that would try to rekindle themselves treacherously, against habits that would soon reaffirm themselves, against prejudices that did not want to die: all things that were much more vague, deceiving, and fleeting.

Moreover, it was a question of fighting among ourselves and within ourselves not only to destroy but to clarify, affirm, and create; not to abandon ourselves to the comfortable exaltation of ideals we had coveted for such a long time, not to be content with words and phrases, but to renew ourselves, keeping ourselves "alive." In short, it was a question of not letting the flame of a unified and fraternal humanity that we saw born on 10 September, and that has guided and sustained us for twenty months, be extinguished in the dead air of a normality that has only apparently been regained.

---

[19] On 29 April 1945, the Germans killed sixty-six citizens in this Piedmontese town.

I knew that—even if the marvelous unity that had united almost all people in those days died in the fervor of victory—we would be there in numbers to fight this difficult battle. Friends, companions of yesterday, would be those of tomorrow as well. But I also knew that the struggle would not be a single effort, it would not have its own unique, immutable face like before, but would be shattered into a thousand forms. Painstakingly, tormentedly, through diverse experiences, accomplishing different tasks, whether they be modest or important, everyone would have to pursue their own truth and their own life.

All of this frightened me. For a long time that night—which should have been one of relaxation and repose—I tormented myself, wondering if I would know how to be worthy of this future, rich in difficulties and promises, that I was preparing myself to face with trembling humility.

28 April 1949

INDEX OF NAMES

INDEX OF PLACES*

---

* All locations are in Italy unless otherwise noted.